Palmyra and the East

STUDIES IN PALMYRENE ARCHAEOLOGY AND HISTORY

Founding Editor

Professor Rubina Raja, *Centre for Urban Network Evolutions, Aarhus University, Denmark*

Advisory Board

Professor Nathanael Andrade, *Binghamton University, New York, USA*
Professor Maura K. Heyn, *University of North Carolina, Greensboro, USA*
Dr Emanuele Intagliata, *Università degli Studi di Milano, Italy*
Professor Ted Kaizer, *Durham University, UK*
Professor Eivind Heldaas Seland, *University of Bergen, Norway*
Dr Jean-Baptiste Yon, *Institut français du Proche-Orient, Beirut, Lebanon*

VOLUME 6

Previously published volumes in this series are listed at the back of the book.

Palmyra and the East

Edited by

Kenneth Lapatin
and Rubina Raja

BREPOLS

British Library Cataloguing in Publication Data

A catalogue record for this book is available from the British Library.

© 2022, Brepols Publishers n.v., Turnhout, Belgium

All rights reserved. No part of this publication may be reproduced,
stored in a retrieval system, or transmitted, in any form or by any means,
electronic, mechanical, photocopying, recording, or otherwise,
without the prior permission of the publisher.

D/2022/0095/11
ISBN: 978-2-503-59825-3

Printed in the EU on acid-free paper

Contents

List of Illustrations.. vii

List of Abbreviations.. xiii

Introduction — Palmyra and the East: Reassessing an Oasis City
   and its Cultural Relations
     KENNETH LAPATIN and RUBINA RAJA xv

Part I. Language, History, and Trade

1. Language as Power: Aramaic at (and East of) Palmyra
     CATHERINE E. BONESHO... 3

2. Palmyra's Maritime Trade
     KATIA SCHÖRLE 23

3. From Palmyra to India: How the East Was Won
     JEAN-BAPTISTE YON 29

4. Palmyra and the Sasanians in the Third Century AD
     TOURAJ DARYAEE 39

5. Zenobia and the East
     NATHANAEL J. ANDRADE 45

6. The Fate of Palmyra and the East after AD 273: A Few Remarks on Trade,
   Economy, and Connectivity in Late Antiquity and the Early Islamic Period
     EMANUELE E. INTAGLIATA 59

Part II. Art and Archaeology

7. Palmyrene Funerary Art between East and West:
Reclining Women in Funerary Sculpture
RUBINA RAJA 71

8. Ashurbanipal and the Reclining Banqueter in Palmyra
MAURA K. HEYN 97

9. So-Called 'Servants' or 'Pages' in Palmyrene Funerary Sculpture
FRED ALBERTSON 109

10. Notes on Some Palmyrene Religious Imagery
TED KAIZER 127

11. A Palmyrene Child at Dura-Europos
LISA R. BRODY 139

12. Edessa and the Sculpture of Greater North Mesopotamia
in the Romano-Parthian Period
MICHAEL BLÖMER 155

Index 179

List of Illustrations

1. Language as Power: Aramaic at (and East of) Palmyra — *Catherine E. Bonesho*

Figure 1.1.	Distribution of Palmyrene Aramaic inscriptions according to *PAT*.	4
Figure 1.2.	Close-up of distribution of Palmyrene Aramaic inscriptions in the Ancient Near East.	6
Figure 1.3.	The Palmyrian Tariff (*PAT* 0259). Panels one and two of the Tariff Inscription. Palmyra. 137. Marble. Inv. no. DV-4187.	12
Figure 1.4.	*PAT* 1097–98: relief with Palmyrene Aramaic inscriptions from the Temple of Gadde in Dura-Europos.	14
Figure 1.5.	*PAT* 1089: relief with Palmyrene Aramaic and Greek visually parallel inscriptions from the Temple of Zeus Kyrios in Dura-Europos.	15
Figure 1.6.	*PAT* 1085: bilingual Greek and Palmyrene Aramaic inscription from the Mithraeum of Dura-Europos with visually primary Palmyrene Aramaic inscription.	16
Figure 1.7.	*PAT* 1078: Greek and Palmyrene Aramaic inscription of Dura-Europos dedicated to Nemesis with visually primary Greek inscription.	17
Figure 1.8.	*PAT* 1080: relief of Herakles with Greek and Palmyrene Aramaic texts from Dura-Europos.	19

3. From Palmyra to India: How the East Was Won — *Jean-Baptiste Yon*

Figure 3.1.	*IGLS* xvii.16 = *PAT* 1352. Malikû son of Nešâ, builder of a temple of Bel.	29
Figure 3.2.	A leopard hunt, Palmyra, vicinity of the Allat sanctuary.	31
Figure 3.3.	*RTP* 285, 'Nanai, Shaknai, auxiliary of Babylon'.	32
Figure 3.4.	Cantineau 1931, 139, no. 18 = *PAT* 2754. Inscription of Alexandros sent as an envoy by Germanicus.	34

4. Palmyra and the Sasanians in the Third Century AD — *Touraj Daryaee*

Figure 4.1.	Arsacid mints.	40

5. Zenobia and the East — *Nathanael J. Andrade*

Figure 5.1.	Coin of Aurelian, ANS 1944.100.32846.	46
Figure 5.2.	Horse armour excavated at Dura-Europos.	48
Figure 5.3.	Mosaic showing an archer killing Persian tigers.	49
Figure 5.4.	Relief of figures wearing Syro-Mesopotamian tunic and trousers.	50

6. The Fate of Palmyra and the East after AD 273 — *Emanuele E. Intagliata*

Figure 6.1. Plan of the site. Monuments discussed in the text: 1. Great Colonnade; 2. Suq; 3. Annexe of the Agora; 4. Sanctuary of Baalshamin; 5. Camp of Diocletian. 59

Figure 6.2. The Camp of Diocletian, view of the stretch of the *Via Praetoria* from the *Groma* to the *Forum*. 60

Figure 6.3. Route from Palmyra to Hit. 63

7. Palmyrene Funerary Art between East and West — *Rubina Raja*

Figure 7.1. Sarcophagus lid with a seated female, two standing individuals, a reclining female, and a reclining male. From the Tomb of Aʿailamî and Zebidâ, west necropolis. 72

Figure 7.2. Fragmented sarcophagus lid with a reclining female. From the Tomb of Aʿailamî and Zebidâ, west necropolis. 72

Figure 7.3. Fragmented sarcophagus lid with the torso of a reclining female. From the Tomb of Aʿailamî and Zebidâ, west necropolis. 73

Figure 7.4. Fragmented sarcophagus lid with the lower body of a reclining female. From the Tomb of Aʿailamî and Zebidâ, west necropolis. 73

Figure 7.5. Complete sarcophagus with a banqueting scene on the lid, depicting a seated and a reclining female, and busts on the box. From the Tombeau de l'Aviation, south-east necropolis. 74

Figure 7.6a. Complete sarcophagus with a banqueting scene on the lid, a religious scene on the front of the box, and a reclining female on the side of the box. 75

Figure 7.6b. Side view of the sarcophagus box with a reclining female and a standing servant. 75

Figure 7.7. Banquet relief with a standing and reclining female. 76

Figure 7.8. Banquet relief with a standing and reclining female. 77

8. Ashurbanipal and the Reclining Banqueter in Palmyra — *Maura K. Heyn*

Figure 8.1. Wall-panel: banquet scene with Ashurbanipal and his queen. North Palace, Nineveh. 645–635 BC. 97

Figure 8.2. Banquet relief. Palmyra. 98

Figure 8.3. Funerary relief of Abuna, daughter of Nabuna, *c.* AD 170–230. Palmyra. Limestone with traces of red paint. 99

Figure 8.4. Funerary relief. Palmyra, *c.* AD 125–150. 99

Figure 8.5. Banquet scene of Malkû, Palmyra. National Museum of Damascus 100

Figure 8.6. Relief, funeral banquet, *c.* AD 200–250, limestone. 102

Figure 8.7. Funerary relief. Probably Palmyra, *c.* second to third centuries AD. 102

LIST OF ILLUSTRATIONS

Figure 8.8. Funerary relief of a banquet scene. Limestone, *c.* AD 200–273...................103

Figure 8.9. Clay tessera with banquet scene. Probably Palmyra, *c.* first to second centuries AD...103

Figure 8.10. Skyphos, 100–50 BC, silver..................104

Figure 8.11. Phiale Mesomphalos, 525–450 BC, silver..................104

9. So-Called 'Servants' or 'Pages' in Palmyrene Funerary Sculpture — *Fred Albertson*

Figure 9.1. Sarcophagus with scene of sacrifice, from Tomb 176, Palmyra. Limestone, *c.* AD 230..................109

Figure 9.2. Detail of Fig. 9.1, sacrifice with attendants carrying offerings..................109

Figure 9.3. Sarcophagus depicting the departure for a hunt, from the Exedra of Julius Aurelius Maqqai, Tomb of ʿAtênaten, Palmyra. Limestone. After AD 229..................110

Figure 9.4. Fragment of a sarcophagus depicting two attendants, from the Exedra of Julius Aurelius Maqqai, Tomb of ʿAtênaten, Palmyra. Limestone. After AD 229..................110

Figure 9.5. Sarcophagus depicting two attendants and a camel, from the Polish Excavations of the Camp of Diocletian, Palmyra. Limestone, *c.* AD 220..................111

Figure 9.6. Sarcophagus depicting six attendants, from the Tomb of Aviation, Palmyra. Limestone, *c.* AD 220..................112

Figure 9.7. Sarcophagus depicting attendants at a banquet, from the Tomb of Julius Aurelius Marona, Palmyra. Limestone. After AD 236..................112

Figure 9.8. 'Small banquet relief', from Palmyra. Limestone, *c.* AD 200–225..................114

Figure 9.9. Stele with Yarḥai and attendant carrying writing implements, from Palmyra. Limestone, *c.* AD 230–250..................115

Figure 9.10. *Loculus* plaque of Malkû, son of Malê, from Palmyra. Limestone, *c.* AD 120–140....116

Figure 9.11. Pilaster capital with offering scene to Abgal, from the Temple of Abgal and Maʾan, Khirbet Semrin. Limestone, *c.* AD 200..................116

Figure 9.12. 'Small banquet relief', from Palmyra. Limestone, *c.* AD 230..................118

Figure 9.13. Relief of the priest Narkissos, entrance to the Lower Great Temple, Niha..................118

Figure 9.14. 'Small banquet relief', from Palmyra. Limestone, *c.* AD 230..................119

Figure 9.15. Stele with two male children, from Palmyra. Limestone, *c.* AD 150–200..................119

Figure 9.16. 'Otes-fresco', from room K of the Temple of the Palmyrene Gods, Dura-Europos. Fresco, *c.* AD 220. Now lost, preserved through excavation photograph..................121

Figure 9.17. Short side of sarcophagus, reclining woman with attendant, from Tomb 176, Palmyra. Limestone, *c.* AD 230..................122

Figure 9.18. Short side of sarcophagus, woman with camel, from Tomb 176, Palmyra. Limestone, *c.* AD 230..................123

10. Notes on Some Palmyrene Religious Imagery — *Ted Kaizer*

Figure 10.1. Statue of Jupiter Optimus Maximus Heliopolitanus from as-Sukhnah............128

Figure 10.2. Statue of Jupiter Optimus Maximus Heliopolitanus from as-Sukhnah............128

Figure 10.3. Relief of she-wolf from the Temple of Bel at Palmyra............................129

Figure 10.4. Relief of she-wolf from the Temple of Bel at Palmyra............................129

Figure 10.5. Arch with bust opposite eastern nymphaeum, opening up street leading from colonnade to agora. View towards the north........................130

Figure 10.6. Detail of bust on Fig. 10.5...130

Figure 10.7. Detail of bust on Fig. 10.5...130

Figure 10.8. Arch with bust opposite eastern nymphaeum, opening up street leading from colonnade to agora. View towards the south........................131

Figure 10.9. Detail of bust on Fig. 10.8...131

Figure 10.10. Detail of bust on Fig. 10.8...131

Figure 10.11. Arch with bust in western half of colonnade. View towards the north..............132

Figure 10.12. Detail of bust on Fig. 10.11..132

Figure 10.13. Arch with bust in western half of colonnade. View towards the south..............133

Figure 10.14. Ruins of the eastern nymphaeum with bust..133

Figure 10.15. Cornice above central door of scaenae frons, entering from colonnade............134

Figure 10.16. Cornice originally above entrance to so-called Caesareum........................135

Figure 10.17. Drawing by Cassas of a frieze with three busts..................................135

11. A Palmyrene Child at Dura-Europos — *Lisa R. Brody*

Figure 11.1. Regional map and city plan of Dura-Europos.....................................139

Figure 11.2. Upper fragment of figure of a Palmyrene child..................................140

Figure 11.3. Lower fragment of figure of a Palmyrene child..................................140

Figure 11.4. Figure of a Palmyrene child..140

Figure 11.5. Plan of Blocks G1–G8 in Dura-Europos Excavation................................141

Figure 11.6. Figure of a Palmyrene child from Dura-Europos, Yale University Art Gallery. AD 100–150...142

Figure 11.7. Mary and James Ottaway Gallery of Ancient Dura-Europos.........................143

Figure 11.8. Figure of a Palmyrene child from Dura-Europos..................................143

Figure 11.9. Figure of a Palmyrene child from Dura-Europos..................................144

Figure 11.10. Silver bracelet with carnelian intaglio from Dura-Europos, Yale University Art Gallery. Second or early third century AD......144

Figure 11.11. Palmyrene funerary relief with a man and his two nephews, Seattle Art Museum. Second century AD......145

Figure 11.12. Palmyrene funerary relief with a brother and a sister, The State Hermitage Museum, St Petersburg, *c.* AD 114......146

Figure 11.13. Palmyrene funerary relief with a mother and child, British Museum, London, *c.* AD 184......146

Figure 11.14. Palmyrene funerary relief of a family, Metropolitan Museum of Art, New York. Second or third century AD. Museum Purchase in 1902......147

Figure 11.15. Palmyrene funerary relief of a mother and two children, Harvard Art Museums. Mid-second century AD......148

Figure 11.16. Graph showing clusters of stable isotope ratios for limestone objects from Durene and Palmyrene quarry sources......150

Figure 11.17. Figure of a Palmyrene child from Dura-Europos photographed with Visible-Induced (infrared) Luminescence (VIL)......152

12. Edessa and the Sculpture of Greater North Mesopotamia in the Romano-Parthian Period — *Michael Blömer*

Figure 12.1. Map of ancient northern Mesopotamia and north Syria......158

Figure 12.2. Column monuments of the third century AD on the citadel of Şanlıurfa......159

Figure 12.3. View of Sumatar from the west with the höyük at the centre......160

Figure 12.4. Statue of a nobleman from Osrhoene, limestone, second–third centuries AD......161

Figure 12.5. Statue of an archer, from Edessa, limestone, second–third centuries AD......162

Figure 12.6. Statue of a nobleman, Bir el-Kantari, limestone, second–third centuries AD......162

Figure 12.7. Fragmented statue from Ain Arous, limestone, whereabouts unknown......163

Figure 12.8. Funerary banquet scene, tomb of Seluk, Kırk Mağara necropolis, Edessa, second–third centuries AD......163

Figure 12.9. Funerary banquet scene, Kırk Mağara necropolis......163

Figure 12.10. Funerary relief with a male half figure, Edessa, limestone, second–third centuries AD......164

Figure 12.11. Funerary relief......164

Figure 12.12. Funerary stele of Šalmat and Rabbayta, limestone, second–third centuries AD......165

Figure 12.13. Votive stele......165

Figure 12.14. Funerary mosaic with funerary banquet scene, Edessa, second–third centuries AD, now lost......166

Figure 12.15. Funerary mosaic of Aphtuha and his family, Edessa, second–third centuries AD.....167

Figure 12.16. Cave sanctuary at Sumatar, rear wall with niche flanked by cultic standards and adorants, third century AD..168

Figure 12.17. Open-air sanctuary with rock-cut reliefs and inscriptions at Sumatar...............168

Figure 12.18. Funerary statue..170

Figure 12.19. Rock reliefs in the necropolis of Hilar, second–third centuries AD.................171

List of Abbreviations

AE	*L'année épigraphique*
Anas. Per.	Flusin, B. (ed.). 1992. *Saint Anastase le Perse et l'Histoire de la Palestine au début du VIIe siècle* (Paris: Éditions du Centre national de la recherche scientifique).
App., B Civ.	Appianus, *Bella civilia*
Cass. Dio	Cassius Dio
CIL	*Corpus inscriptionum latinarum*
CIS	Chabot, J.-B. (ed.). 1926–1951. *Corpus inscriptionum Semiticarum*, II.3: *Inscriptiones Palmyrenae*, fasc. 1–4 (Paris: e Republicae typographeo).
FHG	Müller, K. 1841–1873. *Fragmenta historicorum Graecorum*, 5 vols (Paris: Firmin Didot).
IGLS	Yon, J.-B. 2012. *Inscriptions grecques et latines de la Syrie*, XVII.1: *Palmyre* (Beirut: Institut français du Proche Orient).
IGR	Toutain, J. and others. 1906–1927. *Inscriptiones graecae ad res romanas pertinentes* (Paris: Leroux).
IJO Syria	Noy, D. and H. Bloedhorn (eds). *Inscriptiones Judaicae Orientis*, III: *Syria and Cyprus*, Texts and Studies in Ancient Judaism, 102 (Tübingen: Mohr Siebeck).
ILS	Dessau, Hermann. 1892–1916. *Inscriptiones latinae selectae*, 3 vols (Berlin: Weidmann).
Inv.	*De inventione*
Ioh. Mal.	Iohannes Malalas, *Chronographia*, ed. H. Thurn (Berlin: de Gruyter, 2000); *The Chronicle of John Malalas*, trans. E. Jeffreys, M. Jeffreys, and R. Scott (Melbourne: Australian Association for Byzantine Studies, 1986).
Jos., *Ant. Iud.*	Josephus, *Antiquitates Iudaicae*
PAT	Hillers, D. R. and E. Cussini. 1996. *Palmyrene Aramaic Texts* Baltimore: Johns Hopkins University Press).
Philostr., *VA*	Philostratus, *Vita Apollonii*
Plin., *HN*	Plinius maior, *Naturalis historia*
Procop., *Aed.*	Procopius, *De aedificiis*
RIC	Mattingly, H. and others. 1923–1967. *The Roman Imperial Coinage*, 7 vols (London: Spink).
RTP	Ingholt, H., H. Seyrig, and J. Starcky. 1955. *Recueil des tessères de Palmyre*, Bibliothèque archéologique et historique, 58 (Paris: Geuthner).
SEG	*Supplementum epigraphicum graecum*
SHA, *Aur.*	Scriptores historiae Augustae, *M. Aurelius*
SHA, *Gall.*	Scriptores historiae Augustae, *Gallieni duo*
SHA, *Tyr. Trig.*	Scriptores historiae Augustae, *Triginta Tyranni*
SHA, *Valer.*	Scriptores historiae Augustae, *Valeriani duo*
Stra.	Strabo
Sync.	Syncellus
Theoph., *Chr.*	Theophanes, *Chronographia*, ed. C. de Boor (Leipzig: Teubner, 1884).
Zos.	Zosimus

Introduction — Palmyra and the East: Reassessing an Oasis City and its Cultural Relations

Kenneth Lapatin
J. Paul Getty Museum (KLapatin@getty.edu)

Rubina Raja
Aarhus University, Centre for Urban Network Evolutions (UrbNet) (Rubina.raja@cas.au.dk)

The papers presented in this volume stem from an international scholarly symposium of the same title, held at the Getty Villa in Los Angeles, 18–19 April 2019.[1] Convening such a gathering to explore the relations of the fabled Syrian desert city with the arts and cultures of civilizations further to the east, at a North American museum sited on the Pacific coast, whose architecture famously replicates that of an ancient Roman luxury villa on the Bay of Naples, may seem counter-intuitive. However, the symposium, co-funded by the J. Paul Getty Museum and the Carlsberg Foundation, was conceived in conjunction with the exhibition Palmyra: Loss and Remembrance (18 April 2018 to 27 May 2019),[2] one of the first in Getty's Classical World in Context series, which seeks to elucidate contacts and exchanges between the ancient Greeks, Etruscans, and Romans, who are physically represented by artefacts in the museum's permanent collection, and their neighbours. The exhibition, like the symposium, was co-organized by the editors and resulted from the collaboration between their institutions and the Ny Carlsberg Glyptotek in Copenhagen (NCG), which possesses the largest collection of Palmyrene sculpture outside of Syria,[3] the Getty Research Institute (GRI), which has substantial holdings of early printed books and recently acquired the earliest known photographs of the site, and the Cantor Arts Center at Stanford University, which lent a part of a Palmyrene relief acquired by Leland Stanford, jr. in the early 1880s that was, during the run of the exhibition and subsequently in Copenhagen, temporarily rejoined to a fragment from the NCG.[4] The work undertaken within the framework of the Palmyra Portrait Project headed by Rubina Raja since 2012 contributed to the development of the idea behind the symposium. Within the project, currently in its final stages of publication, approximately four thousand Palmyrene portraits, most of which stem from the funerary sphere, have been collected.[5] The various publications of these portraits and themes concerning them since 2012 have contributed significantly to a new understanding of the art and culture of Palmyrene society in the first three centuries AD and have led to a push for a re-evaluation of the way in which we study portrait culture outside of the core of the Roman world in the centuries when Rome dominated large parts of the Mediterranean world.[6]

The acquisition by the GRI in 2015 of twenty-nine photographs of Palmyra taken by the French naval officer Louis Vignes in 1864 and the subsequent mounting of the Getty's first online exhibition, The Legacy of Ancient Palmyra, which featured the photos alongside a wealth of additional documentary material, was an inspiration for the exhibition of actual artefacts at the Getty Villa together with a much smaller selec-

---

[1] See <https://www.getty.edu/museum/programs/lectures/palmyra_symposium.html> [accessed 10 October 2021].

[2] See <http://www.getty.edu/art/exhibitions/palmyra_sculpture/> [accessed 10 October 2021].

[3] See Raja 2019a.

[4] See Albertson, Lapatin, and Raja 2019.

[5] <https://projects.au.dk/palmyraportrait/> [accessed 10 October 2021]; also see the 2021 volumes published in the newly established series Studies on Palmyrene Archaeology and History (SPAH): Heyn and Raja (eds) 2021; Raja and Steding (eds) 2021; Raja and Sindbæk (eds) 2021; Bobou and others 2021; Romanowska, Bobou, and Raja 2021; Raja, Bobou, and Romanowska 2021; Bobou, Raja, and Romanowska 2021 for some of the main results of the project.

[6] See, for example, now Blömer and Raja (eds) 2019b; Raja (ed.) 2019; Raja 2019b; Blömer and Raja 2019a.

tion of books and photographs. The online exhibition has recently been enlarged, translated into Arabic, and renamed Return to Palmyra.[7] We are grateful to its curators, Fran Terpak and Peter Bonfitto, as well as NCG curator Anne Marie Nielsen and Cantor curator Elizabeth Mitchell for facilitating our work. Thanks are also due to past and present directors of the abovementioned institutions, Christine Buhl Andersen in Copenhagen, James Cuno, Thomas Gaehtgens, Mary Miller, and Timothy Potts in Los Angeles, and Susan Dackerman in Palo Alto, as well as many members of their staffs. We are especially indebted to colleagues in the Public Programs and Visitors Services departments at the Getty Villa and in the Centre for Urban Network Evolutions (UrbNet) at Aarhus University, particularly Lisa Guzzetta, Heather Leisy, and Christina Levisen, for their diligent and successful efforts to ensure that the symposium itself ran smoothly. In September 2019 the Ny Carlsberg Glyptotek opened the door to the largest Palmyra exhibition, when the museum for the first time put on display almost the entire Palmyrene collection in the special exhibition The Road to Palmyra, co-curated by Anne Marie Nielsen and Rubina Raja.[8] In this exhibition, attention was also given to the unique nature of Palmyra's art and archaeology in the first three centuries AD and the city's relationships with the East and the West over time. In connection with the exhibition, a public symposium was held in January 2020, organized by Anne Marie Nielsen and Rubina Raja, at which Kenneth Lapatin spoke about the earlier exhibition at the Getty Villa. This symposium underlined the close collaborations, both between the institutions and between the scholars involved in the research on Palmyra.

Because the arts of Palmyra, particularly its wealth of funerary portraiture, as well as its distinctive cultural mix of architecture, religion, and society, have frequently been compared to those of Rome and the West, the less fully explored relations between Palmyra and the East were chosen as the topic of the symposium in Los Angeles.[9] The ancient oasis site was a significant point of contact between the Roman and Parthian Empires, and has long been the focus of studies of cross-cultural encounters, for it was a locus of the movement of goods, peoples, and ideas between the Mediterranean and the Near East, India, and even China.[10] Thus, in their symposium presentations and the revised and elaborated written essays gathered here, experts from diverse disciplines explore Palmyrene links with the East, as expressed through the art, architecture, social, economic, and religious life of the city across the first three centuries of our era, when it flourished, before the sack by the troops of the Roman emperor Aurelian, after Zenobia had successfully conquered large parts of the territory, surrounding the city in all directions — north, south, east, and west. The papers gathered here focus on evidence from Palmyra and beyond in the light of new knowledge, and inform us about the dynamic relationships of Palmyrenes with their neighbours, particularly in the East — relationships that were as intense and tense as those that the city had with Rome, one notable difference being that Parthia and other Eastern civilizations were considerably closer to Palmyra.

While the oasis city has often been described as a melting pot that simply adopted and adapted what it could from other cultures, research over the past decades has made it clear that Palmyrene culture was distinct, and that Palmyrenes positioned themselves, variously 'code-switching' in modern parlance, to a much greater degree than hitherto thought.[11] The intention of the symposium and the papers presented here is to explore such developments and trends in greater detail, addressing a variety of topics, ranging from Palmyra's position on the Silk Roads, its languages and inscriptions, history, politics, and religion, to its distinctive and increasingly well-known funerary art. The outbreak of the unrest in Syria and the following civil war, which is still ongoing after more than a decade of intense battles in the country, has over the years not only led to the largest humanitarian crisis and displacement of people from their homes since the world wars, but has also led to the demolition and destruction of the country's rich cultural heritage. Therefore, a continuous and renewed focus on the cultural heritage of Syria and its importance as part of the world's heritage is also of concern to us. With this publication, we hope to bring new perspectives to the forefront, reminding readers that this devastating situation is still ongoing and that the cultural heritage of this coun-

---

[7] See <https://www.getty.edu/research/exhibitions_events/exhibitions/palmyra/> [accessed 10 October 2021].

[8] Nielsen and Raja 2019.

[9] Ingholt 1928; Colledge 1976; 1987; 1996. Also see the collection of articles in Sommer and Sommer-Theohari (eds) 2020, an edited volume that stems from a symposium entitled Palmyra: Orient: Okzident, held in Oldenburg, at which Rubina Raja gave the keynote lecture.

[10] For a recent monograph on the archaeology and history of Palmyra, see Raja 2021a.

[11] For example: Raja 2021b.

try, where some of the earliest civilizations in the world have their origins, is suffering and that we through publication of the rich archaeology and history of the region might be able to contribute to raising awareness of this situation.

The volume is divided into two parts, the first addressing Language, History, and Trade, the second Art and Archaeology. We open with Catherine E. Bonesho's examination of 'Language as Power: Aramaic at (and East of) Palmyra'. Recognizing that Palmyra lay not only at the intersections of empires but also at the intersections of languages, Bonesho traces the occurrences of Palmyrene Aramaic far beyond the borders of the ancient city, across the Roman Empire as well as further east, and analyses how the language was used and presented in conjunction with the more common imperial languages, Greek and Latin, not just as a means of conveying information but also as a mechanism for asserting a distinct Palmyrene identity. Thus, she offers a reconceptualization of Palmyrene Aramaic as a language of identity and power. She further argues that visual trends in the presentation of Greek and Aramaic bilingual inscriptions at Palmyra (and Dura-Europos) reveal that after Hadrian's visit to the city in the mid-second century AD, Palmyrenes may have responded to pressures to more fully incorporate Greek by simultaneously monumentalizing Palmyrene Aramaic, mimicking the monumentality of Hellenistic epigraphic traditions, showcasing the power and prestige of their own language, and establishing it as one of equal (or higher) standing.

In Chapter 2, Katia Schörle explores the activities of Palmyrene traders — not, as customary, in their role as caravan drivers across the desert, but at sea, challenging common preconceptions. By exploring the maritime routes and the impact which this sort of trade had on Palmyra's development and status as a city with worldwide connections, new perspectives are shed on the way in which the Palmyrene elite acted, not only within the context of local Palmyrene society but also outside, in maritime-trade relations — which were, for the large part, undertaken along the shores of the Red Sea and Indian Ocean.

Jean-Baptiste Yon looks further east in Chapter 3 — to India, first interrogating the evidence for Palmyrene contacts with the East at an early date through the evidence of Hellenistic-era pottery found at the site, then examining how under the Seleucids the city seems to have become a point of entrance and a gateway to Asia from and for Rome and the Mediterranean world. Excavation of the area called 'Hellenistic city' revealed that Palmyra was linked with the Mediterranean for exchange, specifically through finds of amphorae, which denote the importation of wine, from at least the third century BC, while Mesopotamian and local wares were also abundant. Meanwhile, architecture, particularly the form of the Temple of Bel, provides ample proof of Mesopotamian influence, specifically links to Babylonia. Onomastics, too, provide solid evidence of the depth of the links between different sub-regions, which only continued as Palmyrenes forged stronger ties with Greeks and Romans to the west.

In Chapter 4, Touraj Daryaee addresses 'Palmyra and the Sasanians in the Third Century AD', drawing on the evidence of inscribed coins and historical texts. While the Arsacid and Roman Empires allowed Palmyra and other 'caravan cities' to function as important trade centres, the Sasanians changed this balance of power, doing away with local powers and buffer states as part of a policy aiming to control the economy of the region. They reduced the role of proxies, establishing new trading centres, destroying old ones, and disrupting established trade routes. Thus, Daryaee suggests, Palmyrene expansion in the third century AD was less of an attempt to fill a political vacuum, and more intended to protect their economic well-being against the Sasanians.

Nathanael Andrade observes in Chapter 5 that although Queen Zenobia is depicted in ancient and late antique propagandistic source material as a fundamentally eastern figure, the imperial titles that she adopted for herself and her son, with the obvious exception of 'king of kings', were overwhelmingly embedded in Roman paradigms. But while a wealth of scholarship has accordingly situated her within the context of the Roman Empire, he asks what actually was Zenobia's relationship with the peoples of the East, including the Persians? Andrade examines Zenobia's brief reign (AD 268–272) by situating it within the political, religious, and socio-economic contexts of Iran and the hinterland of Asia, and further analyses the written sources, particularly the *Historia Augusta*, Peter the Patrician, the so-called *Continuator Dionis*, and the *Acts of Thomas*, as well as the evidence of inscriptions, onomastics, and numismatics, that linked Zenobia and her Palmyrenes to Persians, Parthians, or Arabs.

Part 1 concludes with Emanuele Intagliata's examination of the 'Fate of Palmyra and the East after AD 273', focusing on trade, economy, and connectivity in Late Antiquity and the Early Islamic period. The destruction of the city after the fall of Zenobia marked the end of long-distance trade and its commercial prosperity and the beginning of a new phase. Economic vitality dramatically decreased, and the city's cultural and commercial links with the East became weaker. The Palmyrene urban elite, which had been one of the main agents of the city's success as a caravan centre, disappears from the archaeological and epigraphic records. But this did not necessarily translate into the total demise of the settlement, for Palmyra survived throughout Late Antiquity as a crucial military base along the eastern Roman frontier and as a regional religious and economic engine. It is only from the early seventh century AD, Intagliata argues, when former political and administrative boundaries collapsed after the Persian and Islamic conquests, that Palmyra's links with the East were truly revitalized. Intagliata's essay surveys the archaeological data, inscriptions, and written sources, focusing specifically on the settlement's shifting connections with the East in Late Antiquity and the Early Islamic period, when Palmyra evolved from a Roman garrison town to a small, but thriving, local economic centre with wider connections attested by literary, numismatic, and architectural evidence.

Rubina Raja opens Part 2 with a contribution that addresses the motif of the reclining woman in the funerary art of Palmyra. This rare motif, which seems out of context in a strictly patriarchic societal structure, which Palmyra adhered to, tells us more about the inner-working of the city's elite than much other material — archaeological and written. While the public sculpture of the city to a high degree adhered to trends recognizable both in the West and the East, the funerary sculpture makes up a lavish group of material through which we can study the private sphere of the Palmyrene elite. Within the vast corpus, several groups of outlier motifs can be identified, and the motif of the reclining woman is one of the more intriguing. Shown in full-blown private settings, surrounded by luxury objects and wearing rich textiles and jewellery, which often came from the East, these images of women underline the rich culture of the upper classes in Palmyra, who drew on traditions — cultural and societal — also stemming from the East.

Maura Heyn, in Chapter 8, re-examines J.-M. Dentzer's seminal article on the reclining banqueter motif in Sasanian royal iconography and its connection to a similar scene from Nineveh featuring the Neo-Assyrian king, Ashurbanipal, and his wife banqueting in a garden. Despite the chronological distance separating these examples, Dentzer had asserted that the enduring popularity of the reclining banqueter motif, including at Palmyra, hearkened back to and relied on the pose of the Neo-Assyrian king and its association with royal or aristocratic status. Ubiquitous in the Mediterranean and Mesopotamian regions in the first millennium BC, and popular in Palmyra, with over one hundred examples dated as early as AD 40, the banquet scene presents Heyn with an opportunity to juxtapose the modes of presentation from the different regions. She carefully examines attributes, gestures, and dress associated with reclining figures in Palmyrene tombs and finds a strong affiliation of this status-marking iconography with the eastern tradition.

Fred Albertson re-evaluates 'So-Called "Servants" or "Pages" in Palmyrene Funerary Sculpture'. Such young male figures appearing as attendants in scenes of sacrifice, banqueting, and preparation for the hunt on Palmyrene sarcophagi and banquet reliefs had been identified by Harald Ingholt and others as servants, pages, or slaves, but while certainly of lower status than the banqueters and priests whom they serve, there is, in fact, little evidence to suggest that the adolescent individuals depicted originated from a lower social order. Indeed, actual representations of master and slave are virtually unknown at Palmyra, and certain aspects of their iconography suggest that these attendants, all depicted as beardless, youthful males, belong to an age- and gender-specific group. They also sport distinctive local hairstyles and forms of dress associated with equestrian gods of the desert. These limited, defining features can be linked to Persian/Parthian/Sasanian royal and divine iconography, again suggesting the intention to visually categorize a distinctive group — and one of high social and political status. Albertson proposes that, at Palmyra, such figures are religious attendants similar to the *camilli* of Roman religion, not slaves at all but young individuals drawn from elite families performing duties in an official capacity, comparable, at least in function, to *acolytes* recorded at other sites in Syria and northern Mesopotamia.

In Chapter 10, Ted Kaizer offers discussions on and reinterpretations of some of the religious images from Palmyra by focusing on objects which are not usually considered in discussions of the religious life of the city. By doing so Kaizer — once again — brings to the forefront the fact that Palmyra's religious life was tremendously rich and that we should be careful not to study it within preconceived frameworks developed to fit the overall schemes of how we usually understand Roman religion. While we know that the religious life of Palmyra was extremely diverse and drew on traditions both from the East and the West, there is often a tendency to play up the evidence showing the influence from the Roman world, for the simple reason that this evidence is often more readily available to scholars of the classical world. Therefore, it is refreshing and necessary to be reminded that there is another and much more complex side to the story.

'A Palmyrene Child at Dura-Europos' is the focus of Lisa Brody's contribution in Chapter 11, which closely examines a fragmentary statue excavated in 1932 at the site some 230 km east of Palmyra. Three fragments, now reconstituted in the Yale University Art Gallery, were found in disparate locations, and the figure represented, preserved from shoulders to feet, stands frontally with arms in front of the body, dressed in a long chiton and mantle, wearing a necklace, bracelets, and ring, and holding a bird in the right hand and a bunch of grapes in the left. For Brody, this modest statue, about which many questions remain unanswered, is a vehicle to address questions about the interaction between Palmyra and Dura-Europos. Where was the object carved? Why were the fragments dispersed? What were the statue's original context and function? Even the gender of the figure, once thought to represent a girl, is now open to investigation. Drawing upon on iconographic as well as scientific evidence, Brody presents a new analysis of this statue — one of the few free-standing sculptures from Dura-Europos and one of the strongest artistic links between Dura and Palmyra — exploring more deeply the cultural connections between the two cities. Recent isotopic analysis indicates that the figure was carved of Palmyrene limestone, but does not reveal where or by whom the statue was fashioned.

Our volume closes with Michael Blömer's wide-ranging essay, 'Edessa and the Sculpture of Greater North Mesopotamia in the Romano-Parthian Period', which begins north of Palmyra at Edessa, today modern Şanlıurfa in Turkey, one of the most important centres of ancient Mesopotamia and the capital of the kingdom of Osrhoene. Blömer discusses the growing corpus of funerary sculpture and funerary mosaics from that site and from Hatra, to the south-east, and its relation to the sculpture of Palmyra. He notes that both Edessean and Palmyrene statues and reliefs, as well as finds from Hatra and Dura-Europos, have long been cited as examples of Parthian art, whose defining features have been identified as frontality, spirituality, and a veristic, ornamental, linear style evolved from an oriental Hellenism, but that recent studies have questioned the very idea of Parthian impact on the art of the Syrian Desert and Mesopotamia. Palmyrene art, meanwhile, has come to be viewed as an original creation that merges Roman and Graeco-Semitic traditions. With further, more in-depth studies of the sculpture of early first-millennium Mesopotamia, where Blömer concludes the sculptural habit was more pervasive during the Romano-Parthian period than has so far been postulated, still more fruitful comparisons will become possible.

As described above these contributions reach far and wide in an attempt to outline and push borders of how we in the future can study Palmyrene art, archaeology, and history not only as products of being situated 'in between' empires, but rather with a point of departure in the unique local situation which forged a society that was highly aware of its own traditions and identities and whose members used their knowledge of the world around them to express their own ways of doing things. With this volume, we hope to bring new evidence to the forefront of continued discussions of the rich oasis city of Palmyra and its wide-ranging cultural and religious life in the Roman period.

Works Cited

Albertson, A., K. Lapatin, and R. Raja. 2019. 'Rejoining a Palmyrene Funerary Relief: *Postscriptum*', *Zeitschrift für Orient-Archäologie*, 12: 168–83.

Blömer, M. and R. Raja. 2019a. 'Shifting the Paradigms: Towards a New Agenda in the Study of the Funerary Portraiture of Greater Roman Syria', in M. Blömer and R. Raja (eds), *Funerary Portraiture in Greater Roman Syria*, Studies in Classical Archaeology, 6 (Turnhout: Brepols), pp. 5–26.

—— (eds). 2019b. *Funerary Portraiture in Greater Roman Syria*, Studies in Classical Archaeology, 6 (Turnhout: Brepols).

Bobou, O., R. Raja, and I. Romanowska. 2021. 'Historical Trajectories of Palmyra's Elites through the Lens of Archaeological Data', *Journal of Urban Archaeology*, 4: 153–66.

Bobou, O. and others. 2021. *Studies on Palmyrene Sculpture: A Commented Translation of Harald Ingholt's 1928 'Studier over Palmyrensk Skulptur'*, Studies in Palmyrene Archaeology and History, 1 (Turnhout: Brepols).

Colledge, M. A. R. 1976. *The Art of Palmyra* (London: Thames and Hudson).

—— 1987. 'Parthian Cultural Elements at Roman Palmyra', *Mesopotamia*, 22: 19–28.

—— 1996. 'Roman Influence in the Art of Palmyra', *Annales archéologiques arabes syriennes*, 42: 363–70.

Heyn, M. and R. Raja (eds). 2021. *Individualizing the Dead: Attributes in Palmyrene Funerary Sculpture*, Studies in Palmyrene Archaeology and History, 3 (Turnhout: Brepols).

Ingholt, H. 1928. *Studier over Palmyrensk Skulptur* (Copenhagen: Reitzel).

Nielsen, A. M. and R. Raja. 2019. *The Road to Palmyra* (Copenhagen: Ny Carlsberg Glyptotek).

Raja, R. 2019a. *Catalogue: The Palmyra Collection; Ny Carlsberg Glyptotek* (Copenhagen: Ny Carlsberg Glyptotek).

—— 2019b. 'Funerary Portraiture in Palmyra: Portrait Habit at a Crossroads or a Signifier of Local Identity?', in M. Blömer and R. Raja (eds), *Funerary Portraiture in Greater Roman Syria*, Studies in Classical Archaeology, 6 (Turnhout: Brepols), pp. 95–110.

—— 2021a. *Pearl of the Desert: A History of Palmyra* (Oxford: Oxford University Press).

—— 2021b. 'Negotiating Social and Cultural Interaction through Priesthoods: The Iconography of Priesthood in Palmyra', in J. Hoffman-Salz (ed.), *The Middle East as Middle Ground? Cultural Interaction in the Ancient Middle East Revisited* (Vienna: Holzhausen), pp. 129–46.

—— (ed.). 2019. *Revisiting the Religious Life of Palmyra*, Contextualizing the Sacred, 9 (Turnhout: Brepols).

Raja, R., O. Bobou, and I. Romanowska. 2021. 'Three Hundred Years of Palmyrene History: Unlocking Archaeological Data for Studying Past Societal Transformations', *PlosOne*, 16.11: e0256081 <doi.org/10.1371/journal.pone.0256081>.

Raja, R. and S. M. Sindbæk (eds). 2021. *Journal of Urban Archaeology*, 3.

Raja, R. and J. Steding (eds). 2021. *Production Economy in Roman Syria*, Studies in Palmyrene Archaeology and History, 2 (Turnhout: Brepols).

Romanowska, I., O. Bobou, and R. Raja. 2021. 'Reconstructing the Social, Economic and Demographic Trends of Palmyra's Elite from Funerary Data', *Journal of Archaeological Science*, 133: 105432.

Sommer, M. and D. Sommer-Theohari (eds). 2020. *Inter duo imperia: Palmyra between East and West* (Stuttgart: Steiner).

Part I
Language, History, and Trade

1. Language as Power: Aramaic at (and East of) Palmyra

Catherine E. Bonesho
University of California, Los Angeles (bonesho@ucla.edu)

Introduction and Problem

The ancient Syrian city of Palmyra lay not only at the intersections of empires but also at the intersections of languages. Situated between the Roman and Parthian Empires, Palmyra was a prominent trading site or caravan city, where spices, silk, and other objects were sold and traded. Because of its location in the 'in-between', Palmyra exhibits inscriptions in more than one language. Palmyrene Aramaic, Greek, and Latin inscriptions are found there, with Palmyrene Aramaic being the most commonly used language for inscriptions. However, Palmyrene Aramaic inscriptions, dating from the first century BC to the third century AD are found not only at Palmyra itself but also in neighbouring regions, including the Levant, throughout the reaches of the former Roman Empire, as well as east of Palmyra in places like Dura-Europos. Palmyrene Aramaic as a language therefore functions beyond the limits of the city of Palmyra itself.

The continued use of Palmyrene Aramaic throughout the Mediterranean and ancient Near East by Palmyrenes instead of Greek or Latin has typically been seen as exceptional. Though other groups, such as the Nabateans, continue to hold on to their respective dialects of Aramaic, the Palmyrenes are most noted for the use of their dialect even when living as far away from Palmyra as Roman Britain. Several scholars have noted the resilience of Palmyrene Aramaic at Palmyra and abroad in the face of the imperial languages of Greek and Latin. Fergus Millar observed that 'in Palmyra alone, of all the cities in the [Roman] Empire, one could see a series of public inscriptions in both Greek and a Semitic language, in parallel, which lasted for almost three centuries'.[1] Maryline Parca notes that 'unlike other Greek cities in the region, its [Palmyra's] people continued to use their native Palmyrene'.[2] Finally, J. N. Adams argues that Palmyrene Aramaic and Latin bilingual inscriptions are evidence that 'unlike many of the speakers of the vernacular languages who came into contact with the Romans, they [the Palmyrenes] held on to their original linguistic identity, even when they were far from home and participating in Roman institutions'.[3]

Palmyrene Aramaic and Palmyra are, according to these scholars, the exception to the rule of the general adoption of Greek or Latin in the Greek and Roman East. Though the observation that Palmyra and its language are exceptional in the ancient Near East is apt, in this study, I argue that this observation follows from an *a priori* assumption that Greek generally has to be everyone's lingua franca after the annexation of parts of the ancient Near East by Alexander. This assumption leads to such questions like 'why does the city of Palmyra not adopt Greek?' or 'why do the Palmyrenes hold on to their native language even when living abroad?' These questions inevitably locate Palmyra and its language from the perspective of the so-called 'West'.

However, I argue for a fundamental reframing of studying language use in the ancient Near East, viewing Palmyrene Aramaic and its use from the perspective of the 'East', instead of the 'West'. Essentially, Greek or Latin as lingua franca need not be seen as inevitable. Indeed, Aramaic survives and, at times, flourishes well past the arrival of Alexander. Numerous documents and larger corpora attest to the continued use of Aramaic in the Hellenistic period, including the Aramaic documents

---

* I would like to thank Rubina Raja, Kenneth Lapatin, the J. Paul Getty Museum, and the Palmyra Portrait Project for organizing the Palmyra and the East symposium, as well as the other symposium participants. I benefited greatly from my colleagues' comments, as well as their papers, particularly those of Ted Kaizer, Rubina Raja, and M. Rahim Shayegan. Chance McMahon, Liane Feldman, Kevin Mattison, and Julianna Smith are also deserving of recognition for their time and advice on this study. Any errors in the piece remain my own.

---

[1] Millar 2006, 290. Andrade (2013, 179–80) writes 'Aramaic speech and writing [...] distinguished the Palmyrenes from many (but not all) civic Greeks of Syria'.

[2] Parca 2001, 71.

[3] Adams 2003, 247.

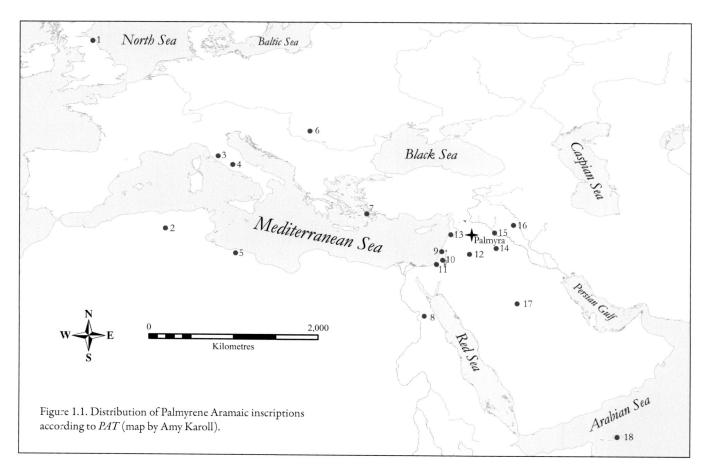

Figure 1.1. Distribution of Palmyrene Aramaic inscriptions according to *PAT* (map by Amy Karoll).

of Qumran.[4] The use of Aramaic dialects in the ancient Near East too continues well past the Hellenistic period, evidenced in numerous dialects and corpora, including Syriac, Jewish Palestinian, and Babylonian Aramaic, and Nabataean Aramaic, among many others.[5] There are plenty of examples of literary works and inscriptions, both public and private, that showcase Aramaic as a productive language in the ancient Near East even after the advent of Greek in the region.

Palmyrene Aramaic must be understood in this larger context of Aramaic dialects in the Roman Near East. The maintenance of Palmyrene Aramaic inscriptions at Palmyra and abroad thus should not merely be understood as just another means of presenting information but also as a means for Palmyrenes to maintain and distinguish their Palmyrene identity in contrast to the Greeks and Romans. Furthermore, I argue that trends in the material presentation of Greek and Aramaic bilingual inscriptions at Palmyra and Dura-Europos reveal that Palmyrenes respond to pressures to more fully incorporate Greek after Hadrian's visit to the city in the mid-second century AD through the monumental use of Palmyrene Aramaic. Their response simultaneously mimics the monumentality of Hellenistic epigraphic traditions and establishes Palmyrene Aramaic as a language of equal (or higher) standing to Greek.

The goals of this study are twofold: first, to reorient the use of Palmyrene Aramaic away from Latin and Greek, and second, to decipher why and how Palmyrene Aramaic continued to be used throughout the Roman world (contrary to west-centric expectations) and what this says about Palmyra, the identity of its citizens, and the status of Palmyrene Aramaic. Towards these respective goals, I provide an overview of the Palmyrene Aramaic corpus to show that it is used not only at the city of Palmyra but also west and, notably, east of the city; second, I perform a macroscopic study of the material presentation of the visuality or material presentation of the bilingual Greek and Palmyrene Aramaic inscriptions found at Palmyra and at Dura-Europos.

---

[4] On the popularity of Aramaic during the Hellenistic period, see Machiela 2018.

[5] On the various dialects of Aramaic used in the Near East, during the Hellenistic, Roman, and late antique periods, see Gzella 2015, 212–381. On the continued use of Aramaic under Arab rule, see Hoyland 2004. On Syriac and Greek influence, see Butts 2016.

The Palmyrene Aramaic Corpus: Both West and East

Before turning to the material presentation of Palmyrene texts, it is first necessary to introduce the geographic scope of the Palmyrene Aramaic corpus.[6] The purpose of this overview is to highlight the range in geographic location of Palmyrene Aramaic, both west *and* east of Palmyra. This use of Palmyrene Aramaic east of the city and in the surrounding regions helps to reconstruct the function and utility of Palmyrene Aramaic in the ancient Near East.

In order to visualize the extent of the geographic breadth in which Palmyrene Aramaic inscriptions were found, I include two maps below: the first locates Palmyrene Aramaic inscriptions found throughout the Roman Empire and ancient Near East (Fig. 1.1), and the second zooms in to show the degree to which Palmyrene Aramaic extended east of Palmyra (Fig. 1.2). In my descriptions of the various locations of this material, I indicate location on the map by its assigned number.[7]

Unsurprisingly, most Palmyrene Aramaic inscriptions come from the city of Palmyra itself. These inscriptions are of a variety of genres, including funerary, dedicatory, honorific, and graffiti. Many inscriptions incorporate other languages as well, notably Greek and Latin, functioning as bilingual or trilingual inscriptions.[8] For example, the famous Tariff inscription, *PAT* 0259, dating to AD 137, during the reign of the emperor Hadrian, includes both Greek and Palmyrene Aramaic in its presentation of taxes on traded goods (Fig. 1.3).[9] Overall, the vast majority of inscriptions in Palmyra, including those found attached to tombs, are written in Palmyrene Aramaic. Additional inscriptions are found in the immediate surrounding region. According to *PAT*, more than eighty inscriptions (*PAT* 1663–1747) are found in the area just outside of the city (the Palmyrene, as well as other nearby sites; not noted on map), including a Greek and Palmyrene Aramaic inscription commemorating Wahaballat, the son of the prominent Palmyrene ruler Zenobia (*PAT* 0317) found at al-Kerasi, just west of Palmyra.[10]

Palmyrene Aramaic inscriptions can also be found all over the former Roman Empire. Most of these inscriptions are bilingual, with a co-text of either Greek or Latin. Starting in the west, a Latin and Aramaic inscription (*PAT* 0246) commonly known as the Regina inscription is found in Roman Britain (Location 1).[11] An additional six Palmyrene Aramaic texts are from the area of modern Algeria (Location 2), four of which are bilingual Latin and Palmyrene Aramaic inscriptions.[12] Continuing east, four Palmyrene Aramaic bilingual inscriptions have been found in Italy, both along the Appian Way (Location 3) and in Rome (Location 4), where there is evidence for a Palmyrene community, including *PAT* 0247, a Greek and Palmyrene Aramaic bilingual dedicatory inscription.[13] Moving east toward Palmyra, other Palmyrene Aramaic inscriptions can be found in modern Libya (Location 5). In Roman-period Dacia (modern Romania) (Location 6), Palmyrenes, who were part of a Roman military unit left behind six Palmyrene Aramaic inscriptions, four of which also include a Latin text.[14] Palmyrene Aramaic inscriptions have also been found on the island of Cos and elsewhere in Greece (Location 7).[15] Finally, two possible Palmyrene Aramaic texts have been found in Egypt (Location 8).[16]

---

[6] My survey of Palmyrene inscriptions is mostly based on the collation by Hillers and Cussini 1996, *Palmyrene Aramaic Texts*, hereafter abbreviated as *PAT*. I follow their numeration, whenever possible. Yon 2013 provides an appendix of inscriptions not included in *PAT*. See also Al-Asʿad, Gawlikowski, and Yon 2012. For the Greek and Latin inscriptions of Palmyra, see Yon's (2012) *Inscriptions grecques et latines de la Syrie*, XVII.1: *Palmyre*, hereafter abbreviated *IGLS*.

[7] Cussini (2016) provides a very helpful survey of Palmyrene Aramaic, including its locations.

[8] On use of Latin and Greek at Palmyra specifically, see Al-Asʿad and Delplace 2002; Yon 2008. On Latin and Palmyrene bilingual inscriptions, see Bonesho 2019; Hutton and Bonesho 2015; Adams 2003, 247–64.

[9] For translations of and scholarship on the inscription, see Shifman 2014; Healey 2009, 164–205; and Teixidor 1983.

[10] Healey 2009, 158–61; Dijkstra 1995, 167–70; and Swain 1993.

[11] On *PAT* 0246, see Wright 1878; Birch 1878; Adams 1998; Hutton and Bonesho 2015, 270–84; and Bonesho 2019, 217–18.

[12] The texts found in Algeria are *PAT* 0253–0255, *PAT* 0990, and Albertini 1931, 29–30. See Chabot 1932.

[13] The other Palmyrene inscriptions found in Italy are *PAT* 0248–0250. On these inscriptions, see Bonesho 2019; Hutton and Bonesho 2015, 273–84; and Adams 2003, 248–53. On Palmyrenes in Rome, see Dirven 1999, 175–80; and Fowlkes-Childs 2016.

[14] Hutton (2019) argues that the Palmyrenes of Dacia 'retained a culturally-specific scribal tradition and that, minimally, one member of the army unit was capable of at least modestly competent writing' (182). For more on the Dacian inscriptions, see Hutton 2019; and Kaizer 2004, 565–69.

[15] *PAT* 1616 is a bilingual dedicatory inscription. On other inscriptions found in neighbouring regions of Greece, see Cussini 2016, n. 28.

[16] The inscriptions found in Egypt are *PAT* 1613 and *PAT* 0256, the latter of which includes a Greek co-text.

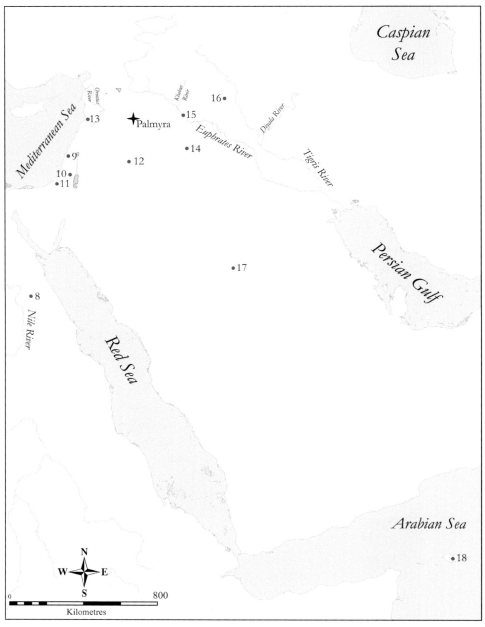

Figure 1.2. Close-up of distribution of Palmyrene Aramaic inscriptions in the Ancient Near East (map by Amy Karoll).

Palmyrene Aramaic inscriptions are not just found in the Greek and Roman West or at Palmyra. They are also found abroad in the ancient Near East (Fig. 1.2).

Palmyrene inscriptions have also been discovered throughout the Levant. There are ten monolingual Palmyrene Aramaic inscriptions found in the catacombs of Beit-Shearim (Location 9).[18] Palmyrene Aramaic inscriptions are also found in the city of Jerusalem, as well as just north of the city (Location 10). A Greek and Palmyrene Aramaic bilingual inscription was reused and found in the Negev near Haluza (Location 11).[19] South-west of Palmyra, there is a single dedicatory graffito found at Wadi Miqat in north-eastern Jordan (Location 12). Returning north, at Akkar, Lebanon, one also finds a longer dedicatory inscription in Palmyrene Aramaic (Location 13).

Palmyrene Aramaic inscriptions are also located east of Palmyra. Thirteen texts are found in modern Iraq in the Wadi Hauran, about 350 km south-east of Palmyra, including two bilingual Aramaic and Safaitic inscriptions (Location 14).[20] The city of Dura-Europos, approximately

Studies that discuss the extent of Palmyrene Aramaic inscriptions beyond Palmyra have typically focused on the inscriptions in the Mediterranean and Roman worlds, with these texts being used as evidence for the Palmyrenes maintaining their linguistic identity. For example, Adams, in his division of Palmyrene Aramaic into the categories of 'at Palmyra' and 'Abroad', only lists texts from 'the West' as abroad texts.[17] However,

---

[17] Adams 2003, 248–60; contra Adams, see Bonesho 2019.

[18] The inscriptions found at Beit-Shearim are *PAT* 0132–0141 (Mazar and others 1973; and Mazar 1985, 293–99).

[19] Naveh and Ustinova 1993. As Naveh and Ustinova comment, it is notable that this inscription is in Palmyrene Aramaic as 'in Haluza one would expect to find a Nabatean rather than a Palmyrene inscription' (91).

[20] Zerbini (2016) argues that these graffiti 'attest to the seasonal migration of a tribal group [...] the script, the onomastics, the *strategeia* of *PAT* 2732 and the likely mention of the "gods of Palmyra" in *PAT* 2740 all point to a Palmyrene cultural background for this group' (327).

240 km east of Palmyra, has an extensive corpus of Palmyrene Aramaic texts, numbering over sixty, which include monolingual inscriptions, as well as a few bilingual inscriptions that include Greek (Location 15).[21] The inscriptions from Dura-Europos are found in a variety of buildings and contexts, including at the site's Mithraeum, the Temple of Adonis, the Temple of Zeus Kyrios-Baalshamin, and private homes. Continuing east, an inscription is found at Hatra (Location 16), approximately 600 km east of Palmyra (*PAT* 1604).[22] In modern Saudi Arabia, south-east of Palmyra, there are two Palmyrene Aramaic inscriptions (Location 17).[23] Finally, a dedicatory Palmyrene Aramaic text inscribed on wood is found on the island of Soqotra (Location 18).[24] Therefore, Palmyrene Aramaic is not limited to Palmyra, but can be found farther east. It seems that Palmyrene Aramaic was one of Palmyra's exports.

As the foregoing survey has illustrated, the breadth of the use of Palmyrene Aramaic is vast. This breadth requires a stronger explanation than reading Palmyrene Aramaic inscriptions merely as maintenance of linguistic identity. Studies that offer this limited explanation and regard Palmyrene Aramaic as an 'exception' typically view Palmyra from the perspective of the Latin West (or the Greek East). By reframing the discussion of Palmyrene Aramaic to also look east, we are better able to assess for the scale of Palmyrene Aramaic in Antiquity and to decipher how Palmyrene Aramaic functioned and why Palmyrenes continued to use it even when abroad.

Methods

To answer the question about the function of Palmyrene Aramaic, I incorporate the field of sociolinguistics and an analysis of the materiality of Palmyrene Aramaic inscriptions. By focusing on how Palmyrene commissioners of inscriptions presented their native language on its own, as well as with other languages, and by contextualizing Palmyrene Aramaic in the larger use of Aramaic dialects in the ancient Near East, I offer a reconceptualization of Palmyrene Aramaic as a language of identity and power for Palmyrenes.

As William Schniedewind shows in his sociolinguistic study of Hebrew, 'language is used in social contexts for communicating needs, ideas, and emotions'.[25] Palmyrene Aramaic is no exception. The use of a language or script on an object, either on its own or in tandem with others, has already been shown to inscribe meaning. This is especially the case with script choice, as Mark Sebba describes: 'visual features of writing can be used to index a group (to whom the writing is attributed) even for those who do not know the language, or script, in question.'[26] The association of script and group is particularly relevant for the study of Palmyrene Aramaic, whose Semitic script differs not only from Greek and Latin script but also from other dialects of Aramaic in Antiquity. Scholars have already noted this particular function of Palmyrene Aramaic, including Adams, who argues that Palmyrene Aramaic inscriptions in Roman Britain acted as a 'symbolic display of the writer's ethnic identity'.[27] However, a further indication of how language and script are used for inscribing meaning can be found in the material presentation of the inscriptions on the object.

One means by which I analyse the Palmyrene Aramaic inscriptions is to concentrate on their material presentation or visuality, following recent analyses that emphasize spatiality and physicality in the study of ancient inscriptions. As Edmund Thomas and others have shown, an inscription's respective texts, images, and spatial context are closely linked and affect how an inscription is seen and interpreted.[28] In previous studies, I have proposed that if one zooms out to analyse the material presentation of an object and its inscriptions it is possible to determine the *visuality* of an inscription, simply, how the commissioners of these inscriptions or texts may have intended the objects and their texts to be seen.[29] By incorporating the materiality of inscribed objects into the analysis of language use, one is able to access how different languages were used and assessed, and what using these languages intended to project to the audience.

I have argued that one particular feature of materiality, namely the relative visuality of the texts of bilingual or trilingual inscriptions, can be used to elucidate the

---

[21] For more on these inscriptions and the Palmyrene community living at Dura-Europos, see Dirven 1999.
[22] On Palmyrenes in Hatra, see Dirven 2013.
[23] Milik and Starcky 1970; and Winnett and Reed 1973, 89.
[24] Gorea 2020.

[25] Schniedewind 2013, 15.
[26] Sebba 2015, 219.
[27] Adams 2003, 248.
[28] Thomas 2014. In regard to materiality and ancient Near Eastern studies, see Smoak and Mandell 2016; 2018.
[29] Bonesho 2019.

relative status of the languages. On objects with more than one text, the text that is presented in the most visually dominant way is 'visually primary'. One benefit of this sort of visual analysis is that it does not merely concentrate on textual or linguistic data that may have been inaccessible to the average passer-by. Rather, this type of analysis shows the multitude of ways an ancient person would have interacted with an inscription, regardless of their level of literacy. A commissioner may mark a visually primary text by a variety of means, including the relative positioning of texts on an object, the relative size of the texts and their graphemes, and the inclusion of decorative frames.

For monolingual inscriptions, determining what text is visually primary is quite simple; regardless of the workmanship of a monolingual Palmyrene Aramaic inscription or graffito, the placement of the text on the object, or the script used, Palmyrene Aramaic is the intended primary text of sight. Thus, I can make the very obvious statement that the many Palmyrene Aramaic monolingual inscriptions at Palmyra are intended to showcase Palmyrene Aramaic. Bilingual and trilingual texts are more complicated. Some are relatively straightforward. For example, the Habibi inscription, *PAT* 0250, found in Rome, places its Latin text at the top of the object with a larger text size, making it visually primary with the Palmyrene Aramaic as visually secondary. The various inscribed texts of an object can thus be ranked in terms of their visuality. Some objects, however, do not privilege a specific text; instead, the inscriptions are presented in a parallel manner and are thus visually equal.

But what is the significance of the visual primacy (or the visual ranking) of inscriptions, especially in a multilingual environment that is dealing with the influence of imperial hegemony? Instead of seeing visual primacy as the result of arbitrary decisions on the part of the commissioner or artisan responsible for the texts' production, I have previously argued that a focus on visuality can actually illuminate Palmyrene attitudes towards Roman imperialism.[30] I now provide a brief summary of this study as it illuminates the variation one sees in terms of material presentation of Palmyrene Aramaic alongside the Greek language.

The corpus of Latin and Palmyrene Aramaic bilingual inscriptions is rather small, with approximately twenty bilingual (and sometimes trilingual with an additional Greek text) inscriptions found throughout the former Roman Empire. Despite the many differences of these inscriptions and the broad geographical distribution of their provenance, they all have one feature in common. From the Habibi inscription of Rome and the Regina inscription of Roman Britain (*PAT* 0246), to the Latin and Palmyrene Aramaic inscriptions of Palmyra, all of these objects mark the Latin text as visually primary compared to the Palmyrene Aramaic text and, in the trilingual inscriptions, to the Greek text as well. The visual primacy of the Latin text over Palmyrene Aramaic is thus consistent both west of Palmyra throughout the reaches of the Roman Empire and at the city of Palmyra itself.

But what is the significance of this visual primacy of the Latin text and the secondary place of Palmyrene Aramaic? Using Homi Bhabha's notion of hybridity, I have argued elsewhere that visually primary Latin texts act as a way for Palmyrenes to display some assimilation into Roman social structures. However, the commissioners of these inscriptions do not just provide a Latin text; the Palmyrene Aramaic text is also visible, displaying a hybrid object that showcases both Romanness and Palmyrene Aramaic identity:

> The hybridity present in these Latin and Aramaic bilingual texts [...] is a byproduct of both assimilation and resistance to Roman imperialism — by including the Palmyrene Aramaic as secondary to the Latin text, the Palmyrene commissioner destabilizes, in some way, Roman power and its influence on Palmyrene culture, whether it be at Palmyra or in Rome. These inscriptions and their material presentation then display a complicated identity — they perform Romanness while also implicitly challenging Romanness, colonialization, and empire.[31]

Furthermore, the Palmyrene Aramaic inscription acts as a marker of identity for Palmyrenes living abroad. This is evident on Palmyrene Aramaic and Latin inscriptions in which the Latin text specifically identifies a commissioner as a Palmyrene, whereas the Aramaic text does not need to because the script itself acts as a marker (see, for example, the Regina inscription). It appears then that both in Rome, thousands of kilometres away from Palmyra, and at Palmyra itself, the continued use of and material presentation of Palmyrene Aramaic vis-à-vis Latin is best understood as Palmyrenes distinguishing their status as Palmyrene from the Romans of the West. An analysis of inscriptions' material presentation, then, can reveal how ancient groups understood or sought to portray themselves.

---

[30] Bonesho 2019.

[31] Bonesho 2019, 227.

Therefore, an analysis of the material presentation, specifically the relative visuality of inscriptions, can be used to illuminate Palmyrene attitudes about imperial hegemony. Moreover, an analysis of relative visuality can also aid in the determination of how the Palmyrenes understood their own language. I now turn to my analysis of the material presentation of Palmyrene Aramaic, especially in relation to Greek, at the city of Palmyra.

Palmyrene Aramaic and its Visuality

The visuality of Palmyrene Aramaic at the city of Palmyra is undeniable. The copious amount of Palmyrene Aramaic inscriptions, numbering in the thousands, speaks to the importance of the language for the identity of the city. Palmyrenes and others utilized the language and/or script of Palmyrene Aramaic on funerary, dedicatory, honorary, and other genres to communicate in the broader landscape of the city. But how did Palmyrene Aramaic come to hold this status?

As Gzella has argued, after the fall of the Seleucid kingdom:

> the emancipation of local dialects of Aramaic [like Palmyrene Aramaic] and their promotion to written idioms partly reflects a wave of national, or 'ethnic', and cultural self-assertion that consciously aimed to downgrade Greek influence at a moment when the control exercised by the Hellenistic ruling dynasties of Palestine, Syria, and Mesopotamia became weaker.[32]

This development also led to distinct script forms among Aramaic dialects, meaning Palmyrene Aramaic script and many of its various developments are peculiar to Palmyrene Aramaic, though the script shows similarity to other Aramaic scripts of the region.[33] Overall, the shared phonetic features among these Aramaic dialects and the sheer number of Palmyrene Aramaic inscriptions in the region suggest that Palmyrene Aramaic acted as an 'official idiom' at Palmyra and in the surrounding region.[34] Other evidence for the use of Palmyrene Aramaic as the common or spoken language of Palmyra can be found on graffiti and tesserae found in the city as many include brief Palmyrene Aramaic notations.

Palmyrene Aramaic served a variety of public and private functions at Palmyra. For example, inscriptions are used on funerary and dedicatory inscriptions, as well as to describe the sale of tombs or the activities of prominent leaders, including members of the trade caravan. Probably one of the larger parts of the corpus is funerary inscriptions. Most of these texts are monolingual and only include Palmyrene Aramaic.[35] Palmyrene citizens, depicted on their funerary busts and influenced by Greek, Roman, Parthian, and Arabic styles, chose to have their funerary busts inscribed with the language of their city. As Gzella argues, the funerary epigraphic tradition of Palmyrene Aramaic functions beyond a mere vernacular and showcases Palmyrene Aramaic as a 'prestige language [...] deemed suitable for public representation'.[36] For example, a funerary inscription currently held at the Harvard Museum of the Ancient Near East, HSM 1894.3.1, tells us of a certain Malē in a monumental style of Palmyrene Aramaic script.[37] Overall, the language of Palmyrene Aramaic is used throughout the city. Indeed, the choice to inscribe Palmyrene Aramaic in the city, both inside and outside of buildings, authenticates Palmyrene Aramaic and promotes its further use. Walking through the city of Palmyra showcases Palmyrene Aramaic, as just that, *Palmyrene*.

However, Palmyrene Aramaic is not alone. Other languages are also present at Palmyra, notably Greek and Latin, which figure into the public inscriptions, both as monolingual inscriptions, and as part of bilingual and trilingual inscriptions. For example, the Palmyrene Aramaic version of the Tax Tariff (discussed below) was set up publicly with a Greek counterpart as a monumental administrative record of the municipal taxes on trade goods. The use of the Greek language on predominately public inscriptions has led some scholars to assume that Palmyra was a de facto bilingual city in terms of epigraphic traditions. For example, David G. K. Taylor argues that 'at Palmyra there were two H[igh] varieties, Greek and Aramaic [...], which had equal public status'.[38] However, there are indications that Palmyrene Aramaic was the more prominent language of the city, especially before the advent of the Roman emperor Hadrian and

---

[32] Gzella 2015, 214–15.

[33] Gzella 2015, 251–52.

[34] Gzella 2015, 249. Because of the shared features of Aramaic dialects in the region, Gzella argues 'that Aramaic was widely used as a vernacular in Palmyra' (252). Another example for Palmyrene Aramaic as a regional dialect is its use by a Nabatean on an inscription at Palmyra (*PAT* 0319).

[35] Greek is also used on some funerary inscriptions, such as the funerary inscription for Viria Phoebe and Gaius Vurus (*IGLS* 401).

[36] Gzella 2015, 254. The topic of Aramaic as a prestige language has been the subject of some debate, see Gzella 2015, 165.

[37] Cussini and others 2018.

[38] Taylor 2002, 320. Adams (2003) too understands Palmyra as a bilingual city (34 n. 98).

the increased influence of Greek networks.[39] Indeed, as Taylor has noted, 'from the available evidence it would appear that Greek never fully displaced Aramaic, which continued to be used for official purposes'.[40] The evidence of inscriptions support this. While the number of Palmyrene Aramaic texts numbers over 2500, the number of Greek inscriptions is much lower, at 524. And of the total 524 Greek inscriptions found at Palmyra and in the immediate surrounding area, 227 (43 per cent) are bilingual inscriptions that also include Palmyrene Aramaic. Therefore, even though Greek is undoubtedly present and public at the city, it is often accompanied by Palmyrene Aramaic. On the other hand, Palmyrene Aramaic inscriptions more commonly stand on their own.[41] Overall, the prevalence of both Greek and Palmyrene Aramaic begs the question of why some languages are used over another. One possible answer is that, as Nathanael Andrade argues, 'Greek or Aramaic usage could highlight significant cultural difference'.[42] One means by which to determine this cultural difference is an analysis of the inscriptions' material presentation or visuality.

Unlike the corpus of Palmyrene Aramaic and Latin bilingual inscriptions, which shows unity in its material presentation, Greek and Palmyrene Aramaic inscriptions vary, regardless of their location. For example, the two Greek and Palmyrene Aramaic bilingual inscriptions found in Rome exhibit divergent material presentations: *PAT* 0247 displays the Greek inscription as visually primary, while *PAT* 0249 displays the Palmyrene Aramaic inscription as primary. Similar variations occur at Palmyra and in the surrounding areas; however, there are trends to be discovered among the epigraphic remains that can reveal Palmyrene language ideology.[43]

It is not Palmyrene Aramaic but Greek inscriptions that are overwhelmingly presented as visually primary on bilingual inscriptions. For example, the honorific inscription of *PAT* 1374 has the Greek text fill the entirety of the top panel and the top two lines of the bottom panel, while the fragmentary Aramaic inscription is found below the Greek text on the bottom panel and on the side of the column console. Here, Greek is the visually primary text. Another example, *PAT* 0258, a dedicatory inscription to Baalshamin found at Et-Tayyibe, displays the Greek and Palmyrene Aramaic inscriptions within a larger frame. The much longer Greek inscription is displayed on the top of the object, with a larger grapheme size than the Palmyrene Aramaic graphemes. The Palmyrene Aramaic inscription, though smaller and placed below the Greek, appears well executed. Both Greek and Palmyrene are featured, but the former is most visually prominent. Overall, of the 227 bilingual and trilingual inscriptions that include Greek and Palmyrene Aramaic texts, 73 per cent showcase Greek as visually primary compared to Palmyrene Aramaic.[44] Despite a lack of uniformity, Greek texts are more often than not visually primary to the Palmyrene Aramaic text in bilingual inscriptions found at Palmyra in all periods.

The privileging of the Greek components of bilingual inscriptions over Palmyrene Aramaic at Palmyra on such a grand scale can be read as one means by which Palmyrene citizens marked their Greekness. The visual primacy of Greek texts in the public sphere of the city, as well as other linguistic and epigraphic features, mimic larger Greek epigraphic habits in the Mediterranean and showcase their assimilation into Greek networks in the eastern Mediterranean.[45] By incorporating Greek into the texts of the city so publicly, the Palmyrenes are marking their city as Greek. However, similar to the Latin and Palmyrene Aramaic inscriptions discussed above, these inscriptions do not merely provide Greek, they also provide Palmyrene Aramaic as visually secondary to the Greek. The Palmyrenes, have an epigraphic habit that in the words of Millar, is 'a borrowing from the wider Greek

---

[39] See Andrade 2013, 171–210.

[40] Taylor 2002, 320. Other scholars have noted that at Palmyra Greek seems to be relegated to more public inscriptions (many times with a corresponding Palmyrene Aramaic inscription) while Aramaic is used for funerary and religious inscriptions.

[41] As Andrade (2013) shows: 'Bilingualism in inscriptions or alternating employment of Greek or Aramaic in different contexts, for instance, constituted visible and material embodiments of the cultural tensions lingering in Roman imperial Palmyra' (179).

[42] Andrade 2013.

[43] Stuckenbruck (2016) has also found variation at Palmyra and Dura-Europos in terms of what he calls the 'physical juxtaposition' of the Greek and Palmyrene Aramaic texts. He writes: 'The spatial relationship between the versions is, to be sure, variously represented, for example, with the Greek above the Aramaic, the Aramaic above the Greek, side by side on the same face of stone, front and back, or on different faces of a console' (178).

[44] For some of the inscriptions, it is difficult to determine visually primacy, either because the inscriptions are fragmentary or because photographs are unavailable.

[45] Taylor (2002) also finds the language of the Greek inscriptions to be of 'good quality, conforming to contemporary literary standards' and concludes that Greek was learned through a more formal education (318).

world, but in a unique bilingual form'.[46] The Aramaic text thus marks the object and the commissioners as a sort of hybrid, with the Palmyrene Aramaic text destabilizing and subverting Greek influence at Palmyra. These bilingual inscriptions and their material presentation thus indicate cultural tension and simultaneously make the claim that, in the words of Andrade: 'All citizens were Palmyrene, and they belonged to a Greek politeia.'[47]

Despite the prevalence of Greek, there are examples of Palmyrene Aramaic presented as visually primary at Palmyra. For example, *PAT* 1352, an honorific inscription reused at the Temple of Bel, is found on a column console. The console has two panels, with the upper panel being larger and jutting out. The six-line Palmyrene Aramaic inscription fills the entirety of the upper panel and continues on the first line of the lower panel. The three-line Greek inscription falls under the Palmyrene Aramaic. Despite the texts having similar size graphemes, the Palmyrene Aramaic text's more prominent position on both panels of the console indicates that *PAT* 1352 intends the Palmyrene Aramaic text to be visually primary. The bilingual inscriptions of Palmyra that present Aramaic as visually primary are relatively rare, with only sixteen total of the 227 bilingual (and trilingual) inscriptions.[48] These inscriptions are found in a variety of locations, including the Temple of Bel and in various necropolises. The inscriptions date from the first century AD through the early third century; however, of the ten of these inscriptions that can be dated either by the content of the inscription or on stylistic grounds, eight date to the first century or early second century AD. The dated tomb foundation inscriptions, for example, all date to the first century AD. Though the data is limited, it appears that displaying Palmyrene Aramaic as visually primary over Greek was more common before Hadrian's efforts to more fully incorporate Syria into the Greek East. The people of Palmyra later responded to these efforts, and more fully integrated Greek (and Latin) into their epigraphic practices.[49]

I now turn to the last category of bilingual inscriptions' presentation at Palmyra, those that make Palmyrene Aramaic visually parallel or equivalent to Greek. Bilingual inscriptions do not always have a visually primary text. Indeed, some objects purposefully display the Greek and Palmyrene Aramaic texts as parallel or equivalent to one another in their visuality. At times, some of these inscriptions may slightly lean toward one language as primary; however, various components of the presentation, such as including portions of texts on the same line, suggest that the two texts lean towards visual parallelism. At Palmyra, this sort of presentation does not occur often (approximately thirty-two of the 227 bilingual Greek and Palmyrene Aramaic inscriptions), but it is present throughout the city, in a variety of locations and in a variety of genres of inscriptions. Of the thirty-two inscriptions, twenty-six are dated either explicitly in the inscription or are able to be dated by stylistic features, and of those, eighteen date to the second century, with the majority (sixteen) dating after Hadrian's visit to Palmyra and the height of the caravan trade.[50] The other dated inscriptions that present Greek and Aramaic as visually parallel date to the first half of the third century. Though the objects that display Palmyrene Aramaic and Greek as equals are rare, they, like their Greek visually primary counterparts, confirm that Palmyrenes adopted components of Greek culture and simultaneously maintained their own Palmyrene traditions.

An example of Palmyrene Aramaic and Greek being presented visually parallelly is *PAT* 1378 (*IGLS* 222), found in the north-eastern part of the agora and dating to AD 199. The Aramaic and Greek texts are presented side by side, with Aramaic on the right, and Greek on the left. The Greek text is composed of seven total lines with one line on the upper rim, five lines on the main panel, and one line on the lower rim. The Aramaic text,

---

[46] Millar 2006, 230.

[47] Andrade 2013, 204.

[48] These inscriptions are (based on *IGLS*, respective date in parentheses): *IGLS* 16 (AD 24); *IGLS* 17 (AD 24); *IGLS* 318 (AD 39); *IGLS* 40 (late first, early second century); *IGLS* 537 (AD 59); *IGLS* 402 (AD 67); *IGLS* 461 (AD 79–80); *IGLS* 512 (AD 98); *IGLS* 449 (AD 136 per Milik); *IGLS* 427 (AD 150–180); *IGLS* 428 (AD 170–200); *IGLS* 377 (AD 225); *IGLS* 481 (undated); *IGLS* 525 (undated); *IGLS* 330 (undated); *IGLS* 562 (undated).

[49] There are other epigraphic trends found at Palmyra noted by scholars. For example, Stuckenbruck notes: 'Greek summaries of longer Aramaic versions are attested at Palmyra only in inscriptions that preserve dates before the third century [...] By contrast, those inscriptions with Aramaic summaries of longer Greek versions [...] tend to be later' (2016, 183).

[50] These inscriptions are: *IGLS* 178 (AD 113–114); *IGLS* 350 (AD 121); *IGLS* 145 (AD 130–131); *IGLS* 150 (AD 132); *IGLS* 183 (mid-second century); *IGLS* 413 (mid-second century); *IGLS* 424 (AD 147); *IGLS* 426 (AD 140–160); *IGLS* 524 (AD 138); *IGLS* 529 (AD 143); *IGLS* 532 (AD 150–170); *IGLS* 533 (AD 160–190); *IGLS* 560 (mid-second century); *IGLS* 542 (AD 185); *IGLS* 523 (AD 186); *IGLS* 403 (AD 191); *IGLS* 222 (AD 199); *IGLS* 82 (AD 201); *IGLS* 429 (AD 200–220); *IGLS* 473 (AD 212); *IGLS* 257 (AD 214); *IGLS* 543 (AD 218); *IGLS* 477 (AD 224); *IGLS* 472 (AD 236); *IGLS* 479 (AD 252); *IGLS* 475 (undated); *IGLS* 520 (undated); *IGLS* 522 (undated); *IGLS* 415 (undated); *IGLS* 554 (undated).

Figure 1.3. The Palmyrian Tariff (*PAT* 0259). Panels one (left) and two (right) of the Tariff Inscription. Palmyra. 137. Marble. Inv. no. DV-4187 (image is taken from <www.hermitagemusum.org>, courtesy of The State Hermitage Museum, St Petersburg, Russia).

with a total of eight lines, has one line on the upper rim, the next two lines on the rounding above the main panel, and five lines on the main panel. Greek and Palmyrene Aramaic here are monumentally parallel, with no text being visually primary.

The most famous example of visual parallelism on Greek and Palmyrene Aramaic inscriptions is provided by the Tariff Inscription (*PAT* 0259), which has four panels of Greek and Palmyrene Aramaic texts (Fig. 1.3). The four panels of text are set up on the same horizontal axis with the main heading of both the Greek and Palmyrene Aramaic text located at the top of the second panel from the left, with the Greek text as the topmost language of these headings. The texts then move logically to the leftmost panel, which includes the date of the tariff, as well as the names of officials. In this section the Greek text is positioned above its corresponding Palmyrene text. However, the leftmost panel (panel one) is where this relative positioning ends. For the other three panels, the Palmyrene Aramaic and Greek texts that provide the specific details of the tariff are provided in parallel. The second panel from the left (with headings) provides the remainder of the Aramaic inscription, with panels three and four providing the rest of the Greek text. The largest sections of both the Palmyrene Aramaic and Greek texts are presented immediately next to one another, in a relatively equal manner visually. Though there are various features of the text that may seem to visually privilege the Greek text over the Aramaic, such as the Greek heading being placed above the Aramaic heading, other features seem to indicate the privileging of the Palmyrene Aramaic. For example, the Tariff's Palmyrene Aramaic text is presented with a slightly larger grapheme size than the Greek graphemes (approximately 15 per cent larger). Additionally, other than the headings and description of the decree, for which the Greek is given first, the remainder of the inscription, which includes the details of the specific taxes, provides the Palmyrene Aramaic prior to the Greek inscription. Overall, though there are features of the Tariff Inscription that privilege one text over the other, unlike many of the other bilingual texts we have access to, the Tariff Inscription presents the Palmyrene Aramaic and Greek texts as visually parallel. The sort of visual equivalency in presentation on these inscriptions brings to mind the United Nations' 'Standards of Multilingualism' for online publications which suggests a menu of language options in order to 'to ensure the full and equitable treatment of all the official languages'.⁵¹ Are the Palmyrenes too giving their language equal treatment as an 'official' language?

Though the objects that display Palmyrene Aramaic and Greek as equals are rare, they, like their Greek visually primary counterparts, confirm that Palmyrenes adopted components of Greek culture and simultaneously maintained their own Palmyrene traditions. Andrade has argued that the very bilingual nature of the Tariff Inscription, and its other Greek and native Palmyrene features, for example, 'exemplifies how the Greek civic processes of Palmyra simultaneously referenced, internalized, and compensated for, the cultural tensions so prevalent in Palmyrene society'.⁵² I argue that the material presentation of the Tariff Inscription and the other parallel presented inscriptions too showcases the Palmyrenes' delicate balance of Greek and Palmyrene cultures.

All of the Greek and Palmyrene bilingual inscriptions, not just those that are visually parallel, offer insight into the Palmyrene reception of Greek culture. While the inclusion of Greek texts on any inscription in Palmyra undoubtedly points to the increased cultural capital of the Greek language in the city, especially in the mid-second century, it also is indicative of Palmyrene mimicry of Greek (and Roman) epigraphic practice. By including Greek texts, the Palmyrenes are emulating the use of Greek because of its associated prestige and potentially because of its status as a lingua franca in other regions of the ancient Near East. However, in the vein of Bhabha, this emulation is imperfect.⁵³ These inscriptions do not merely include Greek, they also include Palmyrene Aramaic, an imperfect emulation of Greek epigraphic practice. Though the Greek and Palmyrene bilingual inscriptions (and the Greek monolingual inscriptions) are indicative of Greek influence in the city, there are indications of a push-back against these influences in the material presentation of inscriptions in the city.

It is at this point that the visually parallel Greek and Palmyrene Aramaic inscriptions can be used to elucidate Palmyrenes' views of their own language. The thirty-two visually parallel inscriptions mostly date to after Hadrian's visit to Palmyra in AD 129 and likely reflect responses to his and others' efforts to increase Syria's Greek qualities. These inscriptions present the languages as equal side-by-side languages. If the more pronounced inclusion of Greek is a result of the mimicking of Greek epigraphic practice, then what is the effect of presenting Palmyrene Aramaic as an equivalent alongside Greek? I would argue that this presentation has two effects. The first is that it upsets the mimetic of Greek epigraphic practice at Palmyra. Instead of merely adopting Greek inscriptions outright, the Palmyrenes continue to include Palmyrene Aramaic both because of its utility as a vernacular and because it is *their* language, the language of Palmyrene identity.

A second effect of the visual parallelism of Greek and Palmyrene Aramaic inscriptions that follows from this is a strategic presentation of language status. While the inclusion of Greek mimics Greek epigraphic practice, so too does the inclusion of Palmyrene Aramaic as a lapidary inscription. Gzella describes how as late as the second century AD Palmyrenes and other groups

> adopted the Hellenistic 'epigraphic habit', that is, the custom of erecting statues and inscriptions in public in honour of themselves and their peers [...] [but] they often used their recently-formalized Aramaic dialects instead of or besides Greek in order to demonstrate their economic power and cultural prestige.⁵⁴

The Palmyrene mimicry of the Greek monumental tradition thus, at least in part, influenced the Palmyrenes to monumentalize their Aramaic dialect. However, this influence can also be found on the visually parallel Greek and Palmyrene Aramaic inscriptions. As Gzella argues, the choice to inscribe Palmyrene Aramaic instead of Greek was meant to showcase power and prestige, but so too does the choice to inscribe these languages in a parallel fashion.

I argue that the parallel presentation of Greek and Palmyrene Aramaic reveals an attempt to make Palmyrene Aramaic an equivalent to the prestige language of Greek in the region. The commissioners of the thirty-two visually parallel inscriptions appropriate Greek epigraphic habits to make a claim that the language of Palmyrene Aramaic is equivalent to Greek and that it too is or at least should be a language of power in the region. They also assert Palmyra's power and influence in the region as equivalent to those of the Greeks, and possibly as an alternative to the Greeks. Palmyrene Aramaic would thus function similarly to Coptic, in that,

---

51 'Minimum Standards of Multilingualism for United Nations' Websites', United Nations <https://www.un.org/en/multilingualism-web-standards> [accessed 10 October 2021].

52 Andrade 2013, 188.

53 On mimicry as imperfect, see Bhabha 1994.

54 Gzella 2015, 215. It is important to acknowledge (and Gzella does) that this monumental tradition is also influenced by earlier West Semitic traditions.

Figure 1.4. *PAT* 1097–98: relief with Palmyrene Aramaic inscriptions from the Temple of Gadde in Dura-Europos (© WPAIP, by Catherine E. Bonesho and Nathaniel Greene with permission of Yale University Art Gallery).

the increased cultural capital of Greek in the second century and Palmyrene mimicking of that epigraphic tradition and elevation of their understanding of Palmyrene Aramaic, is one possible explanation for Palmyrenes holding on to their language abroad. To determine how Palmyrene Aramaic was viewed outside of Palmyra, I now move east to the city of Dura-Europos to determine how the Palmyrenes living there displayed their Aramaic dialect.

according to Jean-Luc Fournet, Coptic 'developed and attempted to undermine the monopoly that the Greek language had held for centuries as the official language [of Egypt]'.[55] Palmyrene Aramaic and its marked script thus continue to function as a marker of Palmyrene identity and of Palmyra's unique and powerful standing in the Levant. The parallel visual presentation simultaneously functions to equate Greek and Palmyrene Aramaic *and* to mark Palmyrene Aramaic as in some sense anti-Greek, at least in the sense that it upsets Greek's supposed monopoly as a language of power in the region. The material presentation of these inscriptions reveals Palmyrene attitudes toward their own language, specifically, their efforts to elevate their Aramaic dialect, efforts which seem to have worked.

Though it is difficult to ascertain whether the parallel presentation was a result of a conscious strategic endeavour to raise Palmyrene Aramaic to the equivalent of Greek, the dating of most of the visually parallel inscriptions to after Hadrian's visit to the city suggests that this presentation, at least in part, responds to increased Greek influence. This is not to say that the increased influence of Greek is the sole reason why Palmyrene Aramaic becomes so prevalent. Certainly, Palmyrene Aramaic develops from the rich Semitic epigraphic tradition in the ancient Near East. However,

Visuality East of Palmyra at Dura-Europos

Dura-Europos, overlooking the banks of the Euphrates River, at various stages was under the control of the Greeks, the Romans, the Parthians, and the Sasanians, and thus the archaeological evidence and epigraphic record showcase the amalgam of contacts in the ancient Near East. One indication of a multicultural Dura-Europos is the plurality of languages preserved at the site. As Ted Kaizer writes: 'Dura-Europos was rich in gods and rich in languages.'[56] At Dura-Europos there is evidence of the languages of Greek, Palmyrene Aramaic, Syriac, Hatrean and other Aramaic dialects, Latin, Parthian, Middle-Persian, Safaitic, and Hebrew.[57] However, this does not mean all languages functioned equally at the city. Throughout most of Dura's history, Greek was the primary language of writing for both public and private purposes.[58]

Though Greek was dominant at Dura-Europos, Palmyrene Aramaic also enjoyed use in the city and is the only dialect of Aramaic that makes substantial appearance, likely because of the Palmyrene population living there.[59]

---

[55] Fournet 2020, 1–2.

[56] Kaizer 2009, 235.

[57] Kaizer 2009, 235.

[58] Gzella 2015, 247. Through the Parthian and Roman periods of the city, Greek continued to be dominant.

[59] Dirven 1999.

1. LANGUAGE AS POWER: ARAMAIC AT (AND EAST OF) PALMYRA

Figure 1.5. *PAT* 1089: relief with Palmyrene Aramaic and Greek visually parallel inscriptions from the Temple of Zeus Kyrios in Dura-Europos (© WPAIP, by Catherine E. Bonesho and Nathaniel Greene with permission of Yale University Art Gallery).

The majority of these inscriptions are monolingual, though some are bilingual, with an additional Greek inscription.[60] Unlike Italy and elsewhere in the western Mediterranean with Palmyrene populations, there are many monolingual Palmyrene inscriptions at Dura-Europos.[61] For example, within the Temple of Gadde, two reliefs, dating to AD 159, contain a total of five monolingual Palmyrene Aramaic inscriptions (*PAT* 1094–96 and *PAT* 1097–98 [Fig. 1.4]).[62] In a city in which Greek leans towards being the predominant language, these monolingual Palmyrene Aramaic inscriptions seem to mark spaces like the Temple of Gadde as Palmyrene, though not necessarily exclusively. The visuality of these monolingual Palmyrene Aramaic inscriptions is, just that, Palmyrene Aramaic. Far from home, east of Palmyra, the Palmyrenes of Dura-Europos continue to not just hold on to their Palmyrene epigraphic traditions but mark them prominently.[63]

In addition to the monolingual Aramaic inscriptions, there are a few Palmyrene Aramaic and Greek bilingual texts found at Dura-Europos.[64] Much like the Palmyrene Aramaic and Greek bilingual inscriptions found at Palmyra, the bilingual texts at Dura-Europos exhibit variety in their material presentation. The earliest of these inscriptions is *PAT* 1089, dating to AD 31 (Fig. 1.5). The inscription, located in the Temple of Zeus Kyrios, presents the Greek and Palmyrene Aramaic texts on the right and left, respectively, in a parallel manner on the bottom panel, though there is also a remnant of another Greek text at the top of the relief. According to Lucinda Dirven, the iconography and inscription are prominently influenced by Palmyrene, as well as local Durene traditions, with Greek being a sort of secondary influence.[65] Indeed, some of the inscriptions' features, such as the date being later in the Greek text (akin to the Palmyrene epigraphic habit) suggest that Greek is added to the object in order to, in the words of Dirven, 'adapt […] to the situation in Dura-Europos, where Greek was the main language'.[66] Unlike the parallel Palmyrene Aramaic and Greek inscriptions at Palmyra that date to the second century AD, which I have argued reflect Palmyrene efforts to make their language equivalent to Greek, the parallel texts of *PAT* 1089 of Dura-Europos instead suggest that Greek was added because of the Greek-speaking locale of Dura-Europos.

---

[60] On the Semitic texts of Dura-Europos, including the Palmyrene texts, see Buisson 1939; and Bertolino 2004. On the bilingual Greek and Palmyrene inscriptions of Dura-Europos, see Stuckenbruck 2016, 177–89.

[61] *PAT* 1117, a Palmyrene Aramaic graffito transcribed into Greek characters, potentially indicates the utility of Palmyrene Aramaic at Dura-Europos.

[62] On these reliefs, see Dirven 1999, 100. One of the reliefs, depicting the Gad of Dura, was likely made in Palmyra and brought to Dura-Europos.

[63] This coalesces, in part, with the finding of Stuckenbruck (2016), who plausibly finds that the 'Dura-Europos inscriptions reflect some of the patterns of bilinguality and language contact that characterised the texts from Palmyra' (189).

[64] The bilingual texts are *PAT* 1078, 1080, 1085, 1089, 1090, 1092, 1093, 1111, 1119, 2831, and 2832. A couple of the corresponding Greek texts have not been included in *PAT*.

[65] Dirven 1999, 212–18.

[66] Dirven 2011, 205. See also Stuckenbruck 2016, 184–85.

Figure 1.6. *PAT* 1085: bilingual Greek and Palmyrene Aramaic inscription from the Mithraeum of Dura-Europos with visually primary Palmyrene Aramaic inscription (© WPAIP, by Catherine E. Bonesho and Nathaniel Greene with permission of Yale University Art Gallery).

Two other dedicatory inscriptions are found in Greek and Palmyrene Aramaic in Dura-Europos. The first, *PAT* 1085, dates to AD 168 (Fig. 1.6). The Palmyrene Aramaic inscription, located directly beneath the relief of Mithras within a *tabula ansata*, is not only the longer inscription, but it is also intended as the visually primary inscription of the object, compared to the shorter Greek text, which runs vertically on the left side of the relief, outside of the border. Stuckenbruck rightly sees the longer Palmyrene Aramaic inscription compared to the very brief Greek text, which only names the dedicant, as reflective of the tendency at Palmyra to have Greek summaries of longer Aramaic inscriptions prior to the third century AD.[67] In the case of text length then, there is evidence that the Palmyrenes of Dura-Europos remain influenced by Palmyrene epigraphic traditions. I argue that the material presentation of this inscription confirms Stuckenbruck's finding. It is not just the content or length of these inscriptions that shows influence from Palmyra, but also how these inscriptions are presented by their commissioners. I suggest that one reason that the Palmyrene inscription of *PAT* 1085 is more visually prominent than the Greek inscription is because of efforts to raise Palmyrene's status in the mid-second century AD in response to growing Greek influence.

Another bilingual inscription is found at the main gate of Dura-Europos, dating to AD 244, and is dedicated to Nemesis (*PAT* 1078; Fig. 1.7). The inscriptions are both included on a panel below the relief with clear guidelines for both the Palmyrene Aramaic and Greek. The Greek text occupies the entirety of the first two lines, with one word found on line three. The Palmyrene Aramaic text fills the rest of line three and the whole of line four. Overall, though both texts are composed by a skilled hand, the Greek not only has a larger grapheme size, but also appears as the topmost text, making the Greek text more visually primary than its Palmyrene counterpart. Providing a visually primary Greek inscription in mid-third-century Dura-Europos, coalesces with the evidence from Palmyra that during this time, the Greek language enjoyed more prominence.[68]

---

[67] Stuckenbruck 2016, 183.

[68] Through linguistic analysis Stuckenbruck (2016) similarly finds that 'towards the end of the era of Palmyrene self-rule, Greek was gaining a certain ascendancy in relative length as well as in the influence it exerted on many parallel Aramaic texts through increasing numbers of loan words' (189). He points to the transliteration of the name Nemesis from Greek into Palmyrene Aramaic as further evidence of this phenomenon.

Finally, there are numerous bilingual graffiti found at Dura-Europos (*PAT* 1092, 1093, 1111, and 1119). Many of these graffiti are found on the famous 'Banquet Scene', with both Greek and Palmyrene Aramaic being used to label figures. While some graffiti are quite fragmentary and are thus difficult to determine visuality, others, including *PAT* 1119, present Greek and Palmyrene Aramaic as visually parallel.

Though the visuality of the Durene bilingual inscriptions do not completely coalesce with the visuality of Palmyrene inscriptions, I argue that the material presentations of the inscriptions certainly reflect similar motivations, just in different cities with different linguistic features. While the bilingual Greek and Palmyrene Aramaic inscriptions of Palmyra overwhelmingly present Greek as visually primary, there are some trends to be found in the epigraphic data. Those inscriptions that present Palmyrene Aramaic as visually primary tend to date to the first century AD, while those which display Palmyrene Aramaic and Greek as visually parallel tend to date to the mid-second century AD, after Hadrian's visit to the city and Roman efforts to more fully Hellenize the region. This movement of Palmyrene Aramaic as visually equivalent to Greek reflects the likely push-back to Hadrian's visit and the increased Greek influence, with the Palmyrenes effectively commissioning inscriptions to make the claim that Palmyrene Aramaic is just like Greek. Though the epigraphic data for this sort of bilingual visuality in Palmyrene Aramaic and Greek is very limited at Dura-Europos, one sees analogous usage of visuality there.

However, the visuality at Dura-Europos displays somewhat differently because of the fact that Dura-Europos has Greek as its predominant language. Therefore, in the first century AD when Aramaic is more commonly displayed as visually primary at Palmyra, the prevalence of Greek at Dura-Europos moves the Greek up to visual parallelism. In the mid-second century AD, when Greek and Palmyrene Aramaic inscriptions are more often displayed as visually parallel at Palmyra, one finds that Palmyrene Aramaic has become more visually primary at Dura-Europos. Both at Palmyra and at Dura-

Figure 1.7. *PAT* 1078: Greek and Palmyrene Aramaic inscription of Dura-Europos dedicated to Nemesis with visually primary Greek inscription (© WPAIP, by Catherine E. Bonesho and Nathaniel Greene with permission of Yale University Art Gallery).

Europos, Palmyrene Aramaic is displayed prominently in response to Greek influence. At Palmyra, though visually primary Palmyrene texts more commonly date to the first century, the vast majority of inscriptions still display Greek primarily. However, in response to increased Greek influence in the mid-second century, both at Palmyra and at Dura-Europos, the Palmyrenes push back and display their Aramaic dialect more prominently. Finally, the inscriptions of the late third century AD in both cities, reflect the growing prevalence of Greek by displaying Greek as visually primary. An analysis of the visuality of bilingual inscriptions from Palmyra and Dura-Europos suggests that the Palmyrenes of Dura-Europos were in continued contact with the epigraphic habits of Palmyra. Indeed, as Stuckenbruck argues:

> at Dura-Europos we are not dealing with a Palmyrene community which, despite any traits acquired through its socio-religious context, had broken off from Palmyra

itself. Instead, the Palmyrene residents of Dura-Europos, at least linguistically, continued to orientate themselves around and draw from Palmyra as their 'mother city'.[69]

But by imitating the Palmyrene epigraphic habit, the Durenes do more than just show influence, they also showcase the views of the language of Palmyrene Aramaic in the ancient Near East.

Conclusions

Karen Stern has previously argued that graffiti and other writings act as more than just 'tags' or mindless writing; rather 'local populations used common and socially acceptable media to compete with one another'.[70] According to Stern, the relative placement of two texts on an object can be indicative of competition. For example, *PAT* 1080 is a Palmyrene Aramaic text seemingly secondarily attached to a Greek inscription on a relief of Herakles found near the Palmyrene Gate (Fig. 1.8). Here the writers of the Aramaic text compete with the visuality of the Greek inscription found at the bottom of the relief by providing an Aramaic text in the middle of the relief by Herakles' thighs in slightly larger graphemes than those of the Greek inscription. Though the relief seems to have been commissioned to have Greek inscribed at the base of the object, the addition of Palmyrene Aramaic draws attention away from the Greek. There are numerous reasons for this sort of competition, including the documentation of devotion or to mark a space as Palmyrene, but I have argued that the placement of Greek and Palmyrene Aramaic on objects in a particular manner is simultaneously indicative of language ideology and competition.[71] What Stern's analysis so aptly shows us is that ancient people used graffiti and other inscriptions 'to exhibit their devotions to a deity, their imperatives to comfort or protect dead ancestors, and their factional and civic pride'.[72] The visuality of Palmyrene Aramaic both at Dura-Europos and Palmyra showcases this last use of ancient texts, whereby Palmyrenes strive both abroad and at home to show the utility and power of their own language. For many Palmyrenes, they need not adopt Greek in their inscriptions because they already have a language that competes with Greek in Palmyrene Aramaic.

---

[69] Stuckenbruck 2016, 189.
[70] Stern 2014, 152.
[71] On the graffiti of Dura-Europos, see also Baird 2011, 49–68.
[72] Stern 2018.

Returning to the main question at hand, why do Palmyrenes hold on to their language? First, this is a poorly phrased question. Palmyrenes are not the only ancient Near Eastern group to continue to use Aramaic in the Hellenistic and Roman periods, they just happen to do it on a large scale and across large geographical areas. This article seeks to redress the issue of Palmyrene language ideology in two ways. First, this article reorients scholarly discussions of Palmyrene Aramaic to its Near Eastern context. Previous studies, including my own, have tended to concentrate on Palmyrene Aramaic bilingual inscriptions west of Palmyra, commenting on the Palmyrene propensity to hold on to their language rather than to adopt only Greek or Latin. However, as I have emphasized, Palmyrene Aramaic inscriptions are found both west *and* east of Palmyra and the Palmyrene epigraphic habit, in part, reflects the Aramaic traditions of the ancient Near East. Previous studies have typically assumed that a Palmyrene must necessarily adopt Greek or Latin when abroad; however, one must not assume that the adoption of Greek was inevitable for those living under Greek and Roman influence. Therefore, this study underscores the relevance of the language politics of Palmyrene Aramaic at Palmyra and elsewhere in the region.

Second, this article shows how an analysis of the visuality of Palmyrene Aramaic inscriptions reveals attitudes about one's own language, especially when living under imperial rule. Unlike the Latin and Palmyrene Aramaic texts that have similar material presentation regardless of their provenance, Greek and Palmyrene Aramaic inscriptions found at Palmyra, Dura-Europos, and in the Mediterranean have quite disparate displays. Despite this lack of unity, there are trends in the visuality of Greek and Palmyrene Aramaic inscriptions at Palmyra that suggest different phases in Palmyrene attitudes towards Greek influence in the city. Though the bilingual inscriptions found at Palmyra overwhelmingly provide Greek as the visually primary text, I have found two trends: Palmyrene Aramaic is more likely to be provided as visually primary to Greek prior to Hadrian's mid-second-century visit to the city and Roman efforts to incorporate more Hellenistic features into the region; and immediately after Hadrian's visit, providing Palmyrene Aramaic and Greek in a parallel fashion becomes more popular. These trends reflect Palmyrene language ideology. As other scholars have shown, one of the reasons for the Palmyrene epigraphic habit is the mimicking of Hellenistic epigraphic traditions, but this mimetic is not mere copying. Rather, Palmyrenes

Figure 1.8. *PAT* 1080: relief of Herakles with Greek and Palmyrene Aramaic texts from Dura-Europos. Housed at Yale University Art Gallery, no. 1929.373 (photo courtesy of Yale University Art Gallery, public domain).

adapted the Hellenistic tradition and instead of merely showcasing Greek, they chose to highlight their own language of Palmyrene Aramaic. In these presentations, the Palmyrenes literally raise their language to show civic pride and the power of Palmyra in the ancient Near East. The material presentation of the few bilingual inscriptions at Dura-Europos follow similar trends.

Overall, the visuality of Palmyrene Aramaic inscriptions reveals Palmyrene language ideology. In the process of acculturating to Hellenistic epigraphic traditions, the Palmyrenes push back to essentially elevate their language as a visual equivalent of Greek. This visuality is a Palmyrene cultural performance that responds to Roman and other outside pressures and seems to say that Palmyra is a power to be reckoned with. Palmyra's status at the intersection of empires meant that Palmyrene Aramaic could function as a language used in trade, yet Palmyrene Aramaic also functioned to highlight the role of the city of Palmyra, as well as its citizens. Palmyrenes who moved abroad continued this use. They commissioned inscriptions far from Palmyra, because for them Palmyrene Aramaic was already a language meant to showcase civic pride at the crossroads of Palmyra in the face of Greek and Roman influence, so why not continue to do so elsewhere in the ancient world?

Works Cited

Adams, J. N. 1998. 'Two Notes on *RIB*', *Zeitschrift für Papyrologie und Epigraphik*, 123: 235–36.
—— 2003. *Bilingualism and the Latin Language* (Cambridge: Cambridge University Press).
Al-Asʿad, K. and C. Delplace. 2002. 'Inscriptions latines de Palmyre', *Revue des études anciennes*, 104: 363–400.
Al-Asʿad, K., M. Gawlikowski, and J. Yon. 2012. 'Aramaic Inscriptions in the Palmyra Museum: New Acquisitions', *Syria*, 89: 163–83.
Albertini, E. 1931. 'Inscriptions d'El Kantara et de la région', *Revue Africaine*, 72: 193–261.
Andrade, N. 2013. *Syrian Identity in the Greco-Roman World* (Cambridge: Cambridge University Press).
Baird, J. A. 2011. 'The Graffiti of Dura-Europos: A Contextual Approach', in J. A. Baird and C. Taylor (eds), *Ancient Graffiti in Context* (New York: Routledge), pp. 49–68.
Bertolino, R. 2004. *Corpus des inscriptions semitiques de Doura-Europos* (Naples: Instituto Orientale di Napoli).
Bhabha, H. 1994. *The Location of Culture* (London: Routledge).
Birch, W. 1878. 'The Palmyrene Monument Discovered at South Shields', *Journal of the British Archaeological Association*, 34: 489–95.
Bonesho, C. 2019. 'Aesthetic of Empire: Material Presentation of Palmyrene Aramaic and Latin Bilingual Inscriptions', *Maarav*, 23: 207–28.
Buisson, R. 1939. 'Inventaire des inscriptions palmyréniennes de Doura-Europos', *Revue des études sémitiques*, 2: 17–39.
Butts, A. M. 2016. *Language Change in the Wake of Empire: Syriac in its Greco-Roman Context* (Winona Lake: Eisenbrauns).
Chabot, J. 1932. 'Nouvelle inscription palmyrénienne d'Afrique', *Comptes rendus de l'Académie des inscriptions et belles-lettres*, 76: 265–69.
Cussini, E. 2016. 'Palmyrene', in D. Selden and P. Vasunia (eds), *The Oxford Handbook of the Literatures of the Roman Empire* (Oxford: Oxford University Press) <doi.org/10.1093/oxfordhb/9780199699445.013.13>.
Cussini, E. and others. 2018. 'The Harvard Semitic Museum Palmyrene Collection', *Bulletin of American Society of Oversees Research*, 380: 231–46.
Dijkstra, K. 1995. *Life and Loyalty: A Study in the Socio-Religious Culture of Syria and Mesopotamia in the Graeco-Roman Period Based on Epigraphical Evidence* (Leiden: Brill).
Dirven, L. 1999. *The Palmyrenes of Dura-Europos: A Study of Religious Interaction in Roman Syria* (Leiden: Brill).
—— 2011. 'Strangers and Sojourners: The Religious Behavior of Palmyrenes and Other Foreigners in Dura Europos', in L. Brody and G. Hoffman (eds), *Dura Europos: Crossroads of Antiquity* (Boston: McMullen Museum of Art, Boston College), pp. 201–20.
—— 2013. 'Palmyrenes in Hatra: Evidence for Cultural Relations in the Fertile Crescent', *Studia Palmyreńskie*, 12: 49–60.
Fournet, J. 2020. *The Rise of Coptic: Egyptian versus Greek in Late Antiquity* (Princeton: Princeton University Press).
Fowlkes-Childs, B. 2016. 'Palmyrenes in Transtiberim: Integration in Rome and Links to the Eastern Frontier', in D. Slootjes (ed.), *Rome and the Worlds beyond its Frontiers* (Leiden: Brill), pp. 193–212.
Gorea, M. 2020. 'Palmyra and Socotra', in I. Strauch (ed.), *Foreign Sailors on Socotra: The Inscriptions and Drawings from the Cave Hoq* (Bremen: Hempen), pp. 447–87.
Gzella, H. 2015. *A Cultural History of Aramaic: From the Beginnings to the Advent of Islam* (Leiden: Brill).
Healey, J. F. (trans.). 2009. *Textbook of Syrian Semitic Inscriptions*, IV: *Aramaic Inscriptions and Documents of the Roman Period* (Oxford: Oxford University Press).
Hillers, D. and E. Cussini. 1996. *Palmyrene Aramaic Texts*, Publications of the Comprehensive Aramaic Lexicon Project (Baltimore: Johns Hopkins University Press).
Hoyland, R. 2004. 'Language and Identity: The Twin Histories of Arabic and Aramaic (and: Why Did Aramaic Succeed Where Greek Failed?)', *Scripta Classica Israelica*, 23: 183–99.
Hutton, J. 2019. 'The First Palmyrene Aramaic Inscription Discovered at Porolissum [MJIAZ CC 799/2002]', *Acta Musei Porolissensis*, 41: 175–85.
Hutton, J. and C. Bonesho. 2015. 'Interpreting Translation Techniques and Material Presentation in Bilingual Texts: Initial Methodological Reflections', in J. Hutton and A. Rubin (eds), *Epigraphy, Philology, and the Hebrew Bible* (Atlanta: Society of Biblical Literature), pp. 253–92.
Kaizer, T. 2004. 'Latin-Palmyrene Inscriptions in the Museum of Banat at Timişoara', in L. Ruscu and others (eds), *Orbis antiquus: studia in honorem Ioannis Pisonis* (Cluj-Napoca: Nereamia Napocae), pp. 565–69.
—— 2009. 'Religion and Language in Dura-Europos', in H. Cotton and others (eds), *From Hellenism to Islam: Cultural and Linguistic Change in the Roman Near East* (Cambridge: Cambridge University Press), pp. 235–54.
Machiela, D. 2018. 'Situating the Aramaic Texts from Qumran: Reconsidering their Language and Socio-Historical Settings', in C. Wassen and S. W. Crawford (eds), *Apocalyptic Thinking in Early Judaism: Engaging with John Collins' 'The Apocalyptic Imagination'* (Leiden: Brill), pp. 88–109.
Mazar, B. 1985. 'Those Who Buried their Dead in Beth-Shearim', *Eretz-Israel*, 18: 293–99.
Mazar, B. and others. 1973. *Beth Sheʿarim: Report on the Excavations during 1936–1940*, I: *Catacombs 1–4* (New Brunswick: Rutgers University Press).

Milik, J. and J. Starcky. 1970. 'III: Nabataean, Palmyrene, and Hebrew Inscriptions', in F. Winnett and W. Reed (eds), *Ancient Records from North Arabia* (Toronto: University of Toronto Press), pp. 141–63.

Millar, F. 2006. *Rome, the Greek World, and the East*, III: *The Greek World, the Jews, and the East*, ed. H. M. Cotton and G. M. Rogers, Studies in the History of Greece and Rome (Chapel Hill: University of North Carolina Press).

'Minimum Standards of Multilingualism for United Nations' Websites', United Nations <https://www.un.org/en/multilingualism-web-standards> [accessed 10 October 2021].

Naveh, J. and Y. Ustinova. 1993. 'A Greek-Palmyrene Aramaic Dedicatory Inscription from the Negev', '*Atiqot*, 22: 91–96.

Parca, M. 2001. 'Local Languages and Native Cultures', in J. Bodel (ed.), *Epigraphic Evidence: Ancient History from Inscriptions* (London: Routledge), pp. 57–72.

Schniedewind, W. 2013. *A Social History of Hebrew: Its Origins through the Rabbinic Period* (New Haven: Yale University Press).

Sebba, M. 2015. 'Iconisation, Attribution and Branding in Orthography', *Written Language & Literacy*, 18: 208–27.

Shifman, I. S. 2014. *The Palmyrene Tax Tariff*, ed. J. F. Healey, trans. S. Khobnya (Oxford: Oxford University Press).

Smoak, J. and A. Mandell. 2016. 'Reconsidering the Function of Tomb Inscriptions in Ancient Judah: Khirbet Beit Lei as a Test Case', *Journal of Ancient Near Eastern Religions*, 16: 192–245.

—— 2018. 'Literacy beyond Reading, Writing beyond Epigraphy: Multimodality and the Study of Northwest Semitic Inscriptions', *Maarav*, 22: 79–112.

Stern, K. 2014. 'Inscription as Religious Competition in Third-Century Syria', in J. Rosenblum, L. Vuong, and N. DesRosiers (eds), *Religious Competition in the Third Century C.E.: Jews, Christians, and the Greco-Roman World* (Gottingen: Vandenhoeck & Ruprecht), pp. 141–52.

—— 2018. *Writing on the Wall: Graffiti and the Forgotten Jews of Antiquity* (Princeton: Princeton University Press).

Stuckenbruck, L. 2016. 'The Bilingual Palmyrene-Greek Inscriptions at Dura-Europos: A Comparison with the Bilinguals from Palmyra', in T. Kaizer (ed.), *Religion, Society and Culture at Dura-Europos* (Cambridge: Cambridge University Press), pp. 177–89.

Swain, S. 1993. 'Greek into Palmyrene: Odaenathus as "Corrector Totius Orientis"?', *Zeitschrift für Papyrologie und Epigraphik*, 9: 157–64.

Taylor, G. K. 2002. 'Bilingualism and Diglossia in Late Antique Syria and Mesopotamia', in J. N. Adams, M. Janse, and S. Swain (eds), *Bilingualism in Ancient Society: Language Contact and the Written Word* (Oxford: Oxford University Press), pp. 298–331.

Teixidor, J. 1983. 'Le Tarif de Palmyre, I: un commentaire de la version palmyrénienne', *Aula Orientalis*, 1: 235–52.

Thomas, E. 2014. 'The Monumentality of Text', in J. Osborne (ed.), *Approaching Monumentality in Archaeology* (Albany: SUNY Press), pp. 57–82.

Winnett, F. and W. Reed. 1973. 'An Archaeological-Epigraphical Survey of the Ḥāʾil Area of Northern Saudi Arabia', *Berytus*, 22: 53–114.

Wright, W. 1878. 'Note on a Bilingual Inscription, Latin and Aramaic, Recently Found at South Shields', *Transactions of the Society of Biblical Archaeology*, 6: 436–40.

Yon, J. 2008. 'Bilinguisme et trilinguisme à Palmyre', in F. Biville, J.-C. Decourt, and G. Rougemont (eds), *Bilinguisme gréco-latin et épigraphie: actes du colloque, Lyon, 17–19 mai 2004*, Collection de la Maison de l'Orient méditerranéen: série épigraphique, 37 (Lyon: Maison de l'Orient méditerranéen), pp. 195–211.

—— 2012. *Inscriptions grecques et latines de la Syrie*, XVII.1: *Palmyre*, Bibliothèque archéologique et historique, 195 (Beirut: Institut français du Proche Orient).

—— 2013. 'L'épigraphie palmyrénienne depuis *PAT*, 1996–2011', *Studia Palmyreńskie*, 12: 333–79.

Zerbini, A. 2016. 'Human Mobility in the Roman Near East: Patterns and Motives', in L. Ligt and L. Tacoma (eds), *Migration and Mobility in the Early Roman Empire* (Leiden: Brill), pp. 305–44.

2. Palmyra's Maritime Trade

Katia Schörle

Aix Marseille Université, CNRS, CCJ, Aix-en-Provence, France (katia.schorle@cnrs.fr)

Introduction

Palmyra's exceptional status as a city in the Roman East, its wealth and diversity in architecture, funerary art, sculpture, or religion were deeply embedded in its particular status as a city connecting East and West. The city is often associated with the concept of the caravan city, which through long-distance terrestrial commerce connected the Roman Empire with the Far East. It is in some ways a useful concept, yet it certainly needs elaboration, since that was not Palmyra's only strength. On a local scale, Palmyra was remarkably successful in managing the diversity of its territories and its associated resources as much as creating successful conditions for strengthening its position as a central marketplace in the wider region, and its general prosperity as a city was based on the management of its hinterland resources. Its outstanding wealth, however, was in part linked to its long-distance commercial activities with the East, via the Euphrates and the Parthian world, and to commercial ties with or products originating all the way from India and the furthest provinces of China.[1] Some of it was certainly via terrestrial routes, but in this article I would like to specifically explore the maritime routes and how these may have had an impact on Palmyra's development and status as an city with worldwide connections. Palmyra was never connected to the sea, and was not a maritime city *stricto sensu*, but its economic success was deeply linked to its involvement in maritime trade.

Of Silk and Pearls

Palmyra's involvement in trade with the East between the first and third centuries AD is epigraphically well attested, and although the items traded with the East are never listed in any of the known inscriptions, they clarify the range of Palmyra's geographic areas of commercial interest and social networks. They suggest that the city's commercial attention shifted from the more northerly towns of the Euphrates, towards the Persian Gulf cities of Vologesias and Spasinou Charax and the wider Indian Ocean as a combination of change of political importance and commercial strategy, with the transhipment of goods onto rafts for quicker and cheaper transport to further markets.[2]

Cost of transport, and especially terrestrial transport, was certainly one of the challenges the Palmyrenes had to think about in terms of major costs to factor into their activities and final retail prices. The benefits that could be reaped from exotic goods, like silk, pearls, frankincense, diamonds, and other items simply unavailable in the Roman Empire could offset these, but with the annexation of the Nabatean Kingdom and Egypt, merchants in the Roman Empire had direct access to much cheaper maritime routes with fewer middlemen likely to inflate prices. Above all, sea-going ships of high tonnage meant that the quantities that could be shipped via sea far outstripped the quantities that caravans could bring in: while it only takes five camels to displace one ton of goods, one two-hundred-ton or five-hundred-ton ship equates to a caravan of a thousand camels or more. While we know that caravans could be quite large, such as the caravans travelling to Petra, which according to Strabo were no less numerous than a sizeable army force (Stra., *Geography* XVI.4.23), they ultimately could not compete with the multitude of ships that we have every reason to believe annually left the harbours of the Red Sea.[3]

---

[1] Schmidt-Colinet 1995; Schmidt-Colinet, Stauffer, and al-Asʿad 2000; Żuchowska 2013.

[2] On geographical routes: Seland 2011; 2015; 2016.

[3] Stra., *Geography* II.5.12. on 120 ships leaving annually from Myos Hormos. While the debate is about whether the ships are only those from Myos Hormos or a combined number of ships leaving Myos Hormos and Berenike, there are few reasons to disbelieve the number as a whole given the scale of archaeological data discovered in the Eastern Desert and its harbour cities. Adams 2007, 80 for the average camel load (*c.* 430 lbs, equivalent to 195.45 kg).

While it is difficult to prove with concrete archaeological evidence, it is most likely that one of the ways for the Palmyrenes to remain competitive over time was to pay particular importance to items of small size and weight but of particularly high value rather than other, heavier Eastern items such elephant tusks, slaves, or pepper, which we know were transported in bulk quantities (pepper in particular) via the Eastern Desert of Egypt harbours.[4]

In terms of items of light weight and high value, two items particularly fit that bill: silk, and pearls. Silk was produced in large quantities in China under the Han Empire, which developed not only a highly organized system via official workshops called the Eastern and Western Weaving Chambers in the capital city of Chang'an, but also by actively developing silk-producing areas in the North China Plain and the middle region of the Yellow River. As Żuchowska points out, the change in pace of technological development and textile diversification clearly happened at a dynamic period, when boosting textile production capacities seems to have been the objective.[5] The scale and rise in tributes paid to northern tribes give an idea of production capacity and surplus: between 51 BC and 1 BC, the Han dynasty increased production capacity, and went from paying c. 2.7 tons of silk yarn and 8000 silk items to 13.5 tons of silk yarn and 30,000 silk textiles in annual tributes to a northern tribe[6] — a tribute or gift in raw silk which alone is worth about 1450 million sesterces based on the Edict of Diocletian were it meant for the Roman Empire. This stands in stark contrast with Pliny's numbers that the commerce with the East annually drained the Roman Empire of a 100 million sesterces,[7] which seems ridiculously small in comparison, were it not for the fact that silk had a much higher value in the Roman Empire than in the Han Empire, and that the simple monetary conversion therefore does not quite work. The size of the tribute, however, gives a sense of scale of production capacity and potential export capacities towards the East and the Roman Empire, either via the terrestrial routes, but importantly also via the maritime routes, since Han documents underline that the trade was operated by foreign merchant boats.[8] One major outlet of trade was via India, and while it would seem that the northern ports were those busiest at importing and exporting silk from the ancient port cities of Barygaza,[9] Bakare,[10] and Barbarikon,[11] even southern harbours such as Muziris and Nelkunda[12] were shipping silk. These highly appreciated Chinese silk products made from the silkworm *Bombyx mori* were shipped on to the Roman world, along with products made from local Indian silkworm species. Branded as Chinese, Indian production also fed into the wider market of the Roman Empire.[13] Ancient Indian literature, in particular Kautilya's *Arthasastra*, but also epigraphic and archaeological evidence make it abundantly clear that local production of silks was produced by silkworms other than the *Bombyx*, and proved to be a lucrative business.[14] Interestingly, these produced silks of different qualities and colours, and must have been sold onwards and perhaps even appreciated for these specific qualities. Importantly, as

---

[4] De Romanis 2015; 2020.

[5] Żuchowska 2013.

[6] Żuchowska 2013, 138. Six thousand catties and thirty thousand catties (450 g) of silk yarn, respectively. During negotiations concerning his plans to renounce the sack of Rome in AD 410, along with a hefty price in gold and silver Alaric also demands silk tunics, four thousand of them (Zos. v.40–41).

[7] Plin., *HN* XII.41, 83–84.

[8] *Book of Han*, *Han Shu* XXVIII; Żuchowska 2013, 140.

[9] *Periplus Maris Erythraei* 49, as export, silk (Σηρικὸν) and silk thread (Νῆμα). See also *Periplus Maris Erythraei* 64 in reference to China (Thîna): 'Beyond this region, immediately under the north, where the sea terminates outwards, there lies somewhere in Thîna a very great city, not on the coast, but in the interior of the country, called Thîna, from which silk, whether in the raw state or spun into thread and woven into cloth, is brought by land to Barugaza through Baktria, or by the Ganges to Limurikê.'

[10] *Periplus Maris Erythraei* 56; fine silk cloth (Ὀθόνια Σηρικὰ). The *Periplus* mentions that 'the ships which frequent these ports are of a large size', though on account of the need to ship pepper which is 'bulky'.

[11] *Periplus Maris Erythraei* 39, Chinese furs and Chinese silk threads (Σηρικὰ δέρματα and Νῆμα Σηρικὸν) exported from there.

[12] *Periplus Maris Erythraei* 56.

[13] I fully agree with Evers's (2017, 158) remark that 'some of the silk textiles available at Barygaza and other South Asian ports although labelled "Chinese silk," sêrikon, in the *Periplus*, might have been of local Indian craftsmanship, as might some of the thread, nêma, for all we know'. Several silk *negotiatores* (*negotiator sericarius*) are known, in Rome (*CIL* VI.09678) and in the wealthy nearby town of Gabii, among which Epaphroditus (*CIL* XIV.02793, *CIL* XIV.02812; see also Evers 2017, esp. 62–66).

[14] On the *Arthasastra*, and the fact that it is a compilation of texts ranging from the fourth century BC to the third to fourth centuries AD, McClish 2019; on silks, qualities, and colours, Indian geographic origins, and literary references in Kautilya, Varadarajan 1998. Albeit slightly later than our period of interest, the Mandrasor inscription and the Temples of Aulikara testify to the importance of the silk weavers' guild, who built a temple of the sun god there in AD 437.

discussed further below, northern India was one of the regions that Palmyrenes specifically targeted as one of their new regions of commercial operations, and we know of Palmyrene boats and merchants that operated there. That silk, or rather silks of different styles and makes, were therefore one of the types of goods brought back to Palmyra or sent onwards to Egypt and the Red Sea via the maritime route and not just the terrestrial routes, is entirely compatible with the data at hand; the silk found in Palmyrene tombs therefore either arrived by land, or was shipped in via India.

Pearls were amongst the most precious Eastern imports from the wider Indian Ocean. Knowledge of pearls in the Mediterranean basin began before the Hellenistic period, but with Alexander the Great's conquest of the East, their accessibility and desirability only increased. Androsthenes of Thasos, who accompanied Alexander's fleet commander Nearchus along the coast from Indus to Tigris, and Chares of Mytilene mention pearls found in oysters in the Indian Ocean and the seas 'adjacent to Armenia, Persia, Susa and Babylon', a clear indication of the role that the Indian Ocean, Black Sea, and of course the Persian Gulf played in the acquisition of luxury goods for the West. Like silk, the lightness and value of pearls made them particularly well suited to profitable long-distance trade. And likewise, while the pearl trade was an important aspect of regional trading dynamics, archaeological finds are relatively rare.[15] Palmyrene busts from the second century AD, however, frequently represent women with necklaces and earrings that could be made of either beads of metal, textile, or glass, or pearls. The Fayyum portraits also frequently depict pearl jewellery, as does the Severan Tondo from Berlin, which illustrates best the use pearls as an elite status marker. Because the colours of the Fayyum portraits and the Tondo are intact, there is little doubt about the representation of pearls on them. Still, we have to be very careful with the Fayyum representations as they are funerary portraits, so carefully crafted representations of social status and social convention, or wishful social status for the afterlife.[16] However, D. Hope's synthesis of finds and potential identification of pearls in archaeological finds as well as on all available types of media (sculpture, numismatics, mosaics, etc.) convincingly makes the point that we do see pearls in the historical and archaeological record much more frequently than we may think.[17]

These pearls fed into the greater Roman Mediterranean pearl market and supplied a sophisticated network of known pearl sellers who handled pearls in Rome and the provinces.[18] At Rome, most pearl sellers known to us were located on the Via Sacra,[19] such as Euhodus whose tomb on the Via Appia describes him as a pearl trader of the Via Sacra. Several Calpurnii are known from the Via Sacra: one of them is L. Calpurnius Nicaei filius Cornelia Antiochus L. Calpurnius Antiochus, probably connected to Calpurnius Capitolinus, to whom eastern Mediterranean traders — in particular those from Alexandria, Asia Minor, and Syria — made a dedication in Puteoli, Rome's harbour of the East on the Bay of Naples. Other *margaritarii* are also attested, in the Velabrum, who were probably operating by the Porticus Margaritaria. Perhaps the most concrete and tangible evidence of some of the pearl traders' influence and wealth is that concerning a late second- to third-century pearl trader from Rome, Manius Publicius Hilarus, whose remarkably vivid portrait bust, the only one of a pearl trader we know of, in some ways best personifies and embodies the pearl trade, which otherwise might seem rather 'invisible'. Several inscriptions concerning Publicius give us a sense of his wealth, status, or connections in Rome, as he is known for having built or renovated at his expense a basilica on the Caelian Hill in Rome, the Basilica Hilariana. Likewise, he had sufficient influence or had rendered sufficient favours, that the members of Rome's *collegium dendrophorii* dedicated a statue to him.[20]

These pearl traders depended on a wide commercial network to bring pearls to Rome or other major marketplaces in the empire. A majority of pearls came from the wider Indian Ocean, and the Persian Gulf, the destination of Palmyrene caravans. The port city of Spasinou Charax, the most common destination on the Persian Gulf mentioned in the Palmyrene caravan inscription, might have been a major intermediary pearl market for

---

[15] Hope 2019–2020 for an overview of all known pearls found in the West.

[16] On this, including the evidence of fake pearls, and generally on pearls coming in via the Red Sea of Egypt, see Schörle 2015.

[17] Hope 2019–2020.

[18] Schörle 2015.

[19] *CIL* VI.9545–49; 33872; 37804; *CIL* X.6492.

[20] *CIL* VI.30973b. 'M(anio) Poblicio Hilaro | margaritario | collegium dendrophorum | Matris deum M(agnae) I(daeae) et Attis | quinq(uennali) p(er)p(etuo) quod cumulata | omni erga se benignitate | meruisset cui statua ab eis | decreta poneretur.' On Hilarus's career and building activities in Rome, see Perez Gonzalez 2017 and Tran 2006, 177, 195, 201, and esp. 247–48.

the Persian Gulf and Indian trade during the Roman period, as strongly suggested by the continuation of a pearl market tradition in the Sassanid and Early Islamic periods in the nearby town of Ulla. It is equally suggestive that Palmyra's connections include strategic places not only in terms of maritime routes but also access to pearls. The connections to the isle of Tylos, modern Bahrain, are well attested, with the presence on Tylos of a Palmyrene satrap with relations to his home city in AD 131. Two other Palmyrenes are known as archons on the island, and one of the tombs of the Janussan cemetery on Bahrain may also be that of a Palmyrene official. While residing on the island, these Palmyrenes would also have provided traders with important social connections or logistical assistance, and presumably promoted Palmyrene interests, given the honours they received back in Palmyra. In its heyday of pearl fishing in the nineteenth century, the Bahrain pearl fleets gathered several thousands of pearl oysters per day, although pearl yields per day were quite low, though sufficient after several months at sea. Bypassing an intermediary marketplace and having access to Bahrain, implied that Palmyrenes could have stronger control of the buying and selling prices of pearls. Both items of trade, silk and pearls, therefore, bring us back to the question of maritime trade, with which they are deeply embedded.

The Maritime Connection

Palmyrenes had connections on the Euphrates, and on islands of the Persian Gulf, but that still leaves the ships needed to confirm their commercial ventures. To develop a true maritime commercial network, Palmyrenes needed to own sea-going vessels rather than merely trading. Perhaps one of the most telling pieces of evidence is a funerary relief from the city of Palmyra itself. The funerary relief of Julius Aurelius Marona (tomb no. 150) of AD 236 shows a merchant with a ship in the background, expressing the Palmyrene merchant's interest in maritime trade or even perhaps the ownership of a sea-going vessel. It had been suggested in earlier literature that the relief was perhaps for navigating along the Euphrates,[21] but in fact the technical details of the ship relief are against this interpretation. What had been interpreted as long oars are in fact rudders typical of Roman-era sea-going vessel. A further argument is that the fluvial craft-building tradition consists of rafts and mainly flat-bottomed and small ships to cope with shallows and rocks, and difficult sailing conditions for larger vessels. Several other inscriptions confirm the investment in sea-going vessels rather than fluvial interest alone. A dedication from AD 157 mentions merchants who went to Scythia (northern India) in the boat of Honaino, son of Haddudan,[22] a clear Palmyrene name and hence ownership. Likewise, another inscription, also from AD 157 concerns merchants coming back from Scythia on the ship of Beelaios Kyrou. A third one equally mentions the land of Kushan, which implies a maritime voyage, and further demonstrates the trend in ownership of seafaring vessels by the Palmyrenes.[23] What does that tell us? It tells us that the Palmyrenes gradually invested in a stronger maritime presence in the Persian Gulf and Indian Ocean as a way to conquer part of the lucrative market in Eastern goods. By the second century AD, Palmyrenes relied on the island of Bahrain as a port of call for Palmyrene vessels for their activities in the Persian Gulf, such as perhaps the acquisition of pearls, but also as a way of assisting travellers on their way to India.

In the Indian Ocean, recent discoveries have shown that the island of Socotra was a regular haunt for sailors from the entire Indian Ocean area. Socotra is a major island in the Indian Ocean situated at the tip of the Horn of Africa. The island serves as an essential stopping place for any sailors travelling between India, East Africa, and the Red Sea, since sailors can wait for the winds to change in their favour, as the trickiest part of navigation in the area is mastering the monsoon winds and transiting into the Bab el Mandeb Strait, where the current and winds are very different. On the north-eastern tip of the island, known in ancient times as Dioscourides, a well-preserved Palmyrene tablet was found in a two-thousand-metre-long cave that contained over two hundred graffiti in various Brahmi, Bactrian, Greek, Axumite, and South Arabian scripts, which have been dated to between the second century BC and the second century AD. The wooden tablet, with a dedication dated to AD 258 in Palmyrene Aramaic, clearly records the presence on the island of a Palmyrene named Abgar.[24] The fascinating new evidence shows a Palmyrene presence around the Arabian Peninsula, and further strengthens the hypothesis that regular circumnavigation of the Arabian Peninsula is not to be excluded.

---

[21] Smith 2013, 78 fig. 3.9.

[22] *Inv.* x.96.

[23] *Inv.* x.91 and 95, *Inv.* vi.14 for the inscription reinterpreted as saying Kushan (rather than Choumanes).

[24] Evers 2017, 136.

A further two inscriptions firmly anchor the Palmyrenes' presence and activities in the Red Sea and Egypt, one at Koptos and one at Denderah.[25] The inscription at Koptos makes it clears that the dedication was from the 'the merchants from Hadriane Palmyra', so Palmyra itself, but as it mentions 'Palmyrene ship-owners on the Red Sea', there was also a maritime community independently operating in the Red Sea, though in association with Palmyrene traders from the homeland. Having a community in these two places on the Nile facilitated the commercial interests of the community as a whole. From owning ships and going to India to the wider Indian Ocean and even Egypt, Palmyrenes took over the entire maritime chain of Indian Ocean supplies, a process that can be described as vertical and horizontal integration economic strategies, as I have discussed elsewhere.[26] The result, however, was a strong maritime presence across the Persian Gulf, the Indian Ocean, as well as the Red Sea and several crucial islands such as Bahrain or Socotra.

Conclusion

To sum up some of the evidence examined, this overview shows that in symbiosis with the development of their long-distance desert trade, Palmyrenes developed extensive maritime connections and were indirectly interested in the maritime sphere, mainly through the ownership of sea-going vessels and social connections to people or places along the coasts of the Indian Ocean or the Red Sea of Egypt. Through their social network and their long-distance ties, the Palmyrenes developed several competitive advantages, either by taking over different phases of the process of bringing goods from the point of origin to the selling point by developing their presence along the Euphrates, and the Persian Gulf and Indian Ocean, or by focusing on high-value and low-weight items such as silk and pearls. Goods such as these were ideally suited for long-distance trade, especially along routes that still required long overland distances combined with maritime trade. What this paper has shown, however, is that by analysing Palmyra's relationship with the sea, the role of Palmyra's maritime trade as well as its overall importance for the city's mercantile economy come into much sharper focus.

---

25 *SEG* 34.1593 = I.Portes 103 and *CIS* II.3190.
26 Schörle 2017.

Works Cited

Adams, C. 2007. *Land Transport in Roman Egypt: A Study of Economics and Administration in a Roman Province* (Oxford: Oxford University Press).

De Romanis, F. 2015. 'Comparative Perspectives on the Pepper Trade', in F. De Romanis and M. Maiuro (eds), *Across the Ocean: Nine Chapters on Indo-Roman Trade* (Leiden: Brill), pp. 127–50.

——2020. *The Indo-Roman Pepper Trade and the Muziris Papyrus* (Oxford: Oxford University Press).

Evers, K. G. 2017. *Worlds Apart Trading Together: The Organisation of Long-Distance Trade between Rome and India in Antiquity* (Oxford: Archaeopress).

Hope, D. 2019–2020. 'Pearls Found in Ancient Greek and Roman Contexts in the Mediterranean', *Mediterranean Archaeology*, 32/33: 23–122.

McClish, M. 2019. *The History of the Arthaśāstra: Sovereignty and Sacred Law in Ancient India (Ideas in Context)* (Cambridge: Cambridge University Press).

Pérez González, J. 2017. 'Manius Publicius Hilarus: del comercio de perlas a la construcción de la Basilica Hilariana. El Culto de Atis y Cibele en la Roma Altoimperial', *Classica et Christiana*, 12: 251–79.

Schmidt-Colinet, A. 1995. 'The Textiles of Palmyra', *ARAM*, 7: 47–51.

Schmidt-Colinet, A., A. Stauffer, and K. Al-As'ad. 2000. *Die Textilien aus Palmyra: Neue und alte Funde* (Mainz: Von Zabern).

Schörle, K. 2015. 'Pearls, Power and Profit: Mercantile Networks and Economic Considerations on the Pearl Trade in the Roman Empire', in F. De Romanis and M. Maiuro (eds), *Across the Ocean: Nine Essays on Indo-Mediterranean Trade* (Leiden: Brill), pp. 43–54.

——2017. 'Palmyrene Merchant Networks and Economic Integration in Competitive Markets', in H. F. Teigen and E. H. Seland (eds), *Sinews of Empire: Roman Networks in the Near East and Beyond* (Oxford: Oxbow), pp. 147–54.

Seland, E. H. 2011. 'The Persian Gulf or the Red Sea? Two Axes in Ancient Indian Ocean Trade, Where to Go and Why', *World Archaeology*, 43: 398–409.

——2015. 'Palmyrene Long-Distance Trade: Land, River, and Maritime Routes in the First–Third Centuries CE', in M. N. Walters and J. P. Ito-Adler (eds), *The Silk Road: Interwoven History*, I: *Long-Distance Trade, Culture and Society* (Cambridge: Cambridge Institutes Press), pp. 101–30.

——2016. *Ships of the Desert and Ships of the Sea: Palmyra in the World Trade of the First Three Centuries CE* (Wiesbaden: Harrassowitz).

Smith, A. 2013. *Roman Palmyra: Identity, Community, and State Formation* (Oxford: Oxford University Press).

Tran, N. 2006. *Les membres des associations romaines: le rang social des 'collegiati' en Italie et Gaules sous le Haut-Empire*, Collection de l'École française de Rome, 367 (Rome: École française de Rome).

Varadarajan, L. 1998. 'Silk in Northeastern and Eastern India: The Indigenous Tradition', *Modern Asian Studies*, 22: 561–70.

Żuchowska, M. 2013. 'From China to Palmyra: The Value of Silk', *Swiatowit*, 11 (52)A: 133–54.

3. From Palmyra to India: How the East Was Won

Jean-Baptiste Yon
CNRS, Institut français du Proche-Orient
(Ifpo), Beirut (jean-baptiste.yon@cnrs.fr)

Figure 3.1. *IGLS* XVII.16 = *PAT* 1352. Malikû son of Nešâ, builder of a temple of Bel (photo: author).

Introduction

In November AD 24, a group of traders in Babylon gave thanks to one Malikû son of Nešâ son of Bôlḥâ for his generosity in the building of a temple of the god Bel (Fig. 3.1).[1] From the place of discovery of the text (the sanctuary of this same god, at Palmyra) and the language used (Palmyrene Aramaic), one might think the traders were of Palmyrene origin and that the reference is to the temple of Palmyra. This inscription is very telling of the links between Palmyra and the East. A few place names appear, and we have some traces of the events, but only from a Palmyrene perspective. The other side of the relation remains unknown. Yet, inscriptions from Palmyra, mostly from the second century AD, tend to show an apparent domination by the caravan city of Eastern trade, including Indian trade. This is the part on which all the narrative for the history of Palmyra — and for parts of the Roman trade with the East — is built.

Actually, evidence from the Gulf itself or from India is lacking. As a whole, as is well known, ancient literary evidence did not mention Palmyra and its trade, except for the historian Appian. The reality of the links with the East in an earlier period is mostly proven by indirect evidence. Only archaeological studies, that of ceramics mostly, allow a more precise understanding of the nature of relations between Palmyra and the East in the Hellenistic and Roman period, while the epigraphic documentation is sparse for the earlier period and very partial in its nature.

In his *Roman Near East*, Fergus Millar stressed the

> very limited and precise character of our evidence and [by] the fact that it is all function of the evolution of the city itself, with its (lost) public statues and (surviving) honorific inscriptions. So, for instance the centrality of the cult of Bel at Palmyra may well be due to Babylonian influence. But the cult was already established at least half a century (and probably longer) before we happen to have explicit evidence of trading contacts with Babylonia.[2]

In the following contribution, I intend to focus on two series of questions. The first point will deal with questions of chronology and review the evidence for connections with the East during the Hellenistic and Early Roman period at Palmyra. As is well known, the very existence of Palmyra was a function of its location on a short cut between Euphrates and central Syria. It could be argued that any development of the city was impossible to separate from the existence of links both with Mesopotamia and the Mediterranean. There were clear Mesopotamian connections at Palmyra, as is evidenced from at least the early first century AD, by inscriptions and by the use of the name of the god Bel — as noticed by Fergus Millar in the extract just mentioned. Other clues could be other gods' names (Nabu or Nanai), architectural features, such as the layout of the Sanctuary of

---

[1] *IGLS* XVII.16 = *PAT* 1352: t[g]ry' klhwn dy bmdynt bbl 'All the traders who are in the city of Babylon'.

[2] Millar 1993, 330.

Bel. But one cannot trace these connections to an actual starting point or pinpoint a date for the arrival of Bel or any other event. Only ceramics found on the site clearly point back to the third and second centuries BC with dated evidence. It shows an alternation of periods when Eastern influences are stronger and of periods of clear Mediterranean dominance.[3] The second point will focus on the first steps of Palmyrene trade with the East, in the context of the end of the Seleucids and of the arrival of Rome. In a way, Palmyra became a point of entrance and a gateway to Asia from the Mediterranean and the Roman Empire. However, the integration of the city into this empire may have constituted only a stage from the point of view of trade, at the beginning of the first century AD, after a long process of development at Palmyra, which benefited from the combination of the sedentarization of nomads, a process of urbanization, and favourable ecological conditions.

Before Rome: A Review of the Evidence

In the present state of the written documentation, it is not possible to go back beyond the first century BC, but the Palmyrene expansion was preceded by contacts in the Hellenistic era, as can be shown by a short review of the evidence. For example, the often-cited extract of Appian is very telling of the state of our documentation. It is revealing, in that it stops at the border of the empire and may conflate different time periods, as it could be a reference to the time of Antonius or to the time of Appian himself, more than one century later (c. 95–c. 165). It clearly shows the role of Palmyrenes, according to Appian or his source,[4] but it would be dangerous to draw more information from the text, the only one of its kind. In contrast, archaeology has more to show in order to explain the links between Palmyra and Mesopotamia and the East in the Hellenistic period.

Archaeological Material

From the ceramics of the Hellenistic period found in the excavations of the area called 'Hellenistic city', it is clear that Palmyra was linked with the Mediterranean for exchange, specifically amphorae, which mean importations of wine, since at least the third century BC:

> Local productions as well as imported fabrics of the 3rd up to the middle of the 2nd century BC have a high affinity to the eastern Mediterranean area. It is only from 150 BC onwards that South Mesopotamian influences are visible within the pottery material, becoming increasingly important over the years.[5]

Yet, at the same period, artefacts imported from the Mediterranean or made locally according to a more or less Western fashion are noticeable in the material, especially lamps of the mid-second century BC or Eastern terra sigillata.[6] A similar picture is obtained from the discoveries made in the 1950s in the excavations of the Sanctuary of Baal-Shamin, specifically when a second-century BC tomb was discovered underneath the temple itself.[7] The excavations of the earliest levels in the sanctuary have revealed artefacts, such as lamps, pottery, alabaster vases, jewels, and coins dated to the second part of the second century BC or to the beginning of the following century. Those artefacts were for the most part imported from Mesopotamia, and to a lesser extent from western Syria.[8] What is clear by a review of the material is that Mesopotamian and local productions were clearly abundant in the earliest levels in this area of the site, which means the second part of second century BC or the beginning of the following century.[9] Then the situation seems to be more balanced, with local and Mediterranean material for the greater part, but with important importations from the East.

Art and Architecture

In the case of sculpture, the turning-point and the adoption of frontality, characteristic of Palmyrene art in much of the period, must have come a little later, at the beginning of the common era. As shown by a relief found near the Sanctuary of Allat (Fig. 3.2), the profile view, gen-

---

[3] For a cautious view on the emergence of Palmyra as a major actor on the trade routes: Kaizer 2015, a review article of Schmidt-Colinet and As'ad (eds) 2013, with a very useful survey of the relevant bibliography. For Palmyrene trade in general, the classic contribution of Gawlikowski 1994 (with bibliography) and recently Seland 2016.

[4] App., *B Civ.* v.9: Ἔμποροι γὰρ ὄντες κομίζουσι μὲν ἐκ Περσῶν τὰ Ἰνδικὰ ἢ Ἀράβια, διατίθενται δ' ἐν τῇ Ῥωμαίων. 'Being merchants, they bring the products of India and Arabia from Persia and dispose of them in the Roman territory' (trans. White 1913, 391).

---

[5] Römer-Strehl 2013, 31.
[6] Römer-Strehl 2013, 270.
[7] Fellmann 1970.
[8] Gawlikowski 1970, 108.
[9] Fellmann 1970, 31–32, 48.

3. FROM PALMYRA TO INDIA: HOW THE EAST WAS WON

Figure 3.2. A leopard hunt, Palmyra, vicinity of the Allat sanctuary. See Gawlikowski 2009 (photo: M. Gawlikowski).

eral in the arts of the ancient Near East, was commonly applied in the archaic sculptures.[10] It was replaced in the 30s of the first century AD by the ubiquitous convention of strict frontality, which may have reached the Roman province of Syria from Parthian Mesopotamia. As has been proved for quite some time now, the term 'Parthian art' is a misnomer and should be taken to designate the art of some of the western provinces of the Parthian kingdom, namely central and northern Mesopotamia, and a part of Elymais in south-west Iran. In any case, it clearly links Palmyra in the very early first century AD to a culture common to a part of Mesopotamia.

Architecture, especially the Temple of Bel, gives ample proof of this Mesopotamian influence, this time with links to Babylonia. The stepped merlons and the entrance off-centre in one long side reflected a Mesopotamian tradition. The almost complete absence of remains of earlier religious monuments makes it impossible to decide whether it is a new development in the local architectural tradition. Although it is possible that in the original project for the temple only the northern adyton with an entrance opposite was planned, in the decoration references are made to mythological figures and episodes which could be Mesopotamian in origin.[11] If the date of the reliefs can be surmised, the date of the introduction of the related myths cannot be defined. The same is true for the principal figure, who gave its name to the temple and appears in the earliest dated Aramaic inscription from Palmyra, namely the god Bel.

Babylonian Religion in the Roman East and at Palmyra

As has often been suggested,[12] the antique figure of a local great god, called Bol, has been given a new name, Bel, from the name of the great god of Babylon Bel Marduk. If it does not make Bol-Bel a Mesopotamian god, it is a direct consequence of the widespread influence of Babylonian culture and religion. As the decline of Babylon has long been dated to the Hellenistic period, the tendency was to date the possible influence to a rather early period, as in the following:[13]

> Il faut certainement admettre avec H. Seyrig que l'antique Bôl ait été rebaptisé d'après le grand dieu de Babylone ; le nom nouveau aurait été adopté au IIIe siècle a. C. avec l'apparition de Palmyre sur les chemins du commerce international.

However, cuneiform tablets from the Esagila, the temple dedicated to Bel Marduk, the protector god of Babylon, mean that it may still have functioned in the first century BC and perhaps even later.[14] Besides, the cult of Bel was much more widespread and was not restricted to Palmyra: according to Jacob of Serug, the god was worshipped at Edessa.[15] It is evidenced at Assur,[16] but not at Hatra, despite its sporadic presence in local ono-

---

10 Gawlikowski 2009, with relevant bibliography; Dirven 2016. I owe the beautiful photograph of the relief to the generosity of M. Gawlikowski.

11 On the Temple of Bel: Seyrig, Amy, and Will 1968–1975. See as well Pietrzykowski 1997 for the chronology.

12 Gawlikowski 1973; 1990, 2609; Kaizer 2002, 71–72.

13 Gawlikowski 1973, 63, with reference to Seyrig 1971, 85–87.

14 Boiy 2004; Clancier 2007, 46–47, 55–64. On later attestations of the cult in the Mandaic texts: Müller-Kessler and Kessler 1999.

15 Jacob of Sarug's *memra* (metrical homily) *On the Fall of the Idols* (edition by Martin 1875, 110, l. 51, and 131).

16 Inscriptions A7 and A15 (*bl mrlh'* 'Bel lord of the gods'): see Beyer 1998, 12–14.

Figure 3.3. *RTP* 285, 'Nanai, Shaknai, auxiliary of Babylon' (photo: Presses de l'Ifpo).

mastics.[17] But northern Mesopotamia was not the only region where the cult is attested, as Bel was the great god of Apamea of Syria, where he took an oracular character.[18] Under his name with or without the addition of the name 'Zeus', he was worshipped as well in other places in the western part of the Near East, at Kilis and Tell Arr in Cyrrhestica, at Safita in central Syria, and even in the south, at Shaqqa, and probably at Ascalon on the coast.[19] Likewise, other Mesopotamian gods were worshipped at Palmyra and other parts of Roman Syria, such as Nabu, the son of Bel Marduk, and Nanai.[20] In the same manner as Bel, Nabu's cult is rather widespread in Roman Syria as shown by onomastics.[21] Actually, that a Mesopotamian origin can be ascribed to several gods does not mean that they were thought of as unquestionably Mesopotamian by the Palmyrenes. Yet, we have a clear case for the cult of Nanai, explicitly linked with Babylon by a tessera: together with another divine figure — Shaknai — they were designated as 'auxiliaries of Babylon' (Fig. 3.3).[22]

Another point must be stressed: Mesopotamian traditional onomastics are rare — rather than absent — at Palmyra, which is more or less true for all the region west of the Euphrates where Aramaic names prevailed from the end of the Hellenistic period onwards. Traditional Mesopotamian names were obviously more numerous in Ashur, and even in Hatra,[23] but even at Edessa those names were very rarely attested. There, only the name *srkn* may be related to the Akkadian name Šarrukinu, the name of the famous king Sargon of Akkad.[24] Syrian examples were almost non-existent, except for a text engraved on a statue of a priest, probably from Hierapolis of Syria, with the name Bedanos, which could be interpreted as *byd'nw* 'By the hand of the god ANU', a supreme god of Sumerian origin, whose primary cult centre was at Uruk.[25] Only at Dura, on the western bank of the Euphrates, but very close to Mesopotamia, the names Μηκανναια (and Μηκατναναια), traditional in this surrounding region and in a part of the local population, probably had an Akkadian origin (Mê-qatê-Nanâ), as did Βηλοοβασσαρος or Αδαδγαβαρος, with close parallels in Neo-Babylonian texts.[26]

What has to be underlined, as shown amply by the geography of the cult of Bel in the Late Hellenistic and Roman periods, is that the subregions of the Near East

---

[17] Beyer 1998, 146.

[18] As attested by the literary sources (Cass. Dio LXXIX.8.5–6: ὁ Ζεὺς ὁ Βῆλος ὀνομαζόμενος καὶ ἐν τῇ Ἀπαμείᾳ τῆς Συρίας τιμώμενος 'Zeus called Belos, honoured in Apamea in Syria'; see LXXIX.40.4) and the epigraphy (Rey-Coquais 1973, 66: ἐπὶ [κελεύ]σεως θεοῦ μεγίστου ἁγίου Βήλου 'by order of the great holy god Belos').

[19] Kilis, *IGLS* I.174 ([Β]ήλῳ θεῷ 'to the god Belos'); Tell Arr, *SEG* XXXII.1447 (Δὶ Βηλέῳ θεῷ 'to Zeus Belos the god'); Hebbé near Safita, *IGLS* VII.4049; Shaqqa, *IGLS* XVI.501 = *SEG* VII.1007; *IGR* I.1092, a citizen from Ascalon makes a dedication in Egypt (Canopus) in the name of Heracles Belus (θεὸν πάτρι[όν] μου Ἡρ[ακ]λῆ Βῆλον ἀνείκητον 'my ancestral god Heracles Belos unvanquished').

[20] Gawlikowski 1990, 2645–46.

[21] Nabu: Νεβουχηλος at Dura, Yon 2018, 144–45; Βαρναβος, Birtha *IGLS* I.126.

[22] *RTP* 285 = *PAT* 2264 (*nny škny šy't bbl*).

[23] Ashur: many theophoric names of the god Ashur, see Beyer 1998, 145–46 (e.g. '*srḥdyn* = Aššur-aḫa-iddina 'Ashur has given a brother'); Hatra, *ttny*, H 66, or *nbwdyn*, H 279a or H 310.

[24] Drijvers and Healey 1999, 169 (Am3). As for Βηδανος *infra*, the Mesopotamian etymology for the name is far from certain.

[25] *SEG* XXVI.1653, Νικοφῶν Βηδανου ὁ καὶ Σεν<ε>κᾶς 'Nikophôn son of Bedanos, also called Seneca'. Curiously this man had a Greek name, while his father had a Mesopotamian name, but his other name was of Latin origin.

[26] Grassi 2012 with references; Yon 2018, 134, 147.

from the Mediterranean to Mesopotamia had a common frame of reference.[27] Onomastics, despite local particularities, is a good example of the depth of the links between those different subregions, as is language. One clear case is that of Dura, where the earliest Aramaic text was almost contemporaneous with the beginning of Aramaic epigraphy at Palmyra.[28] It has been suggested with good arguments that the inscription from Dura was not actually in Palmyrene Aramaic but in a local dialect closely related to it.[29] At the same time, or a little later, in Edessa, then in Ashur and in Hatra, Aramaic is epigraphically attested.[30] Aramaic was also spoken (and presumably written) in Lower Mesopotamia, where the roads of trade led. Personal names in Cyrrhestica, Emesene, or in southern Syria during the Roman period show links with Palmyra and its region, and with Edessa, Osrhoene, and northern Mesopotamia as well.[31]

Unquestionably, other factors played a bigger part in the development of Palmyrene trade, but this dimension of an Aramaic *koine* has to be underlined when one is to understand the links between Palmyra and its neighbours.

Two conclusions can be drawn from the above. First, in the context of the disintegration of the Seleucid Empire and the loss of the region west of the Euphrates by the Seleucids, Palmyra seems to have taken advantage of this relative new freedom, just as the coastal Phoenician cities did in the second century BC. Rather unexpectedly, after the change that came with the Parthian conquest of Mesopotamia, relations intensified with the territory east of the Euphrates. This may have been caused by the unstable situation in the West. Second, Palmyrene trade has to be seen in a larger context, namely that of the relations between the Roman Empire and the Parthians, as the first written data on the Palmyrene presence at Dura were concurrent with the earliest inscriptions at Palmyra and with the attack on Palmyra by Mark Antony's soldiers. In addition, one has to see it as well in the context of a north Mesopotamian and central Syrian *koine*. The tantalizing piece of information given by Appian tallies in a way with the situation on the middle Euphrates as reported by Strabo, in that it stresses the role of steppe dwellers in facilitating the trade. Reference is made to camel-drivers who keep halting-places:

Ἡ ὁδός ἐστι διὰ τῆς ἐρήμου μέχρι Σκηνῶν, ἀξιολόγου πόλεως ἐπὶ τοὺς τῆς Βαβυλωνίας ὅρους ἐπί τινος διώρυγος ἱδρυμένης. Ἔστι δ' ἀπὸ τῆς διαβάσεως μέχρι Σκηνῶν ἡμερῶν πέντε καὶ εἴκοσιν ὁδός. Καμηλῖται δ' εἰσί, καταγωγὰς ἔχοντες τοτὲ μὲν ὑδρείων εὐπόρους, τῶν λακκαίων τὸ πλέον, τοτὲ δ' ἐπακτοῖς χρώμενοι τοῖς ὕδασι. Παρέχουσι δ' αὐτοῖς οἱ Σκηνῖται τήν τε εἰρήνην καὶ τὴν μετριότητα τῆς τῶν τελῶν πράξεως, ἧς χάριν φεύγοντες τὴν παραποταμίαν διὰ τῆς ἐρήμου παραβάλλονται, καταλιπόντες ἐν δεξιᾷ τὸν ποταμὸν ἡμερῶν σχεδόν τι τριῶν ὁδόν. Οἱ γὰρ παροικοῦντες ἑκατέρωθεν τὸν ποταμὸν φύλαρχοι, χώραν οὐκ εὔπορον ἔχοντες, ἧττον δὲ ἄπορον νεμόμενοι, δυναστείαν ἕκαστος ἰδίᾳ περιβεβλημένος ἴδιον καὶ τελώνιον ἔχει, καὶ τοῦτ' οὐ μέτριον.

(The road runs through the desert to Scenae, a noteworthy city situated on a canal towards the borders of Babylonia. The journey from the crossing of the river to Scenae requires twenty-five days. And on that road are camel-drivers who keep halting-places, which sometimes are well supplied with reservoirs, generally cisterns, though sometimes the camel-drivers use waters brought in from other places. The Scenitae are peaceful, and moderate towards travellers in the exaction of tribute, and on this account, merchants avoid the land along the river and risk a journey through the desert, leaving the river on the right for approximately a three days' journey. For the chieftains who live along the river on both sides occupy country which, though not rich in resources, is less resourceless than that of others, and are each invested with their own particular domains and exact a tribute of no moderate amount.) (XVI.1.27, trans. Jones 1930, 235)

The date of the events described is unknown (that of Strabo himself, of Poseidonios, his source, one century earlier?), but it is in a way a fairly accurate description of what is usually reconstructed for Palmyra in a slightly later period. The integration of Palmyra in the Roman Empire, most probably during the second decade of the first century AD, brought a major change.

Rome and Palmyrene Eastern Trade

Roman Diplomacy

Indeed, Palmyra was doubtless soon integrated into the networks of Roman diplomacy. Several documents give information on the role of Germanicus, nephew of Tiberius. It constitutes the first clear steps of the Roman presence in Palmyra. The first document is an inscription in honour of Tiberius, Drusus, and Germanicus, dedicated

---

27 For this and what follows: Yon 2018.
28 *PAT* 1067, dated 33 BC.
29 Bertolino 2004, 34, with relevant bibliography.
30 For Edessa: Drijvers and Healey 1999; for Hatra and Ashur: Beyer 1998.
31 Yon 2018, particularly chapter 2, on the onomastics of the Roman soldiers at Dura.

Figure 3.4. Cantineau 1931, 139, no. 18 = *PAT* 2754. Inscription of Alexandros sent as an envoy by Germanicus (photo: author).

by Minucius Rufus, legatus of the legion X *Fretensis*.[32] It is dated around AD 14–19. The visit of Germanicus to the East had evident political motivations, but economic goals were achieved in the meantime. The famous Tax Law of Palmyra names Germanicus as the author of a letter sent to the publican Statilius. One Statilius Hermes, who built a tomb in Palmyra some decades later, could have been one of his freedmen.[33] Admittedly, in that case, the relation between Germanicus and Palmyrene trade is not explicit, and the Tax Law referred mostly to local trade. Yet, in another case, Germanicus sent a Palmyrene, Alexandros, to several Oriental kingdoms (Fig. 3.4).[34] Among them were Orobazes, king of Mesene, and Shamshigeram of Emesene, which is a little bit more problematic. The name Shamshigeram refers probably to the king of the same name mentioned by Josephus[35] (curiously the mention of his name is missing in the *PAT* edition), but one may wonder why Germanicus had to use a Palmyrene as an envoy to a city 150 km west of Palmyra. It indicates at least some degree of integration, as Alexandros is the first of the Palmyrenes to have a Greek name. It could be interpreted as well as the sign of a period of transition in the city itself.

The Role of Palmyrenes

We can come back now to the inscription mentioning Babylon: the benefactor is one Malikû, son of Nešâ son of Bôlḥâ, who is called Ḥašaš. The family is well known during these years, especially a brother, Ḥašaš, who made peace between two tribes (his own, the Benê Komarê, and the Benê Mathabôl).[36] Malikû contributed to the construction of a sanctuary of Bel, in those years which corresponded to Palmyra's integration into the empire. One possibility is that the sanctuary of the god could have been located in Babylon, as the god was of Mesopotamian origin.[37] We know of other great Palmyra notables who contributed in the second century to religious constructions outside Palmyra; the caravan chief Soados, another great benefactor, was honoured in a caravanserai some 30 km from Palmyra, around the middle of the century, with a tantalizing reference in the inscription to the construction of a Temple of the Emperors.[38] However, in the case of Malikû, the location of the inscription and the testimony of other texts show that the Temple of Palmyra is a serious candidate. The Palmyra merchants of Babylon therefore undoubtedly wanted to demonstrate their pat-

---

[32] *IGLS* XVII.3.

[33] Tax Law, *CIS* 3913 = *PAT* 0259. See now Shifman 2014. For the freedman: *IGLS* XVII.400.

[34] Cantineau 1931, 139, no. 18 = *PAT* 2754.

[35] Jos., *Ant. Iud.* XVIII.335; XIX.338.

[36] *CIS* 3915 = *PAT* 0261.

[37] For this interpretation: e.g. Hauser 2007.

[38] Found at Umm al-'Amad, in the desert south-east of Palmyra: κτίσαντα | [ἐ]ν Ὀλογα[σί]ᾳ ναὸν τῶν Σε]βαστῶν, 'having founded at Vologesias a Temple of the *Augusti*', *SEG* VII.135, with commentary and references in *IGLS* XVII.127 and 150.

riotism and piety by paying these honours, which was also a way of conciliating a great notable of their city of origin. Afterwards, the city of Babylon no longer appears in the Palmyra documentation, perhaps because the caravan roads had moved south. It should be noted that at a time when the documentation of trade is not very rich, the large Mesopotamian city was the seat of a probably quite prosperous Palmyrene community. Another similar inscription, badly damaged, is difficult to interpret, but the general meaning is clear, thanks to the two corresponding versions.[39] The Greek and Palmyrene merchants who were in Seleukeia honoured Yedî'bel for his contribution to the construction of a temple of Bel. The restitution of the word ἔμποροι, 'merchants', for the first line of the Greek text is not assured, but the two groups based in Seleukeia were probably active in trade (at least the Palmyrenes). The identification and the exact localization of the toponym, *slwky'* transcription of the Greek form 'Seleukeia', are more problematic. The great Mesopotamian city, Seleukeia on the Tigris, needs to be taken into consideration as it was on the road to the Gulf, and as most of the cities mentioned later in the caravan inscriptions were located in the same zone. Nevertheless, the toponym was very common in the region and there are other possibilities.[40] What is clear in the early documentation is that there were no references to Rome in the inscriptions dealing with trade, before a much later date, namely the year AD 135, when a centurion, Iulius Maximus, received the thanks of the members of a caravan for his help. As is often the case, the inscription is too short to call for any firm conclusions on what Iulius Maximus had done.[41]

A Turning-Point: The End of the First Century BC – Early First Century AD

A deeper look into the documentation shows that the organization of trade in the first century remains at best elusive. Admittedly, there was a first mention of a wall and of taxes on camels in AD 10/11, manifesting a civic organization of some kind and its interest in trade, and most importantly in the taxes that came with it:[42]

[At] this wall, the taxes of the camels, so much as above the tax due to the Assembly of all the Palmyrenes, [are for] 'Atenatan b. Kaffatut b. Bar'a and for Yamliku his son, [both] from the tribe of Bene Mita, in the year 322.

One is reminded of the text of Strabo on the exaction of 'tribute', which from the point of view of local communities may have been a legal tax, as shown by the very word used by Strabo, τελώνιον.[43] Other documents of the same period give information on local authorities and officials, such as the treasurers in an inscription of AD 25.[44] Interestingly the term caravan itself — the word is *synodia* in Greek — is not mentioned before the year AD 112.[45] Up until then, trade was made only by merchants (*emporoi* or *taggarê*) appearing often as a group, as they did in Babylon or Seleucia, without a more specific term. Some undated inscriptions with the word 'caravan' may be earlier than 112, but definitely belong to the same period, at the end of the first or at the beginning of the second century.[46] Later, the wording of caravan inscriptions points to the caravans as an expression of the city as an institutional reality.[47] One cannot stress enough the fact that this evolution was concurrent with the evolution of the community of Palmyrenes into a city where institutions were modelled on those of Greek cities of the Mediterranean world.[48]

This evolution resulted in a peak in the mid-second century with several Palmyrenes endowed with power of different kinds in the Gulf.[49] This part is well known, and I will not stop on this. The other side of the situation is worth looking into. Despite the documentation, Palmyrenes were not the only ones on the trade routes of the East, and they must have had competitors.[50] In

---

[39] *IGLS* XVII.24 = *PAT* 0270: *[tdmry'] wywny' dy bslwky'* 'The Palmyrenes and the Greeks who are in Seleucia' (the word 'Palmyrenes' is restored by comparison with the Greek version, where the word 'Seleukeia' is no longer extant).

[40] Cohen 2013, 98–100, 104, 156–73 for cities with names formed on the personal name Seleucus. Seleukeia on the Tigris is the most well attested.

[41] *IGLS* XVII.209 = *PAT* 1397.

[42] *PAT* 2636: *ktl' dnh dy blwy' dy gmly' dy l' l mnh dy blw gbl*

tdmry' klhwn 'l 'tntn kptwt br br'' w'l ymlkw brh dy mn bny myt' lyqrhwn šnt 323.

[43] XVI.1.27. Lidell Scott translates the word τελώνιον as 'customs-duty'.

[44] *IGLS* XVII.17 = *PAT* 1353.

[45] *IGLS* XVII.242.

[46] One such example is *IGLS* XVII.244 = *PAT* 0309.

[47] See e.g. *IGLS* XVII.127, 'the caravan of all the Palmyrenes' ἡ [...] συνοδία πάντων Παλμυρηνῶν, *[šyrt' dy] tdmr klh*, dated June 144.

[48] Sartre 1996 = 2014, 293–319.

[49] Soados, endowed with some kind of power (δυναστεία), *SEG* VII.135 (see above); Ιαραιον Νεβο[υ]αβαδ]ου - - - σατρά[π]ην Θιλουανων Μεερεδατου βασιλέως Σπασινου Χάρακος 'Yarḫaî son of Nebûzabad [...], satrap of the Thilouanoi for Meheredates, king of Spasinou Charax', *IGLS* XVII.245.

[50] For overviews: Young 2001; Tomber 2008; Seland 2016; Schörle (in this volume).

the first century, trade through the Nabatean kingdom was thriving. During most of the Roman period, the Egyptian trade and the Red Sea were the main thoroughfare between Rome and the East. In the period when Palmyrene trade was first attested as such (first half of the first century AD), the *Periplus Maris Erythraei* ('Voyage around the Red Sea') provides evidence of the sea routes from Egypt to India, through the Red Sea and around the Arabian Peninsula.[51] For a later period, at least from the second to the third centuries, there is evidence for customs officials at Zeugma on the Euphrates border,[52] evidencing at least some sort of trade by land routes, through northern Mesopotamia, resembling the itineraries first mentioned by Strabo.[53] From the end of the second century, when conditions became difficult for the Palmyrenes in Mesopotamia with the Parthians and then with the Sassanids, it induced new trajectories for Palmyrene trade, by way of Egypt and the Red Sea. For this, inscriptions of Palmyrene soldiers, traders, and travellers from Egypt and Socotra are the main sources of evidence.[54]

Earlier, at the turn of the era, the first stages of Palmyrene trade with the East were linked with the new political situation created by the arrival of the Parthians, the collapse of the Seleucid Empire, and then by the Roman conquest. These conditions must be seen against the background of a cultural *koine* linking the population of Palmyra with Mesopotamia *and* with the West, as is shown by onomastics or by some cults. Not surprisingly, the rise of Palmyra was associated with that of other cities in the region, the turning-point being apparently the arrival of Rome and its slow takeover of the roads and territories of the Near East, but such a rise had been prepared in the vacuum occasioned by the fall of the Seleucids. In a way, what makes the difference for Palmyra is an exceptionally well-preserved documentation: there were presumably other trade routes, other caravans; Palmyra was only the tip of the iceberg, the most visible for the modern eye. This fact has to be considered as well.

---

[51] Boussac, Salles, and Yon (eds) 2012.

[52] Philostr., *VA* 1.20, ὁ τελώνης ὁ ἐπιβεβλημένος τῷ Ζεύγματι 'the tax collector stationed at Zeugma'.

[53] Bernard 2005, for the possible reconstruction of such itineraries. Admittedly, the evidence is sparse and one has to rely mainly on earlier and later evidence to reconstruct the routes of the Roman period.

[54] Yon 2016 and 2018, 32–39, on Palmyrene relations with Egypt and India.

Works Cited

Bernard, P. 2005. 'De l'Euphrate à la Chine avec la caravane de Maès Titianos (c. 100 ap. n. è.)', *Comptes rendus des séances de l'Académie des inscriptions et belles-lettres*, 149: 929–69.

Bertolino, R. 2004. *Corpus des inscriptions sémitiques de Doura-Europos*, Supplementi agli Annali: Sez. Orientale, 94 (Naples: Istituto orientale di Napoli).

Beyer, K. 1998. *Die aramäischen Inschriften aus Assur, Hatra und dem übrigen Ostmesopotamien (datiert 44 v. Chr. bis 238 n. Chr.)* (Göttingen: Vandenhoeck & Ruprecht).

Boiy, T. 2004. *Late Achaemenid and Hellenistic Babylon*, Orientalia Lovaniensia analecta, 136 (Leuven: Peeters).

Boussac, M.-F., J.-F. Salles, and J.-B. Yon (eds). 2012. *Autour du Périple de la mer Érythrée*, Topoi Supplément, 11 (Lyon: Société des amis de la bibliothèque Salomon Reinach).

Cantineau, J. 1931. 'Textes palmyréniens provenant de la fouille du Temple de Bel', *Syria*, 12: 116–42.

Clancier, P. 2007. 'La Babylonie hellénistique: Aperçu d'histoire politique et culturelle', *Topoi*, 15: 21–74.

Cohen, G. M. 2013. *The Hellenistic Settlements in the East from Armenia and Mesopotamia to Bactria and India*, Hellenistic Culture and Society, 54 (Berkeley: University of California Press).

Dirven, L. 2016. 'The Problem with Parthian Art at Dura', in T. Kaizer (ed.), *Religion, Society and Culture at Dura-Europos*, Yale Classical Studies, 38 (Cambridge: Cambridge University Press), pp. 68–88.

Drijvers, H. J. W. and J. F. Healey (eds and trans.). 1999. *The Old Syriac Inscriptions of Edessa and Osrhoene: Texts, Translations and Commentary*, Handbuch der Orientalistik, 1.42 (Leiden: Brill).

Fellmann, R. 1970. *Le sanctuaire de Baalshamin à Palmyre*, V: *Les inscriptions*, Bibliotheca helvetica romana, 10 (Neuchâtel: Institut suisse de Rome).

Gawlikowski, M. 1970. *Monuments funéraires de Palmyre* (Warsaw: Państwowe Wydawnictwo Naukowe).

—— 1973. *Le Temple palmyrénien: étude d'épigraphie et de topographie historique*, Palmyre, 6 (Warsaw: Państwowe Wydawnictwo Naukowe).

—— 1990. 'Les dieux de Palmyre', in H. Temporini and W. Haase (eds), *Aufstieg und Niedergang der römischen Welt*, II.18.4 (Berlin: De Gruyter), pp. 2605–58.

—— 1994. 'Palmyra as a Trading Centre', *Iraq*, 56: 27–33.

—— 2009. 'A Lonely Hunter from Palmyra', in J. M. Burdukiewicz and others (eds), *Understanding the Past: Papers Offered to Stefan K. Kozłowski* (Warsaw: Center for the Research on the Antiquity of Southern Europe, 2009), pp. 123–29.

Grassi, G. F. 2012. *Semitic Onomastics from Dura Europos: The Names in Greek Script and from Latin Epigraphs* (Padua: Sargon).

Hauser, S. 2007. 'Tempel für den palmyrenischen Bel', in R. Rollinger, A. Luther, and J. Wiesehöfer (eds), *Getrennte Wege? Kommunikation, Raum und Wahrnehmung in der Alten Welt*, Oikumene, Studien zur antiken Weltgeschichte, 2 (Frankfurt: Verlag Antike), pp. 57–84.

Jones, H. L. (trans.). 1930. *The Geography of Strabo*, VII: *Books 15–16*, Loeb Classical Library, 241 (Cambridge, MA: Harvard University Press).

Kaizer, T. 2002. *The Religious Life of Palmyra: A Study of the Social Patterns of Worship in the Roman Period*, Oriens et Occidens, 4 (Stuttgart: Steiner).

—— 2015. 'On the Origin of Palmyra and its Trade', *Journal of Roman Archaeology*, 28: 881–88.

Martin, J.-P. H. 1875. 'Discours de Jacques de Saroug sur la chute des idoles', *Zeitschrift der deutschen morgenländischen Gesellschaft*, 29: 107–47.

Millar, F. 1993. *The Roman Near East (31 BC–AD 337)*, Carl Newell Jackson Lectures (Cambridge, MA: Harvard University Press).

Müller-Kessler, C. and K. Kessler. 1999. 'Spätbabylonische Gottheiten in spätantiken mandäischen Texten', *Zeitschrift für Assyriologie und Vorderasiatische Archäologie*, 89: 65–87.

Pietrzykowski, M. 1997. *Adyta światyń palmyreńskich: studium funkcji i formy; Les adytons des temples palmyréniens; forme et fonction* (Warsaw: Archet).

Rey-Coquais, J.-P. 1973. 'Inscriptions grecques d'Apamée', *Annales archéologiques arabes syriennes*, 23: 39–84.

Römer-Strehl, C. 2013. 'Keramik', in A. Schmidt-Colinet and W. Al-Asʿad (eds), *Palmyras Reichtum durch weltweiten Handel: Archäologische Untersuchungen im Bereich der hellenistischen Stadt*, II: *Kleinfunde* (Vienna: Holzhausen), pp. 7–80.

Sartre, M. 1996. 'Palmyre, cité grecque', *Annales archéologiques arabes syriennes*, 42: 385–405.

—— 2014. *L'historien et ses territoires: choix d'articles*, Scripta antiqua, 70 (Bordeaux: Ausonius).

Schmidt-Colinet, A. and W. Al-Asʿad (eds). 2013. *Palmyras Reichtum durch weltweiten Handel: Archäologische Untersuchungen im Bereich der hellenistischen Stadt*, 2 vols (Vienna: Holzhausen).

Seland, E. H. 2016. *Ships of the Desert and Ships of the Sea: Palmyra in the World Trade of the First Three Centuries CE*, Philippika, 101 (Wiesbaden: Harrassowitz).

Seyrig, H. 1971. 'Antiquités syriennes, 93: Bêl de Palmyre', *Syria*, 48: 85–114.

Seyrig, H., R. Amy, and E. Will. 1968–1975. *Le temple de Bêl à Palmyre*, 2 vols, Bibliothèque archéologique et historique, 83 (Paris: Geuthner).
Shifman, I. S. 2014. *The Palmyrene Tax Tariff*, ed. J. F. Healey, trans. S. Khobnya, Journal of Semitic Studies Supplement, 33 (Oxford: Oxford University Press).
Tomber, R. S. 2008. *Indo-Roman Trade: From Pots to Pepper*, Duckworth Debates in Archaeology (London: Duckworth).
White, H. (trans.). 1913. *Appian: Roman History*, I: *Books I–VIII*, Loeb Classical Library, 2 Cambridge, MA: Harvard University Press.
Yon, J.-B. 2016. 'Organization and Financing of Trade and Caravans in the Near East', in J. L. Garcia Moreno (ed.), *Dynamics of Production in the Ancient Near East, 1300–500 BC* (Oxford: Oxbow), pp. 345–55.
—— 2018. *L'histoire par les noms : histoire et onomastique, de la Palmyrène à la Haute Mésopotamie romaines*, Bibliothèque archéologique et historique, 212 (Beirut: Presses de l'Institut français du Proche-Orient).
Young, G. K. 2001. *Rome's Eastern Trade: International Commerce and Imperial Policy, 31 BC–AD 305* (London: Routledge).

4. Palmyra and the Sasanians in the Third Century AD

Touraj Daryaee
University of California, Irvine (tdaryaee@uci.edu)

In the third century AD with the rise of Ardaxšīr, son of Pābag, a local potentate from the province of Pārs, major changes took place in the political landscape of the Near East. After Ardaxšīr defeated the Arsacid king of kings, Ardawān/Artābanus V in AD 224 at the Plain of Hormozgān in the central Iranian Plateau, he claimed kingship of *Ērānšahr* (Iranian Empire).[1] He began to subdue the regions previously controlled by the Arsacid Empire and took steps to control both sides of the Persian Gulf,[2] and challenged the Roman Empire in Mesopotamia and Syria.[3] Ardaxšīr and his son, Šāpūr I, who took the greater title of 'king of kings of Iranians and non-Iranians', laid siege to what have been called caravan cities of Dura-Europos, Hatra, and Palmyra.[4]

But the question is: Why did the Sasanians take steps which seem 'aggressive' or 'predatory' toward these caravan towns? More specifically, why was the lucrative Palmyran trade so suddenly disrupted by Ardaxšīr and the Sasanians? This is even more puzzling, since scholars such as F. Millar have stated that the Sasanians saw the Euphrates as the boundary between Rome and *Ērānšahr*, and that the Sasanians never really tried to control the regions west of the Euphrates.[5] Were the actions of Ardaxšīr and Šāpur really predatory in nature or were they attempting to restore the Achaemenid territory which Alexander had wrested away, or were there other reasons to be considered?[6]

So far the reasons for Sasanian activities beyond the Tigris and into Syria against caravan towns have been explained by most scholars based on the premise of Sasanians regaining Achaemenid territories, or pushing the Romans back from the Near East.[7] I would like to provide yet another suggestion and place the Sasanians in a different light and discuss the Sasanian grand strategy in the third century AD, which affected the caravan cities of Syria, specifically Palmyra. But in order to make sense of the move on the part of the Sasanians into Syria, we must set the Parthian or Arsacid world vis-à-vis Dura, Hatra, and Palmyra.

Instructive as to the economic interests and activities of the Arsacids are their mint locations and trade routes. In a recent work by F. Sinisi, it has been shown that the main mints of the Arsacids (Fig. 4.1) show an East–West route which is in line with the economic activity of the empire. The presence of Arsacid coins in the caravan cities also attests to the economic connections with the eastern empires. If we think of the Silk Road trade that was taking place, beginning with the Arsacid Mithridates I, it makes sense that the Arsacids were the in-between power in the Indo-Chinese and the Roman world of trade. The Arsacids acted as the middle empire, which attempted to control the trade, both on land and on sea to benefit their own economic interest in the global economy of Antiquity.

In regard to the caravan cities, Hatra had been an Arsacid town which allowed them to operate economically with the western Mediterranean. Pliny in the first century already recorded that Hatra was one of the eighteen kingdoms of the Arsacid Empire,[8] which must then be considered one of the (Parthian) *katak-xwatāy* 'house-lords/petty kingdoms'[9] of the Arsacids. By the second century AD, Hatra had reached the peak of its prosperity, and both the Arsacids and the Romans ben-

---

* I would like to thank Professor Rubina Raja for the invitation to the conference on Palmyra and the East at the J. Paul Getty Museum and its publication.

[1] Daryaee 2012, 4.

[2] Piacentini 1985, 57.

[3] Wiesehöfer 1986; Millar 1993, 148–49.

[4] Rostovtzeff 1932; for the Sasanian offensive against these cities see, Gagé 1964, 142–53.

[5] Millar 1993, 73.

[6] There is a lively discussion of Sasanian aims, which includes Kettenhofen 1984, 177–90; Wiesehöfer 1982; Daryaee 2006; and Shayegan 2011.

---

[7] Potter 1987, 156–57.

[8] Plin., *HN* vi.112.

[9] Nyberg II 1974, 116.

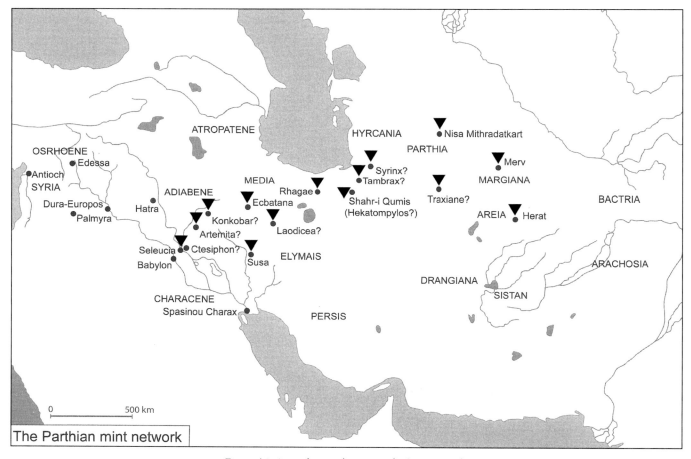

Figure 4.1. Arsacid mints (courtesy of Fabrizio Sinisi).

efited from its position as a caravan trade town. Ardaxšīr in the third century laid siege to the town, but like his Roman counterpart a century earlier he was unable to take the city. It is only close to the end of the city's life in AD 235[10] that a Roman legion was stationed there to protect it from the Sasanians.[11] No doubt for the townspeople and probably whatever Arsacid allies remained in the town, Romans were chosen over the Sasanians. The onomastics of Hatra, along with its art, suggest a considerable number of Iranian and Arsacid names, among them: Aspād, Afrahāṭ, Aštāṭ, Valagaš, Vorōd, Mihrā, Mihradāt, Manēš, Nōxdārā, Sanaṭrūq, Tīridāt.[12]

The city had been part of the Arsacid orbit of influence, and it did fall into the hands of the Romans, but it was never really destroyed by either side. If this city was under Arsacid influence, then it is no surprise that the Sasanians attempted to put an end to it. Ardaxšīr and his son, now co-regent, Šāpur I took the town in AD 240, and destroyed the city and put an end to the kingdom of Hatra. The siege plan of the Sasanians and the time it took for the fall of Hatra demonstrated the amount of the resources and commitment that the Persians invested in bringing down the city.[13] The Manichean Codex of Cologne describes the moment for this end like this:

> in the year in which Dariadaxir (Ardaxšīr), the king of Persia, subjugated the city of Hatra, and in which Sapores (Šāpūr), his son assumed the mighty diadem in the month Pharmuti on the [eighth] day according to the moon (17/18 April 240).[14]

Dura-Europos came under Arsacid control in 113 BC, only to be taken by the Romans in the second century AD. It was during Arsacid times that the town grew and in a sense had an international population, where it became an important caravan town and stop for trading parties. Again, the abundance of Iranian names and

---

10 Wiesehöfer 1982, 437.
11 Jakubiak 2015, 473.
12 Schmitt 2003.

13 Hauser 2009, 128–29.
14 Dodgeon and Lieu 1991, 33.

Arsacid coins finds, along with finds of Iranian deities, suggests a strong Arsacid presence. More important is a title that appears both at Dura and Palmyra, namely *argbed*, whose meaning and function much ink has been spilled on. In a Greek parchment from Dura-Europos dated to AD 121, the title *arcapates* is given to the eunuch Phraates (Parthian Frahāt), a member of the staff of the Arsacid governor Manesos.[15]

Architecturally and artistically, Dura is strongly influenced by the Arsacids, notably visible from the frescos at the Synagogue of Dura, and the Mithraeum. One cannot miss the biblical figures, all dressed in contemporary, i.e. Arsacid, costumes.[16] In AD 256 Šāpur I successfully laid siege to the city, occupied it for several months, and then had its population deported and the city abandoned altogether.[17] This is indeed a strange move on the part of the Persian king, but I believe, again, that it is part of the overall grand strategy. If the city was to be ransacked and destroyed, the city would not have been kept so meticulously for the rediscovery and study by archaeologists of the twentieth century.

Palmyra, the main topic of this paper, was one of the famed caravan towns which profited from the Roman-Arsacid trade network. While Palmyra was independent of the Arsacids, there is still discernible artistic influence.[18] The Arsacids allowed this trade centre to operate, which connected it to the Persian Gulf, through the city of Spasinu Charax.[19] Once the Romans incorporated the Nabatean kingdom in AD 106, Palmyra was the sole beneficiary of this long-distance trade, from the mouth of the Persian Gulf.[20] The existence of Palmyrene traders and their inscriptions suggests the importance of this trade connection with the Arsacid Empire, which in effect was a 'network empire'.[21] The kingdom of Characene was under Arsacid control from the end of the second century BC, and was the key entrepôt for long-distance trade eastward. A series of harbours and terminals connected Charax to Bahrain, and Oman to the Indian Ocean trade posts.

Periplus,[22] observing the importance of this area, states that beyond the Strait of Hormoz is the Persian Gulf where there are market towns designated by law, called Apologus, near Charax Spasini, connecting it to Ommana, where vessels regularly were sent from Barygaza, India.[23] The Palmyrene merchants, or their network, would have reached Barbarikon and Barygaza in the north-east of the Indian subcontinent, with ships sailing regularly from the mid-second century to and from India.[24] The thalassocracy of the Characenians was well known and was supported by the Arsacids, because it benefited them greatly. It was only after Roman aggressions into southern Mesopotamia and Attambelos's allegiance to Trajan that the Arsacids changed the political elite structure of Characene, placing Mithridates, from the Arsacid family, to take control of Characene after AD 131. However, the Palmyrenes were given the privilege of conducting international trade with their merchant organizational system,[25] while the Arsacid family ruled over Characene directly. In a sense the Palmyrene merchants, through the Characene, were in control of the Persian Gulf trade, all the way to Oman (ed-Dur) and the United Arab Emirates (Dibba and Mleiha), under the watchful eye of the Arsacids in the second century AD.[26]

Thus, the Arsacids had been able to graft an economic connection from the eastern Mediterranean through their empire on land, all the way to India, via the Persian Gulf. While the Palmyrenes benefited from and controlled such economic might, it was the Arsacids who held important ties to the caravan towns with their men in place and their connections, from Dura, Hatra, and Palmyra to the Persian Gulf and beyond. This political and economic system was beneficial for all the parties involved and provided wealth and an order in the ancient Near Eastern world. The Arsacid Empire had been able to have deep ties and influence in these areas and was able to graft together local kingdoms, creating what has been called a 'Parthian Commonwealth'.[27] This is a type of rule which is part of the Arsacid imperial ideology and system of kingship which in Pahlavi texts came to be known as *Kadag-xwadāyīh* and later in Arabic and Persian, *Mulūk al-tawāyīf*. This form of rule is made clear politically and economically, in the way in which the Arsacid family became the de facto rulers in Georgia as Aršakianis, until the coming of the Khosrowids in Georgia; and as the Aršakunis in Armenia in the

---

15 Welles, Fink, and Gilliam 1959, 115, no. 20, line 4; Frye 1962, 352–53; Chaumont 1986.

16 Levit-Tawil 1983, 60.

17 Daryaee 2010, 34–35.

18 Seyrig 1950, 6.

19 Gawlikowski 1994, 28–29.

20 Hansman 1991.

21 Gregoratti 2019, 53.

22 Schoff 1912, 35–36.

23 Gregoratti 2018, 55.

24 Gregoratti 2018, 59.

25 Gregoratti 2018, 63.

26 Gregoratti 2018, 64.

27 De Jong 2015, 127.

Caucasus in the fifth century AD. The dynastic connections brought power and influence in the Caucasus for the Arsacids, both political and economic allegiance. On the other hand, it was the economic influence that was wielded by Arsacids over Mesopotamia and Syria in such cities as Dura-Europos, Hatra, and Palmyra which allowed them to benefit as an empire.

With the coming of Ardaxšīr I in the third century AD, the Sasanians needed not only to disrupt such well-organized trade routes and connections that were in the hands of the Arsacids, but also establish new towns and new trade routes in order to completely destroy any possibility of Arsacid resurgence or control, be it politically or economically. This is part of the grand strategy of the Sasanian Empire, as well as pushing the Romans beyond the Euphrates, which has been interpreted as 'aggressive', in the third century AD.

The Sasanians were attempting to control the economy of the region by themselves and were not interested in allowing proxies to take control, as the Arsacids had done before them. One of the early activities of Ardaxšīr is that he took it upon himself to control all of the coast of the Persian Gulf. Sanatroq, the king of Bahrain, was defeated, followed by the king of Oman, named 'Amr b. Wāqed Hemyari, and Oman which had become nominally independent from the Arsacids, was reconquered by the Sasanians.[28] The control of Oman is already mentioned in the Šāpūr I at Ka'be-ye Zardošt inscription (ŠKZ I.1–3), as *Mazūnšahar* in the third century, being part of the empire of *Ērānšahr*.[29] Furthermore, in the only geographical Pahlavi text from Late Antiquity, the *Šahrestānīhā ī Ērānšahr* (passage 52), it is stated that Ardaxšīr 'appointed Ōšag of Hagar as margrave [over the] Dō-sar and Bor-gil by the wall of the Arabs'.[30] This direct control by the Sasanians at the mouth of the Persian Gulf was probably due to the presence of Arsacids in Charax and their connections for the Sasanians.[31]

Ardaxšīr conquered Charax and renamed it Astarā-bād-Ardaxšīr (Karkh Maysān), and other port cities were also established by the Sasanians in the Persian Gulf. In the Pahlavi text, the *Kārnāmag ī Ardaxšīr ī Pābagān* (*Vitae of Ardašīr, Son of Pābag*),[32] the port city of Boxt-Ardaxšīr 'Saved Ardaxšīr'[33] is first mentioned, which later came to be known as Būšehr. In this Pahlavi text, Ardaxšīr is saved from the Arsacids by staying here and hence, establishing a fire temple, and naming it as 'saved by Ardašīr'. This story may inform us that Būšehr was really an independent port from that of the Arsacids that had been in use before. The plethora of Zoroastrian finds, such as ossuaries dated from the third to the seventh centuries AD,[34] provides evidence of the importance of the port of Būšehr for the Sasanian period.

This port, along with another one named Rēw-Ardaxšīr, 'Splendid Ardaxšīr' (Rīšahr), is mentioned by Pseudo-Movses Khorene as the best source of pearls, suggesting the importance of commerce for the Sasanians.[35] Although only a Sasanian fort has so far been found at the port of Siraf, this may show the importance the Sasanians attributed to controlling the sea in this area for economic activity.[36] There are more Sasanian ports and forts on the Eastern Arabian Peninsula, such as Fayluj, which are securely dated only from the Sasanian period and not before it.[37] This fact indicates that the Sasanians created new ports to be in their hands, while disrupting the old routes which were in the hands of the Arsacids and their allies.

Hence, I would like to suggest two reasons why the Sasanian Empire assumed a different form of rule over a large portion of the Near East. With the waning of the decentralized conglomeration of Arsacid petty kings, a much more centralized system took form, which came to be known as *Ērānšahar*. Šāpūr I's victories in the West, beyond Mesopotamia under the king's sway, were the new vision of holding an empire together. This new Iranian empire did not tolerate loosely held kingdoms who held economic lifelines without direct control of the empire and without a central state in the pre-modern sense. When it came to the issue of Palmyra, an episode told by Peter the Patrician,[38] about the correspondence of Septimius Odeanathus with Šāpūr I is instructive:

> he [Odeanathus] sent magnificent gifts and other goods which Persia was not rich in, conveying them by camels. He also sent letters expressing entreaty and saying that he had done nothing against the Persians. Shapur, however, instructed the slaves who received the gifts to throw them into the river and tore up and crushed the letters.

---

28 Gregoratti 2011, 224.
29 Huyse 1999, I, 22–24.
30 Daryaee 1992, 20.
31 Potts 2012.
32 Grenet 2003.
33 Asmussen 1989.
34 Simpson 2014, 81; 2019, 123.
35 Potts 2009.
36 Whitehouse 2009, 341.
37 Al-Jahwari and others 2018.
38 *FHG* IV, frag. 10, 187; Smith II 2013, 167.

How are we to understand this seemingly rash behaviour on the part of the Persian king? Let me provide another episode from late Sasanian history, which may give us some clues. The Sasanian Empire attempted to control the silk industry and silk trade directly[39] during the reign of Khosrow I in the sixth century AD. This is the time when the Sogdian merchants met the Persian king on the eastern boundaries of the empire, and Cosmas Indicopleustes states that at that time the Sasanians received most of their silk through caravan routes, and not the sea.[40] Menander (Frg. 10.1) states that Maniakh, the Sogdian envoy to the Persian king, wanted to gain permission to sell the raw silk, to have free access to the Sasanian Empire. Khosrow I, the great Persian king of kings, then bought the silk, 'paying the fair price for it, and [burning] it in the fire before the very eyes of the envoys'.[41]

I believe what this passage is telling us is that the Sasanians were not going to allow the Turks via the Sogdian traders to take control of the silk trade and move through the roads which the Sasanians controlled to the West. The burning of the raw silk was a symbolic act of informing the Sogdian traders and their Turkish overlords that it was only under Sasanian control and direction that the Silk Road and its silk would be operational. I would make the same case for Peter the Patrician's attestation of the Septimius Odeanathus's request and the Sasanian response of destroying the goods from Palmyra. This public act was meant to be a signal that the trade as it was in Palmyrene hands during the Arsacid period would not continue as such, and that it was the Sasanians who would be in control.

After the coming of the Sasanians to power, between AD 247 and 267,[42] there are only three caravans known to have returned to Palmyra from *Ērānšahar*, which suggests the drastic reduction of this trade route, which was once robust in the Arsacid period. This cutting of trade routes by the Sasanians may be the reason for which Odeanathus launched an attack against the Sasanians, to try to offset the Persian blockade. Such disruption of trade with Charax and the Persian Gulf meant a haemorrhage and economic loss for the Palmyrene kingdom. Then it would be reasonable to think that Odeanathus took on the campaigns that he did, driving deep into Mesopotamia and, according to our sources, even threatening Ctesiphon,[43] to either break the Sasanians into agreeing to open the trade route, or possibly removing them from Mesopotamia altogether.

The Palmyrenes were not filling a political vacuum in the third century before their fall, but, I would suggest, protecting their economic well-being and economic life against the Sasanians, which at first seemed promising and also served Roman interests. When the Romans were beaten by the Sasanians, the Palmyrene victories against Šāpūr only emboldened them against the Romans as well, prompting them to think of a larger position for themselves in the world of Antiquity. However, neither the Romans nor the Sasanians would allow such smaller cities or kingdoms to function independently. While the Sasanians put an end to Dura and Hatra, the Romans under Aurelian did the same after Palmyra began its insubordination in AD 270,[44] and it was taken over in AD 272 with its captured queen, Zenobia.[45]

---

[39] Feltham 2010, 4.
[40] McCrindle 2010, 48; 45–46; de la Vaissiere 2004.
[41] Blockley 1985, 113.

[42] Smith II 2013, 176.
[43] Fevrier 1931, 79–90; Shahid 1994, 437–38.
[44] Stoneman 1992, 119, 117.
[45] Sartre 2005, 358.

Works Cited

al-Jahwari, N. S. and others. 2018. 'Fulayj: A Late Sasanian Fort on the Arabia Coast', *Antiquity*, 92: 724–41.
Asmussen, J. 1989. 'Bōxt-Artaxšīr', in E. Yarshater (ed.), *Encyclopaedia Iranica*, IV.3 (London: Routledge), pp. 332–33.
Blockley, R. 1985. *The History of Menander the Guardsman* (Liverpool: Cairns).
Chaumont, M.-L. 1986. 'Argbed', in E. Yarshater (ed.), *Encyclopaedia Iranica*, I.4 (London: Routledge), pp. 400–01.
Daryaee, T. (trans.). 2002. *Šahrestānīhā ī Ērānšahr: A Middle Persian Text on Geography, Epic and History* (Costa Mesa: Mazda).
—— 2006. 'The Construction of the Past in Late Antique Persia', *Historia*, 55: 493–503.
—— 2010. 'To Learn and to Remember from Others: Persians Visiting the Dura-Europos Synagogue', *Judaica Cracoviensia*, 8: 29–37.
—— 2012. *Sasanian Persia: The Rise and Fall of an Empire* (London: Tauris).
Dodgeon, M. H. and S. N. C. Lieu. 1991. *The Roman Eastern Frontier and the Persian Wars (AD 226–363): A Documentary History*, pt 2 (London: Routledge).

de la Vaissiere, É. 2004. 'Sogdian Trade', in E. Yarshater (ed.), *Encyclopaedia Iranica* <http://www.iranicaonline.org/articles/sogdiana-iii-history-and-archeology> [accessed 10 October 2021].

Feltham, H. 2010. 'Lions, Silks and Silver: The Influence of Sasanian Persia', *Sino-Platonic Papers*, 206: 1–51.

Fevrier, J. G. 1931. *Essai sur l'histoire politique et économique de Palmyre* (Paris: Vrin).

Frye, R. N. 1962. 'Some Early Iranian Titles', *Oriens*, 15: 352–53.

Gagé, J. 1964. *La Montée des Sassanides et l'Heure de Palmyre* (Paris: Éditions Albin Michel).

Gawlikowski, M. 1994. 'Palmyra as a Trading Centre', *British Institute for the Study of Iraq*, 56: 27–33.

Gregpratto, L. 2011. 'A Parthian Harbour in the Gulf: The Characene', *Anabasis: Studia classica et orientalia*, 2: 209–29.

—— 2019. 'Indian Ocean Trade: The Role of Parthia', in M. A. Cobb (ed.), *Indian Ocean Trade in Antiquity: Political, Cultural and Economic Impact* (London: Routledge), pp. 52–72.

Grenet, F. 2003. *La geste d'Ardashir fils de Pâbag: Kārnāmag ī Ardaxšēr ī Pābagān* (Paris: Die).

Hansmann, J. 1991. 'Characene and Charax', in E. Yarshater (ed.), *Encyclopaedia Iranica*, v.4 (London: Routledge), pp. 363–65.

Hauser, S. and D. J. Tucker. 2009. 'The Final Onslaught: The Sasanian Siege of Hatra', *Zeitschrift für Orientarchäologie*, 2: 106–39.

Huyse, P. 1999. *Die dreisprachige Inschrift šābuhrs I. an der Kaba-i Zardust (ŠKZ)*, Corpus inscriptionum Iranicarum, 3, I (London: School of Oriental and African Studies).

Jakubiak, K. 2015. 'The Last Days of Hatra: The Story behind the City's Downfall', in A. Tomas (ed.), *Ad fines Imperii Romani: studia Thaddaeo Sarnowski septuagenario ab amicis, collegis discipulisque dedicate* (Warsaw: Institute of Archaeology Warsaw University), pp. 469–75.

Jong, A. de. 2015. 'Armenian and Georgian Zoroastrianism', in M. Stausberg and Y. S.-D. Vevaina (eds), *The Wiley Blackwell Companion to Zoroastrianism* (Malden: Wiley Blackwell), pp. 119–28.

Kettenhofen, E. 1984. 'Die Einforderung des Achämenidenerbes durch Ardašir: Eine interpretatio romana', *Orientalia Lovaniensia periodica*, 15: 177–90.

Levit-Tawil, D. 1983. 'The Enthroned King Ahasuerus at Dura in Light of the Iconography of Kingship in Iran', *Bulletin of the American Schools of Oriental Research*, 250: 57–78.

McCrindle, J. W. (trans.). 2010. *The Christian Topography of Cosmas, an Egyptian Monk* (London: Hakluyt Society, 1897; repr. 2010).

Millar, F. 1993. *The Roman Near East, 31 BC – AD 337* (Cambridge, MA: Harvard University Press).

Nyberg, S. H. 1974. *A Manual of Pahlavi* (Wiesbaden: Harrassowitz).

Piacentini, V. F. 1985. 'Ardashir i Papakan and the Wars against the Arabs: Working Hypothesis on the Sasanian Hold of the Gulf', *Proceedings of the Seminar for Arabian Studies*, 15: 57–77.

Potter, D. 1987. 'Alexander Severus and Ardashir', *Mesopotamia*, 22: 147–57.

Potts, D. T. 2009. 'Maritime Trade I: Pre-Islamic Period', in E. Yarshater (ed.), *Encyclopaedia Iranica* <https://iranicaonline.org/articles/maritime-trade-i-pre-islamic-period> [accessed 10 October 2021].

—— 2012. 'Arabia II: The Sasanians and Arabia', in E. Yarshater (ed.), *Encyclopaedia Iranica* <https://iranicaonline.org/articles/arabia-ii-sasanians-and-arabia> [accessed 10 October 2021].

Rostovtzeff, M. 1932. *Caravan Cities*, trans. D. Talbot Rice and T. Talbot Rice (Oxford: Clarendon).

Sartre, M. 2005. *The Middle East under Rome* (Cambridge: Belknap).

Schmitt, R. 2003. 'Hatra', in *Encyclopaedia Iranica*, in E. Yarshater (ed.), <https://iranicaonline.org/articles/hatra> [accessed 10 October 2021].

Schoff, W. H. (trans.). 1912. *The Periplus of the Erythraean Sea: Travel and Trade in the Indian Ocean by a Merchant of the First Century* (New York: Longmans).

Seyrig, H. 1950. 'Palmyra and the East', *Journal of Roman Studies*, 40: 1–7.

Shahīd, I. 1994. *Byzantium and the Arabs in the Sixth Century*, I: *Political and Military History* (Washington, DC: Dumbarton Oaks).

Shayegan, M. R. 2011. *Arsacids and Sasanians: Political Ideology in Post-Hellenistic and Late Antique Persia* (Cambridge: Cambridge University Press).

Simpson, St J. 2014. 'Old Bones Overturned: New Evidence for Funerary Practices from the Sasanian Empire', in A. Fletcher, D. Antoine, and J. D. Hill (eds), *Regarding the Dead: Human Remains in the British Museum* (London: The British Museum), pp. 77–79.

—— 2019. 'The Land behind Rishahr: Sasanian Funerary Practices on the Bushehr Peninsula', in Y. Moradi (ed.), *AfarinNameh: Essays on the Archaeology of Iran in Honour of Mehdi Rahbar* (Tehran: The Research Institute of Cultural Heritage and Tourism), pp. 111–24.

Smith II, A. M. 2013. *Roman Palmyra: Identity, Community, and State Formation* (Oxford: Oxford University Press).

Stoneman, R. 1992. *Palmyra and its Empire: Zenobia's Revolt against Rome* (Ann Arbor: University of Michigan Press).

Welles, C. B., R. O. Fink, and J. F. Gilliam. 1959. *The Excavations at Dura Europos: Final Report*, V (New Haven: Yale University Press).

Whitehouse, D. 2009. 'Sasanian Maritime Activity', in J. Reade (ed.), *The Indian Ocean in Antiquity* (London: Routledge), pp. 339–49.

Wiesehöfer, J. 1982. 'Die Anfänge sassanidischer Westpolitik und der Untergang Hatras', *Klio*, 64: 437–47.

—— 1986. 'Ardašīr i. History', in E. Yarshater (ed.), *Encyclopaedia Iranica*, II.4 (London: Routledge), pp. 371–76.

5. Zenobia and the East

Nathanael J. Andrade
Binghamton University (nandrade@binghamton.edu)

Introduction

According to our main textual sources for Zenobia of Palmyra, the famed ruler conspired with the Persians against Roman interests at various junctures. Some allegations fall in her reign's final months. As the Roman emperor Aurelian invested her at Palmyra in the summer of 272, Zenobia allegedly taunted him with claims that Persian support was imminent.[1] When she fled the city, she reportedly sought Persian help.[2] But the *Historia Augusta* also implies that Zenobia aligned herself with the Persians immediately after succeeding her murdered husband Odainath in 268 or so. As it claims:

> When Odainath's death was announced to him, Gallienus reasonably prepared a war against the Persians, in vengeance for his father that came too late, and he was behaving like a capable emperor by having his commander Heraclianus gather troops. Still, when this Heraclianus set out against the Persians, he was defeated by the Palmyrenes and lost all the troops that he had prepared. Zenobia was governing the Palmyrenes and most eastern peoples as though as a man.[3]

For reasons that will be described shortly, scholars have recognized this passage to be deeply flawed. But even so, it reflects a tendency in Roman texts to depict the Palmyrenes and the Persians as joined in their efforts to prevent Roman governance in the East. It is also consistent with the *Historia Augusta*'s tendency to portray Zenobia as an eastern, un-Roman foreigner[4] who had a natural affinity with her Persian and Arabian neighbours.

Now, to what extent does this characterization actually reflect the politics of Zenobia and her Palmyra, as opposed to the perspective of her opponents? In this article, I will address this question by examining the relationship of Zenobia's Palmyra with the world of Iran.

Roman Historiography and its Testimony

To begin, we will assess how Zenobia was represented by Roman historiographic texts. While the main sources date after Zenobia's career, they also seem to reflect how her enemies were characterizing her during her lifetime. In fact, they may be mainly responsible for the premise that Zenobia and her Palmyrenes had a natural political affinity with the Persians.

In Roman texts, Zenobia and her husband Odainath receive remarkably inconsistent treatment. A narrative strain represents Odainath and Zenobia, quite accurately, as fighting the Persians precisely when the Roman imperial court struggled to do so.[5] This should not surprise us. Odainath's victories over the Persians are independently documented by later Roman historiography, Palmyrene epigraphy, and the Jewish rabbinic tradition.[6] Yet, we also hear about complicity or collusion. A fragment of Peter the Patrician, an early Byzantine writer, claims that Odainath had tried to make his own treaty with the Persian king Shapur I during one of his invasions of Roman territory, probably in 260.[7] This testimony is, however, uncorroborated, and its value as evidence for Odainath's political goals is dubious, even if it may shed light on some of Shapur's political motivations. It may even reflect a narrative circulated by the imperial court in 267–268 to justify its complicity in an assassination coup against Odainath.[8] Likewise, a passage of the so-called *Continuator Dionis* (who may be the aforementioned Peter the Patrician)[9] claims that a courtier of the emperor Gallienus arranged Odainath's assassi-

---

[1] SHA, *Aur.* XXVII–XXVIII.

[2] Zos. LV; SHA, *Aur.* XXVII.

[3] SHA, *Gall.* XIII.4–5.

[4] SHA, *Tyr. Trig.* XXX.1–2.

[5] Particularly, Sync. 716 (Mosshammer 1984, 466); Zos. I.39.2; SHA, *Valer.* IV; SHA, *Gall.* X.2, X.6, XII.1; SHA, *Tyr. Trig.* XV.1–4, XXX.6–10.

[6] For the details, see Hartmann 2001, 162–85.

[7] *FHG* IV.187; Hartmann 2001, 136–37; Southern 2008, 60–61; Banchich 2015, 115.

[8] Suggested by Andrade 2018a, 147. See however Daryaee (in this volume), which explores how the testimony may have serious historical validity in the context of Shapur's military activity.

[9] *FGH* IV.195. See Banchich 2015, 3–9.

Figure 5.1. Coin of Aurelian, ANS 1944.100.32846 (© American Numismatic Society).

nation because he was plotting revolution, an accusation made with similar phrasing regarding Zenobia's soliciting of Persian support against Aurelian in the *Historia Augusta*.[10] Presumably, such claims of complicity made it easier for the emperor Aurelian to justify his campaigns against Zenobia in 272. But however we understand these narrative traditions, they do beg two questions. What exactly was the relationship of Zenobia's Palmyra with peoples to the east, especially the Persians? How do we sift through these traditions to understand it?

As noted already, the *Historia Augusta* claims that armies of the Roman imperial court and Zenobia clashed shortly after she had assumed power. It states that Gallienus's praetorian prefect Heraclianus initiated a campaign against the Persians but that his army was destroyed by the Palmyrenes led by Zenobia. Scholarship has often commented on the perplexing nature of the passage. The prefect Heraclianus helped murder Gallienus in Milan in the summer of 268; he could not have been commanding an army in Syria before Gallienus's death. This discrepancy has led scholars to theorize that this expedition, while planned, never occurred or that it actually happened after Gallienus's death.[11] But also odd is the statement that Heraclianus went on campaign against the Persians but was confronted by Palmyrenes.[12] What explains it?

In my view, the statement of the *Historia Augusta* reflects the propaganda of the imperial court in the age of Zenobia, which was likening the Palmyrenes to Persians and Parthians in order to disguise a civil war between different Roman factions as a war between the Roman state and a foreign adversary. In tandem with this technique, it was also insisting that the dynasty of Odainath and Zenobia had affinities with the Persian court. Such characterizations emerged on coins minted by the emperor Aurelian shortly after his victories over the Palmyrenes in 272–273 (Fig. 5.1). These showed figures in Parthian garb (or a generic Roman version thereof) who are depicted as captives or as being trampled by Sol Invictus. On these coins, the Parthians represent the Palmyrenes, and intriguingly, after his victories over the Palmyrenes Aurelian even adopted the titles of Parthicus Maximus and Persicus Maximus.[13] Aurelian, however, never really fought against the Persians; these titles conflated the Palmyrenes with the Parthians and Persians who had been the Romans' most potent rivals in the Middle East for centuries.

Such propaganda may in part explain the inscriptions made in Arabian languages in Jordan that appear to describe conflicts between Romans and so-called Persians. It had been fairly conventional for Arabians to describe powerful empires to the east as Persians or Medes (*mdy*) since Achaemenid times. While it is not always easy to place references to Medes in Arabian language inscriptions in context, an intriguing theory is that at least some of them are referring to the Palmyrenes' military activity in south Syria, north Arabia, or Transjordan, which certain Arabian peoples found invasive.[14] To be sure, it is widely known that Zenobia's Palmyra had long-standing interactions with Arabians, some of these being nomads or pastoralists from north Arabia that spent their summers in Palmyra's vicinity.[15] Even so, some Arabian populations probably had serious objections to Palmyrene imperial hegemony, and these are widely deemed to be the kernel of the conflicts of al-Zabba (generally accepted as based on Zenobia) with the Tanukh confederacy in Islamic Arabic historiography.[16] Aurelian's Arabian allies too may have conceived of the Palmyrenes in Persian terms and thus replicated

---

[10] Zos. LV.2; SHA, *Aur*. XXVII–XXVIII.

[11] Hartmann 2006; Potter 2014, 262; Southern 2008, 90; Andrade 2018a, 149–50.

[12] Southern 2008, 89–90; Hartmann 2006, 111–18 instead conceive of a planned joint expedition against the Palmyrenes and the Persians or a war against Persia as a pretext for the reasserting of control over Palmyra. I would, however, suggest that the *Historia Augusta* is conflating the Persians and Palmyrenes, in keeping with the propaganda of the imperial court.

[13] For coins, *RIC* v.1; Kienast 1996, 235 (titles); Potter 2014, 267.

[14] Graf 1989, 152–55. Certain texts discussed by MacDonald 2014, 162 could be referring to conflicts between the Roman imperial court and the Palmyrenes, though he identifies the Persians. See MacDonald, Al-Manaser, and Hidalgo-Chacón Diez 2017, 524, 3351, 8021, 8357–58, and 8361.

[15] Meyer 2016, 92–93.

[16] Hartmann 2001, 280–81, 343–51.

his claim that his invasion of Syria involved a war against Parthians or Persians.

The existing source material, however, disguises a more complicated reality. This is not to say that the Palmyrenes did not share some cultural and political affinities with the Parthians and the Persians. They certainly did, and this presumably made it easier for Zenobia's detractors to conflate the Palmyrenes and the Persians or to suggest some political complicity. But their characterizations were misleading. Much distinguished the Parthians and Persians from the Palmyrenes too.

Persia and Zenobia's Palmyra: Cultural Similarities

But first, let us discuss similarities. It is well known that the Palmyrenes' cultural and religious practices interwove various strands of Aramaean, Arabian, Parthian, and Persian culture and that Aramaic had pride of place at Zenobia's Palmyra. Yet in my view, this did not make the Palmyrenes any less Roman. If anything, it made them very uniquely Roman and reflected the multicultural variations with which Romanness could be expressed.[17] Moreover, cultural affinities and political alignment are not necessarily identical. Amid their cultural eclecticism, the Palmyrenes had fashioned a unique Roman imperial subjectivity by Zenobia's lifetime. We have evidence for the Roman imperial cult, the realignment of Palmyra as a *colonia* modelled on the political forms of Italian cities, and the adoption of Roman imperial titles by Odainath's dynasty to communicate its increasingly autonomous governing authority in the Roman East. These include the titles of senator, *consularis*, *rector* or *corrector* of all the East, and eventually Caesar and Augustus.[18] Nonetheless, the presence of eastern cultural forms at Palmyra, including those exhibited in funerary sculpture, point to long-standing cultural affinities with the world of Iran. It is well known that certain Palmyrenes cultivated forms of dress resembling those to be found among the Parthians, the Persians, or their Mesopotamian subjects.[19] This fact was not lost on the Romans. This is precisely why Aurelian, when he defeated the Palmyrenes in 272 and 273, assumed the epithets of Parthicus Maximus and Persicus Maximus and depicted Sol Invictus with subdued captives dressed like Parthians.

It was, I suspect, also due to analogous mechanisms that later Roman and rabbinic Jewish texts described the Palmyrenes as 'Saracens'.[20] The most famous example arguably comes from the Palestinian Talmud, which describes how Jewish rabbis negotiated with Zenobia and the 'Saracens' of her court regarding a captive.[21] This does not necessarily reflect how Palmyrenes defined themselves. Arabian traditions undoubtedly flourished at Palmyra, and early Arabic texts modelled the figure of al-Zabba on her.[22] These have encouraged perceptions of Zenobia as an Arab nationalist.[23] Yet, no reliable evidence indicates that Zenobia conceived of herself as an Arab.[24] The labelling of 'Saracen', which typifies sources from the fourth century or later, instead emphasized the perceived 'foreignness' of the Palmyrenes and likened them to putatively foreign Arabian peoples understood to be inimical to Roman interests during Late Antiquity. This would explain why some inscriptions endowed Aurelian with the title of Arabicus maximus after his defeating the Palmyrenes in 272, though this title was probably not an official one.[25] Intriguingly, Zenobia had previously given her son the same title, but to celebrate dynastic victories over the nomadic allies of Persians.[26] By contrast, Aurelian's court seems to have conceived of Zenobia's Palmyrenes variously as Parthians, Persians, and Arabians in its propaganda, thus conflating all these distinct peoples.

But what exactly was Zenobia's relationship with the peoples of the East, especially the Persians, and to what extent did they share social, cultural, or religious affinities? Palmyra's inscriptions and material culture provide some hints, but these can also be deceptive. For example, the armies of Odainath and Zenobia contained heavily

---

17   Andrade 2013, 171–210, 314–39; 2018a, 33–55; Smith 2013, 130–32.

18   The bibliography is vast. See foremost Hartmann 2001, 146–61; 2016; Southern 2008, 68–70; and recently Andrade 2018a, 136–37. For imperial cult, Gawlikowski and As'ad 2010.

19   Long 2017; Curtis 2017, 52–67.

20   Hartmann 2001, 88 and 330–32.

21   Jerusalem Talmud, *Terumot*. VIII.10.46b in Guggenheimer 2000–. For Palmyrenes in Jewish sources, Appelbaum 2011.

22   Hartmann 2001, 332–51; Woltering 2014; Sartre-Fauriat and Sartre 2014, 252–58; and Andrade 2018a, 223–25 on Zenobia in the Arabic tradition.

23   Treated as such by Tlass 1985; 1986; 2000; Zahran 2010. Discussed by Woltering 2014, Sartre-Fauriat and Sartre 2014, 253–55; 2016, 21–32, 219–21.

24   Sartre-Fauriat and Sartre 2014, 253–55; 2016, 21–32, 219–38; Andrade 2018a, 54–55, 225–28.

25   Peachin 1990, 92; Kienast 1996, 235. The key inscriptions are *AE* 1936, no. 129 and *ILS* 576.

26   *ILS* 8924 = Bauzou 1998, nos 98, with 99–101; Isaac 1998, 70. Sartre-Fauriat and Sartre 2014, 94–96; Andrade 2018a, 55, 191.

Figure 5.2. Horse armour excavated at Dura-Europos (© Yale University Art Gallery, 1933.680).

armoured soldiers akin to the cataphracts of the Sasanian Persian Empire; they appear in our Latin sources as *clibanarii*. Some have deemed these soldiers to be Persians themselves.[27] Yet, we know that the Romans had begun to assemble such units by the third century.[28] An officer from Mesopotamia named Barsemis, who died in central Europe while serving in the Roman army, had been an officer in one such cataphract unit.[29] The Romans deployed armoured horsemen and horses at Dura-Europos, to defend it from Persians, who captured it in the 250s (Fig. 5.2).[30] The presence of cataphracts in the armies of Odainath and Zenobia probably reflects how they had come to command many of the Roman units in Syria after 260.[31]

By Zenobia's lifetime, certain Parthian or Persian names were appearing in the Palmyrene onomasticon.[32] Their presence is not overwhelming, as most Palmyrene personal names were Aramaic or Arabic in origin.[33] Some enslaved persons were presumably imported by Palmyrenes from Parthian or Sasanian territory.[34] Unfortunately, Palmyrene documents typically are not explicit on their origins. But a papyrus document issued at a village on the Middle Euphrates in 252 bears witness to the acquisition of a woman from Persian territory at Roman Nisibis and her eventual transfer to other areas of Mesopotamia and the Middle Euphrates that the Romans controlled at the time. It reports that a woman named Aurelia Victorina, the wife of a Roman centurion stationed at Nisibis, had purchased a woman with the Persian name of Vardanaia and had given her the Latin name of Diane, after the Roman goddess.[35] Her example provides an inkling of the mechanisms that brought imported slaves from Persian territory into Palmyra, as mentioned in the Palmyrene Tax Law.[36] It also supports not only that slaves with Iranian or common Mesopotamian Aramaic names (like Abdnergal) were imported from Parthian or Persian territory but that many slaves named after Greek gods (like Hermes) had similar origins.[37]

Most significant among Palmyrenes with Iranian names is easily Septimius Worod. Odainath's deputy throughout the 260s, his career is documented by many inscriptions. While carrying various Roman official titles, he also was *argapet*; an Iranian title, its meaning has been debated.[38] The appearance of a certain Worod in the most famous career inscription of Shapur I has led some to surmise that Septimius Worod was born in Persia or otherwise had Persian sympathies. Such premises are unfounded,[39] but his activity, Iranian title, and duties presumably associated with people in the Iranian world who had the same title hint at the eastward-looking

---

[27] Winsbury 2010, 126; Nakamura 1993, 138. But see Hartmann 2001, 99, 385–86.

[28] Eadie 1967; Hartmann 2001, 99; Southern 2008, 45, 71.

[29] *ILS* 2540; Haynes 2013, 92. Also see *P. Oxy* XLI.295.

[30] James 2004, esp. 259; 2011, 307–08.

[31] Hartmann 2001, 99, 138; Southern 2008, 45, 59, and 71.

[32] Yon 2002, 187; 2000, 87–88.

[33] Maraqten 1995; Stark 1971.

[34] Yon 2002, 187, with 262 for a list; 2000, 87–88; Smith 2013, 104–07.

[35] Feissel, Gascou, and Teixidor 1997 (*P. Euphrates* 9).

[36] *Palmyrene Tax Law* III.a.1–10, II.a.206, in Healey 2009, with 191–92.

[37] Yon 2002, 187, on slave names; 2000, 87–88.

[38] *IGLS* XVII.1.63–79; *PAT* 0063. Gnoli 2007, 95–113. On the name Worod, Marcato 2018, 55. See also Daryaee (in this volume) on the title of *argapet*.

[39] Schmidt-Colinet 1992, 40; Hartmann 2001, 203–11; Southern 2008, 74; Sartre-Fauriat and Sartre 2014, 63–70; Andrade 2018a, 139–40. The inscription, discussed in the next section, is in Huyse 1999.

nature of the court of Odainath and Zenobia and its elite.

We can certainly discern the impact of Persian regal traditions on the activity of Odainath and Zenobia. After 260, Odainath emulated his Persian rival Shapur I by adopting the title of 'king of kings' and apparently coaxing his courtiers to adopt his name of Septimius.[40] Zenobia herself noticeably appears to have adopted the name Septimia under these circumstances.[41] Tesserae and a statue portrait that may represent Odainath indicate that he and his son Herodian (otherwise Hairan) wore headgear consistent with Iranian paradigms, or at least Syro-Mesopotamian patterns common in adjacent Persian territory.[42] Zenobia would subsequently claim the title 'king of kings' for her son Wahballath. Even so, such cultural affinity was born in a context of political rivalry. Odainath's household adopted many of these Persian conventions after its victories over the Persians and as a way of expressing superiority to the Persian king of kings.[43] Its activity did not reflect any solidarity with the Persians or signify any sort of political alliance. A famous mosaic thus celebrated Odainath's victories over the Persians, as symbolized by a chimera and Persian tigers (Fig. 5.3).[44] Zenobia herself would confer the title of Persicus maximus upon her son and establish settlements on the Euphrates to deter further inroads from the Persians.[45]

Figure 5.3. Mosaic showing an archer killing Persian tigers (© Michał Gawlikowski and the Polish Mission to Palmyra; photographed by Waldemar Jerke).

Persia and Zenobia's Palmyra: Critical Differences

According to texts in Iranian languages found in central Asia, a figure named Adda visited the royal court of Palmyra and healed the sister of a queen named Tadi. Coptic texts from Egypt likewise mention a mission to Queen Thadamor.[46] Adda was the disciple of Mani, the Iranian founder of the Manichaean religion, and it is commonly accepted that Tadi and Thadamor were based on Zenobia. If this event occurred, it provides some indication for how the cosmic vision of Zenobia's court parted ways with that of the Sasanian Persians. A few years after Manichaean missionaries were being received by Zenobia, the Persian court executed Mani despite having offered him patronage earlier.[47]

Many chapters in this volume, and various works of recent scholarship, have rightfully stressed the cultural affinities that Zenobia's Palmyra bore with the Iranian world to the east and the ways that they participated in a Parthian cultural *koine*.[48] There is no doubt that

---

[40] *IGLS* XVII.1.61; Hartmann 2001, 176–85; Southern 2008, 71–73; Andrade 2018a, 134–35; Potter 2015, 257.

[41] Southern 2008, 4; Sartre-Fauriat and Sartre 2014, 79; Andrade 2018a, 134.

[42] Gawlikowski 2016. For the concept of 'Syro-Mesopotamian', which affords some variation, see Dirven 2011 and Blömer (in this volume).

[43] *PAT* 0317; *IGLS* 17.1.57; Hartmann 2001, 176–85.

[44] Gawlikowski 2005; Gawlikowski and Żuchowska 2010.

[45] *ILS* 8924 = Bauzou 1998, nos 98, with 99–101; Procop., *Aed*. II.8.8–15; Lauffray 1983–1991; Blétry 2015.

[46] Gardner and Lieu 2004, 111–14 for translations.

[47] Gardner and Lieu 2004, 3–8.

[48] De Jong 2013b; Gregoratti 2016.

Figure 5.4. Relief of figures wearing Syro-Mesopotamian tunic and trousers (© Yale University Art Gallery, 1931.118).

Palmyrenes shared many cultural practices, or variations thereof, with Aramaic-speakers in Mesopotamia, including similarities of attire (Fig. 5.4).[49] On occasion, scholars have even suggested that these reflected political choices made due to natural sympathies with eastern societies or increased opposition to the Roman Empire.[50] For the remainder of this article, I will emphasize how the political and religious lives of Zenobia's Palmyra parted ways from those of the Sasanian Persians and the serious perceptions of difference that Zenobia and her court most probably harboured toward the Persian ruling elite (but not necessarily its subjects in Mesopotamia, with whom they had much in common).

To begin our enquiry, we can reflect on inscriptions made at the temple of the god Assur at Assur, in north Iraq, between AD 199 and 227–28, right at the transition from Parthian to Sasanian rule in the region.[51] One of them, from April of 221, involves a dedication that two men made to the temple's primary god.

Likewise, at nearby Hatra, we have evidence for traditional polytheistic practice throughout its clientage to the Parthians and into the opening decades of the third century.[52]

But in the centuries that followed, most traditional polytheism that had persisted in the world of Iran would disappear from public life. What had happened in the interim? As recent scholarship has stressed, the rock-cut inscriptions of the Zoroastrian priest Kerdir in Fars provide a compelling indication and a precursor.[53] In them, the priest boasts of his success, perhaps exaggerated, in suppressing or subordinating various religious groups and establishing Zoroastrian places of worship where idolaters had venerated demons.[54] Because of his inscriptions, Kerdir has earned recognition for his efforts to establish an increasingly coordinated Zoroastrian priestly order that intervened in the religious affairs of Sasanian Persia, principally in the second half of the third century. The support (if measured) that Kerdir enjoyed from Persia's kings is demonstrated by his increasingly elevated titles and authority and by the eventual execution of the prophet Mani. Significantly, Kerdir's own inscriptions indicate that he was active in the very same decades that Odainath and then Zenobia ruled Palmyra.

Of course, the inscriptions of Kerdir have serious limitations as evidence for the period's religious life. No contemporary texts corroborate Kerdir's testimony and self-promotion. He may not have been as effective, or beloved by the Sasanian monarchs, as he claims.[55] Likewise, we have to recognize the Sasanian royal dynasty's own discrepant relationship with Zoroastrianism. The piety of the early Sasanian kings themselves is documented by the foundation of fire altars associated with the royal dynasty and the appearance of fire altars on royal coinages.[56] Yet, this by no means indicates that they shared

---

[49] Curtis 2017 and Long 2017 discuss attire. See Blömer (in this volume) and Dirven 2018 for important insights.

[50] Long 2017, 75–76, 81–82.

[51] Beyer 1998, A6b, A17a–b, A20, A23a–c, A25b–g, A27a–k, A28a–i, A29a–i.z; Haider 2008, 193–201; Dirven 2014, 214–15.

[52] Dirven 2013 for research on Hatra.

[53] Payne 2015, 24–25, 32–33; Panaino 2016, for example.

[54] MacKenzie 1989, 58, who translates one inscription. Also see Gignoux 1991, 69.

[55] Panaino 2016, 113; Myers 2010, 52. I thank Khodadad Rezakhani for his observations on this matter.

[56] De Jong 2013a, 37–42. For coins, Alram, Blet-Lemarquant, and Skjaervø 2007.

Kerdir's particular worldview, accepted his claims to religious authority without a critical eye, or envisioned the supremacy of Zoroastrianism throughout the Persian state.[57] Ultimately, the religious goals of Shapur I, the reigning monarch during the entirety of Odainath's and Zenobia's governance at Palmyra, are unclear. If he had religious ambitions for his empire, it is not certain that Zenobia would have known what they were.

Even so, it is obvious enough from Shapur's own royal inscriptions, and the volatility of the Euphrates frontier in the 250s–260s, that the activity of the Sasanian royal dynasty represented a palpable threat to Palmyra's security. Shapur did in fact deport people from the populations of cities that he occupied in Roman Syria and Mesopotamia,[58] and the successful campaigns of both his father Ardashir and himself led to the abandonment of cities and thus the desacralization of sanctuaries at Dura-Europos (certainly), as well as Assur and Hatra (presumably).[59] Deportation and coercive abandonment posed obvious dangers to Palmyra's local religious life, along with the unravelling of a Parthian commercial network in Mesopotamia from which the Palmyrenes benefitted.[60] Moreover, Shapur's conception of an ecumene inhabited by Iranians and non-Iranians (which would include the Palmyrenes) had certain religious connotations. He boasted of establishing fire altars in areas that he controlled,[61] and various texts, albeit late, accredit kings as early as Ardashir I with replacing temples of 'idols' with fire temples and elaborate upon the protocols for doing so.[62] At minimum, we could expect the imperial regime to implement financial policies that supported Zoroastrian cult sites and undermined the fiscal basis of a region's traditional cults. To be sure, the third-century Sasanian elite may not have been united, or ambitious, in its religious goals or perceptions. Even so, Kerdir's boasts, even if not representing the dominant vision of his era, presaged the religious trajectory of the Sasanian Empire in the centuries to follow, since subsequent centuries did witness the erosion of polytheism. At the least, Shapur's campaigns were a threat to the continued existence of Palmyra as a city, and thus its religious life.

In this political context, it is possible that Zenobia and other contemporaries on the eastern frontier conceived of certain members of the Sasanian Persian elite as actively privileging Zoroastrian cult in its areas of control. The evidence for this is the apocryphal *Acts of the Apostle Thomas*, a text that was circulating in both Syriac and Greek by the early fourth century. Traditionally theorized to be by origin a Syriac text composed at Edessa in the early third century,[63] a recent theory surmises it to have been a Greek text written somewhere in the second-century Mediterranean.[64] Yet, there is reason to conceive of the text, in its surviving form, as composed in Syriac at Edessa in the mid-to-late third century, and thus in the aftermath of the Persians' initial occupation of the nearby city of Nisibis in 242 and their more enduring reoccupation of it, probably after Shapur's successful invasion of 252 or so (and certainly after 260).[65] Clues for the dating of the text include the tendency for the Greek narrative to depict exchanges in silver bullion where the corresponding Syriac texts describes exchanges in silver. This would seem to situate the Greek version in the context of shifts in the Roman Empire's monetary policy occurring after AD 275 that sometimes made exchanges in silver bullion more expedient than exchanges in silver coins. The Syriac text would be placed some time earlier.[66] Likewise, in instances that the Syriac text uses *rab ḥayla* to describe a general, the Greek version refers to the figure as a *stratelates*, not a *strategos*. This, again, places the Greek version to the late third or early fourth

---

[57] Kreyenbroek 2008.

[58] Huyse 1999, I, nos 30–31.

[59] For desacralization of sanctuaries at Dura-Europos, Coqueugniot 2012, Leriche 2016, 180; Baird 2018, 36–37. By all appearances, Assur, like Hatra, was not inhabited in the Sasanian period. See Downey 1988, 147; Andrae 1933, 2–3; Schlumberger 1970, 113.

[60] See Daryaee (in this volume), along with Daryaee 2020 and Payne 2018, 231–32, 235.

[61] Huyse 1999, I, no. 30–32. Panaino 2016, 115.

[62] Payne 2015, 33; de Jong 2006, 235–38.

[63] Attridge 1990; Myers 2010, 31.

[64] Roig Lanzilotta 2015.

[65] The *Historia Augusta* (*Gall.* x.3) credits Odainath with recapturing Nisibis and Carrhae in a campaign often dated to 262–263. These had been claimed by Shapur by 260 at latest, and more probably by 252. In his career inscription, Shapur noticeably does not mention taking Nisibis in either one of his extensive offensive campaigns against the Romans involving the capture of cities west of the Euphrates, an indication that he had occupied it shortly before his offensive of 252 (or 253) and held it continuously into the 260s. The Persians had initially occupied it briefly during their successful campaign of the early 240s, but the Romans apparently recaptured it. See De Blois 2016, 38–41; Hauser 2013, 136–38; Hartmann 2001, 70–73; Edwell 2008, 169–80; Palermo 2019, 41–49. Al-Tabari, not always an accurate source, places Shapur's capture of Nisibis in the eleventh year of his reign (roughly 252–253), in Bosworth 1999, 28.

[66] Andrade 2018b, 36–42.

century and makes the Syriac version roughly contemporary to Zenobia's adulthood or the aftermath of her rule. Intriguingly, a famous inscription from 271 that celebrates Zenobia exhibits an identical tendency; her generals are called by the term *rb ḥyl'* in Palmyrenean and *stratelates* in the Greek.[67]

This dating and provenance for the *Acts of Thomas* have bearing for how the inhabitants of the Roman Empire's eastern frontier conceived of the Sasanian Persian court. While the first eight 'Acts' into which the text is divided may have to various degrees been adapted from early traditions, Acts 9–13 form a coherent whole that centres on the apostle Thomas's exploits at the court of a king with the Persian name of Mazdai, which of course calls to mind the Zoroastrian god Ahura Mazda.[68] A polytheist figure (whose court worships 'the gods of the East'), he mostly plays the stereotypical role of a pagan oppressor, and to some degree this could reflect a Roman Mesopotamian Christian understanding of Zoroastrians as worshippers of many Iranian gods. Yet, his name and his decision to have the apostle endure a trial by fire seem to reflect an effort to model King Mazdai on contemporary Sasanian royalty or a perception thereof.[69] So does the description of the king's nephew and courtier Karish as his 'second', a term reflecting either how Greeks translated the term *pasgriba*, a figure who acted as the viceroy for the Parthian king,[70] or simply a long-standing perception that an Iranian king always had a 'second'.[71] Moreover, Mazdai's general Siphor appears to have a Greek rendering of the Persian name Shapur, the same borne by Shapur I.[72] Even Mygdonia, the name of the wife of the court noble Karish, happens to be the traditional Greek name of the river running by Nisibis and, by extension, a name for the city.[73] Her name implies an association made by the text's author between the Mesopotamian city of Nisibis and one of its recent Persian occupations.

It accordingly seems that the *Acts of Thomas* is modelling its King Mazdai, heavily fictionalized to be sure, on a certain perception of the Persian governing elite and its religious inclinations that circulated among populations inhabiting the Roman Empire's frontier with Persia. The fact that the Persians effectively occupied Nisibis in the 250s and early 260s would have stimulated greater contemplation of the relationship between the religious lives of Persians and those of their subjects among Edessenes, who were nearby but in Roman territory.[74] After all, Shapur I boasted of establishing fire altars in territories that he controlled in his career inscription, and Kerdir congratulated himself for similar reasons in his inscriptions too.[75] Even if no evidence indicates that such activity happened at Nisibis or elsewhere in what had been Roman territory, at the least the *Acts of Thomas* contains traces of how certain Roman subjects along the eastern frontier were filtering claims of Zoroastrian religious superiority being made by Persian authorities in territory that they had occupied. The king with the name Mazdai thus has Thomas endure a trial by fire in an effort to demonstrate the supremacy of the 'gods of the East'. If such perceptions of contemporary Persians circulated in Upper Mesopotamia in the 250s–270s, they reasonably did so among Zenobia and her Palmyrenes too.

The political and religious trajectories of the Persian Empire and Palmyra during Zenobia's lifetime, meaningfully distinct, have bearing on how we understand the preponderance of Syro-Mesopotamian, Parthian, or Iranian cultural symbols prevalent at Palmyra. It is perhaps obvious, but worth repeating, that such symbols do not correlate to political sympathies with the world of Iran or opposition to the Roman Empire.[76] First, the relationship between culture and political allegiance is actually very complex and unstable, and it can only really be assessed on a case-by-case basis in context. We cannot always be sure what the adoption of, say, clothing styles meant for the political alignment of Palmyrenes at a given time, or even that they endowed such clothing with the cultural significance that we often do.[77] Moreover, even if the Palmyrenes shared cultural affinities or connections with Iranian peoples, there were also some serious cultural differences, whether materially real or merely imagined. By comparison, we know that

---

[67] *IGLS* XVII.1.57.

[68] Myers 2010, 41–42, 51–52. For name, Gignoux, Jullien, and Jullien 2009, 99. Andrade 2018b, 33–34.

[69] *Acts of Thomas* (ed. Wright 1871) p. rpw and št, (ed. Bonnet 1903) 115 and 140. Myers 2010, 41–42, 51–52. Andrade 2018b, 33–34; 2020b.

[70] *Hymn of the Pearl* 42, 48, and 60, in Poirier 1981 and Ferreira 2002. On *pasgriba*, see Gnoli 2002; 2007, 115–21.

[71] Volkmann 1937; Andrade 2020b, 374–75.

[72] Gignoux, Jullien, and Jullien 2009, 126.

[73] Myers 2010, 41–42, though she sees Mygdonia as evidence for composition in Nisibis, not Edessa.

[74] See Myers 2010, 34–44 for the ostensible reflections of Nisibis in the text.

[75] Huyse 1999, I, no. 32; Gignoux 1991, 68–73.

[76] See likewise Blömer's observations (in this volume).

[77] Dirven 2018, esp. 125.

residents of Upper Mesopotamian Edessa participated in a Parthian cultural *koine*, wore variations on Syro-Mesopotamian and Iranian-style attire, and even called heir apparents to the royal throne by an Iranian term.[78] Even so, we have already seen how the *Acts of Thomas* apparently represents how Edessenes were responding to claims of religious superiority posited by Sasanian ruling authorities. Similarly, the Syriac *Book of the Laws of the Countries* shows that some third-century Edessenes conceived of Parthians as foreigners who practised polygamy, of Persians as foreigners who married their mothers, daughters, and sisters, and of Iranian peoples in general as foreigners who fed corpses to animals as part of an independently attested Zoroastrian rite.[79] Despite Palmyra's connections to the cultures of Iran, nothing prevented such views from circulating among the Palmyrenes. After all, like the Edessenes, they were overwhelmingly monogamous, limited their endogamy to the marriage of nieces or cousins, and inhumated their dead in tombs, sometimes after mummifying them.[80]

Second, some of Palmyra's most militaristic conflicts with Persia occurred precisely when depictions of Syro-Mesopotamian, Parthian, or Iranian clothing styles were most popular in the funerary or domestic culture.[81] It was for this reason, as we have seen, that Odainath could adopt Persian symbols of authority amid his combat with Persians and that Palmyrenes could represent him as a man in Iranian dress fighting Persians symbolized by Persian tigers. We know that both Odainath and Zenobia sought to fortify or populate parts of the Euphrates River in spite of the destruction of Roman and even Palmyrene garrisons along it during the 250s.[82] The caravans that are attested during Odainath's governance suggest this,[83] and Zenobia herself founded an eponymous city on the contested Euphrates frontier that enabled her to secure the Palmyrene presence in north Mesopotamia.[84] The Palmyrenes also fought against the Persians with cavalrymen armed as Persian-style cataphracts, as previously mentioned. We can find similar parallels in the example of Hatra. The city was clearly embedded in a Parthian *koine* and had mostly been a client of the Parthians throughout the second century and opening decades of the third.[85] Hatrean sculpture also demonstrates that variations on Syro-Mesopotamian or Iranian clothing styles were very popular, and its architecture was clearly at home in regions governed by Parthians and Persians.[86] The heir apparent of Hatra's royal dynasty, like that at Edessa, was even noticeably described by a Parthian title.[87] Yet, Hatra would find itself in conflict with the Persians throughout the 230s and devastated by them in 240.[88] Its vibrant, polytheistic religious life would virtually end at this time. At third-century Palmyra, Iranian cultural influences probably had little connection to any serious socio-political identification with the contemporary world of Iran. Its practical usages, its connotations of high status, or its occupational associations probably made it desirable.[89]

Finally, as obvious as it may be, it is worth emphasizing that the Parthians and the Persians were distinct peoples who oversaw distinct political systems and had different cosmic views. While the Parthians apparently practised their own strand (or strands) of Zoroastrianism, their Zoroastrianism was fairly loosely coordinated and regionally variable.[90] As such, the Parthian Arsacids intervened very little in the religious lives of their subjects, and in at least some places polytheistic traditions flourished under their rule. The excavations at Dura-Europos and Hatra leave no doubt about this. But when we think of the world of Iran, of Sasanian Persia, during the reigns of Odainath and Zenobia, we witness a different trajectory. Despite various continuities between the Parthian and early Sasanian Empire, the roots were being laid for a religious orientation that would, in the following centuries, pose a threat to traditional polythe-

---

[78] See Blömer (in this volume). For scholarship on Edessa as a Parthian client, Sommer 2018, 228–48; Edwell 2017. Ellerbrock 2015, 197–244 for building, art, and crafts in Parthian Mesopotamia. For the concept of *koine* or commonwealth, see De Jong 2013b. See also n. 87.

[79] Drijvers 1964, 42–44, 48. All of the Syriac *Book*'s statements refer to actual practices of Iranian peoples. On these practices, see Dąbrowa 2016; Boyce 1993; 1995; Skjærvø 2013. Even so, its characterizations of Iranian peoples are consistent with tropes from Greek ethnographic discourse. See Andrade 2020a.

[80] Andrade 2018a, 104–08, 151–61, with bibliography, including Yon 2002 175–80, Smith 2013, 92–95.

[81] Long 2017 treats chronology.

[82] Andrade 2018a, 129–33, 164.

[83] *IGLS* XVII.1.64, 74, 89. Andrade 2018a, 130–31.

[84] Procop., *Aed.* II.8.8–15; Lauffray 1983–1991; Blétry 2015.

[85] De Jong 2013b; Sommer 2005, 355–90; Dirven 2011.

[86] Dirven 2008; Curtis 2017; Ellerbrock 2015.

[87] Gnoli 2002; 2007, 115–21.

[88] Isaac 2013; Hauser 2013; De Blois 2016, 37–38. Dirven 2011, 171–72 even notes that the Parthian practice of dynastic fire worship, if it happened at Hatra, was antagonistic to Ardashir I.

[89] Recent scholarship also stresses these connotations. Long 2017; Curtis 2017.

[90] De Jong 2013a, 31–36; 2008.

ism at places like Palmyra. During Zenobia's lifetime, the Sasanian Persian court's trumpeting of Zoroastrian supremacy may have been perceptible, especially in light of the Persians' presence in parts of Upper Mesopotamia that had belonged to Rome and that Odainath would reclaim in the 260s. This is the aggregate significance of the royal inscriptions of Shapur, the self-promoting texts of the priest Kerdir, the execution of Mani, and the characterization of King Mazdai in the *Acts of Thomas*, all of which belong to the second half of the third century and thus to Zenobia's lifetime. In various ways, the character of King Mazdai appears to represent an Edessene caricature of Persian political and religious figures who shared Kerdir's basic outlook during a time of Persian imperial intervention in Upper Mesopotamia. Zenobia and her Palmyrenes conceivably understood the Persian ruling elite in similar terms at this time too.

If Zenobia deemed Persian imperialism and the religious inclinations of its authorities a threat to Palmyra's traditional polytheism, time would prove her right. In the centuries following Zenobia's life and death, the Sasanian Persian elite incrementally created a coordinated Zoroastrian religious hierarchy whose cosmic vision conceived of Zoroastrian Iranians as the summit of the political order.[91] While deemed subordinate, Jews and Christians were given patronage by the court and co-opted into the fabric of empire; as early as the 250s, Persians at Dura-Europos apparently saw value in the paintings in the Jewish synagogue and wrote favourable graffiti on them.[92] Otherwise, even if there was still some variation among Zoroastrians in the Sasanian Persian Empire, the prevailing perspective increasingly entailed the suppression of traditional polytheist cults and perhaps their reconstitution in other religious frameworks. In the Babylonian Talmud, rabbis assume that they would not routinely encounter traditional idolatry in public spaces.[93] It scarcely leaves a trace in Persian Martyr Acts, which overwhelmingly pits saints against Zoroastrian adversaries.

Zenobia's Palmyra, of course, exhibits no such orientation. Its public cult life also clearly persisted for a century after Zenobia had to leave it, even if it witnessed serious transition too. Only after that did a Christian hegemony rigorously upheld by Roman authorities suppress traditional polytheism, with Christians destroying some temples and converting others into churches.[94] Moreover, right when the Sasanian Persian court was beginning to confront the Manichaeans with violence, Manichaean missionaries were apparently visiting her court and, from there, making substantive inroads in the eastern Roman Empire. True, the aftermath of Aurelian's second capture of Palmyra spelled the end of the city's unique epigraphic and funerary culture.[95] But we should not conceive of the Palmyrenes' political and cosmic vision as intimately aligned with that of the Persians either. Odainath may have tried to make a treaty with Shapur. But any political agreements that the Palmyrenes made with the Persians resulted from pragmatic calculations, not longstanding cultural affinities. The Palmyrenes owed many debts to the world of Iran. Even so, much distinguished them in thought and practice.

---

[91] On which Payne 2015; 2016.

[92] Payne 2015, 32–33; 2016; De Jong 2006. Dirven 2014, 215–16. For continuities in magic bowls: Shaked, Ford, and Bhayro 2013; Moriggi 2014 (no. 8.3). On Dura-Europos's synagogue, *IJO Syria* 177–209 and now Stern 2018, 54–59.

[93] Kalmin 2008, 630.

[94] Kaizer 2010; Andrade 2018a, 217–18; Gawlikowski 2008, 401; Intagliata 2018, 46–64.

[95] Henning 2013; De Jong 2017; 2019.

Works Cited

Alram, M., M. Blet-Lemarquant, and P. O. Skjaervø. 2007. 'Shapur, King of Kings of Iranians and Non-Iranians', in R. Gyselen (ed.), *Des Indo-Grecs aux Sassanides: données pour l'histoire et la géographie historique* (Bures-et-Yvette: Groupe pour l'étude de la civilisation du Moyen-Orient), pp. 11–40.

Andrade, N. 2013. *Syrian Identity in the Greco-Roman World* (Cambridge: Cambridge University Press).

—— 2018a. *The Journey of Christianity to India: Networks and the Movement of Culture* (Cambridge: Cambridge University Press).

—— 2018b. *Zenobia: Shooting Star of Palmyra* (Oxford: Oxford University Press).

—— 2020a. 'Bardaisan's Disciples and Ethnographic Knowledge in the Roman Empire', in A. König, R. Langlands, and J. Uden (eds), *Literature and Culture in the Roman Empire, 96–235: Cross-Cultural Interactions* (Cambridge: Cambridge University Press), pp. 291–308.

—— 2020b. 'Romans and Iranians: Experiences of Imperial Governance in Roman Mesopotamia', in K. Berthelot (ed.), *Reconsidering Roman Power: Roman, Greek, Jewish and Christian Perceptions and Reactions* (Rome: École française de Rome), pp. 361–84.

Andrae, W. 1933. *Die Partherstadt Assur* (Leipzig: Hinrichs).

Appelbaum, A. 2011. 'The Rabbis and Palmyra: A Case Study on (Mis-)Reading Rabbinics for Historical Purposes', *Jewish Quarterly Review*, 101: 527–44.

Attridge, H. 1990. 'The Original Language of the Acts of Thomas', in H. Attridge, J. Collins, and T. Tobin (eds), *Of Scribes and Scrolls: Studies on the Hebrew Bible, Intertestamental Judaism, and Christian Origins* (Lanham: University Press of America), pp. 241–50.

Baird, J. 2018. *Dura-Europos* (London: Bloomsbury).

Banchich, T. (trans.). 2015. *The Lost History of Peter the Patrician: An Account of Rome's Imperial Past from the Age of Justinian* (Abingdon: Routledge).

Bauzou, T. 1998. 'La via nova en Arabie: le secteur nord, de Bostra à Philadelphie', in J.-B. Humbert and A. Desreumaux (eds), *Fouilles de Khirbet es-Samra en Jordanie*, I (Turnhout: Brepols), pp. 101–255.

Beyer, K. 1998. *Die aramäischen Inschriften aus Assur, Hatra und dem übrigen Ostmesopotamien (datiert 44 v. Chr. bis 238 n. Chr.)* (Göttingen: Vandenhoeck & Ruprecht).

Blétry, S. 2015. *Zénobia-Halabiya, habitat urbain et nécropoles* (Ferrol: Sociedade Luso-Galega de Estudos Mesopotámicos).

Bonnet, M. (ed.). 1903. *Acta Philippi et Acta Thomae accedunt Acta Barnabae*, Acta Apostolorum Apocrypha, 2.2 (Leipzig: Teubner).

Bosworth, C. E. (trans.). 1999. *The History of al-Ṭabarī (Taʾrīkh al-rusul waʾl-mulūk)*, V: *The Sāsānids, the Byzantines, the Lakhmids, and Yemen* (Albany: State University of New York).

Boyce, M. 1993 [updated 2011]. 'Corpse', in *Encyclopaedia Iranica*, VI.3 (New York: Columbia University, Center for Iranian Studies), pp. 279–86 <https://iranicaonline.org/articles/corpse-disposal-of-in-zoroastrianism> [accessed 10 October 2021].

—— 1995 [updated 2011]. 'Dog ii: In Zoroastrianism', in *Encyclopaedia Iranica*, VII.5 (New York: Columbia University, Center for Iranian Studies), pp. 461–70 <https://www.iranicaonline.org/articles/dog> [accessed 10 October 2021].

Coqueugniot, G. 2012. 'Des espaces sacrés dans la tourmente: les lieux de culte d'Europos-Doura durant le siège sassanide de la ville (milieu du IIIᵉ siècle de notre ère)', in P. Leriche, G. Coqueugniot, and S. de Pontbriand (eds), *Europos-Doura: Varia*, I (Beirut: Institut français du Proche-Orient), pp. 215–30.

Curtis, V. S. 2017. 'The Parthian Haute-Couture at Palmyra', in T. Long and A. H. Sørensen (eds), *Positions and Professions in Palmyra* (Copenhagen: The Royal Danish Academy of Sciences and Letters), pp. 52–67.

Dąbrowa, E. 2016. 'Kingship ii: Parthian Period', in *Encyclopaedia Iranica* <https://www.iranicaonline.org/articles/kingship-02-parthian-period> [accessed 10 October 2021].

Daryaee, T. 2020. 'Arsacid Economic Activity on the Silk Road', in J. D. Lerner and Y. Shi (eds), *Silk Roads: From Local Realities to Global Narratives* (Oxford: Oxbow), pp. 215–22.

De Blois, L. 2016. 'Rome and Persia in the Middle of the Third Century', in D. Slootjes and M. Peachin (eds), *Rome and the Worlds beyond its Frontiers* (Leiden: Brill), pp. 33–44.

Dirven, L. 2008. 'Aspects of Hatrene Religion: A Note on the Statues of Kings and Nobles from Hatra', in T. Kaizer (ed.), *The Variety of Local Religious Life in the Near East in the Hellenistic and Roman Periods* (Leiden: Brill), pp. 209–46.

—— 2011. 'Religious Frontiers in the Syrian-Mesopotamian Desert', in O. Hekster and T. Kaizer (eds), *Frontiers in the Roman World* (Leiden: Brill), pp. 157–73.

—— 2013. *Hatra: Politics, Culture, and Religion between Parthia and Rome* (Stuttgart: Steiner).

—— 2014. 'Religious Continuity and Change in Parthian Mesopotamia: A Note on the Survival of Babylonian Traditions', *Journal of Ancient Near Eastern History*, 1: 201–29.

—— 2018. 'Palmyrene Sculpture in Context: Between Hybridity and Heterogeneity', in J. Aruz (ed.), *Palmyra: Mirage in the Desert* (New York: Metropolitan Museum of Art), pp. 120–29.

Downey, S. 1988. *Mesopotamian Religious Architecture: Alexander through the Parthians* (Princeton: Princeton University Press).

Drijvers, H. J. W. (ed. and trans.). 1964. *The Book of the Laws of Countries: Dialogue on Fate of Bardaiṣan of Edessa* (Assen: Van Gorcum).

Eadie, J. 1967. 'The Development of Roman Mailed Cavalry', *Journal of Roman Studies*, 57: 161–73.
Edwell, Peter. 2008. *Between Rome and Persia: The Middle Euphrates, Mesopotamia and Palmyra under Roman Control* (London: Routledge).
Edwell, P. 2017. 'Osrhoene and Mesopotamia between Rome and Arsacid Parthia', in J. Schlude and B. Rubin (eds), *Arsacids, Romans, and Local Elites: Cross-Cultural Interactions of the Parthian Empire* (Oxford: Oxbow), pp. 111–36.
Ellerbroek, U. 2015. *Die Parther: Die vergessene Großmacht*, 2nd edn (Darmstadt: Zabern).
Feissel, D., J. Gascou, and J. Teixidor. 1997. 'Documents de archives inédites du Moyen Euphrate (IIIe s. après J.-C.)', *Journal des savants*, 1997: 3–57.
Ferreira, J. (ed.). 2002. *The Hymn of the Pearl: The Syriac and Greek Texts* (Sydney: St Pauls).
Gardner, I. and S. Lieu (trans.). 2004. *Manichaean Texts from the Roman Empire* (Cambridge: Cambridge University Press).
Gawlikowski, M. 2005. 'L'apothéose d'Odeinat sur une mosaïque récemment découverte à Palmyre', *Comptes rendus des séances de l'Académie des inscriptions et belles-lettres*, 149: 293–304.
—— 2008. 'The Statues of the Sanctuary of Allat in Palmyra', in Y. Z. Eliav, E. Friedland, and S. Herbert (eds), *The Sculptural Environment of the Roman Near East: Reflections on Culture, Ideology, Power* (Leuven: Peeters), pp. 397–411.
—— 2016. 'The Portraits of the Palmyrene Royalty', in A. Kropp and R. Raja (eds), *The World of Palmyra* (Copenhagen: The Royal Danish Academy of Sciences and Letters), pp. 126–34.
Gawlikowski, M. and K. al-As'ad. 2010. 'The Imperial Cult in Palmyra under the Antonines', *Studia Palmyreskie*, 11: 43–48.
Gawlikowski, M. and M. Żuchowska. 2010. 'La mosaïque de Bellérophon', *Studia Palmyreskie*, 11: 9–42.
Gignoux, P. (ed.). 1991. *Les quatre inscriptions du mage Kirdīr: textes et concordances* (Leuven: Peeters).
Gignoux, P., C. Jullien, and F. Jullien. 2009. *Iranisches Personennamenbuch*, VII.5: *Noms propres syriaques d'origine iranienne* (Vienna: Österreichische Akademie der Wissenschaften).
Gnoli, T. 2002. 'Pasgriba at Hatra and Edessa', in A. Panaino and G. Pettinato (eds), *Ideologies as Intercultural Phenomena* (Milan: Istituto italiano per l'Africa e l'Oriente), pp. 79–89.
—— 2007. *The Interplay of Roman and Iranian Titles in the Roman East (1st–3rd Century A.D.)* (Vienna: Österreichische Akademie der Wissenschaften).
Graf, D. 1989. 'Zenobia and the Arabs', in D. H. French and C. S. Lightfoot (eds), *The Eastern Frontier of the Roman Empire*, I (Oxford: British Archaeological Reports), pp. 143–67.
Gregoratti, L. 2016. 'Review of Andrew Smith, *Roman Palmyra: Identity, Community, and State Formation*', *Bryn Mawr Classical Review* <http://bmcr.brynmawr.edu/2016/2016-03-08.html> [accessed 10 October 2021].
Guggenheimer, H. (ed. and trans.). 2000–. *The Jerusalem Talmud = Talmud Yerushalmi* (Berlin: De Gruyter).
Haider, P. 2008. 'Tradition and Change in the Beliefs at Assur, Nineveh, and Nisibis between 300 BC and AD 300', in T. Kaizer (ed.), *The Variety of Local Religious Life in the Near East in the Hellenistic and Roman Periods* (Leiden: Brill), pp. 193–207.
Hartmann, U. 2001. *Das palmyrenische Teilreich* (Stuttgart: Steiner).
—— 2006. 'Der Mord an Kaiser Gallienus', in K.-P. Johne, T. Gerhardt, and U. Hartmann (eds), *Deleto paene imperio Romano: Transformationsprozesse des Römischen Reiches im 3. Jahrhundert und ihre Rezeption in der Neuzeit* (Berlin: Steiner), pp. 81–124.
—— 2016. 'What Is It Like to Be Roman in the Age of Crisis? Changing Palmyrene Identities in the Third Century', in A. Kropp and R. Raja (eds), *The World of Palmyra* (Copenhagen: The Royal Danish Academy of Sciences and Letters), pp. 53–69.
Hauser, S. 2013. 'Where Is the Man of Hadr, Who Once Built It and Taxed the Land by the Tigris and Chaboras: On the Significance of the Final Siege of Hatra', in L. Dirven (ed.), *Hatra: Politics, Culture, and Religion between Parthia and Rome* (Stuttgart: Steiner), pp. 119–39.
Haynes, I. 2013. *Blood of the Provinces: The Roman Auxilia and the Making Provincial Society from Augustus to the Severans* (Oxford: Oxford University Press).
Healey, J. F. (trans.). 2009. *Textbook of Syrian Semitic Inscriptions*, IV: *Aramaic Inscriptions and Documents of the Roman Period* (Oxford: Oxford University Press).
Henning, A. 2013. *Die Turmgräber von Palmyra: Eine lokale Bauform im kaiserzeitlichen Syrien als Ausdruck kultureller Identität* (Rahden: Leidorf).
Huyse, P. 1999. *Die dreisprachige Inschrift Šābuhrs I. an der Ka'bai Zardušt (ŠKZ)*, Corpus inscriptionum Iranicarum, 3, 2 vols (London: School of Oriental and African Studies).
Intagliata, E. 2018. *Palmyra after Zenobia, 273–750: An Archaeological and Historical Reappraisal* (Oxford: Oxbow).
Isaac, B. 1998. *The Near East under Roman Rule* (Leiden: Brill).
—— 2013. 'Against Rome and Persia: From Success to Destruction', in L. Dirven (ed.), *Hatra: Politics, Culture, and Religion between Parthia and Rome* (Stuttgart: Steiner), pp. 23–32.
James, S. 2004. *Excavations at Dura-Europos, 1928–1937: Final Report*, VII: *The Arms and Armour and Other Military Equipment* (London: British Museum Press).
—— 2011. 'Dark Secrets of the Archive: Evidence for "Chemical Warfare" and Martial Convergences in Siege-Mines of Dura-Europos', in L. Brody and G. Hoffman (eds), *Dura-Europos: Crossroads of Antiquity* (Chesnut Hill: McMullen Museum of Art), pp. 295–317.

Jong, A. de. 2006. 'One Nation under God: The Early Sasanians as Guardians and Destroyers of Holy Sites', in R. G. Kratz and H. Spiekermann (eds), *Götterbilder, Gottesbilder, Weltbilder: Polytheismus und Monotheismus in der Welt der Antike*, I: *Ägypten, Mesopotamien, Persien, Kleinasien, Syrien, Palästina* (Tübingen: Mohr Siebeck), pp. 223–38.

—— 2008. 'Regional Variation in Zoroastrianism: The Case of the Parthians', *Bulletin of the Asia Institute*, n.s., 22: 17–27.

—— 2013a. 'Religion in Iran: The Parthian and Sasanian Periods (247 BCE–654 CE)', in M. R. Salzman and W. Adler (eds), *The Cambridge History of Religions in the Ancient World*, II: *From the Hellenistic Age to Late Antiquity* (Cambridge: Cambridge University Press), pp. 23–53.

—— 2013b. 'Hatra and the Parthian Commonwealth', in L. Dirven (ed.), *Hatra: Politics, Culture, and Religion between Parthia and Rome* (Stuttgart: Steiner), pp. 143–60.

Jong, L. de. 2017. *The Archaeology of Death in Roman Syria: Burial, Commemoration, and Empire* (Cambridge: Cambridge University Press).

—— 2019. 'Monuments, Landscape, and Memory: The Emergence of Tower-Tombs in Tadmor-Palmyra', *Bulletin of the Institute of Classical Studies*, 62.1: 30–53.

Kaizer, T. 2010. 'From Zenobia to Alexander the Sleepless: Paganism, Judaism, and Christianity at Late Roman Palmyra', in B. Bastl, V. Gassner, and U. Muss (eds), *Zeitreisen: Syrien, Palmyra, Rome* (Vienna: Phoibos), pp. 113–23.

Kalmin, R. 2008. 'Idolatry in Late Antique Babylonia: The Evidence of the Babylonian Talmud', in Y. Z. Eliav and others (eds), *The Sculptural Environment of the Near East: Reflections on Culture, Ideology, and Power* (Leuven: Peeters), pp. 629–58.

Kienast, D. 1996. *Römische Kaisertabelle: Grundzüge einer römischen Kaiserchronologie*, 2nd edn (Darmstadt: Wissenschaftliche Buchgesellschaft).

Kreyenbroek, P. 2008. 'How Pious Was Shapur I? Religion, Church, and Propaganda under the Early Sasanians', in V. S. Curtis and S. Stewart (eds), *The Sasanian Era: The Era of Iran* (London: Tauris), pp. 7–15.

Lauffray, J. 1983–1991. *Halabiyya-Zenobia: place forte du limes oriental et la Haute-Mésopotamie au VIe siècle*, 2 vols (Paris: Geuthner).

Leriche, P. 2016. 'Recent Discoveries concerning Religious Life in Europos-Dura', in M. K. Heyn and A. I. Steinsapir (eds), *Icon, Cult, and Context: Sacred Spaces and Objects in the Classical World* (Los Angeles: UCLA, Cotsen Institute of Archaeology Press), pp. 153–90.

Long, T. 2017. 'The Use of Parthian Costume in Funerary Portraiture at Palmyra', in T. Long and A. H. Sørensen (eds), *Positions and Professions in Palmyra* (Copenhagen: The Royal Danish Academy of Sciences and Letters, 2017), pp. 68–83.

MacDonald, M. C. A. '"Romans Go Home?": Rome and Other "Outsiders" as Viewed from the Syro-Arabian Desert', in J. Dikstra and G. Fisher, *Interactions between Rome and the Peoples on the Arabian and Egyptian Frontiers in Antiquity* (Leuven: Peeters), pp. 145–63.

MacDonald, M. C. A., A. Al-Manaser, and M. del C. Hidalgo-Chacón Diez. 2017. *The OCIANA Corpus of Safaitic Inscriptions: Preliminary Edition* (Oxford: Khalili Research Center) <http://krc.orient.ox.ac.uk/resources/ociana/corpora/ociana_safaitic.pdf> [accessed 10 October 2021].

MacKenzie, D. N. 1989. 'Kerdir's Inscription', in G. Herrmann (ed.), *Naqsh-I Rustam*, VI: *The Triumph of Shapur I* (Berlin: Reimer), pp. 35–72.

Maraqten, M. 1995. 'The Arabic Words in Palmyrene Inscriptions', *ARAM*, 7: 89–108.

Marcato, E. 2018. *Personal Names in the Aramaic Inscriptions of Hatra* (Venice: Ca'Foscari).

Meyer, J. C. 2016. 'Palmyrene: Settlements, Forts, and Nomadic Networks', in A. Kropp and R. Raja (eds), *The World of Palmyra* (Copenhagen: The Royal Danish Academy of Sciences and Letters), pp. 86–102.

Moriggi, M. 2014. *A Corpus of Syriac Incantation Bowls: Syriac Magical Texts from Late-Antique Mesopotamia* (Leiden: Brill).

Mosshammer, A. A. (ed.). 1984. *Georgii Syncelli ecloga chronographica*. Leipzig: Teubner.

Myers, S. 2010. *Spiritual Epicleses in the Acts of Thomas* (Tübingen: Mohr Siebeck).

Nakamura, B. 1993. 'Palmyra and the Roman East', *Greek, Roman, and Byzantine Studies*, 34: 133–50.

Palermo, Rocco. 2019. *On the Edge of Empires: North Mesopotamia during the Roman Period (2nd–4th c. CE)* (Abingdon: Routledge).

Panaino, A. 2016. 'Kirder and the Reorganisation of Persian Mazdeism', in V. S. Curtis and others (eds), *The Parthian and Early Sasanian Empires: Adaptation and Expansion* (London: British Institute for Persian Studies), pp. 53–60.

Payne, R. 2015. *A State of Mixture: Christians, Zoroastrians, and Iranian Political Culture in Late Antiquity* (Oakland: University of California Press).

—— 2016. 'Iranian Cosmopolitanism: World Religions at the Sasanian Court', in M. Lavan, R. Payne, and J. Weiswiler (eds), *Cosmopolitanism and Empire: Universal Rulers, Local Elites, and Cultural Integration in the Ancient Near East and Mediterranean* (Oxford: Oxford University Press), pp. 209–30.

—— 2018. 'The Silk Road and the Iranian Political Economy in Late Antiquity: Iran, the Silk Road, and the Problem of Aristocratic Empire', *Bulletin of the School of Oriental and African Studies*, 81: 227–50.

Peachin, M. 1990. *Roman Imperial Titulature and Chronology, A.D. 235–84* (Amsterdam: Gieben).

Poirier, P.-H. (ed. and trans.). 1981. *L'hymne de la Perle des Actes de Thomas: introduction, texte, traduction, commentaire* (Leuven: Pierier).

Potter, D. 2014. *The Roman Empire at Bay, AD 180–395*, 2nd edn (Abingdon: Routledge).
Roig Lanzillotta, L. 2015. 'A Syriac Original for the *Acts of Thomas*? The Hypothesis of Syriac Priority Revisited', in I. Ramelli and J. Perkins (eds), *Early Christian and Jewish Narrative: The Role of Religion in Shaping Narrative Form* (Tübingen: Mohr Siebeck), pp. 105–34.
Sartre-Fauriat, A. and M. Sartre. 2014. *Zénobie: de Palmyre à Rome* (Paris: Perrin).
—— 2016. *Palmyre: vérités et légendes* (Paris: Perrin).
Schlumberger, D. 1970. *L'Orient Hellénisé* (Paris: Albin Michel).
Schmidt-Colinet, A. 1992. *Das Tempelgrab Nr. 36 in Palmyra: Studien zur palmyrenischen Grabarchitektur und ihrer Ausstattung* (Mainz: Von Zabern).
Shaked, S., J. N. Ford, and S. Bhayro. 2013. *Aramaic Bowl Spells: Jewish Babylonian Aramaic Bowls* (Leiden: Brill).
Skjærvø, P. O. 2013. 'Marriage ii: Next of Kin Marriage in Zoroastrianism', *Encyclopaedia Iranica* <https://iranicaonline.org/articles/marriage-next-of-kin> [accessed 10 October 2021].
Smith, A. 2013. *Roman Palmyra: Identity, Community, and State Formation* (Oxford: Oxford University Press).
Sommer, M. 2018. *Roms orientalische Steppengrenze: Palmyra, Edessa, Dura-Europos, Hatra; Eine Kulturgeschichte von Pompeius bis Diocletian*, 2nd edn (Stuttgart: Steiner).
Southern, P. 2008. *Empress Zenobia: Palmyra's Rebel Queen* (London: Continuum).
Stark, J. 1971. *Personal Names in Palmyrene Inscriptions* (Oxford: Clarendon).
Stern, K. 2018. *Writing on the Wall: Graffiti and the Forgotten Jews of Antiquity* (Princeton: Princeton University Press).
Tlass, M. 1985. *Zanūbiyā malikat Tadmur* (Damascus: Tlass).
—— 1986. *Zénobie: reine de Palmyre* (Damascus: Tlass).
—— 2000. *Zenobia: The Queen of Palmyra* (Damascus: Tlass).
Volkmann, H. 1937. 'Die Zweite nach dem König', *Philologus*, 92: 285–316.
Winsbury, R. 2010. *Zenobia of Palmyra: History, Myth, and the Neo-classical Imagination* (London: Duckworth).
Woltering, R. A. F. L. 2014. 'Zenobia or al-Zabbā': The Modern Arab Literary Reception of the Palmyran Protagonist', *Middle Eastern Literatures*, 17: 25–42.
Wright, W. (ed.). 1871. *Apocryphal Acts of the Apostles: Edited from Syriac Manuscripts in the British Museum and Other Libraries*, I. London: Williams & Norgate.
Yon, J.-B. 2000. 'Onomastique et influences culturelles: Le exemple de l'onomastique de Palmyre', *Mediterraneo antico*, 3: 77–93.
—— 2002. *Les notables de Palmyre* (Beirut: Institut français du Proche-Orient).
Zahran, Y. 2010. *Zenobia: Between Reality and Legend*, rev. edn (London: Stacey).

6. The Fate of Palmyra and the East after AD 273: A Few Remarks on Trade, Economy, and Connectivity in Late Antiquity and the Early Islamic Period

Emanuele E. Intagliata

Università degli Studi di Milano (Emanuele.Intagliata@unimi.it)

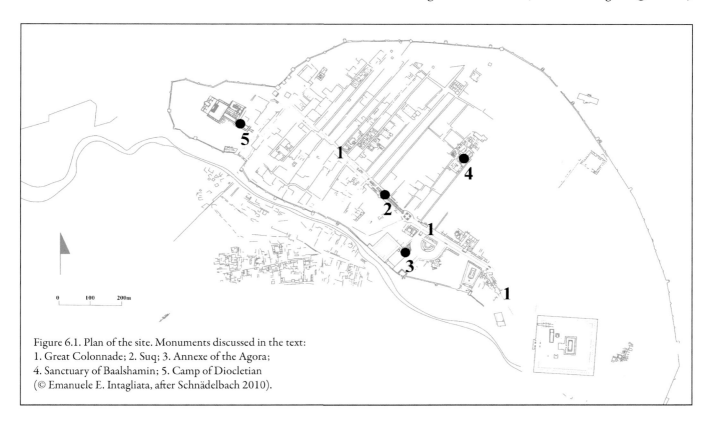

Figure 6.1. Plan of the site. Monuments discussed in the text:
1. Great Colonnade; 2. Suq; 3. Annexe of the Agora;
4. Sanctuary of Baalshamin; 5. Camp of Diocletian
(© Emanuele E. Intagliata, after Schnädelbach 2010).

Introduction

The history of Palmyra after the fall of Zenobia and the second Palmyrene revolt (AD 272–273) is one of survival and transformation. At the end of the third century AD, the city contracted and the area to the south of Wadi al-Qubur was gradually depopulated.[1] The transfer of the *Legio I Illyricorum* to Palmyra affected significantly the role of the city, which transformed to answer the need of a military garrison. In the fifth century AD, the city might have seen a contraction in the number of soldiers hosted within its walls due to the peaceful conditions of that time, but the military remained a constant presence throughout Late Antiquity. Under Justinian, the number of soldiers might have even increased dramatically; Palmyra is reported by written sources to have been home to a *numerus* of soldiers, *limitanei* (frontier troops), as well as the *dux* of Emesa,[2] who was possibly residing there with a large retinue.

It was certainly not the first time that Palmyra saw soldiers within its walls. A permanent garrison is known to have been quartered in the city since at least the mid-second century AD.[3] However, it is only at the end of the third century AD that the archaeological record allows us to see clearly the impact of the military in the townscape. A monumental military camp was constructed in the western corner of the city — the so-called Camp of Diocletian — on the slope of a hill (Fig. 6.1.5 and Fig. 6.2).

---

[1] Note, however, that some areas of the Hellenistic quarter remained occupied: Schmidt-Colinet and al-Asʿad (eds) 2013.

[2] Ioh. Mal. XVII.2; Theoph., *Chr.* I.174.

[3] Yon 2008.

Figure 6.2. The Camp of Diocletian, view of the stretch of the *Via Praetoria* from the *Groma* to the *Forum* (© PAL.M.A.I.S. Missione Acheologica Italo-Siriana, Università degli Studi di Milano).

Despite the fact that the camp employs abundantly reused material from earlier buildings, the compound is by far one of the most monumental and architecturally elaborate structures of its type in the Syrian stretch of the eastern Roman frontier. An inscription reporting the construction of the fortress by Sossianus Hierocles (*praeses provinciae* — provincial governor) provides an important clue on its chronology, which could be pinpointed to AD 293–303.[4]

It was not only the townscape that was altered considerably by the installation of a garrison at Palmyra, but also its economy. With the end of Zenobia's territorial expansion, Palmyra lost its international trading role; its priority was now no longer that of appeasing the western Mediterranean (or the Syrian local market)[5] with exotic goods from the East, but, rather, to feed its inhabitants and its newly installed garrison with the necessary commodities to survive. This is not to say that trade disappeared after AD 273, but that the trading links of Palmyra underwent a considerable reshuffle in which the East, and particularly caravan trade with the East, does not seem to have any longer played a major role. Besides the Aurelianic events, the reason for this must be sought in the changed geopolitical circumstances of this time — as will be shown below.

Our understanding of trade to, from, and through Palmyra in Late Antiquity and the Early Islamic period is hindered at the outset by the limited amount of data available in the published archaeological record. Not only do bulk finds not seem to have been the subject of major typological studies, but, when they have been, pottery and glass types have not allowed for catching important nuances in dating, since some vessels seem to have been used without interruptions throughout this period.[6] In addition, without trace element characterization, the provenance of these artefacts remains mostly unknown. Information about the origin of small finds in modern literature is limited. An exception are coins, which provide us with important clues on the high level of connectivity of this site with the rest of the empire.[7] To shed more light on trade after Zenobia, we are, therefore, inevitably left mostly with written sources and historically driven speculations — with all the problems that these entail.

---

[4] *IGLS* XVII.1, 112–14; however, cf. Reddé 1995.

[5] Gawlikowski 2016, 24; cf. Seland 2016, 53.

[6] Publications on bulk finds have increased in the past decade. See recently Intagliata 2014; Cerutti 2014; Romagnolo 2012; Römer-Strehl 2013; Ployer 2013. On late antique glass, see also the important study of Gawlikowska and al-Asʿad 1994.

[7] See e.g. Gawlikowski 2014.

6. THE FATE OF PALMYRA AND THE EAST AFTER AD 273

This chapter aims to explore the fate of Palmyra and the East between AD 273 and the end of the Umayyad caliphate (AD 750). Although emphasis will be put on trade (and the absence thereof), it will also touch upon connectivity in a broader sense and, thus, discuss evidence for travel. We will then conclude that trade connections with the East may have drastically halted after the defeat of Zenobia only to resume in the Early Islamic period, when Palmyra was no longer a frontier city. Nonetheless, throughout Late Antiquity, the memory of the route (or route networks) connecting the settlement with the East was not completely forgotten.

Late Antiquity

Short- to Long-Distance Trade: The Absence of the East in the Archaeological Record

The garrison stationed at Palmyra after the end of the third century AD functioned as an important economic engine for the settlement throughout Late Antiquity. In addition to providing services, the inhabitants supported the soldiers with much needed foodstuff and other supplies.[8] The oasis of Palmyra and its hinterland certainly played a pivotal role in this. Schlumberger's theory on the depopulation of the Palmyrene after AD 273 and the end of its prosperity[9] has recently been reviewed by Syro-Norwegian surveys in the northern Palmyrenides. These have confirmed the existence of a dense network of sites between Palmyra and Isryie surviving well after the Aurelianic events.[10] Previous research had also identified isolated and fortified sixth-century farmsteads to the south of the settlement at al-Sukkariyya and al-Bazuriyya — some twenty kilometres from Palmyra.[11] One could presume that contacts between these rural realities and the settlement were rather frequent and that Palmyra must have acted as an important regional market for selling or buying local and regional commodities.[12]

Nonetheless, we could also not exclude that agricultural products were imported from further afield.[13]

As for long-distance trade, caravan trade between Palmyra and the East ceased after AD 273.[14] The latest piece of evidence proving the existence of Palmyrene caravan trade is an inscription dated to AD 260–267 in honour of Septimius Worod, who, in holding the title of *archemporos* (chief of the merchants), is reported to have brought back to the city caravans at his own expenses.[15] No evidence of caravan trade is known after this date, and the silence of the archaeological and inscriptional record on this regard has been taken as proof of the collapse of trading links between Palmyra and the East from the late third century AD.[16] The oft-quoted piece of evidence that substantiates the absence of links with the East is the treaty of Nisibis signed between Diocletian and Narses in AD 299, which, among other things, rendered Nisibis the sole trading point between the two empires.[17]

As has already been emphasized in modern literature,[18] the fate of the caravan trade was sealed by changed geopolitical circumstances. For the caravan trade to function in the liminal areas between the two empires, Palmyra needed to count upon secure relationships with local nomadic communities. If this could be arranged in the Roman period, the transformation of the political landscape after AD 272–273 made this impossible. Indeed, it was probably one of these tribes that might have plotted with Aurelian against Zenobia and the Palmyrene power for the capitulation of the city.[19] Throughout Late Antiquity, but especially in the fourth and sixth centuries AD, the Syrian frontier remained a fighting ground between Rome and Persia, which waged war against each other through proxies (the Lakhmids on the Persian side and the Tanukhids, the Salihids, and the Jafnids on the Roman one).

The changed role of the city might have had important repercussions in the Palmyrene society, where the old aristocratic elite gradually disappeared from the scene. This social reshuffle was likely caused only in

---

[8] The only evidence suggesting a potential transaction was brought to light by Wiegand and his team in 1902. This is an ostracon bearing the lettering *MOD LIX* (mod[ii]) (*c.* 513 kg) and interpreted by the excavators as the receipt for a transaction for a load of foodstuff (barley?) sold to the soldiers stationed in the Camp of Diocletian: Lehner 1932, 107 n. 1. The Camp of Diocletian was provided with a granary: Gawlikowski 1986.

[9] Schlumberger 1951, 133.

[10] Meyer 2017, with extensive bibliography.

[11] Genequand 2003 38–43; 2012, 33 with extensive bibliography.

[12] Genequand 2012, 36.

---

[13] Meyer 2017, 54.

[14] Young 2001, 182–84; Seland 2016, 86.

[15] *IGLS* XVII.1.67.

[16] Seland 2016, 86.

[17] See Seland 2016, 86, Sartre-Fauriat and Sartre 2008, 93; Gawlikowski 1983, 68.

[18] Seland 2016, 86–87.

[19] Intagliata 2018a, 98.

part by the slaughters of the inhabitants following the events of AD 272–273. In fact, the aristocracy is attested in the city in the immediate Aurelianic aftermath in the inscriptional evidence. Septimius Haddudan is reported as an 'illustrious senator' and symposiarch in the Sanctuary of Bel as early as March 273 — i.e. after the Zenobian events.[20] Several members of the tribe of the Maththabolioi are reported to have restored the 'basilica' of Arsu in AD 279–280.[21] Nonetheless, the private residential buildings of the former aristocratic elite were gradually abandoned in Late Antiquity to be occupied by squatters. Had the Palmyrene upper classes continued living in Palmyra, one would have seen the same process of beautification of private buildings visible in other sites, such as at Antioch and Apamea.[22] It seems clear, therefore, that this social change occurred gradually and not abruptly. It is possible that the end of the lucrative caravan trade, which was most likely considered a much respected activity,[23] was one of the causes behind this change.

One should note that long-distance trade to or through Palmyra in this period is not well attested overall. Unsurprisingly, the very few pieces of evidence of late antique medium-to-long-distance trade suggest links with the West rather than the East. These include pottery from northern Syria and liturgical commodities.[24] Glass, like pottery, could likely have been produced at Palmyra.[25] However, there is also evidence to suggest a glass trade possibly originating from the Syrian coast.[26] The connection with the West appears to be substantiated by numismatic evidence (esp. mint marks)[27] as well as inscriptional evidence.[28]

---

[20] Gawlikowski 1973, 78.

[21] *IGLS* XVII.1, ns 80–81.

[22] Intagliata 2018a, 43–45.

[23] Gawlikowski 2016, 25.

[24] Cerutti 2014; Michałowski 1960, 212; Intagliata 2018a, 8; Galavaris 1970, 121–22 (bread stamps). The same picture can be seen in the Palmyrene. At Qasr al-Hayr al-Sharqi, excavations have brought to light fine ware and transport containers proving links between this site and western Syria, Asia Minor, Africa, and Gaul (Genequand 2012, 194). Fieldworks at Umm el-Tlel have revealed the presence of transport containers from the north-eastern Mediterranean and western Asia Minor (LRA 1 and LRA 3) (Majcherek and Taha 2004, 232–33).

[25] Gawlikowska (2015, 292) reports of 'most probably late' lumps of glass found in the Annexe of the Agora (Fig. 1.3).

[26] Gawlikowska and al-As'ad 1994, 33.

[27] Intagliata 2018b.

[28] Note, in particular, the funerary inscription dedicated to a

Late Antiquity: The End of Palmyra and the East?

Caravan trade with the East might have ceased, but it is most likely that the route connecting Palmyra with the Euphrates did not completely die out in Late Antiquity. There is at least one piece of written evidence suggesting connection between Palmyra and the East after AD 273. This is found in a compilation of stories dedicated to St Anastasius. The passage in question reports how a monk was instructed to reach Dastagerd in Persia, take custody of the remains of the body of the holy man, and move it to Jerusalem. For this task, the monk decided to move north and, thence, enter the Roman Empire from Palmyra, thus considerably extending the length and time of his travel. The portage was carried out with the support of the phylarch (φύλαρχος) of the Saracens, who granted him safe passage to Palmyra after the monk 'had been staying long with them in their camps'. From Palmyra, where the relic performed a miracle,[29] the monk proceeded to the west to Arados (potentially via Emesa). The episode is dated to between spring 630 and November 631 — that is, no more than four years before the capitulation of Palmyra at the hands of Khalid b. al-Walid and his force.[30]

The reason behind the monk's decision to cross the Syrian steppe through Palmyra may have been motivated by geopolitical factors — the presence of allied Saracens in the area that could grant safe passage, as opposed to the south — but also by the existence of a known route. The reliability of this text can justifiably be questioned. However, for the scope of this discussion, it is irrelevant whether the portage of the relics actually occurred. What is more important is that the writer of the miracles knew that it was possible to reach Persia via Palmyra at that time and that this area was under the control of allied *Saracenoi*.

The course of the route in question is not known, nor is the route mentioned in any other late antique written sources. It seems reasonable to believe, however, that part of it followed the same route that had been used

---

certain Anamos, clibanarus of Palmyra in the Tomb of the Prophets at Jerusalem: Clermont-Ganneau 1899, 367–68. The network of routes connecting Palmyra with other cities of Syria was still very much alive and continued being in use throughout Late Antiquity and the Early Islamic period (Intagliata 2018a, 2–8). On the Tabula Peutingeriana and the road link between Palmyra and Damascus, see Mior 2016.

[29] *Anas. Per.* I.129–30.

[30] *Anas. Per.* I.102–04; English translation in Intagliata 2018a, 135, nos 26–27 reported in Appendix below.

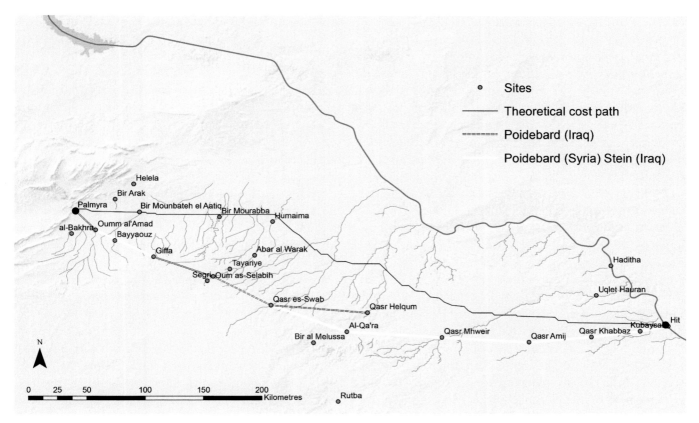

Figure 6.3. Route from Palmyra to Hit (© Jørgen Christian Meyer and Eivind Heldaas Seland, basemap © ESRI 2014; after Meyer and Seland 2016, fig. 4, with permission).

by Palmyrene merchants to cross the Syrian steppe and reach the Euphrates in the Roman period. The Roman caravan route has been recently identified by Meyer and Seland through a study of published archaeological evidence and network analyses (Fig. 6.3).[31]

This route would experience construction activities after the Islamic conquest, as discussed below. Rather than a rediscovery in the Early Islamic period, it is possible that this track remained trodden and well known throughout Late Antiquity, by which time its caravan role had, however, long disappeared.

The Early Islamic Period until the Collapse of the Umayyad Dynasty

The history of Palmyra in the first half of the seventh century was marked by two significant turning points. The first was the short Sasanian occupation of Syria between AD 613 and 628 by which Palmyra passed to Persian hands. Of this occupation, nothing is known through written sources or the archaeological evidence.

The second event, the Islamic takeover, is better known thanks to a set of problematic written sources. According to their reports, in AD 634 one of the generals of Abu Bakr, Khalid b. al-Walid, besieged the settlement and conquered it by treaty. Most written sources seem to agree that the inhabitants did not attempt to push back the invaders, but that they opened the gates without a fight.[32] Archaeological evidence has so far confirmed this version of the story. As opposed to the Aurelianic events of AD 272–273, whose destructions are visible in the archaeological record, no destruction layers have so far been attributed by excavators to this episode. It is possibly this smooth transition between powers that allowed Palmyra to maintain its freedom of religion and, we believe, its economic status quo.

In this period and until the capitulation of the Umayyad dynasty at the hands of the Abbasids, the settlement survived and may have also experienced a surge in occupation. The Camp of Diocletian, which had lost

---

[31] The authors concluded that: 'the restrictions imposed by topography and availability of water would lead to the existence of one and only one major caravan route' (Meyer and Seland 2016, 511).

[32] There are, however, exceptions. See Intagliata 2018a, 104–05.

its military purpose, was abandoned, but the necessity of the people of Tadmur to find a safe place to live within the urban limit brought some inhabitants to encroach upon the space left unoccupied in the *Via Pretoria* and *Via Principalis* of the camp.[33] The occupation saw the construction of new private residential buildings and productive areas, mostly with reused architecture robbed from former buildings. Rather than an urban decline, one might see in these activities a proof of the vitality of the Palmyrene urban community.

A Suq was constructed in the westernmost section of the Great Colonnade (Fig. 6.1.2). This expanded considerably the available market space, which could also count upon the earlier Roman shop installed behind the colonnades of the main thoroughfare.[34] The new shopping area consisted of forty-seven new stores opening towards the north and installed within the central carriageway. The building of this compound occurred gradually and not suddenly. This is suggested by the varied building techniques used for its construction as well as the varied plan of the shops. The organic building of the eastern section of the Great Colonnade may have reflected the growing need of the inhabitants to sell and buy goods.

Transactions were not only limited to the public space, but they may also have occurred in private settings. The excavations of the northern courtyard of the Sanctuary of Baalshamin (Fig. 6.1.4) by the Swiss team lead by Paul Collart uncovered a Greek ostracon listing a number of individuals, possibly debtors or creditors, followed by the abbreviation 'nou' (for 'noummi') and a number that indicates the sum of money due, which is between 100 and 385. The inscription was found during the excavation of Building C and has been dated by Dunant to the seventh century AD.[35] A second inscription on a vessel was uncovered during the excavation of Building B. This is in Arabic and, as opposed to the earlier ostracon, it was meant to occupy the whole outer surface of a closed vessel. The existence of the vessel was noted down in Collart's diary,[36] but the piece has never been published by the excavators. The five photographs taken of the vessel in 1956 are now stored at the Fonds d'Archives Paul Collart and are currently being studied. Again, the inscription appears to list individuals, but this time next to the word Dirham and a number. The content closely recalls, therefore, the seventh-century ostracon and proves continuity in the occupation and types of activities conducted in the compound. The inscription is palaeographically datable to the eighth century, and the script is consistent with an Umayyad chronological horizon (Ghali Zuhur-Adi, personal communication). The plan of Building C, which is situated against the former northern portico of the Great Colonnade, strongly recalls that of other private residential buildings in the Palmyrene.[37]

In the Early Islamic period, Palmyra must have relied heavily on commodities produced either locally or regionally. The Palmyrene hinterland appears densely occupied after the Islamic conquest. Evidence for medium-to-long distance trade is, however, only sporadically attested. Genequand, writing on the material found at Qasr al-Hayr al-Sharqi, has reported on the existence of amphorae from Palestine, pottery from Jordan and northern Syria, steatite vessels from the Hijaz, and foodstuff from western Syria.[38] It is reasonable to assume that the same goods would have reached Palmyra.

The changed geopolitical circumstances meant that Palmyra was no longer situated on a fighting ground between two powers. It is in this period that connections between Palmyra and the East resumed, as is clearly visible in the numismatic record.[39] Albeit rarely, travel from Palmyra to the East is also reported in written sources. Theophanes, for example, recounts that after a fight with Marwan, the last Umayyad caliph, the rebel Suleyman 'escaped first to Palmyra then to Persia'.[40]

The route through the Syrian steppe to the Euphrates is the best indicator for this renewed activity. A number of sites situated along this route experienced building in the Islamic period. At Qasr al-Swab, Qasr Khabbaz, and Qasr Amij, for example, are the remains of enceintes with three-quarter-of-a-circle corner bastions and semicircular interval bastions protruding outward. In one of these sites, Qasr Khabbaz, A. Stein could even identify the remains of a small mosque situated close to the entrance gate. Although their dating has never been precisely pinpointed, these buildings are distinctively associable with the so-called desert castles appearing in the Syrian steppe in the Umayyad period. Their existence must have heav-

---

[33] Michałowski 1960, 70–75; 1962, 54–77; 1963, 41–60; see short summary in Intagliata 2018a, 35–36.

[34] Al-As'ad and Stępniowski 1989.

[35] Dunant 1975, 127.

[36] Collart 1956, 17 September 1956.

[37] Intagliata 2017, with bibliography.

[38] Genequand 2012, 195; Genequand and others 2010, 210–11.

[39] Intagliata 2018a, 7–8; see Gawlikowski 2014 — on the end of an 'insular economy' in early Islamic times, see more generally Bessard 2013.

[40] Theop., *Chr.* 1.422; trans. Hoyland 2011, 258.

ily relied upon the route where they were situated, to the extent that these enceintes are traditionally believed to have been small road stations.[41]

The connection between Palmyra and the Euphrates continued throughout the period that followed and until very recently. As late as 1899, in discussing the economy of Palmyra, Von Oppenheim would write that, until some decades earlier the market of this settlement was flourishing because of its position in the trade between Damascus and the Euphrates. However, at this time, Palmyra had already lost its trading role to the advantage of Deir ez-Zor.[42]

Conclusion

Archaeological evidence on the trade and economy of Palmyra in Late Antiquity and the Early Islamic period is patchy and incomplete. In this chapter, several conclusions have been put forward based on a cross-examination of the published archaeological record and written sources. In Late Antiquity, the economy of Palmyra must have depended heavily on its hinterland. Short-distance trade between Palmyra and its surroundings would have assured the necessary food commodities to Palmyra's inhabitants and its garrison. Long-distance trade is barely visible in our archaeological and historical record between the fourth and sixth centuries AD. However, it is undoubted that trading links with the East had been severed by the dramatic Aurelianic events of AD 272–273. This might have also caused a gradual reshuffle in the social composition of the Palmyrene urban community, whereby the former aristocratic elite gradually disappeared.

Despite this, the knowledge of the route networks connecting Palmyra with the Euphrates presumably did not die out, as evidenced by a late written source reporting the portage of the relics of St Anastasius from Dastagerd in Persia to Jerusalem through Palmyra. The reliability of the source may be questioned, and the episode might even not have happened. However, it is indicative of the writer of this collection knowing that travelling to Persia through Palmyra was possible and that the area was under the control of allied *Saracenoi*.

In the Early Islamic period, connections between Palmyra and the East likely resumed thanks to the newly established geopolitical scenario of the seventh century AD. At that time, the economy of Palmyra might have been thriving, the construction of a Suq, an open market, in the central stretch of the Great Colonnade, and inscriptions on pottery being the most significant proofs of this to date. Although there is no direct evidence for trade with the East at Palmyra, from the seventh century, numismatic evidence proves the abundant circulation of small coinage minted in the East. It is likely that the ancient route in use for caravan trade before the Aurelianic event resumed its use at this time. Proof of this is the evidence for Early Islamic occupation along its course, which included at least two desert castles at Qasr al-Swab and Qasr Khabbaz.

Acknowledgements

This work was supported by the Danish National Research Foundation under the grant DNRF119 — Centre of Excellence for Urban Network Evolutions (UrbNet). I am very grateful to Calum Maciver (University of Edinburgh) for his help in translating the Greek (see Appendix below and Intagliata 2018a, 135, nos 26–27); to Ghali Zuhur-Adi for his hints on the chronology of the Arabic inscription found in the northern courtyard of the Sanctuary of Baalshamin; to Michael Blömer and Julia Steding for inspiring discussions on late antique connectivity through the Syrian steppe at UrbNet; to Jørgen Christian Meyer and Eivind Heldaas Seland for allowing me to reproduce Fig. 6.3; and to Rubina Raja and Kenneth Lapatin for inviting me to the conference at the Getty Villa in Los Angeles, from which this volume stems. Any mistakes, however, remain wholly my own.

---

[41] Genequand 2012, 143, 186–87, 193; Meyer and Seland 2016, 503, 505 with further bibliography. Other sites along its course were believed by Stein to be generically Islamic in date (these include Qasr Helqoum and Qasr al-Rah: Gregory and Kennedy 1985, 207–10, 225–27; Meyer and Seland 2016, 504–07).

[42] Van Oppenheim 1899, 317. I am grateful to Michael Blömer for this reference.

Appendix

Anas. Per., 1.102–04

Αὐτοὶ μὲν οὖν τιμήσαντες τὸ λείψανον τοῦ μάρτυρος ὡς εἰκὸς ἦν καὶ παραδεδωκότες τὸν ἀδελφὸν τῷ τῶν Σαρακηνῶν φυλάρχῳ ἐξέπεμψαν ἐν εἰρήνῃ μετὰ καὶ γραμμάτων ἰδίων πρὸς τὸν ἀποστείλαντα. Ὁ δὲ φύλαρχος διὰ τῆς ἐρήμου ἀπεκατέστησεν τὸν ἀδελφὸν μέχρι Παλμύρης, χρονίσαντα μετ'αὐτῶν ἐν ταῖς παρεμβολαῖς. Κἀκεῖθεν ἀπελθὼν εἰς Ἄραδον καὶ ἐμβὰς ἐν πλοίῳ, ἦλθεν ἕως Τύρου.

Therefore, after having venerated the relic of the martyr appropriately and after having left the brother in the hand of the phylarch of the Saracens, they sent him away in peace with personal letters for the person who had sent him. The phylarch led the brother, who had been staying long with them in their camps, across the desert to Palmyra. From there, he left to Arados, embarked on a ship and reached Tyre.

Anas. Per., 1.129–30

Ἐν Παλμύρᾳ τῇ πόλει

Λαβὼν οὖν ὁ προρρηθεὶς μοναχὸς τὸ ἅγιον λείψανον καὶ τῇ ὁδῷ κεχρημένος ἐπὶ τὴν ἁγίαν Χριστοῦ τοῦ Θεοῦ ἡμῶν πόλιν καταλαμβάνει ἐν Παλμύρᾳ τῇ πόλει. Ἐξῆλθον δὲ οἱ τῆς πόλεως εἰς προσκύνησιν τοῦ ἁγίου λειψάνου· ἐν οἷς νεώτερός τις ἔχων τοὺς ὀφθαλμοὺς πεφυσημένους ἵστατο κλαίων καὶ δεόμενος τοῦ μάρτυρος, ὅπως ἵλεως γένηται αὐτῷ ὁ Θεὸς δι'αὐτοῦ καὶ ἰάσηται αὐτοῦ τὴν πήρωσιν. Τοῦ δὲ ἀδελφοῦ τὴν αἰτίαν τῆς νόσου πυνθανομένου καὶ πόσον χρόνον ἔχει ἀσθενῶν, εἶπον οἱ τῆς πόλεως πρὸς αὐτόν. 'Τετραετῆ τοῦτον ἔχει χρόνον μὴ βλέπων καὶ πᾶσαν τὴν ὕπαρξιν αὐτοῦ ἰατροῖς προσαναλώσας, τέλος γέγονεν τυφλός.' Ὁ δὲ ἀδελφός φησι πρὸς αὐτόν· Ἐὰν πιστεύσῃς τῷ Θεῷ ὅτι δύναται σε περιοδεῦσαι, ὄψει τὴν δόξαν αὐτοῦ διὰ τοῦ ἁγίου Ἀναστασίου.' Ὁ δὲ ἔκραξε λέγων· 'Ναὶ πιστεύω.' Λέγει οὖν αὐτῷ πάλιν· 'Χρέος οὖν σε νηστεύειν καὶ ἐκδέχεσθαι τὴν χάριν τοῦ Θεοῦ.' Κἀκεῖνός φησιν· 'Ἀπὸ πάντων ὡς ἂν εἴπῃς μοι ἀπέχομαι, ἀπὸ δὲ οἴνου πολλὰς ἡμέρας φυλάξασθαι οὐ δύναμαι.' Καὶ ὁ πρεσβύτερος εἶπεν πρὸς αὐτόν. 'Οὐδὲ μέχρις ἑβδόμης ἡμέρας;' Καὶ ἔφη· 'Ναί.' Ἔσχεν δὲ ἔξωθεν τῆς τιμίας θήκης μικρὰν μερίδα ὁ ἀδελφός, ἣν λαβὼν καὶ ἀπομυρίσας δέδωκεν αὐτῷ ἐντειλάμενος ἀνοίγειν τοὺς ὀφθαλμοὺς αὐτοῦ καὶ ὑπαλείφειν τὰς κόρας. Καὶ ἀπελθὼν ἐποίει καθὼς ἐνετείλατο αὐτῷ καὶ μετὰ τὴν ἑβδόμην ἡμέραν ἦλθεν ὑγιὴς αἰνῶν καὶ δοξάζων τὸν Θεὸν καὶ τὸν αὐτοῦ μάρτυρα Ἀναστάσιον.

At Palmyra

The monk, then, the one we spoke about, took the holy relic and praying on the road to the holy city of Christ our God, reached the city of Palmyra. The inhabitants of the city went out to adore the holy relic. Among them was a young man whose eyes were swollen and who implored the martyr that God would be merciful to him through him and that he would heal his infirmity. When the monk asked the cause of the disease and how long he had been sick, the people of the city replied: 'he has not been able to see for four years, after having spent all his fortune on medicines, in the end he became blind'. The monk asked him 'if you believe that God can heal you, you will see his glory through St Anastasius'. And he replied crying: 'yes, I believe!'. He then told him: 'then it is necessary that you fast and that you wait the grace of God'. And he said: 'I will abstain myself from anything you say; but I am not able to keep myself from wine for many days'. The monk asked him: 'not even for at least seven days?'. He replied: 'yes'. The monk had, besides the precious box, a small parcel that he opened and having taken a balm, he gave it to him, with instructions to open his eyes and scrub it on his pupils. He then left, doing what he was told and after seven days he was healed, praising and glorifying God and his martyr Anastasius.

Works Cited

al-Asʿad, K. and F. M. Stępniowski. 1989. 'The Umayyad Suq in Palmyra', *Damaszener Mitteilungen*, 4: 205–23.

Bessard, F. 2013. 'The Urban Economy in Southern Inland Greater Syria from the Seventh Century to the End of the Umayyads', in L. Lavan (ed.), *Local Economies? Production and Exchange of Inland Regions in Late Antiquity* (Leiden: Brill), pp. 377–421.

Cerutti, A. 2014. 'Preliminary Data for the Brittle Ware from the New Excavations in the South-West Quarter of Palmyra (Syria)', in N. Poulou-Papadimitriou, E. Nodarou, and V. Kilikoglou (eds), *LRCW 4: Late Roman Coarse Wares, Cooking Wares and Amphorae in the Mediterranean; Archaeology and Archaeometry; The Mediterranean; A Market without Frontiers* (Oxford: Archaeopress), pp. 643–48.

Clermont-Ganneau, S. C. 1899. *Archaeological Researches in Palestine during the Years 1873–1874: With Numerous Illustrations from Drawings Made on the Spot by A. Lecomte du Noüy*, I (London: Palestine Exploration Fund).

Collart, P. 1956. *Excavation Diary* (unpublished, Fond d'Archives Paul Collart, University of Lausanne).

Dunant, C. 1975. 'Les inscriptions sur céramique', in C. Dunant and R. Fellmann (eds), *Le sanctuaire de Baalshamin à Palmyre*, VI: *Kleinfunde/Objets divers* (Rome: Institut suisse de Rome), pp. 119–28.

Galavaris, G. 1970. *Bread and the Liturgy: The Symbolism of Early Christian and Byzantine Bread Stamps* (Madison: University of Wisconsin Press).

Gawlikowska, K. 2015. 'The Glass Industry in Palmyra', *Syria*, 95: 291–98.

Gawlikowska, K. and K. al-Asʿad. 1994. 'The Collection of Glass Vessels in the Museum of Palmyra', *Studia Palmyreńskie*, 9: 5–38.

Gawlikowski, M. 1973. *Palmyre*, VI: *Le temple Palmyrénien: études d'épigraphie et de topographie historique* (Warsaw: Państwowe Wydawnictwo Naukowe).

—— 1983. 'Réflexions sur la chronologie du sanctuaire d'Allat à Palmyre', *Damaszener Mitteilungen*, 1: 59–67.

—— 1986. 'Palmyre (mission Polonaise)', *Syria*, 63: 397–99.

—— 2014. 'Le trésor Sasanide', in A. Krzyżanowska and M. Gawlikowski (eds), *Monnaies des fouilles Polonaises à Palmyre*, Studia Palmyrenskie, 13 (Warsaw: Warsaw University Press, Polish Centre of Mediterranean Archaeology), pp. 61–120.

—— 2016. 'Trade across Frontiers: Foreign Relations of a Caravan City', in J. C. Meyer, E. H. Seland, and N. Anfinset (eds), *Palmyrena: City, Hinterland and Caravan Trade between Orient and Occident; Proceedings of the Conference Held in Athens, December 1–3, 2012* (Oxford, Archaeopress), pp. 19–28.

Genequand, D. 2003. 'Project "implantations umayyades de Syrie et de Jordanie": rapport de la campagne de prospection (Juin-Juillet 2002)', *SLSA: Jahresbericht*, 2002: 31–68.

—— 2012. *Les établissements des élites omeyyades en Palmyrène et au Proche-Orient* (Beirut: Institut français du Proche Orient).

Genequand, D. and others. 2010. 'Rapport préliminaire des campagne 2008 et 2009 de la mission archéologique Syro-Suisse de Qasr al-Hayr al-Sharqi', *SLSA: Jahresbericht*, 2009: 177–219.

Gregory, S. and D. Kennedy. 1985. *Sir Aurel Stein's Limes Report*, British Archaeological Reports, International Series, 272 (Oxford: British Archaeological Reports).

Hoyland, R. (trans.). 2011. *Theophilus of Edessa's Chronicle and the Circulation of Historical Knowledge in Late Antiquity and Early Islam*, Translated Texts for Historians, 57 (Liverpool: Liverpool University Press).

Intagliata, E. E. 2014. 'The White Ware from Palmyra (Syria): Preliminary Data from the New Excavations in the South-West Quarter', in N. Poulou-Papadimitriou, E. Nodarou, and V. Kilikoglou (eds), *LRCW 4: Late Roman Coarse Wares, Cooking Wares and Amphorae in the Mediterranean; Archaeology and Archaeometry; The Mediterranean; A Market without Frontiers* (Oxford: Archaeopress), pp. 649–55.

—— 2017. 'The Post-Roman Occupation of the Northern Courtyard of the Sanctuary of Baalshamin in Palmyra: A Reassessment of the Evidence Based on the Documents at the Fonds d'Archives Paul Collart, Université de Lausanne', *Zeitschrift für Orient-Archäologie*, 9: 180–99.

—— 2018a. *Palmyra after Zenobia (273–750): An Archaeological and Historical Reappraisal* (Oxford: Oxbow).

—— 2018b. 'Pinpointing Unrest at Palmyra in Early Islam: The Evidence from Coin Hoards and Written Sources', *Études et travaux*, 31: 183–96.

Lehner, H. 1932. 'Zur Bauinschrift des Diocletianslagers', in T. Wiegand (ed.), *Palmyra: Ergebnisse der Expeditionen von 1902 und 1917* (Berlin: Keller), pp. 106–07.

Oppenheim, M. F. von. 1899. *Vom Mittelmeer zum Persischen Golf durch den Haurän, die Syrische Wüste und Mesopotamien* (Berlin: Reimer).

Majcherek, G. and A. Taha. 2004. 'Roman and Byzantine Layers at Umm el-Tlel: Ceramics and Other Finds', *Syria*, 81: 229–48.

Meyer, J. C. 2017. *Palmyrena: Palmyra and the Surrounding Territory from the Roman to the Early Islamic Period* (Oxford: Archaeopress).

Meyer, J. C. and E. H. Seland. 2016. 'Palmyra and the Trade Route to the Euphrates', in S. Abouzayd (ed.), *The Decapolis: History and Archaeology; Hatra, Palmyra and Edessa; Contacts and Cultural Exchanges between Cities in the Fertile Crescent before Islam* (Oxford: Aram), pp. 497–523.

Michałowski, K. 1960. *Palmyre*, I: *Fouilles Polonaises 1959* (Warsaw: Państwowe Wydawnictwo Naukowe).
—— 1962. *Palmyre*, II: *Fouilles Polonaises 1960* (Warsaw: Państwowe Wydawnictwo Naukowe).
—— 1963. *Palmyre*, III: *Fouilles Polonaises 1961* (Warsaw: Państwowe Wydawnictwo Naukowe).
Mior, P. 2016. 'The Road from Palmyra to Damascus in the Tabula Peutingeriana', in J. C. Meyer, E. H. Seland, and N. Anfinset (eds), *Palmyrena: City, Hinterland and Caravan Trade between Orient and Occident; Proceedings of the Conference Held in Athens, December 1–3, 2012* (Oxford: Archaeopress), pp. 49–57.
Ployer, R. 2013. 'Gläser', in A. Schmidt-Colinet and W. al-Asʿad (eds), *Palmyras Reichtum durch weltweiten Handel: Archäologische Untersuchungen im Bereich der hellenistischen Stadt*, II (Vienna: Holzhausen), pp. 127–205.
Reddé, M. 1995. 'Dioclétien et les fortifications militaires de l'Antiquité Tardive: quelques considérations de méthode', *Antiquité Tardive*, 3: 91–124.
Romagnolo, M. 2012. 'Dati preliminari sui vetri dell'edficio con peristilio di Palmira (Siria)', in A. Coscarella (ed.), *Il vetro in Italia: testimonianze, produzioni, commerci in età basso medievale; il vetro in Calabria; vecchie scoperte, nuove acquisizioni; atti XV Giornate Nazionali di Studio sul Vetro A.I.H.V.* (Cosenza: Università della Calabria), pp. 599–604.
Römer-Strehl, C. 2013. 'Keramik', in A. Schmidt-Colinet and W. al-Asʿad (eds), *Palmyras Reichtum durch weltweiten Handel: Archäologische Untersuchungen im Bereich der hellenistischen Stadt*, II (Vienna: Holzhausen), pp. 7–80.
Sartre-Fauriat, A. and M. Sartre. 2008. *Palmyre: la cité des caravanes* (Paris: Gallimard).
Schlumberger, D. 1951. *La Palmyrène du Nord-Ouest: villages et lieux de culte de l'époque impérial; recherches archéologiques sur la mise en valeur d'une région du désert par les Palmyréniens* (Paris: Geuthner).
Schmidt-Colinet, A. and W. al-Asʿad (eds). 2013. *Palmyras Reichtum durch weltweiten Handel: Archäologische Untersuchungen im Bereich der hellenistischen Stadt*, 2 vols (Vienna: Holzhausen).
Schnädelbach, K. 2010. *Topographia Palmyrena*, I: *Topography* (Bonn: Habelt).
Seland, E. H. 2016. *Ships of the Desert and Ships of the Sea: Palmyra in the World Trade of the First Three Centuries CE*, Philippika, 101 (Wiesbaden: Harrassowitz).
Yon, J.-B. 2008. 'Documents sur l'armée romaine à Palmyre', *Electrum*, 14: 129–47.
Young, G. K. 2001. *Rome's Eastern Trade: International Commerce and Imperial Policy 31 BC–AD 305* (London: Routledge).

Part II
Art and Archaeology

7. Palmyrene Funerary Art between East and West: Reclining Women in Funerary Sculpture

Rubina Raja

Aarhus University, Centre for Urban Network Evolutions (UrbNet) (Rubina.raja@cas.au.dk)

Palmyrene Art: Transforming the Way We View Local Art Forms

Palmyrene art produced in the first three centuries AD has received the attention of art historians and archaeologists for more than a century.[1] However, most often the art of Palmyra — including the thousands of portraits — has been studied through the lens of the city's relation to Rome — whose political dominance it was under in the first three centuries AD — the era from which most of its archaeological record stems.[2] Yet, it is worth noting that Palmyra geographically speaking was located much closer to Parthia — whose influence it, of course, also was under — both in terms of politics and culture.[3] It is not surprising, however, that the art of this oasis city has been studied mainly within the framework of the Roman world, since the study of provincial art (in itself a problematic term) — that is, the art of the Roman provinces — is a research focus that has been strong for several decades. Studying art from outside of Rome more or less purely as a product of the influence of Roman domination has until recently been the main way of accessing and understanding this art, and has immensely affected the ways in which art — also from the eastern provinces — has been perceived, disseminated in scholarship, and taught to students.[4]

While there can be no doubt that Palmyrene art and its development naturally stood under the influence of the cultural spheres with which it was in contact, the Roman influences have been given undue preference over the connections with the East, leading to a skewed picture of the rich and varied art forms of Palmyra and their development over the first three centuries AD. While this is one side of the story, the other side is that when studying any category of art from a perspective that primarily takes its point of departure in examining the influence of one specific cultural realm on another local setting, this will happen to the detriment of the understanding of the local setting. In fact, the point of departure must first and foremost be to understand the local setting and then branch out from there in order to situate the local developments and responses to outside influences. Recently, new trends in the way that we study art from outside Rome as classical archaeologists have indeed begun to make their imprint on scholarship, and new agendas are currently being set for new lines of enquiries, which over time will pave the way for new insight into the understanding of art forms and their styles and local choices made.[5]

Representations of Women in Palmyrene Art

In the last decade, Palmyrene funerary art has, for example, received much renewed attention through the Palmyra Portrait Project within the framework of which all known funerary sculpture has been collected in a database.[6] The database has given the opportunity to study several aspects of the funerary art as well as trends and developments in an entirely different light than hitherto possible, since the database allows us to draw out particular groups of sculptural material and study them in their own right. Among other themes, the representations of women in the funerary art has

---

[1] Ingholt 1928; Colledge 1976. Now also see: Bobou and others 2021; Simonsen 1889; 1889; Wood 1753. Also see: Sartre-Fauriat 2019.

[2] Parlasca 1981; 1985a; 1990; Colledge 1996.

[3] Colledge 1977; 1987.

[4] For example, the contribution on sculpture in the Roman Near East in the *Oxford Handbook of Roman Sculpture* is almost exclusively concerned with marble sculpture, disregarding the locally produced sculpture in limestone and basalt, despite the fact that marble was a non-indigenous stone, and most locally produced sculpture of that period was executed in local stone. See Weber 2015.

[5] Blömer and Raja (eds) 2019; Blömer and Raja 2019a; 2019b; Raja 2019a for contributions which also incorporate further references to these debates and discussions.

[6] Raja 2019b; 2019c; 2019d, 2019e. Also now see: Romanowska, Bobou, and Raja 2021; Raja, Bobou, and Romanowska 2021; Bobou, Raja, and Romanowska 2021.

Figure 7.1. Sarcophagus lid with a seated female, two standing individuals, a reclining female, and a reclining male. From the Tomb of Aʿailamî and Zebidâ, west necropolis. Ingholt Archive, Aarhus, PS 529A (© Palmyra Portrait Project and Rubina Raja).

Figure 7.2. Fragmented sarcophagus lid with a reclining female. From the Tomb of Aʿailamî and Zebidâ, west necropolis. Ingholt Archive, Aarhus, PS 529A (© Palmyra Portrait Project and Rubina Raja).

that there was a certain variety in the types of female representations, often with specific contextual connotations, depending on the sphere in which these had originally been displayed.[8] Over the years, articles have been published on hairstyles, special gestures, ornaments, jewellery, and women in constellation with other family members.[9] It has been demonstrated that representations of women developed with respect to styles of clothing and attributes shown, but that the contexts in which women were shown — namely in domestic settings and with a focus on the family and on the role as mother and wife — consistently stayed the same across all three centuries in which the funerary sculpture was produced.[10] These observations make it even more pertinent to bring to the forefront the contexts and scenes in which women are represented in slightly different scenarios, and until now, the group of objects depicting reclining women on couches has not been presented in its entirety.[11]

gained renewed attention, most recently in the 2018 monograph by Signe Krag in which more than seven hundred representations of women were presented in a corpus drawn from the Palmyra Portrait Project database.[7] However, a set of articles on women represented in various contexts have also been published, showing

[7] Krag 2018.

[8] Krag 2016; 2017a; 2017b; 2018; Krag and Raja 2016a; 2017; 2018; 2019a; (eds) 2019b; Cussini 2019a; Henning 2019; Klaver 2019.

[9] Heyn 2010; 2012; 2019.

[10] Krag's publications are the standard works on representations of women in Palmyra with further references: Krag 2016; 2017a; 2017b; 2018. See also: Kaizer 2019; Klaver.

[11] Heyn 2010; 2012; 2019; Krag 2016; 2017a; Krag and Raja 2016a; 2017; 2018; (eds) 2019b.

Figure 7.3. Fragmented sarcophagus lid with the torso of a reclining female. From the Tomb of Aʿailamî and Zebidâ, west necropolis. Ingholt Archive, Aarhus, PS 881 (© Palmyra Portrait Project and Rubina Raja).

Figure 7.4. Fragmented sarcophagus lid with the lower body of a reclining female. From the Tomb of Aʿailamî and Zebidâ, west necropolis (© American Colony Photo Department, photographer. Palmyra. Remains of a tomb temple. Palmyrene type of reclining figures. Syria Tadmur. Tadmur, *c.* 1920–1933. Photograph: <https://www.loc.gov/item/2019706277/> [accessed 10 October 2021]).

This group consisting of thirteen objects makes up the focus of this contribution, in order to discuss the meaning of this otherwise very non-Palmyrene motif.

Banqueting in Palmyra

The banqueting motif in Palmyrene art was widely used in the funerary and religious spheres. There are three main groups of material in which the banqueting motif is often encountered in Palmyra: the sarcophagi lids and so-called banqueting reliefs — both stemming from the funerary sphere — and on the so-called banqueting tesserae used as entrance tickets to religious banquets.[12] However, the two groups of motifs differ in their overall contextual settings. The banqueting scenes in the funerary art focus on family and domestic settings, showing reclining men and women with servants and family members. In the case of the tesserae, the focus is exclusively on reclining Palmyrene priests, who are most often shown alone, but also sometimes reclining two and two together. The meaning of banqueting scenes, both in ancient art in general and in relation to Palmyra specifically, has been treated elsewhere and will therefore not be the topic of this contribution.[13] It suffices to say that banqueting held a central role in elite life in the ancient world on a variety of levels and in a variety of settings, and that Palmyrene society also embraced this custom, whereby the iconography of the banquet came to be a signifier of the importance of family and other socio-cultural settings, such as the religious life.[14]

The Contexts of Objects Depicting Reclining Women in Palmyrene Banqueting Scenes

While women are well represented in the Palmyrene funerary art, and banqueting scenes also are common, motifs including reclining women are rare. The Palmyra Portrait Project database holds only thirteen objects, which show women reclining, out of a total of almost four thousand objects.[15] All thirteen objects, most of which stem from sarcophagi lids, date to the period between the late second century AD and the late third century AD (see Catalogue at the end of this chapter). Eight of these objects are sarcophagi lids or fragments of these (cat. nos 1–8) (Figs 7.1–7.5); one representation

---

[12] For a general introduction and overview of the literature on the banqueting scene in the funerary art, see Audley-Miller 2016. Also see Bobou and Raja (forthcoming). This publication comprises a total of 729 Palmyrene sarcophagi with portrait decoration in different states of preservation (including banqueting reliefs with frames), four fragments of Attic sarcophagi, eleven Palmyrene sarcophagi fragments without portraits, and another twenty-nine sarcophagi that are known only from publications. For recent publications on the tesserae including the banqueting scenes see: Raja 2015a; 2015b; 2016a; 2019f; 2019i; 2020.

[13] Dentzer 1982; Seyrig; Audley-Miller 2016; Cussini 2016; Fabricius 1999; Dunbabin 2010.

[14] Makowski 1985a; 1985b; Gnoli 2016.

[15] Romanowska, Bobou, and Raja 2021 for a summary of results from the Palmyra Portrait Project.

Figure 7.5 Complete sarcophagus with a banqueting scene on the lid, depicting a seated and a reclining female, and busts on the box. From the Tombeau de l'Aviation, south-east necropolis. Ingholt Archive, Aarhus, unnumbered sheet (© Palmyra Portrait Project and Rubina Raja).

is depicted on a short side of a sarcophagus (cat. no. 9) (Fig. 7.6); and four objects are banqueting reliefs, one in a large format (cat. no. 10) and three of a smaller format (cat. nos 11 and 13) (Figs 7.7–7.8).[16] These scenes showing reclining women fall into two categories: 1) banqueting scenes showing a reclining woman together with a reclining man and usually one or several standing family members (cat. nos 1–8 and 10) and 2) a woman reclining by herself on a couch in a domestic, private setting being attended to by a servant (cat. nos 9 and 11–13).

Nine of these thirteen objects are more or less fragmented banqueting scenes, which, apart from one (cat. no. 10), formed part of lavish sarcophagi lids on which family scenes were shown representing the pater familias together with several family members.[17] Originally these now fragmented scenes are likely to have shown women reclining next to men.[18] This conclusion is based on the few objects in which the man is still visible (cat. nos 1 and 7) as well as the general composition of such motifs known from other places in the ancient world. Cat. no. 10, which is a large banqueting relief in which a woman is shown reclining together with a man in a domestic setting, adheres to the motif style shown on the sarcophagi lids. It, however, also differs from the most ordinary banqueting scenes, since the couple, who according to the inscription are siblings — not man and wife — are shown in a private setting as underlined by the large box, potentially for jewellery or other expensive goods, shown on a pedestal to the left in the image. The man is holding a drinking cup in his hand,[19] whereas the woman is not associated with any foodstuff or drinks. This scene is unique, in that it is not a broader family constellation where man and wife are shown together surrounded by family members — rather, it depicts siblings reclining together. Representations of siblings, both shown as children and as adults, are known from

---

[16] Figures are only referenced here and can otherwise be found numbered in the catalogue. Images of eight objects are included in this contribution. These are cat. nos 1–4 (Figs 7.1–7.4), 7 (Fig. 7.5), 11 (Fig. 7.7), and 13 (Fig. 7.8).

[17] Raja 2019b.

[18] Cat. nos 2, 3, 4, 5, 6, and 8 are heavily fragmented. However, judging from the breaks and the approximate sizes of the fragments, it is clear that these belonged to larger banqueting lids and would have been part of larger family constellations, most likely involving several reclining individuals. In particular, the breaks to the left of the reclining women indicate that they originally would have been reclining in front of another person, most likely a man, as seen in other examples in the catalogue.

[19] Also now see Heyn 2021.

7. PALMYRENE FUNERARY ART BETWEEN EAST AND WEST

Figure 7.6a. Complete sarcophagus with a banqueting scene on the lid, a religious scene on the front of the box, and a reclining female on the side of the box. Palmyra Museum, Palmyra, inv. no. 2677B/8983 (© Andreas Schmidt-Colinet).

Figure 7.6b. Side view of the sarcophagus box with a reclining female and a standing servant. Palmyra Museum, Palmyra, inv. no. 2677B/8983 (© Andreas Schmidt-Colinet).

other funerary sculptural constellations in Palmyra.[20] In this case, a piece of textile pinned to the background with rosettes and vegetal motifs is hanging behind the lower head of the man. This piece of textile, which has often wrongly been called a *dorsalium*, is undeniably connected with the funerary sphere and, in this case, indicates that at least the man was deceased.[21]

Four of the objects stem from one and the same grave (cat. nos 1–4), the so-called Tomb Cantineau, an elite grave in the west necropolis of Palmyra. This grave was of the so-called house- or temple-tomb type of a later second-century AD date, and the sarcophagi lids are stylistically dated to the later second century AD into the first part of the third century AD. This grave must certainly have been a family grave, and obviously the motif of women reclining was preferred in some instances by this family. The remaining four objects also have grave provenances and stem from the Tower of Elahbel (cat. no. 5), temple tomb no. 159 (cat. no. 6), temple tomb no. 186 ('Tombeau de l'aviation'), and temple tomb no. 36, respectively. All these graves belong to the most exclusive ones found in Palmyra. And the fact that all fragments apart from one (cat. no. 5) stem from temple tombs, which were the most exclusive sort of grave monuments in the city, underline that the motif showing women reclining on sarcophagi lids was one that was used by the uppermost elite layers in Palmyra. The women wear rich jewellery and clothing. The mattresses they are reclining on are also richly decorated, as are the pillows against which they lean. None of the women hold drinking vessels — only the man preserved in one of the objects holds a drinking cup in his left hand (cat. no. 1).

The second motif group comprises four objects that show women reclining alone in a private setting. These consist of three banqueting reliefs of a smaller size (cat. nos 11–13) and one example stemming from one of the most lavish sarcophagi found in Palmyra, where a woman is shown reclining on one short side of a sarcoph-

---

20 Ringsborg 2017; Krag and Raja 2016a; 2017; 2019a. Also see, for example, Raja 2019e, 98–101 (I.N. 2776) and 222–25 (I.N. 2763). Also see Raja 2019g.

21 Raja 2019g. One other banqueting relief exists which shows a reclining man with a piece of textile hung behind him: Raja 2019g, 145, cat. no. 242. A total of 246 objects (one of which is a wall-painting) exist with these textiles hung behind one or more individuals.

Figure 7.7. Banquet relief with a standing and reclining female. Archaeological Museum, Istanbul, inv. no. 3728/180. Ingholt Archive, Aarhus, PS 529 (© Palmyra Portrait Project and Rubina Raja).

agus (cat. no. 9), potentially the sarcophagus belonging to her husband, who chose to be depicted with his horse in the place where a sitting wife would have usually been depicted.[22] In these scenes, the reclining women are being presented with jewellery, jewellery boxes, and, in one case at least, also a mirror (potentially also a jewellery box — but the object is fragmented) by a servant (cat. no. 12). In two cases, an object is placed in the background on a pedestal between the reclining woman and the servant. In one case, a vase is shown (cat. no. 11), in the other what appears to be a ball of yarn placed in a basket (cat. no. 13). The women are shown situated in rich ambiences with jewellery, clothing of a high standard, reclining on richly decorated mattresses, and leaning against richly decorated pillows. In the cases where the women are reclining alone, there is no active eating or drinking involved in the motif, neither is food nor drink generally represented at all in these scenes. However, in one case, the reclining woman seems to be holding a small fruit of an identified sort in her right hand, which is resting on her right knee (cat. no. 11). In another case, the man reclining together with a woman is shown holding a drinking cup in his left hand (cat. no. 10). The original contexts of the banqueting reliefs are not as straightforward as those of the sarcophagi lid, which certainly stem from funerary contexts. The sarcophagus showing a reclining woman on one short side comes from a known funerary context (cat. no. 9). However, the three banqueting reliefs stem from secondary contexts, but are assumed to originally have come from funerary contexts, based on the fact that other such reliefs have been found in funerary contexts.[23]

Six objects carry inscriptions: three in Greek (cat. nos 1–2 and 7) and three in Palmyrene Aramaic (cat. nos 3–4 and 10). Four of the objects stem from the same tomb (see above), Tomb Cantineau, two Greek and two Palmyrene Aramaic. This is another underlining of the utmost elite context of these objects; not only is the rare reclining female motif used, but it is also combined with inscriptions giving us the names of the individuals portrayed. The Greek inscription, which goes together with the lavish sarcophagus lid (cat. no. 1), apart from naming individuals also tells us that one of the men was a symposiarch — very likely the man reclining together with a woman. The Greek inscriptions on the keys (now lost) on a sarcophagus lid (cat. no. 7) observed by Watzinger and Wulzinger, but not recorded in detail, most likely only held a few words as known from other such contexts.[24] The Palmyrene inscription on the banqueting relief depicting siblings (cat. no. 10) is a standard inscription, simply giving the names of the individuals represented and their father's name.

All thirteen objects date from the late second century onwards, underlining that this motif with a reclining

---

[22] Schmidt-Colinet 2003; 2009; Schmidt-Colinet and As'ad 2007.

[23] Dentzer 1982; Makowski 1985b; Audley-Miller 2016; Cussini 2016; Krag and Raja 2017.

[24] Raja and Yon (forthcoming). Also see Thomsen 2021.

Figure 7.8. Banquet relief with a standing and reclining female. National Museum of Damascus, Damascus, inv. no. 2153. Ingholt Archive, Aarhus, PS 684 (© Palmyra Portrait Project and Rubina Raja).

woman — whether alone or shown together with a man — was only used in Palmyra from this period onwards and only in very few cases. This same pattern of only being used sparingly and being constricted to a certain data range can be traced in the case of other outlier phenomena in Palmyrene sculpture. This, in turn, underlines that trends and fashions were in place, and that certain motifs restricted to a small part of the elite circulated among what might have been extended families or connected families.[25] At least the fact that four objects stem from the same grave (cat. nos 1–4) points in the direction that motifs could be particularly fashionable within some families.

Conclusion: The Socio-Cultural Meaning of the Motif

Having set out the contexts and dates of the thirteen objects, it is time to turn to the socio-cultural meanings which are implied through the depiction of women reclining — either alone or together with men. As has been shown in research over the last many decades, and as has recently been pulled together in two new contributions by Lucy Audley-Miller and Maura Heyn, respectively, the banqueting scenes shown in funerary art in Palmyra are not that straightforward to interpret.[26] In numerous ways, they adhere to motifs known from the broader Graeco-Roman cultural *koine*, but they differ in their basic expressions, since active eating and drinking is never involved, and usually only one of the reclining men holds a drinking vessel or a piece of fruit in one hand. It is clear that the banqueting motifs in Palmyra were connected either to the funerary sphere or to the religious sphere, as also outlined in the introduction to this contribution. Both Audley-Miller and Heyn have recapped the various opinions on whether the banqueting scenes show banquets in the afterlife or funerary banquets or banquets that celebrate dining habits in life. Both come to the conclusion, as do I in earlier publications, that the banqueting motif most likely alludes to the banquet culture connected to events in family and religious contexts. Furthermore, these motifs were connected with the elite strata in Palmyrene society. This is underlined by the fact that the scenes, on the one hand, are found in the graves of the upper classes and, on the other hand, on the tesserae commissioned by the sponsors of the religious banquets, Palmyrene priests, who also were drawn from the upper classes of the local society.[27] As Audley-Miller underlines in her contribution, the banquet scenes were individualized more through choice of clothing, jewellery, and other attributes than through the portraiture, which we know to be highly standardized and very seldomly individualized.[28]

---

[25] Krag and Raja 2016a; 2017; 2018; Raja 2016b; 2017f.

[26] Audley-Miller 2016; Heyn 2021.

[27] Raja 2016b; 2017a; 2017b; 2017c; 2017d; 2017e; 2017f; 2018a; 2019h; 2021a; 2021b.

[28] Audley-Miller 2016.

However, the slight differences in the constellations of the banqueting scenes, such as using the motif with reclining women, was another way of individualizing the otherwise highly standardized banqueting motif. And it is most likely within such a contextual framework that this outlier motif is to be understood. Heyn has written on the meaning of drinking attributes in the Palmyrene banqueting scenes, re-examining several of the objects showing men with drinking vessels in their left hands, but also giving a profound overview of research on the cultural significance of the banqueting scenes in Palmyrene funerary art undertaken until now, as well as reminding us how the banqueting culture was also connected to eastern elite culture and can be traced in the relief scenes from Assyria.[29] Her convincing examples and argumentation remind us that while the Roman cultural *koine* might bring the most handy comparative to mind, there is an entirely different side to the story as well — namely the much older palace banqueting culture of Assyria and Mesopotamia. Palmyrene banqueting scenes certainly drew from these as well, connecting the Palmyrene elite with strong and long manifested ideals of how elite members of society were to represent themselves. However, in this art, no reclining women are encountered. In Graeco-Roman and Etruscan art, there are examples of reclining women in the funerary sphere. Most examples come from Etruscan and Roman contexts, but some sarcophagi from Roman Asia Minor also show women reclining with their husbands at banquets. A few banqueting scenes, but very fragmented examples, are known from mosaics stemming from Edessa. These mosaics also stem from elite grave contexts. So while the banqueting motif used widely in Palmyra — in funerary and religious contexts — was profoundly inscribed into a broader regional context showing knowledge of both Roman and Eastern banqueting traditions — but adapting the motif to the specific local needs — the small group depicting women reclining can best be understood in the wider geographic context of funerary art in the eastern regions, where this motif seems to have worked as an underlining of elite culture and status. This was a culture in which women could be represented reclining alone in domestic settings, displaying their wealth and status, or together with their male family members, which also would have underlined their status in society. The most important thing, however, is perhaps that these images were not visible to all, but restricted to being viewed by certain groups, first and foremost the closest family in the family grave settings that they were intended for. So while they show Palmyrene women in a very different way than we encounter them in the few religious reliefs known from Palmyra showing women entirely veiled, or in a more public setting in Graeco-Roman clothing in the public statuary, their contexts also underline that such images were not for everyone to see. The reclining female motif can perhaps best be compared with those of the mourning mothers, another outlier group, which show mothers who have bared their breasts and scratched their chests so that it bleeds as a sign of mourning.[30] Both motifs would have been provocative to look at — and while the bare-breasted mothers might not be as lavish and high quality as the objects depicting reclining women, both motifs are expressions of elite culture and values that were deeply embedded in the local culture, drawing on a string of influences from both the East and the West.

---

[29] Heyn 2021, 68–71.

[30] For example: Raja 2019e, 226–29, I.N. 1025.

Works Cited

Abdul-Hak, S. 1952. 'L'hypogée de Taai à Palmyre', *Les annales archéologiques arabes syriennes*, 2: 193–251.

Abdul-Hak, S. and A. Abdul-Hak. 1951. *Catalogue illustré du Département des Antiquités Gréco-Romaines au Musée de Damas*, 1 (Damascus: Publications de la Direction Générale des Antiquités de Syrie).

al-As'ad, K. and A. Schmidt-Colinet. 1995. 'Zur Einführung', in A. Schmidt-Colinet (ed.), *Palmyra: Kulturbegegnung im Grenzbereich*, Sonderbände der Antike Welt, Zaberns Bildbände zur Archäologie, 3rd edn (Mainz: Von Zabern), pp. 28–53.

—— 2005. 'Kulturbegegnung im Grenzbereich', in A. Schmidt-Colinet (ed.), *Palmyra: Kulturbegegnung im Grenzbereich*, Sonderbände der Antike Welt, Zaberns Bildbände zur Archäologie, 3rd edn (Mainz: Von Zabern), pp. 36–64.

Albertson, F. C. 2014. 'A Distribution Scene on a Palmyran Funerary Relief', *Antike Kunst: Zeitschrift für klassische Archäologie*, 57: 25–37.

Andrade, N. J. 2013. *Syrian Identity in the Greco-Roman World* (Cambridge: Cambridge University Press).

Audley-Miller, L. 2016. 'The Banquet in Palmyrene Funerary Contexts', in C. M. Draycott and M. Stamatopoulou (eds), *Dining and Death: Interdisciplinary Perspectives on the 'Funerary Banquet' in Ancient Art, Burial and Belief* (Leuven: Peeters), pp. 553–90.

Blömer, M. and R. Raja. 2019a. 'Funerary Portraits in Roman Greater Syria: Time for a Reappreciation', in M. Blömer and R. Raja (eds), *Funerary Portraiture in Greater Roman Syria*, Studies in Classical Archaeology, 6 (Turnhout: Brepols), pp. 1–4.

—— 2019b. 'Shifting the Paradigms: Towards a New Agenda in the Study of the Funerary Portraiture of Greater Roman Syria', in M. Blömer and R. Raja (eds), *Funerary Portraiture in Greater Roman Syria*, Studies in Classical Archaeology, 6 (Turnhout: Brepols), pp. 5–26.

Blömer, M. and R. Raja (eds). 2019. *Funerary Portraiture in Greater Roman Syria*, Studies in Classical Archaeology, 6 (Turnhout: Brepols).

Bobou, O. and R. Raja (forthcoming). *The Palmyrene Sarcophagi*, Sarkofagen Studien (Berlin: German Archaeological Institute).

Bobou, O., R. Raja, and I. Romanowska. 2021. 'Historical Trajectories of Palmyra's Elites through the Lens of Archaeological Data', *Journal of Urban Archaeology*, 4: 153–66.

Bobou, O. and others. 2021. *Studies on Palmyrene Sculpture: A Commented Translation of Harald Ingholt's 1928 Studier over Palmyrensk Skulptur*, Studies in Palmyrene Archaeology and History, 1 (Turnhout: Brepols).

Cantineau, J. 1929. 'Fouilles à Palmyre', *Mélanges de l'Institut français de Damas: section des Arabisants*, 1: 3–15.

—— 1930. 'Inscriptions palmyréniennes', *Revue d'Assyriologie et d'archéologie orientale*, 27: 27–51.

Chehadeh, J. 1987. 'Zu Schmuckdarstellungen auf palmyrenischen Grabreliefs', in E. M. Ruprechtsberger (ed.), *Palmyra: Geschichte, Kunst und Kultur der syrischen Oasenstadt* (Linz: Druck- und Verlagsanstalt Gutenberg), pp. 193–99.

Ciliberto, F. 2017. 'La scultura funeraria di Palmira/ The Funerary Sculpture of Palmyra', in M. Novello and C. Tiussi (eds), *Volti di Palmira ad Aquileia: Portraits of Palmyra in Aquileia* (Rome: Gangemi), pp. 47–57.

Clauss, P. 2002. 'Morire ai tempi di Zenobia', in A. Gabucci (ed.), *Zenobia: il sogno di una regina d'Oriente* (Milan: Electa), pp. 74–99.

Colledge, M. A. R. 1976. *The Art of Palmyra* (London: Thames and Hudson).

—— 1977. *Parthian Art* (London: Elek).

—— 1987. 'Parthian Cultural Elements at Roman Palmyra', *Mesopotamia*, 22: 19–28.

—— 1992. 'La perle du désert de Syrie', *Palmyre: le monde de la Bible*, 74: 44–50.

—— 1996. 'Roman Influence in the Art of Palmyra', *Annales archéologiques arabes syriennes*, 42: 363–70.

Curtis, V. S. 2017. 'The Parthian haute-couture at Palmyra', in A. H. Sørensen and T. Long (eds), *Positions and Professions in Palmyra*, Palmyrene Studies, 2, Scientia Danica, Series H, Humanistica, 4.9 (Copenhagen: The Royal Danish Academy of Sciences and Letters), pp. 52–67.

Cussini, E. 2016. 'Family Banqueting at Palmyra: Reassessing the Evidence', in P. Corò and others (eds), *Libiamo ne' lieti calici: Ancient Near Eastern Studies Presented to Lucio Milano on the Occasion of his 65th Birthday by Pupils, Colleagues and Friends*, Alter Orient und Altes Testament, 436 (Münster: Ugarit), pp. 139–59.

—— 2019a. 'Daughters and Wives: Defining Women in Palmyrene Inscriptions', in S. Krag and R. Raja (eds), *Women, Children, and the Family in Palmyra*, Palmyrene Studies, 3, Scientia Danica, H, Humanistica, 4.10 (Copenhagen: The Royal Danish Academy of Sciences and Letters), pp. 67–81.

—— 2019b. 'Images of Individual Devotion in Palmyrene Sources', in R. Raja (ed.), *Revisiting the Religious Life of Palmyra*, Contextualizing the Sacred, 9 (Turnhout: Brepols), pp. 51–66.

Dentzer, J.-M. 1982. *Le motif du banquet couché dans le Proche-Orient et le monde grec du VII au IV siècle avant J.-C. Rome* (Rome: École française de Rome).

Dunbabin, K. M. D. 2010. *The Roman Banquet: Images of Conviviality* (Cambridge: Cambridge University Press).

Fabricius, J. 1999. *Die hellenistischen Totenmahlreliefs: Grabrepräsentation und Wertvorstellungen in ostgriechischen Städten* (Munich: Pfeil).

Fejfer, J. 2009. *Roman Portraits in Context* (Berlin: De Gruyter).

Finlayson, C. 2002–2003. 'Veil, Turban and Headpiece: Funerary Portraits and Female Status at Palmyra', *Annales archéologiques arabes syriennes*, 45–46: 221–35.

—— 2008. 'Mut'a Marriage in the Roman Near East: The Evidence from Palmyra, Syria', in B. A. Nakhai (ed.), *The World of Women in the Ancient and Classical Near East* (Newcastle-upon-Tyne: Cambridge Scholars), pp. 99–138.

Gawlikowski, M. 1974. *Recueil d'inscriptions palmyréniennes provenant de fouilles syriennes et polonaises récentes à Palmyre* (Paris: Imprimerie nationale).

—— 2010. *Palmyra* (Warsaw: Fundacja Przyjaciół Instytutu Archeologii UW).

Gawlikowski, M. and J. Starcky. 1985. *Palmyre* (Paris: Librairie d'Amérique et d'Orient).

Gnoli, T. 2016. 'Banqueting in Honour of the Gods: Notes on the Marzeah of Palmyra', in A. Kropp and R. Raja (eds), *The World of Palmyra*, Scientia Danica, Series H, Humanistica, 4.6 (Copenhagen: The Royal Danish Academy of Sciences and Letters), pp. 31–41.

Hekster, O. 2008. *Rome and its Empire, AD 193–284* (Edinburgh: Edinburgh University Press).

Henning, A. 2013. *Die Turmgräber von Palmyra: Eine lokale Bauform im kaiserzeitlichen Syrien als Ausdruck kultureller Identität*, Orient-Archäologie, 29 (Rahden: Leidorf).

—— 2019. 'The Representation of Matrimony in the Tower Tombs of Palmyra', in S. Krag and R. Raja (eds), *Women, Children and the Family in Palmyra*, Palmyrene Studies, 3, Scientia Danica, H, Humanistica, 4.10 (Copenhagen: The Royal Danish Academy of Sciences and Letters), pp. 19–37.

Heyn, M. K. 2010. 'Gesture and Identity in the Funerary Art of Palmyra', *American Journal of Archaeology*, 114: 631–61.

—— 2012. 'Female Portraiture in Palmyra', in S. L. James and S. Dillon (eds), *A Companion to Women in the Ancient World* (Chichester: Wiley-Blackwell), pp. 439–41.

—— 2019. 'Valuable Impressions of Women in Palmyra', in A. M. Nielsen and R. Raja (eds), *The Road to Palmyra* (Copenhagen: Ny Carlsberg Glyptotek), pp. 175–92.

—— 2021. 'The Significance of the Drinking Attributes in Palmyrene Banquet Scenes', in M K. Heyn and R. Raja (eds), *Individualizing the Dead: Attributes in Palmyrene Funerary Sculpture*, Studies in Palmyrene Archaeology and History, 3 (Turnhout: Brepols), pp. 63–74.

Ingholt Archives <https://doi.org/10.6084/m9.figshare.c.5509725.v1>.

Ingholt, H. 1928. *Studier over Palmyrensk Skulptur* (Copenhagen: Reitzel).

Kaizer, T. 2002. *The Religious Life of Palmyra: A Study of the Social Patterns of Worship in the Roman Period* (Stuttgart: Steiner).

—— 2018. '"Ich bin ein Palmyrener" or "Je suis Tadmor": On How to Be a Proper Citizen of the Queen of the Desert', in J. Aruz (ed.), *Palmyra: Mirage in the Desert* (New York: Yale University Press), pp. 76–89.

—— 2019. 'Family Connections and Religious Life at Palmyra', in S. Krag and R. Raja (eds), *Women, Children, and the Family in Palmyra*, Palmyrene Studies, 3, Scientia Danica, H, Humanistica, 4.10 (Copenhagen: The Royal Danish Academy of Sciences and Letters), pp. 82–94.

Klaver, S. 2019. 'The Participation of Palmyrene Women in the Religious Life of the City', in S. Krag and R. Raja (eds), *Women, Children, and the Family in Palmyra*, Palmyrene Studies, 3, Scientia Danica, H, Humanistica, 4.10 (Copenhagen: The Royal Danish Academy of Sciences and Letters), pp. 157–67.

Krag, S. 2016. 'Females in Group Portraits in Palmyra', in A. Kropp and R. Raja (eds), *The World of Palmyra*, Scientia Danica, Series H, Humanistica, 4.6 (Copenhagen: The Royal Danish Academy of Sciences and Letters), pp. 180–93.

—— 2017a. 'Changing Identities, Changing Positions: Jewellery in Palmyrene Female Portraits', in T. Long and A. H. Sørensen (eds), *Positions and Professions in Palmyra*, Scientia Danica, Series H, Humanistica, 4.9 (Copenhagen: The Royal Academy of Sciences and Letters), pp. 36–51.

—— 2017b. 'Women in Palmyra', in R. Raja (ed.), *Palmyra: Pearl of the Desert* (Aarhus, SUN-Tryk), pp. 56–66.

—— 2018. *Funerary Representations of Palmyrene Women: From the First Century BC to the Third Century AD*, Studies in Classical Archaeology, 3 (Turnhout: Brepols).

Krag, S. and R. Raja. 2016. 'Representations of Women and Children in Palmyrene Funerary Loculus Reliefs, Loculus Stelae and Wall Paintings', *Zeitschrift für Orient-Archäologie*, 9: 134–78.

—— 2017. 'Representations of Women and Children in Palmyrene Banqueting Reliefs and Sarcophagus Scenes', *Zeitschrift für Orient-Archäologie*, 10: 196–227.

—— 2018. 'Unveiling Female Hairstyles: Markers of Age, Social Roles, and Status in Funerary Sculpture from Palmyra', *Zeitschrift für Orient-Archäologie*, 11: 242–77.

—— 2019a. 'Families in Palmyra: The Evidence from the First Three Centuries CE', in S. Krag and R. Raja (eds), *Women, Children and the Family in Palmyra*, Palmyrene Studies, 3, Scientia Danica, H, Humanistica, 4.10 (Copenhagen: Royal Academy of Sciences and Letters), pp. 7–18.

—— (eds). 2019b. *Women, Children and the Family in Palmyra*, Palmyrene Studies, 3, Scientia Danica, H, Humanistica, 4.10 (Copenhagen: The Royal Danish Academy of Sciences and Letters).

Mackay, D. 1949. 'The Jewellery of Palmyra and its Significance', *Iraq*, 11: 160–87.

Makowski, K. C. 1983. 'Recherches sur le tombeau de Aʿailamî et Zebîdâ', *Damaszener Mitteilungem*, 1: 175–87.
—— 1985a. 'La sculpture funéraire Palmyrénienne et sa fonction dans l'architecture sépulcrale', *Studia Palmyrenskie*, 8: 69–117.
—— 1985b. 'Recherches sur le banquet miniaturisé dans l'art funéraire de Palmyre', *Studia Palmyrenskie*, 8: 119–30.
Michalowski, K. 1962. *Palmyre*, II: *Fouilles Polonaise 1960* (Warsaw: Państwowe Wydawnictwo Naukowe).
Milik, J. T. 1972. *Dédicaces faites par des Dieux (Palmyre, Hatra, Tyr) et des thiases sémitiques à l'époque romaine* (Paris: Geuthner).
Miyashita, S. 2016. 'The Vessels in Palmyrene Banquet Scenes: Tomb BWLH and BWRP amd Tomb TYBL', in J. C. Meyer, E. H. Seland, and N. Anfinset (eds), *Palmyrena: City, Hinterland and Caravan Trade between Orient and Occident; Proceedings of the Conference Held in Athens, December 1–3, 2012* (Oxford: Archaeopress), pp. 131–46.
Musée Impérial Ottoman. 1895. *Antiquités himyarites et palmyréniennes: catalogue sommaire* (Constantinople: Musée Impérial Ottoman).
Parlasca, K. 1981. *Syrische Grabreliefs hellenistischer und römischer Zeit: Fundgruppen und Probleme* (Mainz: Von Zabern).
—— 1982. 'Römische Kunst in Syrien', in K. Kohlmeyer and E. Strommenger (eds), *Land des Baal: Syrien, Forum der Völker und Kulturen* (Mainz: Von Zabern), pp. 186–226.
—— 1985a. 'Das Verhältnis der palmyrenischen Grabplastik zur römischen Porträtkunst', *Mitteilungen des Deutschen Archäologischen Instituts: Römische Abteilung*, 92: 343–56.
—— 1985b. 'Roman Art in Syria', in H. Weiss (ed.), *Ebla to Damascus: Art and Archaeology of Ancient Syria; An Exhibition from the Directorate-General of Antiquities and Museums, Syrian Arab Republic* (Washington, DC: Smithsonian Institution Traveling Exhibition Service), pp. 386–415.
—— 1998. 'Palmyrenische Sarkophage mit Totenmahlreliefs: Forschungsstand und ikonographische Probleme', *Sarkophag-Studien*, 1: 311–20.
—— 1990. 'Römische Elemente in der Grabkunst Palmyras', in F. Zayadine (ed.), *Petra and the Caravan Cities: Proceedings of the Symposium Organised at Petra in September 1985* (Amman: Department of Antiquities of Jordan), pp. 191–96.
Raja, R. 2015a. 'Cultic Dining and Religious Patterns in Palmyra: The Case of the Palmyrene Banqueting Tesserae', in S. Faust, M. Seifert, and L. Ziemer (eds), *Antike. Architektur. Geschichte: Festschrift für Inge Nielsen zum 65. Geburtstag* (Aachen: Shaker), pp. 181–200.
—— 2015b. 'Staging "Private" Religion in Roman "Public" Palmyra: The Role of the Religious Dining Tickets (Banqueting Tesserae)', in C. Ando and J. Rüpke (eds), *Public and Private in Ancient Mediterranean Law and Religion* (Berlin: De Gruyter), pp. 165–86.
—— 2016a. 'In and Out of Contexts: Explaining Religious Complexity through the Banqueting Tesserae from Palmyra', *Religion in the Roman Empire*, 2: 340–71.
—— 2016b. 'Representations of Priests in Palmyra: Methodological Considerations on the Meaning of the Representation of Priesthood in Roman Period Palmyra', *Religion in the Roman Empire*, 2: 125–46.
—— 2017a. 'You Can Leave your Hat on: Priestly Representations from Palmyra – Between Visual Genre, Religious Importance and Social Status', in R. L. Gordon, G. Petridou, and J. Rüpke (eds), *Beyond Priesthood: Religious Entrepreneurs and Innovators in the Imperial Era* (Berlin: De Gruyter), pp. 417–42.
—— 2017b. 'To Be or Not to Be Depicted as a Priest in Palmyra: A Matter of Representational Spheres and Societal Values', in T. Long and A. H. Sørensen (eds), *Positions and Professions in Palmyra*, Scientia Danica, Series H, Humanistica, 4.9 (Copenhagen: The Royal Academy of Sciences and Letters), pp. 115–30.
—— 2017c. 'Networking beyond Death: Priests and their Family Networks in Palmyra Explored through the Funerary Sculpture', in E. H. Seland and H. F. Teigen (eds), *Sinews of Empire: Networks in the Roman Near East and Beyond* (Oxford: Oxbow), pp. 121–36.
—— 2017d. 'Priesthood in Palmyra: Public Office or Social Status?', in R. Raja (ed.), *Palmyra: Pearl of the Desert* (Aarhus: SUN-Tryk), pp. 77–85.
—— 2017e. 'Between Fashion Phenomena and Status Symbols: Contextualising the Dress of the So-Called "Former Priests" of Palmyra', in C. Brøns and M.-L. Nosch (eds), *Textiles and Cult in the Mediterranean Area in the 1st Millennium BC* (Oxford: Oxbow), pp. 209–29.
—— 2017f. 'Representations of the So-Called "Former Priests" in Palmyrene Funerary Art: A Methodological Contribution and Commentary', *Topoi: Orient et Occident*, 21: 51–81.
—— 2018a. 'The Matter of the Palmyrene "Modius": Remarks on the History of Research of the Terminology of the Palmyrene Priestly Hat', *Religion in the Roman Empire*, 4: 237–59.
—— 2019a. 'Funerary Portraiture in Palmyra: Portrait Habit at a Crossroads or a Signifier of Local Identity?', in M. Blömer and R. Raja (eds), *Funerary Portraiture in Greater Roman Syria*, Studies in Classical Archaeology, 6 (Turnhout: Brepols), pp. 95–110.
—— 2019b. 'Family Matters: Family Constellations in Palmyrene Funerary Sculpture', in K. Bøggild Johannsen and J. H. Petersen (eds), *Family Lives: Aspects of Life and Death in Ancient Families* (Copenhagen: Museum Tusculanum), pp. 245–70.
—— 2019c. 'Stacking Aesthetics in the Syrian Desert: Displaying Palmyrene Sculpture in the Public and Funerary Sphere', in C. M. Draycott and others (eds), *Visual Histories of the Classical World: Essays in Honour of R. R. R. Smith*, Studies in Classical Archaeology, 4 (Turnhout: Brepols), pp. 281–98.

——2019d. 'Portrait Habit in Palmyra', in A. M. Nielsen and R. Raja (eds), *The Road to Palmyra* (Copenhagen: Ny Carlsberg Glyptotek), pp. 137–54.
——2019e. *The Palmyra Collection* (Copenhagen: Ny Carlsberg Glyptotek).
——2019 f. 'Religious Banquets in Palmyra and the Palmyrene Banqueting Tesserae', in A. M. Nielsen and R. Raja (eds), *The Road to Palmyra* (Copenhagen: Ny Carlsberg Glyptotek), pp. 221–34.
——2019g. 'Reconsidering the *dorsalium* or "Curtain of Death" in Palmyrene Funerary Sculpture: Significance and Interpretations in Light of the Palmyra Portrait Project Corpus', in R. Raja (ed.), *Revisiting the Religious Life of Palmyra*, Contextualizing the Sacred, 9 (Turnhout: Brepols), pp. 67–151.
——2019h. 'It Stays in the Family: Palmyrene Priestly Representations and their Constellations', in S. Krag and R. Raja (eds), *Women, Children and the Family in Palmyra*, Palmyrene Studies, 3, Scientia Danica, H, Humanistica, 4.10 (Copenhagen: The Royal Danish Academy of Sciences and Letters), pp. 95–156.
——2019i. 'Dining with the Gods and the Others: The Banqueting Tickets from Palmyra as Expressions of Religious Individuality', in M. Fuchs and others (eds), *Religious Individualization: Historical Dimensions and Comparative Perspectives* (Berlin: De Gruyter), pp. 243–56.
——2020. 'Come and Dine with Us: Invitations to Ritual Dining as Part of Social Strategies in Sacred Spaces in Palmyra', in V. Gasparini and others (eds), *Lived Ancient Religion* (Berlin: De Gruyter), pp. 385–404.
——2021a. 'Adornment and Jewellery as a Status Symbol in Priestly Representations in Roman Palmyra: The Palmyrene Priests and their Brooches', in M. K. Heyn and R. Raja (eds), *Individualizing the Dead: Attributes in Palmyrene Funerary Sculpture*, Studies in Palmyrene Archaeology and History, 3 (Turnhout: Brepols), pp. 75–118.
——2021b. 'Negotiating Social and Cultural Interaction through Priesthoods: The Iconography of Priesthood in Palmyra', in J. Hoffman-Salz (ed.), *The Middle East as Middle Ground? Cultural Interaction in the Ancient Middle East Revisited* (Vienna: Holzhausen), pp. 129–46.
Raja, R., O. Bobou, and I. Romanowska. 2021. 'Three Hundred Years of Palmyrene History: Unlocking Archaeological Data for Studying Past Societal Transformations', *PlosOne*, 16.11: e0256081 <doi.org/10.1371/journal.pone.0256081>.
Raja, R. and J.-B. Yon (forthcoming). 'Palmyrene Funerary Sculptural Representations with Greek, Latin and Bilingual Inscriptions', *Zeitschrift für Orientarchäologie*.
Ringsborg, S. 2017. 'Children's Portraits from Palmyra', in R. Raja (ed.), *Palmyra: Pearl of the Desert* (Aarhus: SUN-Tryk), pp. 66–75.
Romanowska, I., O. Bobou, and R. Raja. 2021. 'Reconstructing the Social, Economic and Demographic Trends of Palmyra's Elite from Funerary Data', *Journal of Archaeological Science*, 133: 105432.
Rumscheid, J. 2000. *Kranz und Krone: Zu Insignien, Siegespreisen und Ehrenzeichen der römischen Kaiserzeit*, Istanbuler Forschungen, 43 (Tübingen: Wasmuth).
Sartre-Fauriat, A. 2019. 'The Discovery and Reception of Palmyra', in A. M. Nielsen and R. Raja (eds), *The Road to Palmyra* (Copenhagen: Ny Carlsberg Glyptotek), pp. 65–76.
Sartre-Fauriat, A. and M. Sartre. 2008. *Palmyre: La cité des caravanes* (Paris: Gallimard).
Schmidt-Colinet, A. 1992. *Das Tempelgrab Nr. 36 in Palmyra: Studien zur Palmyrenischen Grabarchitektur und ihrer Ausstattung*, 2 vols (Mainz: Von Zabern).
—— 1996. 'Antike Denkmäler in Syrien. Die Stichvorlagen von Louis François Cassas (1756–1827) in Wallraf-Richartz-Museum in Köln', *Kölner Jahrbuch*, 29: 343–548.
—— 1997. 'Aspects of "Romanization": The Tomb Architecture of Palmyra and its Decoration', in S. E. Alcock (ed.), *The Early Roman Empire in the East* (Oxford: Oxbow), pp. 157–77.
—— 2003. *Lokale Identitäten in Randgebieten des Römischen Reich: Akten des internationalen Symposiums in Wiener Neustadt, 24. – 26. April 2003*, Wiener Forschungen zur Archäologie, 7 (Vienna: Phoibos).
—— 2004. 'Palmyrenische Grabkunst als Ausdruck lokaler Identität(en): Fallbeispiele', in A. Schmidt-Colinet (ed.), *Lokale Identitäten in Randgebieten des Römischen Reiches* (Vienna: Phoibos), pp. 189–97.
—— 2009. 'Nochmal zur Ikonographie zweier palmyrenischen Sarkophage', in M. Blömer, M. Facella, and E. Winter (eds), *Lokale Identität im römischen Nahen Osten: Kontexte und Perspektiven* (Stuttgart: Steiner), pp. 223–34, Abb. 221–14.
Schmidt-Colinet, A. and K. Asʿad. 2007. 'Zwei Neufunde Palmyrenischer Sarkophage', in G. Koch (ed.), *Symposium des Sarkophag-Corpus, Marburg 2001*, Sarkophag-Studien, 3 (Mainz: Von Zabern), pp. 271–78.
Seyrig, H. 1951. 'Le repas des morts et le "banquets funèbre" à Palmyre', *Annales archéologiques arabes syriennes*, 1: 32–40.
Simonsen, D. 1889. *Sculptures et inscriptions de Palmyre à la Glyptothèque de Ny Carlsberg* (Copenhagen: Lind).
—— 1889. *Skulpturer og Indskrifter fra Palmyra i Ny Carlsberg Glyptotek* (Copenhagen: Lind).
Sommer, M. 2005. *Roms orientalische Steppengrenze: Palmyra – Edessa – Dura-Europos – Hatra; Eine Kulturgeschichte von Pompeius bis Diocletian*, Oriens et Occidens, 9 (Stuttgart: Steiner).
—— 2017. *Palmyra: Biographie einer verlorenen Stadt* (Darmstadt: Von Zabern).
—— 2018. *Palmyra: A History*, Cities of the Ancient World (Abingdon: Routledge).
Starcky, J. 1941. 'Palmyre: Guide archéologique', *Mélanges de l'Université Saint-Joseph, Beyrouth*, 24: 5–68.

Tanabe, K. (ed.). 1986. *Sculptures of Palmyra*, I, Memoirs of the Ancient Orient Museum, 1 (Tokyo: Ancient Orient Museum).

Thomsen, R. R. 2021. 'Unlocking a Mystery? The Keys in Palmyrene Funerary Portraiture', in M. K. Heyn and R. Raja (eds), *Individualizing the Dead: Attributes in Palmyrene Funerary Sculpture*, Studies in Palmyrene Archaeology and History, 3 (Turnhout: Brepols), pp. 51–63.

Tokyo National Museum. 1977. *The Exhibition of Treasures of Syrian Antiquity* (Tokyo: Tokyo National Museum).

Watzinger, C. and K. Wulzinger. 1932. 'Die Nekropolen', in T. Wiegand (ed.), *Palmyra: Ergebnisse der Expeditionen von 1902 und 1917* (Berlin: Keller), pp. 44–76.

Weber, T. 2015. 'The Near East', in E. A. Friedland, M. Grunow Sobocinski, and E. K. Gazda (eds), *The Oxford Handbook of Roman Sculpture* (Oxford: Oxford University Press), pp. 569–87.

Wielgosz, D. 1997. 'Funeralia Palmyrena', *Studia Palmyrénskie*, 10: 69–75.

Wielgosz-Rondolino, D. 2016. 'Orient et Occident unis par enchantement dans la pierre sculptée: la sculpture figurative de Palmyre', in M. Al-Maqdissi and E. Ishaq (eds), *La Syrie et le désastre archéologique du Proche-Orient: Palmyre citée martyre* (Beirut: Beiteddine Art Festival), pp. 65–82.

Wood, R. 1753. *The Ruins of Palmyra: Otherwise Tedmor in the Desart* (London: Robert Wood).

Yon, J.-B. 2001. 'Stèle funéraire de Malê et Bôlayâ', in J. Charles-Gaffiot, H. Lavagne, and J.-M. Hofman (eds), *Moi, Zénobie reine de Palmyre* (Milan: Skira), pp. 367–68.

—— 2002. *Les notables de Palmyre* (Beirut: Institut français du Proche-Orient).

—— 2012. *Inscriptions grecques et latines de la Syrie*, XVII.1: *Palmyre* (Beirut: Institut français du Proche Orient).

Zahran, Y. 2004. 'Zenobia between Reality and Legend', *Minerva*, 15: 29–32.

Catalogue of the Thirteen Objects Representing Reclining Women in Palmyrene Funerary Art Collected in the Database of the Palmyra Portrait Project

1–8: Women reclining on sarcophagi lids
9: Woman depicted reclining on short side of sarcophagus
10–13: Banqueting reliefs

Cat. No. 1: Sarcophagus lid with banqueting scene

LOCATION: Palmyra Museum, Palmyra, inv. no. —

CONTEXT: West necropolis. Valley of the Tombs. Temple/house tomb no. 85b, Tomb of Aʿailamî and Zebidâ ('Tomb Cantineau').

ACQUISITION HISTORY: —

MEASUREMENTS: Height: 85 cm.

MATERIAL: Limestone, white.

PRESERVATION: All sides are chipped. Portrait A: The upper part is broken off at the base of the neck and at the left wrist. The right arm is chipped. Portrait B: The upper part is broken off at the base of the neck. Heavily chipped and weathered. Portrait C: The upper part is broken off at the base of the neck. Heavily chipped and weathered. Portrait D: The upper part is broken off horizontally across the shoulders. The left arm is broken off. The surface of the chest is chipped. Portrait E: The head is broken off at the base of the neck.

DATE: AD 170–190.

REFERENCES: Ingholt Archives, PS 529A; Cantineau 1929, pl. 2, figs 1.6, 3; Makowski 1983, 186, cat. no. 1, pl. 49, b; Krag 2018, 32 n. 62, 58 n. 304, 62 n. 353, 63 n. 354, 64 n. 361–62, 65 n. 375, n. 378, 66 n. 382, 88 n. 193, n. 195, 89 n. 203, 397, cat. no. 858. Inscription: Cantineau 1930, 38–40, cat. no. 14; Milik 1972, 250; Yon 2012, 333–34, cat. no. 434.

INSCRIPTION:

Script: Ancient Greek. **Location on relief:** On the base of the relief. The location of the inscription is according to Cantineau 1930. According to Makowski (1983) the following inscription belongs to the relief.

[Βωλανος Ζ]ηνοβίου [τοῦ Αιρανοῦ τ]οῦ Μοκιμου τοῦ Μαθθα ΑΚ[-- αἱρεθεὶ]ς συνποσιάρχης ἱερέων [... Δι]ὸς Βή[λου καὶ ---] [---]ς αὐτῷ[--- ἀδε]λφὴ [τοῦ?] Μουκιανοῦ κ[αὶ ---] Καλλίστη θυγάτηρ Ηρ[---] ΥΜΟΥ [---].

Bôlanos son of Zenobios son of Airanes son of Mokimos son of Mattha - - - chosen as symposiarches of the priests of Zeus Belos and - - - for him - - - sister of Mucianus and - - - Kalliste the daughter - - -.

PORTRAIT A – Seated female: The figure is shown in three-quarter view. The right arm is bent and rests on her right thigh. The left arm is raised to the neck. Her legs are bent and the knees are rendered under the drapery. Her feet are obscured by the reclining figure to her left. She wears a veil that is wrapped around her right shoulder. She wears a necklace with a central, rectangular pendant below the collarbone. She wears a tunic and a himation. The folds of the tunic are indicated with oblique grooves. The himation crosses the chest diagonally from the left shoulder to the right side, and covers the left breast. It is fastened with a brooch on her left shoulder (details unclear). The folds of the himation are rendered by curving grooves. With the right hand, she holds a fold, possibly the edge of the veil. The left hand is raised to the height of the neck.

PORTRAIT B – Standing figure: The figure is shown frontally. They are wearing a garment (other details unclear).

PORTRAIT C – Standing figure: The figure is shown frontally. They are wearing a garment (other details unclear).

PORTRAIT D – Reclining female: The figure is shown in three-quarter view. The right arm is extended and rests on his right knee. The outline of the left arm is visible and she holds the arm in front of the chest. The right leg is bent, but the foot is obscured by the left leg. The left leg is slightly bent and the foot is seen in frontal view. She wears a veil. It falls over the right shoulder. She wears three necklaces. The first is worn below the collarbone. It has a wide oval central decoration with an incised border. Its centre is oval-shaped and raised. The second is worn over the breasts. It is composed of a wide hoop and has a crescent-shaped pendant at the centre suspended by a wide sleeve. Below that she wears a necklace composed of a thick chain with a central oval decoration with a beaded border. Rectangular elements are suspended under the pendant. She wears a tunic and a himation. The tunic has short, wide sleeves that fall to the elbows. The folds of the tunic are rendered by curving grooves. Over the tunic she wears a himation that is wrapped under the breasts and covers the body. Part of the himation falls over the cushion in two zigzag-shaped folds. With her right hand, she holds a round object, possibly a fruit. She wears a wide, thick hoop bracelet at the wrist.

PORTRAIT E – Reclining male: The figure is shown in three-quarter view. The arms appear short in relation to the body. The right arm is bent and held to the torso. The left arm is bent in front of the chest. His legs are obscured by the reclining figure to his right. He wears a tunic and a chlamys. The tunic is long sleeved. The folds of the tunic are rendered by curving grooves. Over the tunic, he wears a chlamys that falls over the left shoulder, and covers most of the chest. It is folded around his left arm. A wide fold falls from under the arm along his left side and over the cushions. His right hand rests on his stomach, the index and the little finger are extended. He holds a bowl in his left hand. The index and the little finger are extended.

Cat. No. 2: Sarcophagus lid with banqueting scene

LOCATION: Palmyra Museum, Palmyra, inv. no. —

CONTEXT: West necropolis. Valley of the Tombs. Temple/house tomb no. 85b, Tomb of Aʿailamî and Zebidâ ('Tomb Cantineau').

ACQUISITION HISTORY: —

MEASUREMENTS: Height: 88 cm. Depth: 40 cm. Depth: 19 cm.

MATERIAL: Limestone, white/yellow.

PRESERVATION: The head is broken off horizontally at the base of the neck, the lower part is broken off vertically at the lower part of the legs. The right arm and left lower arm are broken off. The knees are chipped. Multiple cracks run through the figure.

DATE: AD 170–190.

REFERENCES: Ingholt Archives, PS 529A; Makowski 1983, 186, cat. no. 2, pl. 50, a; Schmidt-Colinet 1992, 110 n. 404c, n. 477, pl. 72.a; Krag 2018, 56 n. 290, 58 n. 304, 59 n. 325, 62 n. 353, 64 ns 361–62, 65 n. 374, 384, cat. no. 821. Inscription: Cantineau 1930, 38, cat. no. 13; Milik 1972, 250; Yon 2012, 332–33, cat. no. 432; Krag 2018, 384, cat. no. 821.

OBJECT DESCRIPTION: The object depicts a reclining female. She rests on a thin mattress. The mattress is decorated with an intersecting lozenges pattern with flowers represented in the lozenges. She rests the left arm against two cushions. The cushions are decorated with bands decorated with vegetal motifs set between beaded bands. Curving grooves indicate the texture of the fabric.

INSCRIPTION 1:

Script: Ancient Greek. **Location on relief:** On the edges of the mattress.

[---κ]αὶ Αμαθαης Μουκιανοῦ σύνβιος αὐτοῦ καὶ Βωλ[ανος---]

[---] Amathaes, daughter of Mukianus, her husband and Bolanos [their son?]

CIS no.: —; **PAT no.:** —. According to Milik (1972) this inscription joins with Cantineau 1930, 38, cat. no. 19 (Yon 2012, 332–33, cat. no. 433).

PORTRAIT: The female figure is shown in frontal to three-quarter view. The left arm is bent and raised to the neck. The left leg is bent under the right leg. She wears a veil, which is wrapped around her left shoulder and falls over the back of her right shoulder. A wavy lock of hair falls down the right side of her neck and shoulder. She wears four necklaces. The first is composed of small, round beads, worn at the base of the neck. The second is composed of alternating round and square pendants with beaded borders linked by beaded elements, worn high on the chest. The third is composed of round beads and a central crescent-shaped pendant, worn on the chest. The fourth is composed of a double loop-in-loop chain with a central oval pendant with a beaded border. Three spirally wrapped wires with trefoil-shaped beads at the ends are suspended from the oval pendant. It is hanging low below her chest.

She wears a tunic and a himation. The tunic has a small, round neckline. The folds of the tunic are rendered by curving and oblique grooves. Over the tunic, she wears a himation. It is folded from behind and falls vertically across the torso in a fold with a scalloped edge. The himation is folded around her left arm. Two s-shaped folds fall from under her left arm and proceed downwards at her left side. The himation is rendered as resembling a toga. The folds of the himation are rendered by curving and vertical grooves. The left arm is bent to the chest. She wears a bracelet on her wrist (details unclear).

Cat. No. 3: Sarcophagus lid with banqueting scene

LOCATION: Palmyra, in situ.

CONTEXT: West necropolis. Valley of the Tombs. Temple/house tomb no. 85b, Tomb of Aʿailamî and Zebidâ ('Tomb Cantineau').

ACQUISITION HISTORY: —

MEASUREMENTS: —

MATERIAL: Limestone.

PRESERVATION: The head is broken off at the base of the neck, and the lower part is broken off at the waist. Both arms are broken off.

DATE: AD 180–240.

REFERENCES: Ingholt Archives PS 881; Starcky 1941, 36, fig. 29; Makowski 1983, 186, cat. no. 2, pl. 50, fig. b; Schmidt-Colinet 1992, 110 n. 404c, 120 n. 440d, pl. 72.c; Krag 2018, 56 n. 290, 58 n. 304, 62 n. 353, 64 ns 361–62, 65 n. 374, 102 n. 69, 384, cat. no. 822. Inscription: Cantineau 1930, 41, cat. no. 17; Krag 2018, 384, cat. no. 822.

OBJECT DESCRIPTION: The object depicts a reclining female. She rests the left arm against a cushion. It is decorated with a band with a vegetal motif set between beaded bands.

INSCRIPTION 1:

Script: Palmyrene Aramaic. **Location on relief:** On the garment.

[......] nwr/d zbyd'|byr/d [......]

[......] | ...Zebîdâ |... [......]

CIS no.:: —; **PAT no.:** Inv 4 9e.

PORTRAIT: The figure is shown frontally. The left arm is bent. She wears a veil. It is wrapped around her left lower arm and falls back over the right shoulder. Two wavy locks of hair fall down the right side of the neck and shoulder. The individual strands of hair are rendered by incised lines. She wears five necklaces: one composed of round beads worn at the base of the neck. One composed of a thin loop-in-loop chain with a central, circular pendant with an incised border, worn high on the chest. One composed of round beads with a central, oval pendant with a beaded border, where three spirally wrapped wires ending in round beads are suspended from the pendant. This is worn below the chest. Two necklaces composed of round beads and round pendants decorated with armless busts encircled by beaded edges are worn low on the chest and the pendants are placed at the sides, below each breast. She wears a tunic and a himation. The tunic has a small, v-shaped neckline and short, wide sleeves. The folds of the tunic are rendered by curving and oblique grooves. Over the tunic, she wears a himation that crosses her chest in a curving fold from the right shoulder to the left side and covers the left breast. It is fastened at the left shoulder with a circular brooch with a polygon with curved sides meeting at flat ends, and an inner beaded border. Three s-shaped folds fall from under her left arm and proceed downwards. The folds of the himation are rendered by curving and oblique grooves. She wears an armlet on her right upper arm. It is composed of two entwining wires and is decorated with a large round element.

Cat. no. 4: Sarcophagus lid with banqueting scene

LOCATION: Palmyra, in situ.

CONTEXT: West necropolis. Valley of the Tombs. Temple/house tomb no. 85b, Tomb of Aʿailamî and Zebîdâ ('Tomb Cantineau').

ACQUISITION HISTORY: —

MEASUREMENTS: Height: 61 cm. Width: 100 cm. Depth: 28 cm.

MATERIAL: Limestone.

PRESERVATION: The upper part is broken off at the waist and the feet are broken off. The right hand and the lower left corner of the mattress are chipped.

DATE: AD 180–240.

REFERENCES: Cantineau 1929, 12, pl. 2.2, pl. 3.2; Makowski 1983, 186, cat. no. 3, pl. 50.c; Krag 2018, 58 n. 304, 62 n. 353, 64 ns 361–62, 65 n. 374, 88 n. 193, n. 195, 384, cat. no. 819. Inscription: Cantineau 1930, 41, cat. no. 17; Krag 2018, 384, cat. no. 819.

OBJECT DESCRIPTION: The object depicts a reclining female. The figure rests on a thin mattress decorated with an intersecting lozenges pattern with four-petal flowers in the lozenges. The left side of the mattress is decorated with a wide band with a vegetal motif between beaded bands.

INSCRIPTION:
Script: Palmyrene Aramaic. Location on relief: On the folds of the garment.

[......]NWR/D ZBYDʾ
BYR/D[...]

[......]NWR/D Zebîdâ
BYR/D[...]

CIS no.: —; **PAT no.:** —.

PORTRAIT – Zebîdâ: The legs are bent and the knees are rendered under the drapery. The figure wears a himation that covers his legs. The folds are rendered by curving and oblique folds.

Cat. no. 5: Sarcophagus lid with banqueting scene

LOCATION: Palmyra Museum, Palmyra, inv. no. —

CONTEXT: West necropolis. Valley of the Tombs. Tower tomb no. 13, Tower of Elahbel.

ACQUISITION HISTORY: —

MEASUREMENTS: Height: 76 cm. Width: 130 cm. Depth: 28 cm.

MATERIAL: Limestone.

PRESERVATION: The head is broken off at the base of the neck and the lower part of the figure is broken off below the knees. A large crack is running vertically at the waist. The surface is weathered.

DATE: AD 200–220.

REFERENCES: Makowski 1983, 181 n. 22; Schmidt-Colinet 1992, 110; 1996, 471, fig. 188; Henning 2013, 305–06, cat. S 44, pl. 26, b; Krag 2018, 49 n. 229, 64 ns 361–62, 65 n. 374, 98 n. 28, 103 n. 75, 314, cat. no. 557.

OBJECT DESCRIPTION: The object shows a reclining figure. The figure lies on a mattress decorated with a floral motif, and rests the left arm on two cushions. Each of the cushions has a band decorated with floral motif set between beaded bands. Curving grooves indicate the texture of the fabric.

PORTRAIT: The figure is shown in frontal to three-quarter view. The arms appear short in relation to the body. The right arm is slightly bent and held along the body. The left arm is bent and rests along her side. She wears a tunic and a himation. The tunic has a wide, v-shaped neckline and short, wide sleeves that reach to the elbow. The tunic covers her torso. The folds of the tunic are indicated by curving grooves. Over the tunic, she wears a himation. It is wrapped around her left shoulder and arm, leaving the chest and the hand free. It falls along the left side of his torso where it is folded over the tunic, across her waist and legs. A zigzag-shaped fold falls from under her left hand. The folds of the himation are indicated by curving and oblique grooves. She holds a branch with her right hand. The individual leaves are rendered by incised lines. She holds a fold of the himation with her left hand.

Cat. No. 6: Sarcophagus lid with banqueting scene

LOCATION: Palmyra, in situ.

CONTEXT: North-west necropolis. Temple tomb no. 159.

ACQUISITION HISTORY: —

MEASUREMENTS: —

MATERIAL: Limestone, white/yellow.

PRESERVATION: The head is broken off at the base of the neck, and the lower part is broken off at the waist. Both the right and left lower arm is broken off. The surface is very fragmented.

DATE: AD 220–240.

REFERENCES: Watzinger and Wulzinger 1932, 65; Schmidt-Colinet 1992, 110 n. 404 e, pl. 72.e, Henning 2013, 272; Krag 2018, 58 n. 304, 62 n. 353, 64 ns 361–62, 65 n. 374, 384, cat. no. 823.

OBJECT DESCRIPTION: The object depicts a reclining female. She rests the left arm against a cushion. It is decorated with a band with a vegetal motif between beaded bands. Curving grooves indicate the texture of the fabric.

PORTRAIT: The figure is shown frontally. The left arm is bent and raised to the neck. She wears a veil. It falls over her shoulders. She wears three necklaces. The first is composed of a thin loop-in-loop chain with a central pendant worn low on the neck. The second is composed of round beads and a central, crescent-shaped pendant, worn on the chest. The third is composed of a loop-in-loop chain with a central, oval pendant, worn at the chest. She wears a tunic and a himation. The tunic has a small, v-shaped neckline. The folds of the tunic are rendered by curving and oblique grooves. Over the tunic, she wears a himation. It is folded from behind and across the torso in a curving fold that is wrapped around her left arm. The folds of the himation are rendered by curving and vertical grooves.

Cat. No. 7: Complete sarcophagus with banqueting scene and portrait busts

LOCATION: Palmyra Museum, Palmyra, inv. no. —

CONTEXT: South-east necropolis. Temple/house tomb no. 186 ('Tombeau de l'aviation'/'Tomb Duvaux').

ACQUISITION HISTORY: —

MEASUREMENTS: —

MATERIAL: Limestone.

PRESERVATION: The surface of the sarcophagus is weathered. The upper part of the sarcophagus is broken off. The upper right side and the lower right side of the sarcophagus box are chipped. Portrait A: The head is broken off horizontally at the base of the neck. The surface around the abdomen, right and left arm, and knees are chipped. Portrait B: The head is broken off horizontally at the base of the neck. The right arm has broken off. The tip of the left foot has broken off. The surface of the right leg is chipped. Portrait C: The head is broken off horizontally at the base of the neck. The surface of the lower left arm and attribute is chipped. A large crack runs diagonally from the right side of the neck and through the right arm. Portrait D: The head of the figure is chipped. Portrait E: The head of the figure is chipped. Portrait F: The head of the figure is chipped. Portrait G: The head of the figure is chipped.

DATE: AD 220–240.

REFERENCES: Watzinger and Wulzinger 1932, 70, figs 68–69; Schmidt-Colinet 1992, 107, n. 380g.2, n. 383b, 108 n. 389, 110 n. 403, n. 404d, 121 n. 440g, 125 n. 473, n. 476, 130 n. 479, 135 n. 517, pls 72.d, 73.b; Krag and Raja 2017, 199 n. 24, 204 ns 72–73, 205 n. 75, 207 n. 94, 209 n. 100, 212 n. 126, 220, cat. no. 37; Krag 2018, 28 n. 9, 32 n. 63, 45 n. 193, 46 n. 194, n. 196, 53 n. 258, 58 ns 300–01, 303, n. 307, 59 n. 323, n. 325, 61 n. 334, 62 n. 349, ns 351–53, 63 n. 354, 64 ns 361–62, 65 ns 375–76, n. 379, 66 ns 381–82, 84 n. 304, 89 n. 203, 101 n. 54, 102 n. 69, 103 n. 74, 105 n. 95, 394–95, cat. no. 852.

OBJECT DESCRIPTION: The sarcophagus lid is rectangular in shape and depicts a seated female, a reclining female, and a reclining male. The reclining female rests on a round cushion decorated with a band with a running scroll with rosettes, set between beaded bands. The reclining male rests on a round cushion decorated with a band with leaves arranged in an opposite arrangement on the stem, set between beaded bands. Beneath these figures is a box in the shape of a kline with two mattresses. Between the legs of the kline are four busts; two males, a female, and a male. The thin mattress at the top is decorated with an intersecting lozenges pattern with four-petal flowers with serrated petals in the lozenges. The centre of the petals is rendered by incised lines. At the right side of the kline a fulcrum is shown. The fulcrum is decorated with a four-petal rosette. The lower mattress has three bands. The central band is decorated with a running scroll with rosettes set between beaded bands. The bands on either side are decorated with serrated flowers in an opposite arrangement on the stem and set between beaded bands. Curving grooves indicate the texture of the mattress. The central stretcher of the kline is decorated. The central part is divided into two sections by a horizontal thin line. The upper section is decorated with miniature bunches of grapes. The lower section is decorated with vine leaves on a stem. On either side of the stretcher is a rectangular indentation decorated with a wave pattern. On either side of these are two squared inlays or appliqués. The kline legs are turned. They are composed of a plinth, and above is a convex quarter, a reversed bell-shaped element, a bell-shaped element, a small torus, a ball, a torus, and above the stretcher is a biconical finial. All elements are decorated with a tongue pattern, rendered diagonally on the ball.

According to Watzinger and Wulzinger (1932, 70 fig. 69) one of the figures held three keys in their hand, two of them inscribed.

INSCRIPTION 1:
Script: Ancient Greek. Location on relief: On key to the left.

Transcription:

Translation:

INSCRIPTION 2:
Script: Ancient Greek. Location on relief: On central key.

Transcription:

Translation:

CIS no.: —; **PAT no.:** —

SARCOPHAGUS LID

PORTRAIT A – Seated female: The figure is shown frontally. The left arm is bent and held in front of the torso. Her legs are bent. The left foot is obscured by the right foot of the reclining figure to her left. She wears six necklaces: One composed of small, round beads, worn at the base of the neck. One composed of a loop-in-loop chain with a central oval pendant, worn against the collarbone. Below that, she wears a necklace composed of a thick hoop with a central, crescent-shaped pendant. Directly below that, she wears a necklace composed of small, round beads. Above the breasts she wears an interwoven loop-in-loop chain with a large, central oval pendant with a beaded border. The sixth necklace falls over the breasts: it is composed of large, round beads and has a round medallion with a beaded border and possibly a bust at the centre (details unclear) that falls over the right breast. According to Watzinger and Wulzinger (1932, 70 fig. 68), there is another medallion with a bust at the last necklace. She wears a tunic and a himation. The tunic has short, wide sleeves and ends at the ankles. The folds of the tunic are rendered by curving and oblique grooves. The himation falls diagonally over the torso and covers the legs. She wears a shoe with a round end.

PORTRAIT B – Reclining female: The torso and the upper arms of the figure are shown in frontal view. The right leg is bent and raised. The right arm is bent and rests on the right leg. The left arm rests against a cushion. The left leg is slightly bent, extending along the mattress.

She wears a veil with scalloped edge. It falls over her right shoulder and upper arm. She wears two necklaces: One composed of large, round beads, worn at the base of the neck. The second is composed of alternating round and square bezels with an incised border. The square bezels have attached round beads at their lower side. She wears a tunic and a himation. The tunic has a wide, round neckline and short, wide sleeves with a scalloped edge. At the right side of the chest, the tunic has a band decorated with a vegetal motif extending downwards. The folds of the tunic are rendered by curving and oblique grooves. Over the tunic she wears a himation. It is wrapped around her left shoulder and upper arm. It crosses the chest diagonally and covers the left breast. The upper border of the himation has a scalloped edge. The himation covers her body and ends at her ankles. It is fastened at the left shoulder with a circular brooch with a beaded boarder (details unclear). A wide fold of the himation extends downwards from the left arm and across the cushion and mattress. At the edge, the fold is divided into two s-shaped folds which end with two triangular-shaped tassels or weights. The folds of the himation are rendered by wide, curving and oblique grooves.

PORTRAIT C – Reclining male: The upper torso of the figure is shown in frontal view and the lower torso and arms in three-quarter view. The right arm is bent and held to the torso. The left arm is bent and rests against a cushion. The legs of the figure are not rendered. He wears a tunic and a himation. The tunic has a wide, v-shaped neckline and short, wide sleeves. At the right side of the chest, the tunic has a band decorated with a floral motif between two beaded bands extending downwards. The folds of the tunic are rendered by curving and oblique grooves. Over the tunic he wears a himation. It is wrapped around his left shoulder and arm. It falls in a curving fold across the lower abdomen and covers the lower body. The upper edge is scalloped. A wide fold extends downwards from the left arm and across the cushion and mattress. At the edge, the fold is divided into two s-shaped folds which end with two triangular-shaped tassels or weights. The folds of the himation are rendered by wide, curving and oblique grooves. The right hand lightly pulls the upper edge of the himation. The thumb and the index finger are extended. The outline of a circular object, possibly a drinking bowl, is recognizable at the centre of the chest.

SARCOPHAGUS BOX

PORTRAIT D – Armless bust of priest: The figure is shown frontally, rendered in a clipeus. He wears a tall, cylindrical, flat-top headdress: a Palmyrene priestly hat (visible in outline). He wears a tunic and a chlamys. The tunic has a wide, round neckline. The folds of the tunic are rendered by curving grooves. Over the tunic he wears a chlamys that falls over both shoulders, and covers the chest. It is fastened at the right shoulder with a circular brooch with a beaded band along the outer border. An s-shaped fold falls from under the brooch. The folds of the chlamys are indicated by narrow, deep grooves.

PORTRAIT E – Armless bust of priest: The figure is shown frontally, rendered in a clipeus. He wears a tall, cylindrical, flat-top headdress: a Palmyrene priestly hat (visible in outline). He wears a tunic and a chlamys. The tunic has a small, round neckline. The folds of the tunic are rendered by curving grooves. Over the tunic he wears a chlamys that falls over both shoulders, and covers the chest. It is fastened at the right shoulder with a circular brooch with a beaded band along the outer border. The folds of the chlamys are indicated by narrow, deep grooves.

PORTRAIT F – Armless bust of a female: The figure is shown frontally, rendered in a clipeus. She wears a veil. It falls over the shoulders in a semicircular fold. She wears a thick hoop necklace with a central, round pendant with an incised border at the base of the neck. She wears a tunic. The tunic has a wide, v-shaped neckline. The folds of the tunic are rendered by curving and oblique grooves.

PORTRAIT G – Armless bust of priest: The figure is shown frontally, rendered in a clipeus. He wears a tall, cylindrical, flat-top headdress: a Palmyrene priestly hat (visible in outline). He wears a tunic and a chlamys. The tunic has a small, round neckline. The folds of the tunic are rendered by curving grooves. Over the tunic he wears a chlamys that falls over both shoulders, and covers the chest. It is fastened at the right shoulder with a circular brooch with a beaded band along the outer border. The folds of the chlamys are indicated by narrow, deep grooves.

Cat. no. 8: Sarcophagus lid relief with banqueting scene (reclining female figure)

LOCATION: Palmyra Museum, Palmyra, inv. no. 657/86/II.d. 8.

CONTEXT: West necropolis. Valley of the Tombs. Temple tomb no. 36.

ACQUISITION HISTORY: —

MEASUREMENTS: Height: 86 cm. Width: 119 cm. Fragment: Height: 11 cm. Width: 16.5 cm.

MATERIAL: Limestone, white/grey.

PRESERVATION: A large crack runs diagonally at the thighs of the figure. The lower part is broken off under the knees; the head is broken off at the base of the neck. The right lower arm and the left lower arm is broken off. The surface is weathered and chipped. Fragment: Only the upper part of the hair and headdress is preserved.

DATE: AD 220–240 (Schmidt-Colinet: AD 220–250).

REFERENCES: Schmidt-Colinet 1992, 105, 110, 122, 125, 135, 151–52, cat. no. B 17, fig. 57, pls 45.a–45.b, 45.e; Krag 2018, 58 n. 304, 59 n. 325, 62 n. 353, 64 ns 361–62, 65 n. 374, 384, cat. no. 820.

OBJECT DESCRIPTION: The object depicts a reclining female. She rests on a thin mattress decorated with an intersecting lozenges pattern with rosettes in the lozenges. She rests the left arm on two cushions: The upper one is decorated with a wide band with a vegetal motif between beaded bands. The lower one is decorated with a running scroll with rosettes between beaded bands. Curving grooves indicate the texture of the fabric. A fragment belonging to the object depicts a part of a cushion (according to Schmidt-Colinet 1992).

PORTRAIT: The figure is shown frontally. The right arm is bent and held in front of the torso. The left arm is bent and raised to the shoulder. The left leg is bent under the right leg.

She wears a coiled turban. The coiling of the fabric is indicated by curving grooves. She wears a heavy veil. The hair is parted at the centre of her forehead and brushed to the sides. Individual strands of hair are indicated by incised lines. She wears four necklaces. The first is composed of small, round beads worn at the base of the neck. The second, also worn at the base of the neck, is composed of a twisted hoop with an oval pendant with an incised border, suspended from the centre by a narrow sleeve. The third is composed of alternating circular and square pendants with beaded borders linked together by beaded elements, worn high on the chest. The fourth is composed of a double loop-in-loop chain with a central, oval pendant. The pendant has a beaded border and five rectangular bars are suspended from it.

She wears a tunic and a himation. The tunic has a small, round neckline and short, wide sleeves. The sleeves have a pleated edge. The folds of the tunic are rendered by curving and oblique grooves. Over the tunic, she wears a himation. It is folded over her right shoulder and arm, and is wrapped around the left arm. Two s-shaped folds fall from under her left arm and proceed over the cushions where a small weight is fastened to the left fold. The folds of the himation are rendered by curving grooves.

Cat. no. 9: Complete sarcophagus with banqueting scene and religious scene

LOCATION: Palmyra Museum, Palmyra, inv. no. 2677B/8983.

CONTEXT: Secondary context: Found (10.09.1990) built into temple tomb no. 176.

ACQUISITION HISTORY: —

MEASUREMENTS: Length of box: 232 cm. Width of box: 107 cm. Height of box: 110 cm. Height of figures on box: 70 cm. Length of lid: 226 cm. Width of lid: 97–105 cm. Height of lid: 115 cm (highest point on horse).

MATERIAL: Limestone, white/yellow.

PRESERVATION: The head and the front legs of the horse are broken off. The top right corner under the horse is chipped. The heads of the standing figures are chipped and the surface is weathered. Portrait A: The lower part is broken off diagonally at the knees. The surface of the left leg is chipped. Portrait B and C: Only the bases of the figures are preserved. Portrait D: The head is broken off at the base of the neck. The left lower arm and at the front of the right foot are broken off. Portrait E: The surface is weathered. The upper part is broken off at the waist. Portrait F: A crack runs horizontally through the waist. Portrait G: The surface of the face is shipped. A crack runs diagonally from the right side of the waist and through the head of the calf. Portrait H–K: The surfaces of the faces are chipped. Portrait L: The nose, mouth, and the chin are chipped. Portrait M: The surface is weathered and the head is chipped. Portrait N: The surface of the face is chipped. Portrait O: The surface of the face is chipped. Portrait P: The surface of the face is chipped. The surface is weathered. Portrait Q: The surface of the head is chipped.

DATE: AD 240–273.

REFERENCES: Colledge 1992, 49, fig. 49; al-As'ad and Schmidt-Colinet 1995, 41, figs 48–51; 2005, 42, figs 60–66; Parlasca 1998, 313, pl. 126.1; Rumscheid 2000, 223–24, cat. no. 272, pl. 66, 1; Kaizer 2002, 179, pl. 4; Yon 2002, 132, fig. 35; 2018, 84, fig. 8; Schmidt-Colinet 2004, 193–94, figs 7–10; 2009, 223–27, figs 1–8; Sommer 2005, 199–98, pls 4–5; 2017, 185–86; 2018, 175, fig. 8.3; Schmidt-Colinet and al-As'ad 2007, 271–76, pls 84–89; Hekster 2008, 51, pl. 40; Fejfer 2009, 108, fig. 67; Andrade 2013, 184–85, fig. 14; Wielgosz-Rondolino 2016a, 77–78, fig. 16a–c; Ciliberto 2017, 49, 54, fig. 2; Curtis 2017, 63–64, fig. 15; Raja 2017e, 220–21, 227, cat. no. 19; 2017f, 64–65, 75, cat. no. 19; Krag 2018, 32 n. 63, 49 n. 229, 53 n. 260, 58 n. 304, 62 n. 349, ns 351–53, 64 ns 361–62, 65 n. 367, ns 372–73, 66 n. 382, 73 n. 47, n. 54, 87 n. 183, 103 n. 73, 396, cat. no. 854; Cussini 2019b, 58, fig. 5.5.

OBJECT DESCRIPTION: The sarcophagus is rectangular in shape and depicts the torso and neck of a horse, two standing figures, a reclining figure, and a standing figure. Underneath these figures is a box in the shape of a kline with seven male figures and an animal between the kline legs. On top of the kline are two mattresses. The mattress at the top is decorated with intersecting lozenge pattern with four-petal flowers in the squares. The lower mattress is decorated with five bands. The outer bands are decorated with a running scroll with rosettes, set between beaded bands. The bands on either side of the central one are decorated with lobed leaves in an opposite arrangement on the stem, set between beaded bands. The central band is decorated with four-petal flowers separated by beaded bands. The centre of the flower petals is rendered by fine, incised lines. It is set between beaded bands. Curving grooves indicate the texture of the mattress. The largest figure on the lid, the reclining figure, rests the left arm against a cushion. It is decorated with a band with a sequence of narrow, rib-shaped flowers, six-petal rosettes, and serrated six-petal flowers in circles. The band is set between beaded bands. A folded cloth with tassels lies on top of the cushion.

It is decorated with a floral motif set between beaded bands. A fulcrum is shown at the left side of the kline. It is decorated with a small armless bust of a male (portrait M) rendered in a clipeus. From the fulcrum, a male figure protrudes. The right arm is held along the body and the left is bent. The left leg is bent under the right with the knee pointing forwards. He wears a himation that covers his left shoulder and arm, leaving the chest free. The himation proceeds in a curving fold across his waist, covers his legs, and falls back at his right side. The chest musculature and the navel are rendered by narrow depressions. In his right hand, he holds a large staff that rests against the upper arm. A row of curving grooves is rendered over his head, possibly depicting a garment of another figure. A female figure is positioned over the male figure. She is seated. Her legs are turned towards her right and her torso is turned toward her left. The left arm is bent and raised, and the right arm is lowered at the height of the waist. She wears a chiton.

The central stretcher of the kline is decorated. The central part is divided into two sections by a thin, horizontal line. The upper section is decorated with leaves placed at either end from where a criss-cross pattern extends. The lower section is decorated with a tongue pattern. On either side of the stretcher are rectangular indentations flanked by two square inlays or appliqués. The rectangular indentations are decorated with a wave pattern and the inlays with animals. The kline legs are turned. They are composed of a plinth, above is a concave quarter, a long reversed concave quarter, a concave quarter, a torus, a reversed bell-shaped element, a ball, a biconical element, a reversed concave quarter, and a bell-shaped element. All elements are decorated with a tongue pattern.

At the right side of the sarcophagus lid, a horse is shown. It is fragmented, only the lower part of the neck, the body, and the upper part of the tail is preserved. The chest musculature of the horse is modelled and rendered by deep grooves. The tail is long and voluminous. The individual hairs of the tail are rendered by incised lines. The horse is equipped with a cushioned saddle, a rein at the buttock, and a wide strap around the neck. The saddle cushion is decorated with four-petal flowers in squares separated by beaded bands. The lower part of the pommels at the front and the back of the saddle are preserved. The rein at the buttock is decorated with a wave pattern and circles with a beaded edge. The neck strap is decorated with a scroll with concentric, incised circles. At the middle, the strap is fastened with a circular medallion with a beaded border and a central, undecorated inlay.

The left lateral side of the sarcophagus lid is decorated with a relief divided into two registers. A part of the upper edge is preserved, decorated with a band with oblique grooves. The upper register depicts five figures in architectural aediculae, alternating between triangular and circular pediments supported by columns on bases. Larger figures are shown between the aediculae. The lower register depicts five figures in architectural aediculae, alternating between triangular and circular pediments supported by columns on bases. The lower edge of the sarcophagus lid is decorated with a sequence of squares with four-petal flowers. The midribs of the leaves are incised.

The sarcophagus box depicts seven standing male figures. Between portrait F and G the front legs and part of the torso of an animal are shown frontally. The head of the animal is chipped. The hooves of the animal are rendered, and they have an incised line down the middle, suggesting that the animal is a calf. A small rectangular altar is shown between portrait H and I: the base is composed of two juxtaposed hexagonal plinths, the body is rectangular, and has a trapezoidal upper end, with a circular top. Above the altar, between the heads of portrait H and I, a wreath with a folded cloth underneath is shown. The cloth is folded into two circular loops on either side. Between portrait I and J is a high, cylindrical, flat-top headdress (Palmyrene priestly hat) shown at the height of their heads. It is divided into three sections by two vertical grooves. A wreath with the leaves pointing towards a central medallion is depicted at the middle of the headdress. A folded cloth is shown underneath the headdress. It has two circular, looped folds on either side.

The right lateral side of the sarcophagus box depicts a standing female and a reclining female. The figures are resting on a kline with a mattress. The mattress is decorated with two bands. They are decorated with running scrolls with rosettes. Curving grooves indicate the texture of the fabric. The reclining female rests the right arm against a cushion. The cushion is decorated with a wide, central band (details unclear). The central stretcher of the kline is decorated with two rectangular indentations followed by a square inlay on each side. The central section appears to be decorated (details unclear). The kline legs are composed of two trapezoidal turning. The kline legs are decorated with a tongue pattern. Between the figures, a hexagon-shaped chest placed on a pillar is depicted. The narrow upper part of the chest also, in a hexagon-shape, is decorated with rows of oblique grooves. Each section on the lower part of the chest is decorated with inlays (details unclear).

The left lateral side depicts a standing female and a camel. The camel is rendered in profile. The neck is slender and curving, the body is oval and oblong. The legs are slender. The tail of the camel is crescent-shaped and the hairs are rendered by incised lines. The camel is equipped with a tall saddle covered by a woollen skin, possibly sheep. The texture is indicated by fine, incised lines. On the back of the saddle is a coiled fabric. Underneath the saddle is an embroidered cloth decorated with rhombi. Each diamond has a raised dot at the centre and the edge of the cloth has a beaded band. The saddle is attached to the camel by three lanyards, which form a single band on the belly. The lanyards are covered at the top of the saddle by the skin. On the hip of the camel is a round shield decorated with circular incisions, connected to the saddle by a strap.

SARCOPHAGUS LID

PORTRAIT A – Standing male: The figure is standing with the legs slightly apart. The feet of the figure are obscured by the right foot of the reclining figure to his left. He wears a 'Parthian-style' tunic and 'Parthian-style' trousers. The tunic ends at the knees and has a decorated lower border with a running scroll with rosettes and a beaded band at the hem. He also wears trousers tucked into his boots. Each trouser leg is decorated in the middle with a vegetal motif extending downwards. The folds of the trousers are indicated by wide, curving grooves. He wears ankle-boots.

PORTRAIT B – Standing figure: (Details unclear).

PORTRAIT C – Standing figure: (Details unclear).

PORTRAIT D – Relining male: The figure is shown in frontal to three-quarter view. The right arm appears short in relation to the body. The right arm is extended and rests on his raised right knee. The left arm is bent and held to the chest. His right leg is bent and his foot is resting on the mattress. The left leg is bent under the right leg with the knee pointing outwards.

He wears a 'Parthian-style' tunic, a chlamys, and 'Parthian-style' trousers. The tunic has a wide, round neckline decorated with squares and rhombi. The tunic has long, tight-fitting sleeves. The cuffs of the sleeves are decorated with a beaded band, followed by acanthus leaves, each with two opposite volutes, followed by another beaded band. At the middle, the tunic has a wide band decorated with nude male figures holding baskets and picking grapes, extending downwards. The figures are rendered within concentric circles that are tied together by a vine scroll. Surrounding the circles are vines and bunches of grapes. The tunic ends above the knees and has a decorated border with lobed leaves in an opposite arrangement on a stem, set between beaded bands. At the right thigh, the border of the tunic is folded upwards revealing the inner side. The folds of the tunic are rendered by curving, wide grooves. Over the tunic, he wears a chlamys that falls over both shoulders and covers most of the chest. One edge of the chlamys has a scalloped border decorated with rosettes followed by a beaded band, visible on the fold across the chest and the four folds falling down the left shoulder and along the cushion. Attached to the fold in the middle is a pendant or a weight. It is rendered in the shape of a flower with four lanceolate leaves with a round inlay within. The edge of the fold to the left ends in a tassel. The chlamys is fastened at the right shoulder with a circular brooch (details unclear). A zigzag-shaped fold falls from under the brooch. The folds of the chlamys are rendered by wide, curving grooves. Alongside his right thigh lies an object with a pointed end, a rectangular main body, and a lateral semicircle: a sheathed dagger. He also wears a belt across the lower torso. It is composed of round and square bezels with incised borders linked by beaded elements. The bezels and the strap of the belt are fastened to a star-shaped element. The straps are knotted at the centre with the ends looped under on either side of the knot. A sword is fastened to the belt. It has a pommel decorated with a rosette while the scabbard is decorated with an upper curving rim and a central fuller. The trousers are visible from above the knees. Each trouser leg is decorated with a broad, central band extending downwards, decorated with five-petal flowers in circles, and set between beaded bands. The folds of the trousers are rendered by curving grooves. His trousers are tucked into his round-toe boot. The boot is decorated with vines that meander across the surface. The upper edge is decorated with a panel with squares and rhombi between thin lines, followed by panels with a wave pattern. The boot has a wide band running above the ankle. It is decorated with concentric circles and fastened to the boot with a button in the shape of a rosette.

With his right hand, he holds a pinecone facing downwards. The scales of the pinecone are outlined. At the centre of the chest, the outline of an object, possibly a bowl is recognizable.

PORTRAIT E – Standing male: The figure is shown frontally. The legs are obscured by the reclining figure to his right. He wears a garment, possibly a 'Parthian-style' tunic, which ends at the knees. The lower edge of the tunic has a decorated band (details unclear). The folds of the garment are rendered by oblique grooves.

SARCOPHAGUS BOX

PORTRAIT F – Standing male: The figure is shown in three quarter view. The right arm is bent and held to the chest. The left arm is bent and held out from the body towards the animal. He stands with his legs apart and rests his weight on the right leg. The left leg is slightly bent with the knee rendered under the drapery. His hair is arranged in snail-shell curls around the head. He wears a tunic with short sleeves. The tunic ends at the knees. An overfold, possibly created by a belt, is rendered in a curving line at the waist. The folds of the tunic are rendered by oblique and curving grooves. He does not wear shoes. His right hand is clenched around a thin, oblong object, possibly a dagger.

PORTRAIT G – Standing male: The figure is shown frontally. The head appears to be turned slightly to his right. The right arm is held along the side of the body. The left arm is slightly bent and held out from the body. He stands with his legs apart. He rests his weight on the left leg while the right leg is slightly bent with the knee rendered under the drapery. The neck is short. He wears an undergarment and a tunic. The undergarment has a tasselled edge and is visible proceeding in a diagonal line from the left knee and over the right. The tunic has a wide, round neckline and long, tight-fitting sleeves. An overfold, possibly created by a belt, is rendered in a curving line at the waist. The folds of the tunic are rendered by oblique and curving grooves. He does not wear shoes. With the right hand, he holds the handle of a jug. The jug has an ovoid body and a narrow neck. With the palm turned outwards, he holds the handle of a patera in his left hand.

PORTRAIT H – Standing male: The figure is shown frontally. The head appears to be turned slightly to his right. Both arms are bent and held to the torso. He stands with his legs set apart and rests his weight on the left leg. The right leg is slightly bent with the knee rendered in the drapery. The outline of his hair is recognizable and it appears to be voluminous and reaching the neck. He wears an undergarment and a tunic. The undergarment has a tasselled edge and is visible proceeding in a diagonal line from the left knee and over the right. The tunic has a wide, round neckline and short, loose sleeves. An overfold, possibly created by a belt, is rendered in a curving line at the waist. The folds of the tunic are rendered by oblique and curving grooves. He does not wear shoes. The outline of a rectangular chest is visible at the left side of his waist. With the right hand, he holds the lid of the chest. He holds the bottom of the chest with the left hand.

PORTRAIT I – Standing male: The figure is shown frontally. The right arm is extended and held out from the body. The left arm is bent and held to the torso. He stands with his legs apart. The left leg is slightly bent with the knee rendered in the drapery. He wears a wreath with a central element (details unclear). The neck is wide. He wears a tunic and a toga. The tunic has a wide, round neckline and short sleeves. At the right side of the chest, the tunic has a wide band (clavus) extending downwards. The folds of the tunic are rendered by curving grooves. The toga is folded over his left shoulder and arm, leaving the hand free. A wide fold of the toga is wrapped around his abdomen, coming from the right side and extends downwards with two large, curving folds (the sinus) rendered. The fold (umbo) coming from the left shoulder is folded under the wide fold at the abdomen. The toga ends at the ankles. The folds of the toga are rendered by curving and oblique grooves. He also wears sandals (details unclear). With the right hand he holds a patera above the altar. With the left hand, he holds an oblong object, possibly a book-roll. The index finger is extended.

PORTRAIT J – Standing male: The figure is shown in three-quarter view. Both arms are bent and held to the torso. He stands with his legs slightly apart. He rests his weight on the right leg and the left leg is slightly bent with the knee rendered in the drapery. The outline of the hair is recognizable and appears to have been voluminous and covering the ears.

He wears an undergarment and a tunic. The undergarment has a tasselled edge and is visible proceeding in a diagonal line from the left knee and over the right. The tunic has a wide, round neckline and wide sleeves reaching the elbows. An overfold, possibly created by a belt, is rendered in a curving line at the waist. The folds of the tunic are rendered by oblique and curving grooves. He does not wear shoes. He holds a large bowl filled with round objects, possibly fruit, in his hands.

PORTRAIT K – Standing male: The figure is shown in three-quarter view. The head is seen frontally. The arms are bent and held to the torso. He stands with his legs slightly apart. He rests his weight on the right leg and the left leg is slightly bent with the knee rendered in the drapery. His hair is centrally parted and brushed to each side of the forehead. On the sides of the head, the hair becomes curly and covers the ears. The neck is long. He wears an undergarment and a tunic. The undergarment has a tasselled edge and is visible proceeding in a diagonal line from the left knee and over the right. The tunic has a wide, round neckline and wide sleeves reaching the elbows. An overfold with a tasselled edge, possibly created by a belt, is rendered in a curving line at the waist. The folds of the tunic are rendered by oblique and curving grooves. He does not wear shoes. He is holding a bird in his hands. The individual feathers are outlined by incised lines and the tail by horizontal grooves.

PORTRAIT L – Standing male: The figure is shown frontally. The right arm is extended and held out from the body. The left arm is bent and held to the torso. He stands with his legs apart. He rests his weight on the right leg and the left leg is slightly bent with the knee rendered in the drapery. He wears an undergarment, a tunic, and a himation. The undergarment has a tasselled edge and is visible proceeding in a diagonal line from the left knee and over the right. The tunic has a wide, v-shaped neckline and short, wide sleeves. An overfold with a tasselled edge, possibly created by a belt, is rendered in a curving line at the waist. The folds of the tunic are rendered by oblique and curving grooves. Over the tunic, he wears a himation. It is wrapped around his left shoulder and arm, leaving the left side of the body and the hand free. The himation falls in a wide fold along the left side of the body and falls back at the waist. With the right hand, he holds the handle of a jug. The jug has an ovoid body and a wide neck. With the left hand, he holds the thick fold of the himation. The thumb and the index finger are extended.

PORTRAIT M – Armless bust of a male in fulcrum: The figure is shown frontally, rendered in a clipeus. (Details unclear).

THE RIGHT LATERAL SIDE OF SARCOPHAGUS BOX

PORTRAIT N – Standing female: The figure is shown in three-quarter view. The right arm is bent and held to the torso and the left arm is bent and held out from her body towards the reclining figure. She stands with the legs slightly parted. Her feet are obscured by the reclining female to her left. She wears a tunic and a himation. The tunic has a wide, round neckline and short sleeves. The folds of the tunic are rendered by curving grooves. Over the tunic, she wears an ankle-length himation. It is wrapped around her left shoulder and arm, covering the left breast and the body. The folds of the himation are rendered by curving and vertical grooves. She holds the ends of a necklace in her hands, directing it towards the reclining female to her left. The necklace is composed of a central rectangular pendant and oval pendants on each side. The pendants are linked by beaded elements.

PORTRAIT O – Reclining female: The figure is shown in frontal to three-quarter view. The right arm is bent and rests on her right raised knee. The left arm is bent and raised to the neck. The right leg is bent. The left leg is slightly bent and extended along the mattress. The right foot is obscured by the left leg. She wears a veil. It falls down on each side of the face and back at the shoulders. She wears two necklaces: one composed of round beads in a string worn at the base of the neck. One composed of a loop-in-loop chain with a central, oval pendant. The chain and pendant are linked by oval terminals on each side. She wears a tunic and a himation. The tunic has a wide, v-shaped neckline and short, wide sleeves. The folds of the tunic are rendered by curving and oblique grooves. Over the tunic, she wears a himation. It is wrapped around her left shoulder and upper arm. It proceeds in a curving fold across the chest and covers the left breast and the body. A wide, zigzag-shaped fold of the himation falls from under her left arm across the cushion and the mattress. The edge of the fold is tied into a small knot. The himation ends at the ankles. The folds are rendered by curving and oblique grooves. Her right hand is placed on her right raised knee. She wears a wide hoop bracelet around her right wrist. Her left hand is raised to the neck, and she appears to pull a fold of the veil with her hand.

THE LEFT LATERAL SIDE OF SARCOPHAGUS BOX

PORTRAIT P – Standing female: The figure is shown frontally. The right arm is bent and held away from the body. The left arm is slightly bent and held to the lower body. She stands with her legs apart. She wears a tunic and a himation. The tunic has a wide, round neckline and short, tight-fitting sleeves. The folds of the tunic are rendered by curving grooves. Over the tunic, she wears a himation. It is folded around her left shoulder and upper arm. It proceeds in a slightly curving fold along the left side of the chest and body. Another end of the himation is folded from the right side across the waist, covers the legs, and reaches the ground. The folds of the himation are rendered by deep, diagonal and curving grooves. Her right hand is clenched around a long staff. The left hand is pulling the fold of the himation coming across the waist.

Cat. no. 10: Banqueting relief

LOCATION: National Museum of Damascus, Damascus, inv. no. 18802.

CONTEXT: South-east necropolis. Hypogeum of Taai, west exedra, south section A3.

ACQUISITION HISTORY: —

MEASUREMENTS: Height: 55.5 cm. Width: 82 cm. Depth: 11 cm.

MATERIAL: Limestone, yellow.

PRESERVATION: The right and the upper side of the relief are slightly chipped. Portrait A: The surface of the left knee is chipped.

DATE: AD 220–240.

REFERENCES: Abdul-Hak 1952, 215, 225, 228 n. 2, 230–31, 233–35, 246, cat. no. 20, pl. 2.2; Gawlikowski 1974, 270–71, cat. no. 11; Parlasca 1982, 198, cat. no. 178; 1985b, 399, cat. no. 190; Tanabe 1986, 42, pl. 424; Yon 2001, 367–68, cat. no. 255; Clauss 2002, 92, cat. no. 105; Finlayson 2002–2003, 228, pl. 7; Zahran 2004, 31, fig. 8; Finlayson 2008, 113, fig. 6, 5; Miyashita 2016, 133, fig. 18; Krag 2018, 28 n. 9, 32 n. 62, 56 n. 291, 62 n. 353, 63 n. 354, 64 ns 361–62, n. 365, 65 ns 372–73, 377, 87 n. 182, n. 186, 88 n. 192, 89 n. 203, 90 n. 210, 101 n. 63, 102 n. 66, 103 n. 75, 377, cat. no. 792. Inscription: Abdul-Hak 1952, 234; Gawlikowski 1974, 270–71, cat. no. 11; Yon 2001, 368, cat. no. 255; Krag 2018, 377, cat. no. 792.

OBJECT DESCRIPTION: The relief is rectangular in shape, and depicts a reclining female and a reclining male. Beneath these figures is a mattress. It is decorated with an intersecting lozenges pattern with beaded elements at the intersections. The lozenges have four-petal flowers, with the veins of the petals incised. Behind the reclining male, there is a cloth depicted hanging from two six-petal rosettes. A branch of palm leaves projects upwards and inwards from each rosette. The midribs of the leaves are incised. The folds of the cloth are indicated by curving grooves. The female rests against a cushion. The cushion is decorated with a wide band extending downwards with leaves on a stem. Curving grooves indicate the fabric of the cushion. The male rests on a cushion. The cushion is decorated with a vertical band with lanceolate leaves closely arranged. Curving grooves indicate the fabric of the cushion. To the right of the two figures is a chest on a pedestal. The chest appears to be polygonal (four sides are visible), and has a stepped lid. The upper part of the box is decorated with four horizontal panels decorated with leaves pointing towards a central rosette. The central part has three coffered rectangles. The middle rectangle has a circular incision with a horizontal and vertical rectangular depression, possibly a rendering of a lock or keyhole. The chest has disc-shaped feet.

INSCRIPTION 1:
Script: Palmyrene Aramaic. Location on relief: To the right of reclining female, at the height of her head.

ṢLMT BWLY' BRT| 'G' BR BWRP'.
Image of Bôlayâ, daughter of 'Oggâ, son of Bôrrefâ.

INSCRIPTION 2:
Script: Palmyrene Aramaic. Location on relief: To the right of reclining male, at the height of his head.

ṢLM ML' | BR 'G' | BWRP'.
Image of Malê, son of 'Oggâ Bôrrefâ.

CIS no: —; **PAT no.:** 1802.

PORTRAIT A – Reclining female, Bôlayâ: The torso of the reclining female is shown in frontal view, with her head turned slightly to her right. The lower body and legs are in three-quarter view. The head and left arm appear large. The right arm is bent across the chest. The left is bent and raised to the head, and rests on a cushion. The right leg is bent and the right foot rests on the mattress. The left leg is bent under the right, and the knee is visible under the drapery, pointing forwards. The left lower leg is obscured by the right leg.

She wears three headdresses: a headband, a turban, and a veil. The headband is placed high on her forehead. It is decorated by a central square panel with four-petal flowers with incised midribs, set between two beaded bands. A narrow, plain band runs along the lower border. She also wears a head-chain that is attached under the centre of the turban and runs to the sides disappearing under the veil. It is composed of circular bezels linked by beaded elements. The turban is coiled. It is in a single layer with horizontal grooves indicating the coiling of the fabric. The veil is heavy. It falls behind her shoulders. The hair is visible over her ears where it is brushed back under the head-chain, over the headband, and disappears under the veil. Individual strands of hair are indicated with incised lines. A row of single comma-shaped curls is under the headband. Her face is oval. The eyebrows are slightly curving, rendered by incised grooves starting from the root of the nose. The eyes are almond-shaped with thick upper eyelids. The irises are indicated by incised circles. The earlobes are visible under the hair and she wears dumbbell-shaped earrings. The nose is straight and wide. The alae are incised and the nostrils carved. The mouth is small, with a full lower lip. The chin is pointed. The neck is long, with three curving grooves. She wears four necklaces: a string of small, round beads worn at the base of the neck. A plain hoop necklace with a round pendant with an incised border, perhaps indicating the setting of a stone, suspended from a narrow sleeve, worn at the base of the neck. A chain of alternating square and circular bezels, all with an incised border, perhaps indicating the setting of a stone, joined by beaded elements, worn below the collarbone. A loop-in-loop chain with a circular pendant with an incised border, perhaps indicating the setting of a stone, suspended by a narrow sleeve at the centre, is worn below the collarbone.

She wears a tunic and a himation. The tunic has a small, angular neckline, and short sleeves. The folds of the tunic are rendered by oblique grooves on the chest and sleeve. The himation crosses the chest diagonally from the left upper arm to the right side, and covers most of the left breast. It is folded around the left arm and two edges fall from under the arm onto the mattress in two large, zigzag-shaped folds. The himation covers the lower body and legs, and ends at the ankles with a scalloped edge. The folds of the himation are rendered by curving and oblique grooves. She wears sandals (visible on the right foot). The sandal has a plain strap between the first two toes that runs on either side of the foot. The sole is indicated by a horizontal, incised line. Incised lines indicate the toenails.

Her right hand rests on the cushion, with the fingers slightly extended. She wears a bracelet on her right wrist, composed of plain and beaded wires twisted together. The left hand is held to her face, with the fingers resting against the cheek. The left index finger is extended to the forehead. She wears a bracelet on her left wrist, composed of plain and beaded wires twisted together. She wears a ring on the left little finger: it has a round bezel with an incised border, perhaps indicating the setting of a stone.

PORTRAIT B – Reclining male, Malê: The figure is shown in frontal view. The head appears large. The right arm is slightly bent and held in front of the waist. The left hand is bent in front of the chest and rests on a cushion. His legs are obscured by the reclining figure to his right. His hair is arranged in three rows of snail-shell curls around his head. The individual strands of hair are indicated by incised lines. He wears a wreath high on the head. It has three rows of leaves pointing towards a central rosette. His face is diamond-shaped. The eyebrows are slightly curving, indicated with incised lines starting from the root of the nose. The eyes are almond-shaped with thick upper eyelids. The irises and pupils are depicted with concentric, incised circles. The ears are protruding and the tail of the helix, scapha, and lobe are depicted. The nose is straight and wide. The alae are incised and the nostrils carved. He has a beard: it starts at the temples, covers the outer side of the cheeks, the chin, and the upper lip. The facial hair is rendered by snail-shell curls in the beard and incised vertical lines in the moustache. The mouth is small with a full lower lip. The chin is round. The neck is wide. He wears a 'Parthian-style' tunic and a himation. The tunic has a round neckline decorated with a beaded band. The sleeves are long, the cuffs are decorated with a band of alternating incised circles and squares. The tunic has a wide band with leaves on a curving stem set between two beaded bands, extending downwards from the middle of the neckline. The folds of the tunic are rendered by vertical and oblique grooves. He wears a plain band belt, with a single strap looped under the side. The himation falls over his left shoulder and arm and along the left side of his body. It is folded around his left arm and the edge of the himation continues onto the cushion and mattress in two large, zigzag-shaped folds. With his right hand, he holds an oblong oval object with a pointed end and diamond-shaped pattern, possibly a pinecone. The right index finger and thumb are extended. With the upturned palm of the left hand he holds a bowl with his fingertips. The bowl has a round base indicated by an incised, horizontal line. The body is decorated with hollowed circles, and the rim is indicated with a horizontal, incised line. The upper surface is plain. The nails are indicated with fine, incised lines.

Cat. no. 11: Banqueting relief

LOCATION: Archaeological Museum, Istanbul, inv. no. 3728/180.

CONTEXT: —

ACQUISITION HISTORY: Confiscated in Damascus in 1893.

MEASUREMENTS: Height: 45 cm. Width: 40 cm.

MATERIAL: Limestone, yellow.

PRESERVATION: The right side and lower right corner is chipped. The upper left corner is chipped. Portrait B: The surface of the feet is chipped.

DATE: AD 220–240.

REFERENCES: Ingholt Archives, PS 529; Musée Impérial Ottoman 1895, 72, cat. no. 180; Ingholt 1928, 43 n. 2; Mackay 1949, 164, pl. 53.1; Albertson 2014, 32, appendix 23, pl. 3.3; Krag 2018, 49 n. 229, 53 n. 255, n. 260, 62 n. 353, 64 ns 361–62, 65 n. 372–73, 73 n. 47, 103 n. 73, 375–74, cat. no. 788.

OBJECT DESCRIPTION: The object is rectangular in shape and depicts a standing female and a reclining female. It has an outer plain frame on all four sides. There is an inner frame on the right, upper, and left side, composed of a leaf-and-dart pattern, a plain band, and a beaded band. On the relief background, between the two figures, is a pedestal with a dual plinth and upon this a round vase, possibly a lebes. The vase is decorated with a criss-cross pattern. Beneath the figures is a mattress with three bands: the central one is decorated with a running scroll and six-petal rosettes. The petals of the upper rosette have depressions. The bands on either side are decorated with squares of plain bands, with circles as corners, and central four-petal flowers. The right end of the mattress is indicated by an oval incision. Curving grooves indicate the texture of the fabric. The reclining female rests on two cushions: the upper cushion is decorated with a band of leaves on a stem. The lower cushion is decorated with a band with a running scroll. Curving grooves indicate the texture of the fabric.

PORTRAIT A – Standing female: The figure is shown in frontal view, with the head turned slightly to the left. The right arm is bent and held in front of the torso. The lower legs are obscured by the reclining figure to her left. Her hair is parted at the centre and combed back over the ears. Individual strands of hair are indicated by incised lines. Her face is oval. The eyebrows are curving. The eyes are large and almond-shaped. The eyeballs are blank. The ears are not visible under the hair. The nose is short with a wide base. The alae are incised and the nostrils carved. The mouth is small with thin lips. The chin is oval. The neck is short and has a curving groove. She wears a tunic. The tunic has a small, round neckline and wide sleeves reaching the elbows. A large overfold is depicted across the waist. The folds of the tunic are rendered by curving grooves. With the right hand, she holds a square box in front of her torso. The sides of the box have incised squares and the front side has a five-petal flower in the centre of the square. The lid of the box is indicated by a horizontal, incised line. It is possibly a jewellery box.

PORTRAIT B – Reclining female: The body of the figure is shown in frontal view; the head is turned slightly to the left. The head appears large. The right arm is extended and rests on the right knee. The left arm is bent and raised to the neck, and rests on the cushions. The right leg is bent and raised. The left leg is slightly bent, resting along the mattress, and the knee is rendered under the drapery. The left leg obscures the right foot. She wears three headdresses: a headband, a turban, and a veil. The headband is decorated with square panels with central incised circles, separated by vertical, narrow bands. The turban is coiled. It is composed of one layer, and oblique grooves indicate the coiling of the fabric. The veil is heavy. It falls behind her shoulders. Part of the hair is covered by the headdress: several strands of hair above the ears are pushed back over the headband and disappear under the veil. The individual strands of hair are indicated by incised lines. Her face is oval. The eyebrows are slightly curving. The eyes are round with thick upper eyelids. The eyeballs are blank. The right earlobe is visible and she wears earrings composed of two juxtaposed beads; a round, upper bead and a lower, bell-shaped bead. The nose is short and wide, with incised alae and carved nostrils. The cheeks are fleshy. The mouth is small and the lips are full. The chin is oval. The neck has a horizontal groove. She wears a necklace: a string of round beads worn at the base of her neck. She wears a tunic and a himation. The tunic has a wide, v-shaped neckline and loose sleeves reaching the elbows. The folds of the tunic are rendered as curving grooves on the chest and oblique grooves on the sleeve. The himation crosses the body horizontally just under the breasts, and is folded around the left arm. A fold of the himation falls underneath the left arm onto the cushions and ends in an s-shaped fold. At the corner of the fold is a triangular-shaped object, possibly a tassel. The himation covers her lower body and legs, and ends at the ankles. The folds are rendered by curving grooves. She wears sandals, with the strap fastened between the big toe and index toe. The toes are indicated by deep, incised lines. The right hand rests on the right knee, and she holds a round object with a punch hole, possibly a fruit. The left hand is supporting the head at the chin and cheek. On each wrist she wears a bracelet composed of twisted, plain wires.

Cat. no. 12: Banqueting relief

LOCATION: Palmyra Museum, Palmyra, inv. no. CD 9, CD 42.

CONTEXT: Secondary context: Found (03/04.05.1960) four metres west of the Tetrapylon in the Camp of Diocletian.

ACQUISITION HISTORY: —

MEASUREMENTS: Height: 64 cm. Width: 47 cm. Depth: 16 cm.

MATERIAL: Limestone, yellow.

PRESERVATION: The object is composed of three fragments. The upper and left side is chipped. Portrait A: The lower part is broken off at the chest. Portrait B: The lower right arm and the legs are broken off. The surface of the forehead and of the right hand is chipped.

DATE: AD 220–240.

REFERENCES: Michalowski 1962, 158–59, cat. no. 28, fig. 173; Albertson 2014, 32, appendix 24; Krag 2018, 49 n. 229, 53 n. 255, n. 260, 62 n. 353, 64 ns 361–62, 65 n. 370, 73 n. 47, ns 53–54, 103 n. 73, 376, cat. no. 789.

OBJECT DESCRIPTION: The object is rectangular in shape and depicts a standing female and a reclining female. On the upper and lower side, there is an outer plain frame. On the right, upper, and left side an inner frame is depicted. The inner frame is composed of a leaf-and-dart design, a plain band, and beaded band. Beneath the figures is a mattress. The mattress is decorated with an intersecting lozenges pattern with rosettes and flowers in the lozenges. There are round elements at the corners of the lozenges. The petals of the rosettes have depressions. The reclining female rests on a cushion. Curving grooves indicate the texture of the fabric.

PORTRAIT A – Standing female: The figure is shown in three-quarter view. The left hand is bent and held to the left. Her hair is parted at the centre, and brushed to the sides. It is collected in a round knot in the back. The individual locks of hair are indicated by incised lines. Her face is oval. The eyebrows are curving. She has almond-shaped eyes with thick upper eyelids. The eyeballs appear blank. The earlobes are visible under the hair. The nose bridge is narrow. The mouth is small with full lips. The chin is round. The neck is wide. She wears a tunic. The tunic has a round neckline and is fastened at both shoulders with circular brooches (details unclear). With the left hand, she holds an object: the object is round with a round incision, indicating a round frame. Possibly a mirror or tambourine.

PORTRAIT B – Reclining female: The figure is shown in frontal view, with the head turned slightly to the left. The head appears large. The right arm is slightly bent. The left arm is bent and raised to the head and rests on the cushion. She wears a veil. The veil is heavy and falls over the right shoulder and upper arm and behind the left shoulder. The hair is arranged in crescent-shaped curls and is brushed back under the veil. The individual locks of hair are rendered by incised lines. Her face is oval. The eyebrows are curving. The eyes are large and almond-shaped. The eyeballs are blank. The nose is short, with a wide base. The alae are incised. The mouth is small with full lips. The chin is oval. The neck has a single curving groove. She wears a tunic and a himation. The tunic has a round neckline and sleeves reaching the elbows. The folds of the tunic are rendered by oblique grooves on the chest. The himation is fastened at the left shoulder with a circular brooch (details unclear). It falls along the left arm and is wrapped around her waist. The himation covers the lower body and legs. The edge of the himation is scalloped, indicated on the edge that falls on the mattress. The folds of the himation are rendered by oblique grooves.

With her left hand she touches her cheek and temple. She wears a plain band bracelet on her left wrist.

Cat. no. 13: Banqueting relief

LOCATION: National Museum of Damascus, Damascus, inv. no. 2153.

CONTEXT: —

ACQUISITION HISTORY: —

MEASUREMENTS: Height: 47 cm. Width: 55 cm.

MATERIAL: Limestone, yellow.

PRESERVATION: The upper right corner is broken off. The upper side is chipped. The surface of the right half of the mattress is chipped. Portrait A: The surface of the head and of the right side of body is chipped. Portrait B: The surface of the forehead, nose, mouth, and of the chest is chipped. The right foot is chipped. The lower right arm and the left hand are broken off.

DATE: AD 220–240.

REFERENCES: Ingholt Archives, PS 684; Abdul-Hak and Abdul-Hak 1951, 35, cat. no. 17, pl. 14, 1; Colledge 1976, 63, 79, 132, 136, 139, 150, 155–56, 215, 240–41, pl. 107; Tanabe 1986, 43, pl. 438; Chehade 1987, 193, fig. 1; Albertson 2014, 32, appendix 22; Krag and Raja 2017, 201–02, fig. 3; Krag 2018, 49 n. 229, 53 n. 255, n. 260, 62 n. 353, 64 ns 361–62, 65 ns 372–73, 73 n. 47, n. 53, 103 n. 73, 108 n. 125, 376, cat. no. 790.

OBJECT DESCRIPTION: The object is rectangular in shape and depicts a standing female and a reclining female. There is a plain frame on all four sides of the relief. There is an inner frame on the right, upper, and left side composed of a leaf-and-dart design, a plain band, and a beaded band. The midribs of the leaves are indicated with incised lines. Between the two figures, on the relief background, is a polygonal pedestal with coffers and a dual plinth. On top of this is a round object: the lower half is decorated with a criss-cross pattern, and the upper half has very fine, incised lines. The two halves are separated by two horizontal, narrow bands (according to Colledge 1976, this is a ball of wool). Beneath the figures is a mattress. It is decorated with an intersecting lozenge pattern with six-petal flowers in the lozenges. The corners of the lozenges have round elements. The reclining female rests on a cushion: the cushion is decorated with a band with a running scroll and rosettes. The petals of the rosettes have depressions. Curving grooves indicate the texture of the fabric.

PORTRAIT A – Standing female: The figure is shown in three-quarter view. The arms appear large in relation to the body. The right arm is bent and held in front of the torso. The left arm is bent and held to the left side. She stands with the right foot on the mattress, the left leg and foot are obscured by the reclining figure to her left. Her hair is parted at the centre and brushed back. Individual locks of hair are indicated by wavy, incised lines. The chin is oval and prominent. The neck is wide. She wears a tunic. The tunic has a wide, v-shaped neckline and wide sleeves reaching the elbows. A large round fold of the sleeve at the left arm is rendered on the relief background. A wide, horizontal fold is depicted across the waist. The folds of the tunic are rendered by curving grooves on the chest. With the upturned palm of the left hand, she holds a square box. The box is decorated with incised squares on the front. The lid is lifted and the box is open towards the reclining figure to the left. Two necklaces hang on the outer side of the box: the lower necklace is composed of a loop-in-loop chain with a triangular pendant suspended from the centre. The upper necklace is composed of round beads, with a trapezoidal pendant suspended from the centre.

PORTRAIT B – Reclining female: The figure is shown in frontal view. The head appears large. The arms appear small in relation to the body. The right arm is bent across the torso. The left arm is bent and raised to the neck and rests on a cushion. The right leg is bent and the right foot rests on the mattress. The left leg is bent under the right, and the knee is rendered under the drapery. The lower left leg is obscured by the right leg. She wears three headdresses: a headband, a turban, and a veil. The headband is placed low on the forehead (details unclear). The turban is coiled. It is arranged in a single layer and horizontal grooves indicate the coiling of the fabric. The veil is heavy. It falls behind her shoulders. She also wears a head-chain that is attached under the centre of the turban and runs to the sides disappearing under the veil. It is composed of circular pendants joined by beaded elements. Part of the hair is covered by the headdress: several strands of hair above the ears are pushed back over the headband and disappear under the veil. The individual strands of hair are indicated by incised lines. Her face is oval and the eyebrows slightly curving. The eyes are almond-shaped with thick upper eyelids. She wears dumbbell-shaped earrings. The chin is oval. The neck has a curving groove. She wears a tunic and a himation. The tunic has loose sleeves reaching just below the elbows. The folds of the tunic are rendered by curving grooves on the chest and sleeve. The himation crosses the chest diagonally from the left shoulder to the right side and covers the left breast. It is fastened at the shoulder with a circular brooch with an incised border. A fold of the himation falls along the left side of her body onto the mattress in a zigzag-shaped fold. The himation covers her lower body and legs and ends at the ankles. She wears footwear: a sole is indicated by an incised, horizontal line. The right hand rests on the cushion and the fingers are extended. The left hand lightly pulls the edge of the veil at the height of her neck.

8. Ashurbanipal and the Reclining Banqueter in Palmyra

Maura K. Heyn

The University of North Carolina at Greensboro (mkheyn@uncg.edu)

Figure 8.1. Wall-panel: banquet scene with Ashurbanipal and his queen. North Palace, Nineveh. 645–635 BC (© The Trustees of the British Museum (BM 124920)).

Introduction

Fifty years have passed since the publication of Jean-Marie Dentzer's seminal article on the reclining banqueter in Persian royal iconography and the connection of this motif to the seventh-century BC scene from the palace in Nineveh featuring the Neo-Assyrian king, Ashurbanipal, and his wife banqueting in a garden (Fig. 8.1).[1] It is a famous scene, largely because the head of the Elamite king whom Ashurbanipal has defeated is seen hanging from a tree branch in the garden. Despite the near millennium which separated the Sassanid Persian examples from their purported Neo-Assyrian paradigm, Dentzer argued that the enduring popularity of the image of the reclining banqueter, including at nearby Palmyra, hearkened back to the pose of Ashurbanipal and its association with royal or aristocratic status.[2] In this chapter, I revisit Dentzer's argument regarding the pose of the Neo-Assyrian king as a starting point to interpreting the significance of this motif in Palmyrene funerary sculpture (Fig. 8.2). The banquet scene is ubiquitous in the Mediterranean, and present in Mesopotamia, in the centuries preceding its appearance in Palmyra, and its popularity in Palmyra presents us with an interesting opportunity to juxtapose the modes of presentation from the different regions. Although it is certainly the case that the significance of the scene in Palmyra was context-specific, it is also possible that its perceived provenance added to its effectiveness as a symbol of elite status, as Dentzer argued. There is evidence at Palmyra to support both the idea that the reclining figure motif was meaningful on its own and that this significance was strongly connected to the eastern tradition.

Palmyrene Funerary Sculpture

The most common type of sculpture in the tombs of Palmyra was the high-relief, torso-length portrait (Figs 8.3–8.4). With preserved examples numbering in the thousands, these portraits were a desirable and effective means for the ancient inhabitants of Palmyra to commemorate their dead, celebrate their families, and share or mould their identity.[3] Although not the focus of

---

[1] I would like to thank Rubina Raja and Kenneth Lapatin for the invitation to participate in the day-long event at the Getty Villa and to contribute to this publication. As always, it is an honour.

[2] Dentzer 1971.

[3] The most comprehensive database of these portraits is the

Figure 8.2. Banquet relief. Palmyra. Palmyra Museum, A 218 (photo: the author).

this chapter, the source of the inspiration for this style of funerary portraiture has also been debated, and much of the discussion centres on the eastern or western origin of the frontal portraits. Malcolm Colledge, who wrote the seminal book on the art of Palmyra, identified the source for the relief portraits that sealed the burial niches as Roman.[4] Several earlier scholars argued for an eastern, Parthian, influence on the sculpture, particularly with regard to its strict frontality.[5]

The blended or hybrid nature of Palmyrene art and architecture is a well-known phenomenon. Considering the geographical position of Palmyra as well as the role of its citizens in the caravan trade, this hybridity is not surprising, but equating the significance of the individual blended components with either their geographical origin or meaning in the original location can be problematic.[6] To further complicate matters, Palmyrene artists of the first several centuries AD were drawing motifs from regions where much cultural interchange had already happened, adding another layer of hybridity.[7] The coexistence of Greek, Persian, Semitic, Hellenistic, Arab, and Roman traits, to name just a few, make the identification of a single source for any motif difficult, if not futile. For example, Ernest Will has argued that the banquet scene in the Palmyrene tomb drew its inspiration from funerary reliefs from Hellenistic Asia Minor, which had in turn been inspired by similar, albeit not always funerary, scenes in Greece, which admittedly may have all derived from the original Neo-Assyrian scene with Ashurbanipal and his wife.[8]

Lucinda Dirven has argued that we should move away from ethnic descriptors when speculating about the significance of a particular style in Palmyra, that we are perhaps overemphasizing this aspect of its significance.[9] Along similar lines, Kevin Butcher has pointed out:

> One can try to tease apart the different threads of origins and influences at places like Palmyra and Petra, but the separate influences need not say anything much about what the whole meant to contemporaries. Still less do the influences help to define what is 'real' and what is 'veneer'.

---

forthcoming database from the Palmyra Portrait Project: <https://projects.au.dk/palmyraportrait/about/> [accessed 15 January 2021]; Kropp and Raja 2014.

[4] Colledge 1976, 239; see also Edwell 2019, 119 for a summary of the debate. See Raja 2017a.

[5] Seyrig 1950; Ingholt 1954; Rostovtzeff 1935.

[6] Raja 2015b, 333; Raja 2017a, 343.

[7] Colledge 1976, 241–42; Ingholt 1954.

[8] Will 1951.

[9] Dirven 2018.

When looking for social identities, one has to take into account all of the evidence, which is no easy task. All sorts of cultural symbols – shapes and designs of pottery, funerary rites, images of deities and so on – were manipulated by communities and individuals to express similarities with or differences from others.[10]

Considering these valid concerns, making an argument for the origin of the reclining banqueter motif and, following upon that assertion, the possible significance of this provenance in Palmyra, seems somewhat contradictory. Nevertheless, given the possibility that the (purported) source of the motif added to its efficacy as a demonstration of elite status in the tomb, it is worth considering that the significance of the motif was connected to its regal origins in the East. The attributes, hand gestures, and dress associated with the reclining figures in the Palmyrene tomb suggest a strong affiliation with the eastern iconographic tradition, and the singular prominence of the reclining figure in the various iterations of the banquet scene suggest that its symbolism could be self-contained.

Figure 8.3. Funerary relief of Abuna, daughter of Nabuna, c. AD 170–230. Palmyra. Limestone with traces of red paint. Gift of Edward B. Greene, B.A. 1900 (Yale University Art Gallery [1930.6]).

Reclining Figure Motif

The banquet scene was a popular choice among the Palmyrene elite for representing the family in the tomb in the first three centuries AD, and the reclining figure alone also appears on the tesserae from the sanctuaries in the city. The earliest versions in the funerary sphere appear on the exterior of the tomb, in niches that were strategically placed to be visible to those passing on the nearby roads.[11] The earliest in situ example is the scene on the Tower Tomb of Kithôt, dated to 40 AD.[12] In the scene, placed high on the north-east facade of the tomb and framed by an arched recess,[13] the reclining figure, probably Kithôt, rests on his left elbow and stretches across the kline in the foreground. This recumbent figure clearly dominates the scene, especially as it would have been seen from below. Kithôt's right hand rests on his right thigh, and he presumably held a cup (no longer visible) in his left hand. He wears a long-sleeved tunic over which a cloak is draped, and loose trousers adorned with an embroidered band. Kithôt's three family members,

---

10 Butcher 2003, 332.

11 Makowski 1985a, 72–73. For the importance of the familial tombs as expressions of social status, see Yon 1999.

12 Will 1951; Colledge 1976, 64.

13 Gawlikowski 1970, 147–48.

Figure 8.4. Funerary relief. Palmyra, c. AD 125–150 (The Metropolitan Museum of Art, New York, Bequest of Armida B. Colt, 2011 [2012.454]).

Figure 8.5. Banquet scene of Malkû, Palmyra. National Museum of Damascus. Picture from Ingholt Archive (© Palmyra Portrait Project. By permission of Ny Carlsberg Glyptotek).

his wife and two sons, stand in the background. Both sons wear the cylindrical hat associated with priests in Palmyra and hold banqueting vessels; the son to the left wears a belted, short-sleeved tunic and the son to the right has his cloak draped in the 'arm-sling' arrangement around his right arm. The mother, who is standing on the far right, wears a long-sleeved tunic and cloak, with a veil draped over her head. Niches which probably once contained banquet scenes similar to that on the facade of the Tomb of Kithôt are also seen on several other tower tombs dating to the late first and early second centuries AD.[14] The placement of the inscription under the banquet relief as well as evidence for paint on the figures further emphasizes the importance of the scene for the identity of the family.[15]

When these banquet scenes are placed inside the tombs, early in the second century AD, they retain the basic characteristics of the exterior examples: a prominent, recumbent male (or males) in the foreground, resting his left elbow on the cushion(s) and holding a drinking cup in his left hand in front of his chest (Figs 8.2 and 8.5).[16] His right hand, occasionally holding an attribute such as a leaf or garland, would be casually positioned on the right knee, which was raised to allow the left leg to tuck underneath.[17] These scenes, of which 117 examples are known,[18] also continue to be important status markers, judging from their prominent placement in the tomb where lines of sight and purpose-built niches drew the attention of the visitor. In some cases, the banquet scene would have been the first thing which was seen upon entering the tomb.[19]

---

[14] Will 1951, 84; 1949, 99.

[15] Henning 2019, 160–61.

[16] Heyn 2018, 107.

[17] Colledge 1976, 74.

[18] Raja 2019a. The number is based on Raja's paper 'Palmyran Art and the East' given at the conference from which this volume stems, 'Palmyra and the East' at the Getty Villa, USA, 18 April 2019.

[19] For example, the Hypogeum of Bolbarak (Sadurska and Bounni 1994, 148); and the Hypogeum of the Family of Artaban, son of 'Ogga (Sadurska and Bounni 1994, 39).

8. ASHURBANIPAL AND THE RECLINING BANQUETER IN PALMYRA

The larger-scale banquet scenes were carved in high relief on flat rectangular limestone slabs or on L-shaped slabs that served as sarcophagus lids. A lower slab or the sarcophagus would then be carved to represent the banqueting kline. Armless busts of additional family members were often placed in the space between the carved legs of this couch, and family members were grouped behind the reclining figure in the banquet scene above. Occasionally, figured scenes would appear in the space between the legs of the couch, such as groups of young men wearing matching outfits and holding items appropriate to a banquet or perhaps preparing for a hunt.[20] Two examples also exist of the banquet scene carved on the front of the sarcophagus itself.[21]

Although these large-scale scenes have predictable elements: the reclining figure in the foreground holding a cup and surrounded by members of his family, including his wife or mother seated at his feet, there is a great deal of variety in the different banquet reliefs. This variety is found not only in the placement of the scene, with some displayed individually in niches in the tomb while others were grouped with others in a triclinium or pentiklinium arrangement,[22] but also in the arrangement of family members whose identity is made clear by the accompanying inscriptions. Despite the clear importance of the reclining figure, scenes featuring the recumbent figure alone are very rare, indicating the importance of showing additional family members or attendants.[23]

An example of one these large-scale scenes (Fig. 8.2), which used to be displayed in the courtyard of the Palmyra Museum, is the scene of Barateh and his mother and brothers. Barateh's recumbent figure dominates the scene in a pattern which repeats itself on all other large-scale scenes. He is wearing the 'Parthian' costume: a long tunic, belted at the waist, with embroidery at the hem and cuffs. Under the tunic, Barateh wears trousers decorated with an embroidered band. He also wears chaps over his trousers, and soft, embroidered shoes. He also wears a riding cloak that attached on the right side with a fibula. He wears the priestly headgear on his head: a tall, cylindrical cap adorned with a wreath and a small bust. Barateh's three brothers, who stand behind him in smaller scale, wear a tunic and cloak, with the right arm in the sling created by the draping of the cloak. Thus, their garments differ from that of their brother, a phenomenon which repeats itself in many other banquet scenes. Their mother is seated in a chair at the end of the couch. She is wearing a similar outfit to the wife of Kithôt: a long tunic, over which a cloak is draped and attached at the left shoulder with a fibula. She wears a turban and veil on her head.[24]

An additional example of these popular scenes is the third-century scene from the Hypogeum of Bôlbarak (not pictured).[25] The large, recumbent figure of Bôlbarak, with his huge left hand grasping the drinking vessel, is surrounded by members of his family, but the choice of family members is somewhat unusual. On either side of Bôlbarak are his mother, to his left, and his first wife, likely deceased, to the far right. His second wife stands next to the first, and his son stands next to her.[26] The left hand of the Bôlbarak's son rests on the shoulder of his father. The five busts between the legs of the couch represent Bôlbarak's other children. It was clearly important to represent family members but, given that deceased and living relatives could be included, it is not obvious why Bôlbarak is drawing attention to the women in his family, his two wives and his mother.[27] This scenario might suggest that fathers, if pictured, would recline with their sons in an indication of their status.

There are also abridged versions of the large-scale banquet scene in the Palmyrene tomb, although these are less common. This truncated version of the scene, which features two reclining figures holding a cup in the left hand and seen only from the waist up is a cross between a full-scale banquet and a torso-length relief. Rather than members of the family, these so-called hybrid scenes include a small-scale, full-length figure, presumably an attendant, standing to the side.[28] The Hypogeum of Astor, son of Maliku, located in the south-east necropolis, contained six of these hybrid scenes, none of which bore an inscription.[29] The lack of inscription,

---

[20] Colledge 1976, 78.

[21] One was found in the underground tomb of Lišamš (Ingholt 1938, 107). Another, dated to AD 249/50, was found in a temple tomb (#173b) (Gawlikowski 1970, 133 n. 15).

[22] Colledge 1976, 75.

[23] Raja 2017b, 420 n. 19: only four of the banquet scenes in the Palmyra Portrait Project database represent the reclining figure alone.

[24] Chabot 1922, 112–13.

[25] Palmyra Museum, Palmyra, inv. no. 1795/6644, 1796/6645; Sadurska and Bounni 1994, 142–43, fig. 247.

[26] Sadurska and Bounni 1994, 148.

[27] The importance of representing a large family is made clear by the triclinium in the Hypogeum of Bolha, with twenty-one family members represented (Sadurska 1995, 587).

[28] Colledge 1976, 74.

[29] Sadurska and Bounni 1994, 14–22.

the absence of any female figures, and the presence of the young attendants proffering vases or garlands prompted Sadurska and Bounni to interpret the scenes as an allusion to the sacred banquets in the city and not as a family banquet.[30] It is interesting to consider that the absence of family members implies that a different type of banquet (cultic rather than familial) is represented, especially when the family, even when depicted, do not indicate participation in any way other than their presence.

An additional variation of the banquet scene is the so-called miniature banquet scene (Fig. 8.6): a genre that appears in the second century and reaches its zenith in the third.[31] These scenes are carved on limestone slabs no bigger than those which sealed the *loculi*, and most commonly feature only the main reclining figure, with an attendant or two standing at his feet, though examples do exist of family members included in such scenes. In Figure 8.7, the deceased is depicted with his son and two daughters. In other examples, the deceased is depicted with two attendants (Fig. 8.8) or with his wife.[32] Clearly, various groupings were acceptable in the tomb, but the reclining figure holding a cup is an integral element.

Lastly, reclining figures appear on small, clay tokens, known as tesserae,

Figure 8.6. Relief, funeral banquet, *c.* AD 200–250, limestone (courtesy of the Yale University Art Gallery, purchased for the University by Prof. Rostovtzeff (1931.138)).

Figure 8.7. Funerary relief. Probably Palmyra, *c.* second to third centuries AD (The Metropolitan Museum of Art, New York. Gift of Mr and Mrs Harry G. Friedman, 1955 (02.29.1)).

---

[30] Sadurska and Bounni 1994, 15. Sadurska (1996, 285) also suggested that the smaller-scale banquet scenes with attendants rather than female family members and lacking inscriptions might symbolically represent family members engaged in a perpetual meal with the deceased.

[31] Colledge 1976, 78–79; Makowski 1985b.

[32] For example, on a miniature banquet in the Louvre Museum. First half of third century AD, Palmyra, Syria, Limestone, H. 44 cm; W. 57 cm; D. 21 cm. Acquired in 1890; AO 2000 The epitaph reads 'Image of Maliku, son of Hagegu, son of Maliku, priest of the temple precinct, alas! and Hadira, his wife' <https://collections.louvre.fr/en/ark:/53355/cl010127798> [accessed 24 October 2021]; see also Dentzer-Feydy and Teixidor (eds) 1993.

Figure 8.9. Clay tessera with banquet scene. Probably Palmyra, c. first to second centuries AD (The Metropolitan Museum of Art, New York. Purchase, 1902 (55.109)).

Figure 8.8. Funerary relief of a banquet scene. Limestone, c. AD 200–273, the University of Pennsylvania Museum of Archaeology and Anthropology, Babylonian Expedition to Nippur II, 1890 (image courtesy of Penn Museum, image no. 299131; object no. B8902).

that have been found in the sanctuaries of the city.[33] These clay tokens, of which over 1100 different types are known, seem to have functioned as entrance tickets to sacred banquets in the sanctuaries of the city. In addition to scattered finds and a single cache in the sanctuaries, the largest number of these tokens has been found in the drainage area near the banqueting hall in the Sanctuary of Bel.[34] Banqueting was an important part of Palmyrene religious rituals, and, in addition to the banquet hall in the Sanctuary of Bel, three other banquet halls have been identified in Palmyra, one in the Sanctuary of Ba'alshamin and two outside temple complexes.[35] Palmyrene priests played an important role in organizing and funding these banquets to which entrance was granted only to those with the appropriate tessera.[36] The imagery on these tesserae is a fascinating blend of religious symbols, banqueting imagery, inscriptions, and seal impressions, and one of the most common images on the obverse was that of a Palmyrene priest or two reclining on a kline and perhaps holding a cup in the left hand (Fig. 8.9).[37] The similarity between the reclining figure on the tesserae and the male figures in the funerary reliefs prompted some to speculate that the tesserae were tickets to funerary banquets, but not one has ever been found in a funerary context.[38]

Identification of the Banquet Scene

The type of banquet represented by the funerary scene in Palmyra has been much debated, and certainly its appearance in the tombs muddies the waters of interpretation. It would make sense for a funerary banquet to be represented, given the burial context of the scene as well as the popularity of placing the scenes in the u-shaped triclinium arrangement for dining.[39] However, food is never displayed in these banquet scenes, and the vessels held and displayed are more appropriate for drinking than eating.[40] The depiction of a banquet in the afterworld[41] seems unlikely for similar reasons, lack of food and focus on drinking, and also because some of the family members, whose like-

---

[33] Raja 2015a; 2019b; Ingholt, Seyrig, and Starcky 1955; Seyrig 1937.

[34] Raja 2015a; the cache was found in the Sanctuary of Arsu (Raja 2019b, 224).

[35] Raja 2015a, 190; 2016.

[36] Kaizer 2002, 165, 221–29.

[37] Raja 2019b, 224.

[38] Seyrig 1940, 52.

[39] Colledge 1976, 75.

[40] Colledge 1976, 77; Seyrig 1951, 33–35; Will 1951, 96–98.

[41] Cumont 1942, 421.

Figure 8.10. Skyphos, 100–50 BC, silver (The J. Paul Getty Museum, Villa Collection, Malibu, California, Gift of Barbara and Lawrence Fleischman (96.AM.162.7)).

Figure 8.11. Phiale Mesomphalos, 525–450 BC, silver (The J. Paul Getty Museum, Villa Collection, Malibu, California. Digital image courtesy of the Getty's Open Content Program (68.AM.16)).

nesses were included, were still alive when the banquet scene was carved.[42]

The most agreed-upon conclusion is that the banquet motif served as a convenient excuse to place the family together, dressed in their finest attire.[43] The scene would thus be a 'sculptural memorial' of the happy family life and could serve as a reference to actual familial banquets.[44] While the evidence for banqueting in a private residence is much less abundant than for the sacred banquets, elite houses in Palmyra contained dining rooms with sumptuous decoration: wall paintings, stucco work, floors with opus sectile and mosaic decoration; these were clearly spaces where family banquets could take place.[45] The identification of the funerary scene as a family banquet is also corroborated by wall paintings from a dining room in nearby Dura-Europos, where diners with Palmyrene names are depicted in similar positions and holding drinking cups.[46] While drawing attention to the family group is clearly at work in the Palmyrene tomb, this particular banqueting motif still seems like an odd choice, since many of those depicted do not seem to participate, and are, in fact, somewhat awkwardly included.

The appearance of the motif in both the tomb and on the tesserae from the sanctuaries could indicate that the funerary scenes allude to participation in the banquets to which the tesserae granted access.[47] The similarity of the reclining figures motif is clear. While the conclusion has been reached that the tesserae are not connected to any funerary banquet, the reverse still seems plausible: the motif in the tomb refers to participation in the sacred banquets. It is difficult to account for the presence of women and children in the scenes in the tombs as they would not have participated in the sacred banquets,[48] but if we isolate the reclining figure in the funerary sphere, then a connection is possible. In other words, the tesserae may not have reminded the viewer of a funerary banquet, but the reclining figure motif in the tomb could well have conjured up images of the sacred banquets in the city, high-status events where priests were in positions of authority.[49] As Audley-Miller points out:

> Visual connections with the tesserae may have been useful in emphasising the deceased subjects' priestly role overseeing cult banquets, reminding viewers of their benefactions of wine and food, or loosely recalling their presence at the centre of these occasions.[50]

This connection between the funerary and sacred spheres is strengthened by the other allusions to banquets, such as the rows of young men wearing similar costume and holding banqueting items.[51]

The dress worn by most of the reclining figures might also provide a connection between the funerary and sacred banquets. Broadly, there are two styles of dress worn by the recumbent figures: a tunic with either long or short sleeves over which a cloak would be draped in a style which is described as Graeco-Roman in origin, and an embroidered tunic worn over loose trousers, which are also adorned with ornate bands.[52] Sometimes a long-sleeved coat is worn over the tunic and occasionally a chlamys is added.[53] This latter costume is usually

---

[42] Colledge 1976, 132.
[43] Seyrig 1951, 37.
[44] Ingholt 1970/71, 182–83; Cussini 2016.
[45] Cussini 2016, 147.
[46] Audley-Miller 2016, 563–64; Cussini 2016, 150.
[47] Heyn 2008.
[48] Seyrig 1951, 37.

[49] Kaizer 2002, 165, 221–29; Milik 1972, 279–81.
[50] Audley-Miller 2016, 562.
[51] Will 1951, 96–99; Colledge 1976, 76.
[52] For more on 'Parthian' dress, see Curtis 2017; Long 2017; Taha 1982; Seyrig 1937.
[53] The frequency with which the Parthian dress appears is revealed by a brief survey of fourteen underground tombs which contained banquet scenes (Sadurska and Bounni 1994). Fifty reclining males are depicted in these scenes: thirty-four of them

described as 'Parthian', though 'Mesopotamian' might be a more appropriate adjective.[54] The reasons behind the choice of 'Graeco-Roman' or 'Parthian' attire in the funerary portraits are not obvious, although patterns in the way that certain clothing items are worn would suggest that it was not entirely a capricious choice.[55] For example, when the male members of the family or the accompanying attendant wear the so-called Parthian costume in the funerary banquet scene, they are also usually holding banqueting items, suggesting an association between costume and sacerdotal activities.[56] Additionally, when priests are depicted wearing the tall and cylindrical cap that identifies them as priests in both the torso-length reliefs as well as the banquet scenes, they seem to have shaved their heads, as no hair is visible.[57] Moreover, images of priests performing sacrifices on one of the peristyle beam reliefs from the Temple of Bel seem to indicate that the individual pairs of priests wear matching outfits.[58] It would therefore not seem unreasonable to assume that the dress worn in the funerary banquet scenes, if these scenes allude to banquets in the sanctuaries of the city, would strengthen the reference to sacred banquets.

The cup held by the reclining figure represents an additional opportunity to add variety to the scene but is also clearly an integral element to its meaning: in all of the different iterations of the scene, a drinking cup almost always appears in the hand, usually the left, of the reclining figure.[59] There are two types of cups displayed in the Palmyrene banquet scene: the skyphos, with its origins in the West, and the phiale, with a clear eastern pedigree.[60] The skyphos is a deep, two-handled cup with a pedestal (Fig. 8.10). Some of the skyphoi in the Palmyrene scenes bear no decoration (Fig. 8.2), but others are decorated with rosettes (Figs 8.5 and 8.7) or oblique slashes. The other common vessel, the phiale, has a wide and shallow profile, without handles (Fig. 8.11). Like the skyphoi, these phialai can be rendered without decoration (Fig. 8.6) or adorned with a honeycomb (Fig. 8.8) or lozenge pattern. Traditionally associated with Achaemenid Persians, the phiale shows up in Greek symposium scenes as a drinking vessel but was much more commonly used in the Greek world for libations.[61] Although there is some evidence of the phiale being used for a libation in Palmyra,[62] its function as a drinking vessel in the Palmyrene banqueting scenes is clear. The evidence for these skyphoi and phialai, likely made of gold or silver (Figs 8.10–8.11), is restricted to the funerary art in Palmyra, since they have not been found in archaeological excavations, but the pottery that has been found at the site includes imported vessels from East and West.[63]

The manner with which the phiale is held in the Palmyrene reliefs provides further evidence of incorporating motifs from the East; indeed, the pedigree of this hand position can be traced back to the banqueting scene of Ashurbanipal at Nineveh (Fig. 8.1). In her analysis of symposium scenes in western Anatolia from the sixth to the fourth centuries, Margaret Miller noticed that the manner in which the reclining figure balanced his drinking bowl on three fingers fit Xenophon's description of the way in which the phiale was held in the Achaemenid court. According to Miller, this 'practice of holding a drinking bowl on three fingers was a Persian-period refinement of an older Assyrian manner of drinking'.[64] Turning to the Neo-Assyrian relief (Fig. 8.1), it is impossible to see the hand and cup of Ashurbanipal, obliterated by Elamite vandalism because of the importance of the cup to his identity, but the queen quite clearly holds her cup balanced on the tips of three fingers.[65] The reclining figures in the banquet scenes in Palmyra who display the phiale hold it in much the same way (Figs 8.6 and 8.8), and it seems reasonable to see this manner of holding the cup as eastern in origin and associated with high status. Moreover, the importance attached to the royal cup that would have provoked the Elamites to destroy its image adds an interesting dimension to the importance of the cup for the identity of the reclining male in Palmyra.[66]

---

are in Parthian dress and sixteen are in the Graeco-Roman tunic and cloak. Those in Parthian dress outnumber those in the Graeco-Roman tunic by a ratio of more than two-to-one.

54   Butcher 2003, 329.

55   Heyn 2008.

56   Heyn 2008, 179.

57   Stucky 1973, 175; Ingholt 1934, 33–35; For more on priestly dress, see Raja 2017b.

58   Heyn 2008, 186.

59   Heyn 2021.

60   Miyashita 2016.

---

61   Tsingarida 2009.

62   Mosaic (Palmyra Museum, Palmyra, inv. no. 1686) from the peristyle of a house located east of the Temple of Bel in Palmyra, and dating from c. AD 160–260, depicts the god Asklepios pouring wine from a phiale onto a flaming altar (Colledge 1976, 105, pl. 141).

63   Colledge 1976, 94–95.

64   Miller 2011, 114.

65   Miller 2011, 100.

66   On the significance of the royal cup in Assyria, see Nylander 1999; Stronach 1995; Winter 1986.

Palmyrene men who recline almost always hold a cup in the left hand.[67] Even in the most abbreviated versions of the scene, they hold the cup, and arguably draw attention to it with the gesture of their fingers (Figs 8.2, 8.5, and 8.7).[68] Additional evidence for the importance of the cup for the significance of the scene is found on the rare occasions when women are depicted reclining.[69] These women never hold a cup, which indicates the importance of this attribute for the reclining men in the banquet scenes, although clearly both men and women could communicate high status by reclining.[70]

The attention drawn to the reclining figure in Dentzer's interpretation presents some interesting possibilities for the significance of the banquet scene with male reclining figures in Palmyra. As explained in the introduction, Dentzer argued that the reclining figure motif in the East could be traced back to the depiction of the garden party of Assurbanipal at Nineveh (Fig. 8.1). While the significance of the banquet motif in Palmyra was surely related to its connection to local practices,[71] whether those were family banquets and/or sacred banquets, there is reason to believe that the reclining figure had additional significance on its own. In his argument regarding the symbolism of the reclining figure, Dentzer saw clear points of connection between the Palmyrene figures and Ashurbanipal: he pointed out the schematic position of the legs, the left hand holding the drinking vessel with the right hand posed on the knee, the banqueting couch with its pile of cushions on the right, and the absence of any other banqueting items except the cup.[72] Certainly the position of this figure, his larger scale, his attributes, and often, his dress, set him apart; that the message might have been associated with eastern, regnal, depictions is worth considering, especially since many of these characteristics were also of eastern derivation.

If the reclining figure could be considered as an independent, high-status reference, one could interpret the scene not as representing an event or memorializing a gathering of the family, but rather as a collection of family portraits and symbols that contributed to the prestige of the family.[73] This manner of creating and reinforcing identity through a juxtaposition of images has already been seen on the banqueting tesserae, which were clearly used by those organizing the banquets as illustrations of their status in the community.[74] In other words, instead of imagining the scene as a family moment captured in the equivalent of a photograph, we should see it a collage of images that draw attention to important family members, status-raising activities, and wealth.

In sum, although it is admittedly difficult to tease out an origin for the banqueting motif in Palmyra, when considering its appearance alongside the choice of attributes, the manner in which some of them are held, and the garments worn by certain of the figures, we cannot rule out the East as a source of inspiration. Dentzer's argument regarding the eastern origins for the reclining figure is particularly compelling because of the similar importance granted to this recumbent figure in Nineveh and Palmyra. In the Palmyrene scenes the reclining figure stands out because of its larger scale, its placement in the foreground, and the consistency with which the reclining figure with his cup appears in all the different iterations of the scene in the tomb. The sheer variety of the other elements that are included in these scenes — whether they be the wife or mother at the end of the couch, the surrounding family members, the couch, the

---

[67] Examples of cup held in the right hand: large-scale banquet scenes in the Hypogeum of Bolha (Sadurska and Bounni 1994, figs 233 and 234); miniature banquet in the Hypogeum of 'Aštôr, son of Malikû (Palmyra Museum, Palmyra, inv. no. 1731/6402; Tanabe 1986, fig. 432); miniature banquet in the Cleveland Museum of Art (acc. no. 1964.359); miniature banquet in the Nelson-Atkins Museum of Art (acc. no. 65.2); miniature banquet in the Louvre (AO 4999 — Dentzer-Feydy and Teixidor (eds) 1993, 203 n. 201).

[68] For a similar phenomenon, using hand gestures to draw attention to the attribute in the torso-length relief portraits from Palmyra, see Heyn 2010.

[69] One example is found in the Hypogeum of Ta'aî, and depicts a sister and brother reclining together (Charles-Gaffiot, Hofman, and Lavagne (eds) 2001, 367, fig. 255); a second, featuring a woman reclining alone, is a miniature banquet scene, located today in the Damascus Museum (National Museum, Damascus, inv. no. 2153; Tanabe 1986, fig. 438; Colledge 1976, pl. 107); and a third, on the short end of a sarcophagus in the courtyard of the Palmyra Museum.

[70] For a discussion of gendered implications of body language in Palmyra, see Davies 2017.

[71] Audley-Miller 2016.

[72] Dentzer 1971, 47.

[73] For a similar interpretation of the collection of images on a funerary stele from Smyrna, see the interpretation by Zanker (1993, 221–22) of the relief of Amyntes: 'This example shows especially clearly that we cannot expect a unity of time and space on the reliefs. The artists make allusion to a variety of themes and subjects and arrange the elements at hand so artfully that sometimes a seemingly deliberate narrative context results. In looking at the relief of little Amyntes we are apparently meant simultaneously to remember the child as he was in life, at play, to think of the costly monument that his parents set up to his memory, and to be sadly reminded, by the herm, shield, and wreath, that he died so young.'

[74] Raja 2019b, 231–32.

supplementary figures, or the figural scenes — suggests that the reclining figure does not depend on these additional elements for its significance. It is certainly possible that the pose of the reclining figure and perhaps his garments draw attention to his involvement in religious activities, and that the other elements of the scene, which did not allude to the same activity, provided supplementary though no less important information about his family. Dentzer's argument regarding the reclining banqueter motif allows us to interpret the whole scene as a collage of sorts; a presentation of different elements that conveyed or created the prestige of the family: the banqueter, his couch, his wife, his parents, his children, his activities in the city.

Works Cited

Audley-Miller, L. 2016. 'The Banquet in Palmyrene Funerary Contexts', in C. M. Draycott and M. Stamatopoulou (eds), *Dining and Death: Interdisciplinary Perspectives on the 'Funerary Banquet' in Ancient Art, Burial and Belief* (Leuven: Peeters), pp. 549–86.

Butcher, K. 2003. *Roman Syria and the Near East* (Los Angeles: J. Paul Getty Museum).

Chabot, J.-B. 1922. *Choix d'inscriptions de Palmyre* (Paris: Imprimerie nationale).

Charles-Gaffiot, J., J.-M. Hofman, and H. Lavagne (eds). 2001. *Moi, Zénobie reine de Palmyre* (Paris: Centre culturel du Panthéon).

Colledge, M. A. R. 1976. *The Art of Palmyra* (London: Thames and Hudson).

Cumont, F. 1942. *Recherches sur le symbolisme funéraire des Romains* (Paris: Geuthner).

Curtis, V. S. 2017. 'The Parthian Haute-Couture at Palmyra', in T. Long and A. H. Sørensen (eds), *Positions and Professions in Palmyra*, Palmyrene Studies, 2 (Copenhagen: The Royal Danish Academy of Sciences and Letters), pp. 52–67.

Cussini, E. 2016. 'Family Banqueting at Palmyra: Reassessing the Evidence', in P. Corò and others (eds), *Libiamo ne' lieti calici: Ancient Near Eastern Studies Presented to Lucio Milano on the Occasion of his 65th Birthday by Pupils, Colleagues, and Friends* (Münster: Ugarit), pp. 139–59.

Davies, G. 2017. 'The Body Language of Palmyra and Rome', in T. Long and A. H. Sørensen (eds), *Positions and Professions in Palmyra*, Palmyrene Studies, 2 (Copenhagen: The Royal Danish Academy of Sciences and Letters), pp. 20–36.

Dentzer, J.-M. 1971. 'L'Iconographie iranienne du souverain couché et le motif du banquet', *Annales archéologiques arabes syriennes*, 21: 39–50.

Dentzer-Feydy, J. and J. Teixidor (eds). 1993. *Les antiquités de Palmyre au Musée du Louvre* (Paris: Seuil).

Dirven, L. 2018. 'Palmyrene Sculpture in Context: Between Hybridity and Heterogeneity', in J. Aruz (ed.), *Palmyra: Mirage in the Desert* (New York: Yale University Press), pp. 120–29.

Edwell, P. 2019. 'Palmyra between Rome and the Parthians', in A. M. Nielsen and R. Raja (eds), *The Road to Palmyra* (Copenhagen: Ny Carlsberg Glyptotek), pp. 109–26.

Gawlikowski, M. 1970. *Monuments funéraires de Palmyre* (Warsaw: University of Warsaw).

Henning, A. 2019. 'Houses of Eternity', in A. M. Nielsen and R. Raja (eds), *The Road to Palmyra* (Copenhagen: Ny Carlsberg Glyptotek), pp. 155–72.

Heyn, M. K. 2008. 'Sacerdotal Activities and Parthian Dress in Roman Palmyra', in C. S. Colburn and M. K. Heyn (eds), *Reading a Dynamic Canvas: Adornment in the Ancient Mediterranean World* (Newcastle: Cambridge Scholars), pp. 170–93.

—— 2010. 'Gesture and Identity in the Funerary Art of Palmyra', *American Journal of Archaeology*, 114: 631–61.

—— 2018. 'Embodied Identities in the Funerary Portraiture of Palmyra', in Joan Aruz (ed.), *Palmyra: Mirage in the Desert* (New York: Yale University Press), pp. 110–19.

—— 2021. 'The Significance of Drinking Attributes in Palmyrene Banquet Scenes', in M. Heyn and R. Raja (eds), *Individualizing the Dead: Attributes in Palmyrene Funerary Sculpture*, Studies in Palmyrene Archaeology and History, 3 (Turnhout: Brepols), pp. 63–71.

Ingholt, H. 1934. 'Palmyrene Sculptures in Beirut', *Berytus*, 1: 32–43.

—— 1938. 'Inscriptions and Sculptures from Palmyra II', *Berytus*, 5: 93–140.

—— 1954. *Palmyrene and Gandharan Sculpture: An Exhibition Illustrating the Cultural Interrelations between the Parthian Empire and its Neighbors West and East, Palmyra and Gandhara, October 14 through November 14, 1954* (New Haven: Yale University Art Gallery).

—— 1970/71. 'The Sarcophagus of Be'elai and Other Sculptures from the Tomb of Malkû, Palmyra', *Mélanges de l'Université Saint-Joseph*, 45: 173–200.

Ingholt, H., H. Seyrig, and J. Starcky. 1955. *Recueil des tessères de Palmyre* (Paris: Geuthner).

Kaizer, T. 2002. *The Religious Life of Palmyra: A Study of the Social Patterns of Worship in the Roman Period* (Stuttgart: Steiner).

Kropp, A. and R. Raja. 2014. 'The Palmyra Portrait Project', *Syria*, 91: 393–408.

Long, T. 2017. 'The Use of Parthian Costume in Funerary Portraiture in Palmyra', in T. Long and A. H. Sørensen (eds), *Positions and Professions in Palmyra*, Palmyrene Studies, 2 (Copenhagen: The Royal Danish Academy of Sciences and Letters), pp. 68–83.

Makowski, K. C. 1985a. 'La sculpture funéraire palmyrénienne et sa fonction dans l'architecture sépulcrale', *Studia Palmyrenskie: Études palmyréniennes*, 8: 69–117.

—— 1985b. 'Recherches sur le banquet miniaturisé dans l'art funéraire de Palmyre', *Studia Palmyrenskie: Études palmyréniennes*, 8: 119–30.

Milik, J. T. 1972. *Dédicaces faites par des dieux (Palmyre, Hatra, Tyr) et des thiases sémitiques à l'époque romaine* (Paris: Bibliothèque archéologique et historique).

Miller, M. 2011. '"Manners Makyth Man": Diacritical Drinking in Achaemenid Anatolia', in E. S. Gruen (ed.), *Cultural Identity in the Ancient Mediterranean* (Los Angeles: Getty Research Institute), pp. 97–134.

Miyashita, S. 2016. 'The Vessels in Palmyrene Banquet Scenes: Tomb BWLH and BWRP and Tomb TYBL', in J. C. Meyer, E. H. Seland, and N. Anfinset (eds), *Palmyrena: City, Hinterland and Caravan Trade between Orient and Occident; Proceedings of the Conference Held in Athens, December 1–3, 2012* (Oxford: Archaeopress), pp. 131–46.

Nylander, C. 1999. 'Breaking the Cup of Kingship: An Elamite Coup in Nineveh?', *Iranica antiqua*, 34: 71–83.

Raja, R. 2015a. 'Cultic Dining and Religious Patterns in Palmyra: The Case of the Palmyrene Banqueting Tesserae', in S. Faust, M. Seifert, and L. Ziemer (eds), *Festschrift für Inge Nielsen zum 65. Geburtstag*, Gateways, Hamburger Beiträge zur Archäologie und Kulturgeschichte des antiken Mittelmeerraumes, 3 (Aachen: Shaker), pp. 181–200.

—— 2015b. 'Palmyrene Funerary Portraits in Context: Portrait Habit between Local Traditions and Imperial Trends', in J. Fejfer, M. Moltesen, and A. Rathje (eds), *Traditions: Transmission of Culture in the Ancient World*, Acta Hyperborea, 14 (Copenhagen: Collegium Hyperboreum and Museum Tusculanum Press), pp. 329–61.

—— 2016. 'In and Out of Contexts: Explaining Religious Complexity through the Banqueting Tesserae from Palmyra', in R. Raja and L. Weiss (eds), *The Significance of Objects: Considerations on Agency and Context* (Tübingen: Mohr Siebeck), pp. 340–71.

—— 2017a. 'Powerful Images of the Deceased: Palmyrene Funerary Portrait Culture between Local, Greek and Roman Representations', in D. Boschung and F. Queyrel (eds), *Bilder der Macht: Das griechische Porträt und seine Verwendung in der antiken Welt*, Morphomata, 34 (Paderborn: Fink), pp. 319–48.

—— 2017b. '"You Can Leave your Hat on": Priestly Representations from Palmyra: Between Visual Genre, Religious Importance and Social Status', in R. Gordon, G. Peitridou, and J. Rüpke (eds), *Beyond Priesthood: Religious Entrepreneurs and Innovators in the Roman Empire* (Berlin: De Gruyter), pp. 417–42.

—— 2019a. 'Palmyran Art and the East', paper given at the conference Palmyra and the East, Getty Villa, USA, 18 April 2019.

—— 2019b. 'Religious Banquets in Palmyra and the Palmyrene Banqueting Tesserae', in A. M. Nielsen and R. Raja (eds), *The Road to Palmyra* (Copenhagen: Ny Carlsberg Glyptotek), pp. 221–34.

Rostovtzeff, M. I. 1935. 'Dura and the Problem of Parthian Art', *Yale Classical Studies*, 5: 157–303.

Sadurska, A. 1995. 'La famille et son image dans l'art de Palmyre', in F. E. König and S. Rebetez (eds), *Arculiana: Ioanni Boegli, anno sexagesimo quinto feliciter peracto* (Avenches: LAOTT), pp. 583–89.

Sadurska, A. and A. Bounni. 1994. *Les sculptures funéraires de Palmyre* (Rome: G. Bretschneider).

Seyrig, H. 1937. 'Armes et costumes iraniens de Palmyre', *Syria*, 18: 4–31.

—— 1940. 'Les tessères palmyréniennes et le banquet rituel', in H. Vincent (ed.), *Mémorial Lagrange* (Paris: Gabalda), pp. 51–58.

—— 1950. 'Palmyra and the East', *Journal of Roman Studies*, 40: 1–7.

—— 1951. 'Le repas des morts et le "banquet funèbre" à Palmyre', *Annales archéologiques arabes syriennes*, 2: 32–41.

Stronach, D. 1995. 'Imagery of the Wine Bowl: Wine in Assyria in the Early First Millennium B.C.', in P. E. McGovern, S. J. Fleming, and S. H. Katz (eds), *The Origins and Ancient History of Wine* (Philadelphia: The University of Pennsylvania Museum of Archaeology and Anthropology), pp. 175–95.

Stucky, R. 1973. 'Pretres syriens I: Palmyre', *Syria*, 50: 163–80.

Taha, A. 1982. 'Men's Costume in Palmyra', *Annales archéologiques arabes syriennes*, 32: 117–32.

Tanabe, K. 1986. *Sculptures of Palmyra*, I (Tokyo: Ancient Orient Museum).

Tsingarida, A. 2009. 'À la santé des dieux et des hommes: la phiale: un vase à boire au banquet athénien?', in M.-C. Villanueva-Puig (ed.), *Dossier: images mises en forme* (Paris: L'École des hautes études en sciences sociales), pp. 91–109.

Will, E. 1949. 'La tour funéraire de Palmyre', *Syria*, 26: 87–116.

—— 1951. 'Le relief de la tour de Kithôt et le banquet funéraire à Palmyre', *Syria*, 28: 70–100.

Winter, I. J. 1986. 'The King and the Cup', in M. K. Buccelati and others (eds), *Insight through Images: Studies in Honour of Edith Porada*, Bibliotheca Mesopotamica, 21 (Malibu: J. Paul Getty Museum), pp. 253–68.

Yon, J.-B. 1999. 'La présence des notables dans l'espace périurbain à Palmyre', in C. Petitfrère (ed.), *Construction, reproduction et représentation des patriciats urbains de l'Antiquité au XXᵉ siècle* (Tours: Université François Rabelais), pp. 387–400.

Zanker, P. 1993. 'The Hellenistic Grave Stelai from Smyrna: Identity and Self-Image in the Polis', in A. Bulloch and others (eds), *Images and Ideologies: Self-Definition in the Hellenistic World* (Berkeley: University of California Press), pp. 212–30.

9. So-Called 'Servants' or 'Pages' in Palmyrene Funerary Sculpture

Fred Albertson
University of Memphis, Department of Art (falbrtsn@memphis.edu)

Figure 9.1. Sarcophagus with scene of sacrifice, from Tomb 176, Palmyra. Limestone, *c.* AD 230. Palmyra Museum, Palmyra, inv. no. B 2677/8983 (© Livius.org. CC BY–SA 4.0).

Figure 9.2. Detail of Fig. 9.1, sacrifice with attendants carrying offerings (© Livius.org. CC BY–SA 4.0).

Introduction

Among the figural images depicted in Palmyrene funerary art is a category of young male figures identified as attendants. They appear within a very limited number of narrative scenes: as members of a religious sacrifice, who carry offerings and ritual implements; as bearers of items of food or utensils to be used in a banquet; and as grooms or weapon-bearers in an activity surrounding the preparation for a hunt or the departure of a caravan. Their appearance is confined primarily to sarcophagi, banquet reliefs imitating sarcophagi, and so-called 'small banquet reliefs' — all types which become popular towards the end of the second century AD.

Representations of Attendants

A representative example of this group is found on the front of a sarcophagus in the garden of the Palmyra Museum, discovered in Tomb 176 (Figs 9.1–9.2).[1] Here such attendants participate in a sacrifice. In the centre stands a priest, toga drawn up over his head, pouring a libation over a small altar. He is flanked by three attendants on each side. As is typical of our group, each of these attendants holds some item related to the offering occurring in the centre. From left to right are depicted an attendant leading a bull and holding an axe or mallet in the manner of a Roman *popa*, one holding a *patera* and a pitcher, another carrying an *acerra* (incense box), and then to the right of the sacrificer, an attendant carrying a plate of fruits, another with a bird

---

[1] Palmyra Museum, Palmyra, inv. no. B 2677/8983. Wielgosz 2004, 941–49, fig. 12; Schmidt-Colinet and al-As'ad 2007, 271–76, pls 84–89; Schmidt-Colinet 2009, 223–25, 228–31, figs 1–8; Raja 2019, 123 no. 38.

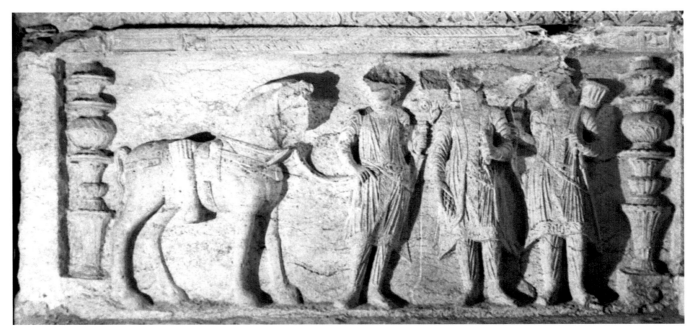

Figure 9.3. Sarcophagus depicting the departure for a hunt, from the Exedra of Julius Aurelius Maqqai, Tomb of ʿAtênaten, Palmyra. Limestone. After AD 229. In situ (Institut français du Proche-Orient: <https://medihal.archives-ouvertes.fr/medihal-00814945v1> [accessed 10 October 2021], under 'Open License')

on a plate, and a final figure bearing a pitcher (Fig. 9.2). A similar scene of sacrifice appears on one other sarcophagus from Palmyra, also in the Palmyra Museum.[2] The front shows two priests conducting the sacrifice, wearing togas drawn over the head in the Roman manner. Each of the priests are accompanied by a female figure, most likely their wives, elegantly dressed in a fringed mantle. At each end appear young males as attendants; the one on the right is carrying a large bowl with fruit, while his counterpart on the left bears an incense box. On the reverse side, another scene of sacrifice occurs, in this instance with only one priest pouring a libation over an altar. The priest is assisted by six figures. The first assistant on the left leads in a bull. He is then followed by individuals carrying a pitcher and a *patera*, an incense box, a plate of fruit, a bird, and a pitcher.

Another sarcophagus on which these attendants are represented is one of three found in the exedra constructed after AD 229 by Julius Aurelius Maqqai, within the Tomb of ʿAtênaten (Fig. 9.3).[3] The bearded figure in

Figure 9.4. Fragment of a sarcophagus depicting two attendants, from the Exedra of Julius Aurelius Maqqai, Tomb of ʿAtênaten, Palmyra. Limestone. After AD 229. Baalbek Museum, Baalbek (Institut français du Proche-Orient: <https://medihal.archives-ouvertes.fr/medihal-00783944v1> [accessed 10 October 2021], with permission).

[2] Palmyra Museum, Palmyra, inv. no. B 2723/9160. Wielgosz 2004, 941, 948; Schmidt-Colinet and al-Asʿad 2007, 276–77, pl. 90; Schmidt-Colinet 2009, 225–27, 232–34, figs 9–14; Raja 2019, 113–19 no. 32.

[3] In situ. Ingholt 1935, 63–67, pls 26–27.1; Colledge 1976,

Figure 9.5. Sarcophagus depicting two attendants and a camel, from the Polish Excavations of the Camp of Diocletian, Palmyra. Limestone, c. AD 220. Palmyra Museum, Palmyra, inv. no. 2093/7431 (© Michael & Carole ALCAMO/ Wikipedia. CC BY–SA 2.0).

the scene is a person of authority, who is shown holding sheaths of grain in his right hand and wearing a long vest-like garment over his tunic and trousers. His priestly cap is placed on one side, balanced by a wreath set on the other. He is accompanied by two attendants; the one on the left holds the reins of a horse, while the one on the right carries a bow and quiver. We can probably assume these are the possessions of our central figure. Colledge identifies the scene as the departure for a hunt,[4] although the lid of this sarcophagus portrays the typical reclining banqueter and the other two surviving but fragmentary sarcophagi from this exedra depict a series of attendant figures carrying items presumably associated with a banquet (Fig. 9.4).[5] In any case, such a 'departure for the hunt' would be unique.

A sarcophagus discovered during the Polish excavations of the Camp of Diocletian displays on the front side a similar scene although a camel has replaced the horse (Fig. 9.5).[6] Consequently, it is most often identified as the departure of a caravan. The deceased is being brought his camel, presumably to highlight his profession as a financier or caravan leader. In this case then, the scene is thought to be biographical. The camels depicted in these scenes, however, are not baggage-carrying animals — they are riding camels, with elaborate saddles, decorative saddle blankets, and a round shield attached at the back.[7] Another fragmentary sarcophagus, found in temple tomb no. 36, relates to the previous, except here a single attendant stands between a horse and a camel.[8] Ultimately, a connection with these scenes to a caravan may be supported by a third example, although fragmentary, found in the Tomb of Julius Aurelius Marona.[9] Here an attendant holds the reins of a horse or camel, whose front hooves are barely extant. The presence of a ship on the right side, however, clearly connects a scene of overland trade to one of seafaring trade, reflecting precisely Palmyra's links to the Mediterranean and the Persian Gulf. Finally, there is the possibility of a third example belonging to this caravan type, the relief from a sarcophagus recently displayed publicly for the first time in the exhibit 'Syria Matters' at the Museum of Islamic Art at Doha.[10] Unfortunately, only a camel is preserved, so there are no accompanying human figures to identify the specifics of the scene.

77–78, fig. 103; Wielgosz 2004, 933, 937–38, fig. 9; Krag and Raja 2017, 217 no. 22; Raja 2019, 122 no. 36, 123, fig. 24.

[4] Colledge 1976, 78.

[5] Ingholt 1935, 67–68, pl. 27.2 (sarcophagi); Krag and Raja 2017, 219 no. 32, fig. 10 (lid).

[6] Palmyra Museum, Palmyra, inv. no. 2093/7431. Michałowski 1962, 143–47 no. 16, figs 158–60; Tanabe 1986, pl. 431; Schmidt-Colinet 1992, 106 n. 377 b, 109, pl. 69d.

[7] Seland 2017, 107–08.

[8] Palmyra Museum, Palmyra. Schmidt-Colinet 1992, 109 no. S5, 127, fig. 59, pl. 33.

[9] Palmyra Museum, Palmyra, inv. no. B 1946/2249. Colledge 1976, 76, fig. 103; Wielgosz 2004, 939–40, fig. 10.

[10] Collection of Sheikh Saoud bin Mohammed al Thani. Christie's New York, 12 June 2002, sale 1091, lot 355; Kohlmeyer 2018, 70 no. 22; Raja 2019, 112 no. 28.

Figure 9.6. Sarcophagus depicting six attendants, from the Tomb of Aviation, Palmyra. Limestone, *c*. AD 220. Palmyra Museum, Palmyra (Institut français du Proche-Orient: <https://medihal.archives-ouvertes.fr/medihal-00779206v1> [accessed 10 October 2021], with permission).

Figure 9.7. Sarcophagus depicting attendants at a banquet, from the Tomb of Julius Aurelius Marona, Palmyra. Limestone. After AD 236. Palmyra Museum, Palmyra (Institut français du Proche-Orient: <https://medihal.archives-ouvertes.fr/medihal-00793932v1> [accessed 10 October 2021], with permission).

Outside of these seven sarcophagi, the remaining number, approximately five or six complete or mostly intact sarcophagus fronts and twenty to twenty-five fragments (denoting fragmentary single figures, complete single figures, or two full-figures) depict an arrangement of standing attendants carrying various items.[11] A sarcophagus front found in the Tomb of Aviation illustrates this scenario, with six attendants, each of whom carries, from left to right, a *patera* and rhyton, a jug and *patera*, a plate with fruits or bread, a jug and an *acerra*, two *infulae* (fillets), and a pitcher (Fig. 9.6).[12] Since the lids associated with Palmyrene sarcophagi are the standard *kline*-type with a reclining banqueter, the subject matter associated with these figures is assumed also to be banqueting and specifically, due to its context within a tomb, a funerary banquet. Two sarcophagi do exist where the setting inferred is assuredly one associated with banqueting.[13] One of these, in the Palmyra Museum, depicts on the left side a table leg adorned with a feline head, in the centre an elaborate stand holding two drinking cups, with the support in the form of a satyr and maenad, and finally on the right a large volute-handled krater. The other example, from the Tomb of Julius Aurelius Marona, places attendants on either side of a similar volute-handled krater encircled by a crown (Fig. 9.7). The attendant to the left stands with a large wineskin at his side. Two *skyphoi* are again set on a stand, supported by a pilaster-shaped leg decorated with sculpted figures (now damaged). Otherwise, the serving figures on sarcophagi, as illustrated by the example from the Tomb of Aviation, are depicted carrying various items that could be associated with such a banquet — garlands and wreaths, ornately decorated rhyta, pitchers, *paterae*, and plates with fruit or an animal. However, especially when dealing with single and partial groups of figures now separated from their original composition, such attendants assigned to banquets could instead have been part of a sacrifice scene.

Questioning the Identification of Attendants as Servants and Slaves

The nature of these attendants was first addressed by Harald Ingholt, in an article published in *Berytus* in 1935. Ingholt labelled these figures 'servants' or 'pages' and identified them as slaves, thus designating them as individuals clearly originating from a lower social order than that of the banqueters and priests they serve.[14] Among his reasons was the lack of inscriptions identifying them as family members, as commonly seen on large banquet reliefs and sarcophagi lids. This article proposes that certain aspects of their iconography suggest otherwise. While other scholars have previously questioned Ingholt's identification of these figures as slaves,[15] this is the first systematic effort to reach an alternative explanation, not only in terms of who these individuals are but also what might be the artistic traditions behind them. The initial argument addresses the issues of gender and age, since the members of this series, without exception, are youthful males depicted without beards. This would suggest that we are dealing with a group in which gender and age were specific requirements for the service they are performing. Additional arguments concern the two distinctive forms of dress and the two distinctive hairstyles that characterize the group. The features of hairstyle and dress are non-Western; they reflect a local tradition associated with equestrian gods of the desert and, I would argue, Palmyra's pre-urban, pre-classical roots. In some cases, these features also may be linked to Persian/Parthian/Sasanian royal iconography. The evidence confirms these attendants are neither slaves nor servants but, on the contrary, are individuals of high social and political status. It is suggested here that at Palmyra what have been previously identified as 'servants' or 'pages' represent, in fact, religious attendants similar to the *camilli* found in Roman religion and comparable, at least in function, to *acolytes* recorded at other sites in Syria and northern Mesopotamia. They therefore represent not slaves but individuals drawn from elite families, performing duties in an official capacity. In many cases, we are probably looking at the adolescent son of the ban-

---

[11] An inclusive catalogue of sarcophagi from Palmyra depicting narrative scenes, including the numerous fragments, is still wanting. Ingholt 1935, 63–75; Colledge 1976, 77–78, 132, 278 n. 253; Parlasca 1984; Schmidt-Colinet 1992, 105–09; Wielgosz 2004; Schmidt-Colinet and al-As'ad 2007; Schmidt-Colinet 2009. I suspect that Colledge's category of 'Serving Youth Stelae' (p. 79) are, in fact, individual figures originating from sarcophagi, which in some cases have been recut with curved tops. Add to the group an example in painting: al-As'ad 2013, 18–19, 24, fig. 7 (from the Tomb of Ḥaṭrai).

[12] Ingholt 1935, 73, pl. 34.1–2; Colledge 1976, 78, pl. 106.

[13] Palmyra Museum, Palmyra: unpublished. Photograph Getty Images n. 111025990. Tomb of Julius Aurelius Marona: mentioned by Will 1951, 98, but otherwise unpublished. Photograph Ifpo-05037 (reproduced here as Fig. 9.7).

[14] Ingholt 1935, 73.

[15] Most notably, Will 1951, 98 n. 2. More recently, Krag and Raja 2019, 252–53.

Figure 9.8. 'Small banquet relief', from Palmyra. Limestone, c. AD 200–225. Cleveland Museum of Art, Cleveland, acc. no. 1964.359 (courtesy of Cleveland Museum of Art, CC0 1.0).

context in the manner of the *marzeah*.[17] From the standpoint of the funerary reliefs themselves, there also remain controversial issues as to the artistic sources behind their representation: whether they reflect a conceptual reference to banqueting, a kind of artistic *topos*, or whether they are documents of an actual ritualistic activity and thus accurately reproducing the ritual itself. As such, I have also decided to avoid an examination of large banquet reliefs and banquet scenes represented on sarcophagi lids. These tend to depict a banquet as the setting for a family portrait — with the patriarch reclining, his wife sitting at his feet, and various sons and daughters standing in between, some holding items of banqueting — but seldom do they depict the act of banqueting, with attendants clearly participating as servers.[18] The objective of this article is simply to examine the group of so-called attendants or serving youths in its entirety in order to determine its common features and then to turn to a few select examples whose unique features may provide some essential clues to answer a specific question — if these are not servants-slaves, then who might they then be?

queter or the priest. The tradition we are examining is to be associated with Palmyra's long-standing cultural links to the East.

To assist in formulating this conclusion, a second group of funerary reliefs, the so-called 'small banquet reliefs', will also be examined (Figs 9.8, 9.12, 9.14).[16] These are small rectangular plaques, roughly 45–50 cm in height and 55–60 cm wide, characterized by their leaf-and-dart and bead mouldings and taking their name from the fact that over two-thirds of the forty or so surviving examples depict a male banqueter being served by a younger male attendant. Thus, this group provides additional comparisons as to the nature of such attendants in connection with banqueting.

Before continuing, it is important to make clear that this article does not attempt to formulate a convincing solution as to the nature of the banquets we are examining: whether what we are viewing are references to cultic dining, taking place in banquet halls within the temple precinct — an activity best represented by the numerous *tesserae* from Palmyra — or a funerary feast, taking place among family members at the tomb or in a more civic

The Image of the Attendant: Gender and Age

The first aspect of these reliefs is that they all depict youthful males. This youthfulness is signified by the fact that, without exception, none of these so-called attendants wears a beard, either on sarcophagi or on the small banquet reliefs. This contrasts with the fact that the persons they serve are often depicted as older individuals, such as the bearded caravan leader represented on the sarcophagus from Diocletian's Camp (Fig. 9.5). This

---

[16] Albertson 2014.

[17] For recent comprehensive studies on Palmyrene banqueting, see Audley-Miller 2016; Cussini 2016; Krag and Raja 2017.

[18] Audley-Miller 2016, 557–58.

might suggest that age, specifically young men or adolescents, was a criterion for being a member of this group.

Secondly, as illustrated by a small banquet relief now in the Cleveland Museum of Art (Fig. 9.8),[19] there are clear instances where the supposed slave would be dressed identically to and as luxuriously as the individual he is serving. One can clearly see on this relief that the only difference in dress is that the reclining male wears a mantle clasped at the right shoulder by a round brooch. Otherwise, the attendant mimics the banqueter in wearing trousers also ornamented with an embroidered floral band down the front and a long-sleeved tunic with an identical floral band decorating the lower hem. These similarities would suggest our server is not intended to be viewed as a person of servile status. In addition, many of these attendants are wearing swords, which seems improbable if they were slaves (Figs 9.3–9.4).

The Image of the Attendant: Dress

Aspects of dress and hairstyle also provide clues as to who these serving youths are and what their social status is. In terms of dress, these attendants wear one of either two types of garments. The most frequent is a long-sleeved tunic, often decorated with embroidery, worn together with trousers and boots (Figs 9.3–9.5). Generally referred to as 'Parthian dress', the term is misleading, as it is a form of dress which can be recognized as indigenous to inland Syria as well. Either label betrays a common source, which is Persia.[20] It is likewise a common form of dress associated with banqueting, often worn by the reclining male banqueter appearing within reliefs (Figs 9.8 and 9.12) and on lids of sarcophagi,[21] although a Greek-style himation over a tunic can also be worn. In the case of the 'small banquet reliefs', however, when the banqueter is wearing Persian dress, the attendant does the same.

The other form of dress for these attendants is a short tunic reaching only to the knees, presumably belted, with an overfold at the waist (Figs 9.2 and 9.6). This is perhaps the one single feature associated with the group that can be described as a Graeco-Roman. What is peculiar to all these figures is that there appears to be an additional undergarment, whose lower hem, visible over

Figure 9.9. Stele with Yarḥai and attendant carrying writing implements, from Palmyra. Limestone, *c.* AD 230–250. Ny Carlsberg Glyptotek, Copenhagen, inv. no. IN 1024 (Ny Carlsberg Glyptotek, Copenhagen/ Anders Sune Berg).

the right knee, is fringed. This fringed undergarment combined with a tunic is extremely scarce at Palmyra. Outside of our attendants represented on sarcophagi, among the few additional examples is the stele in the Ny Carlsberg Glyptotek depicting a certain Yarḥai, identified by the inscription, and his attendant, who stands on the left side, holding Yarḥai's documents, a *scrinium* or *capsa* (a circular container holding papyrus scrolls) and a *polyptychon* (a multi-leafed tablet) (Fig. 9.9).[22] Yarḥai is a person of prominence, conveyed by the presence of his priestly cap sitting on a column in the centre of the composition. The attendant figure who wears a fringed undergarment has been regularly referred to as a servant, due to the simple dress and the fact that in Graeco-Roman representations of such a scene this figure would most likely be a slave.[23] At Palmyra, however, fringed

---

19 Cleveland Museum of Art, Cleveland, acc. no. 1964.359. Vermeule 1981, 386 no. 335 with fig; Parlasca 1984, 285, 287, fig. 2; Albertson 2014, 31 no. 4.

20 Seyrig 1937.

21 Long 2017, 77–82.

22 Ny Carlsberg Glyptotek, Copenhagen, inv. no. IN 1024. Ingholt 1928, 125 n. 2 PS 130; 1935, 73–74, pl. 33.2; Ploug 1995, 255–57 no. 126 with fig.; Raja 2019, 106–07 no. 13, fig. 13.

23 Ingholt 1935, 74; Colledge 1976, 132 n. 450, 143 n. 530; Ploug 1995, 256.

Figure 9.10. *Loculus* plaque of Malkû, son of Malê, from Palmyra. Limestone, *c.* AD 120–140. Limestone. Ny Carlsberg Glyptotek, Copenhagen, inv. no. IN 1050 (Ny Carlsberg Glyptotek, Copenhagen/Anders Sune Berg).

Figure 9.11. Pilaster capital with offering scene to Abgal, from the Temple of Abgal and Ma'an, Khirbet Semrin. Limestone, *c.* AD 200. National Museum, Damascus, inv. no. 2840 (Institut français du Proche-Orient: <https://medihal.archives-ouvertes.fr/medihal-03047482v1>, under 'Open License').

garments, whether a tunic or a mantle, are not associated with either slaves or servants; they are elaborate, if not luxurious garments worn by individuals of position and authority.[24] In addition, our so-called servant on the Copenhagen stele wears a recognizable long single lock of hair flowing over his right shoulder, what has been labelled a 'slave-lock'.[25] While the appearance of such a lock confirms the individual is a young male, there is no confirmation, let alone any evidence, that the person is a slave.[26] Actual representations of master and slave are virtually unknown at Palmyra.[27] One may simply wonder if the function referred to on the Copenhagen stele is intended as an act of assisting a priest, much like the assistants on the two sarcophagi in the Palmyra Museum depicting a sacrifice (Fig. 9.2). As this form of dress is also the same short tunic with fringed undergarment often worn by attendants acting as servers presumably at a banquet, as seen on the sarcophagus from the Tomb of Aviation (Fig. 9.6), it may also be that these individuals carry items more specifically associated with a sacrifice.

The Image of the Attendant: Hairstyle

Not only is the manner of dress associated with these serving youths limited to two selections, but the possible hairstyles are also limited to two. The more common one is arranged as a large, rounded mass of snail-shell or corkscrew curls (Figs 9.1–9.2). The other hairstyle is characterized by a part above the centre of the forehead, from which the hair is brushed laterally towards the temples, terminating at the sides of the head in a mass of snail-shell curls (Figs 9.2, 9.4, 9.8). Both are local. The first — the large circular mass of curls — is seen throughout Syria and northern Mesopotamia, as noted on the

---

[24] Among men, a fringed tunic is worn by priests, especially during the second half of the second century; see Raja 2017, 128, 126, figs 15–16. Women wearing a fringed long-sleeved tunic combine this garment with an extensive array of jewellery, suggesting the wearer is a person of wealth and status. The examples, dating *c.* AD 220–250, are discussed in Ploug 1995, 202–03 under no. 82; Krag 2018, 58 and n. 305 with list.

[25] Colledge 1976, 143, 291 n. 530.

[26] The only other instance at Palmyra is on a male figure, part of a double bust, in the Ny Carlsberg Glyptotek, Copenhagen, inv. no. IN 1153. Ploug 1995, 208–10 no. 85 with fig. See the comments on this relief by Krag and Raja 2019, 252–53, who correctly refute previous identifications of this figure as a slave. Note the connection between this arrangement and the so-called 'child's lock': Ingholt 1938, 138, pl. 49.3–4; Colledge 1976, 143, 291 n. 530.

[27] Ploug 1995, 256.

wall paintings from the synagogue at Dura-Europos and sculptures from Hatra.[28] The other hairstyle — with a central part and corkscrew curls only at the sides — presents a more intriguing situation. Such a hairstyle is reproduced on the *loculus* plaque of Malkû, son of Malê, in Copenhagen (Fig. 9.10).[29] A second example, although slightly looser in its arrangement of the spiralling curls on the sides, appears on the *loculus* bust of the cameleer Shokai, son of Wahbai, son of Malê.[30] These two, and perhaps a third,[31] are the only examples of this distinctive hairstyle on *loculus* reliefs — essentially two or three out of nearly 1200 examples. Although such a hairstyle is extremely rare within the corpus of *loculus* plaques, it is surprisingly more common on sarcophagi, where it appears among our attendants at least four times (Figs 9.2 and 9.4),[32] and on 'small banquet reliefs', where it appears thrice with banqueters[33] and another four times with attendants (Fig. 9.8).[34] It would seem that this hairstyle had a special connection with both a religious sacrifice and banqueting, where it could be worn by both attendants and banqueters.

One of the more striking parallels for this hairstyle is found on the unique silver head of a Sasanian king, perhaps Shapur II, dating to the fourth century AD, now in the Metropolitan Museum of Art in New York.[35] Although its original source is unknown and its original use is problematic, it does link the hairstyle of our Palmyrene attendants to Sasanian and presumably Parthian royalty.

However, this hairstyle is especially noticeable on equestrian divinities represented on Syrian votive reliefs. Such a hairstyle is worn by a horseman decorating either a capital or a statue base that comes from a temple dedicated to Abgal and Ma'an at Khirbet Semrin, about one hundred kilometres north-west of Palmyra (Fig. 9.11).[36] Inscriptions found by Daniel Schlumberger during excavations of the site reveal that this was an active religious centre from the mid-second century to *c.* AD 270.[37] The mounted figure is identified by inscription as the god Abgal, who together with the likes of Ma'an, Azizos, Ashar, Sa'ad, and Shalman, form a group of protective deities found in desert sanctuaries and apparently associated with the less sedentary inhabitants of the rural villages of southern and central Syria.[38] Additional examples of equestrian divinities wearing this hairstyle from Syria may be cited.[39] These reliefs and the one from Khirbet Semrin suggest that this hairstyle reflects a tradition associated with riding figures, with gods of the desert,[40] and with Palmyra's pre-urban roots. Its religious ties to rural sanctuaries speak for an indigenous Syrian source, although its ultimate origin may be traced again to Persia.

The rarity of such an arrangement and its association with religious activities support a conclusion that this hairstyle references something special and is not simply a fashion randomly worn by a servant or even a mere attendant. The additional connection to both kings and divinities suggests that such a hairstyle was appropriate

---

[28] Labelled the 'halo-style' by Colledge 1976, 141, 289 n. 511; Ploug 1995, 174.

[29] Ny Carlsberg Glyptotek, Copenhagen, inv. no. IN 1050. Ingholt 1928, 100 PS 89; Ploug 1995, 74–75 no. 14 with fig.

[30] Palmyra Museum, Palmyra, inv. no. A 202. Seyrig 1933, 158, 167–68 no. 12, pl. 20.1; Charles-Gaffiot, Lavagne, and Hofman (eds) 2001, 342–43 no. 147, fig. on 254 (plaster cast in Museo della Civiltà Romana, Rome) (A. Liberati).

[31] National Museum, Aleppo, formerly collection George Marcopoli. *CIS* 419 no. 4454, pl. 56; Ingholt 1928, 102 PS 107; Bobou and others 2021, 233 PS 107, 400 fig. 111, 510, 540.

[32] 1) Palmyra Museum, Palmyra, inv. no. B 2677/8983, attendant holding bird (Fig. 9.2) (see n. 1); 2) Palmyra, Tomb of ʿAtênaten, Exedra of Maqqai, attendant leading camel (Fig. 9.3) (see n. 3); 3) Palmyra, Tomb of ʿAtênaten, Exedra of Maqqai, sarcophagus fragment with two standing figures (Fig. 9.4); 4) Louvre, Paris, inv. no. AO 15556, sarcophagus fragment with two standing figures: Dentzer-Feydy and Teixidor 1993, 226–27 no. 220.

[33] 1) Palmyra Museum, Palmyra, inv. no. 2253/8113: Charles-Gaffiot, Lavagne, and Hofman (eds) 2001, 344 no. 149, fig. on 248 (J.-M. Dentzer); Albertson 2014, 31 no. 11; 2) Palmyra Museum, Palmyra, inv. no. CD 78/65: Gawlikowski 1984, 107 no. 58, pl. 88.192; Albertson 2014, 31 no. 13; 3) Art Market, Paris: Albertson 2014, 32 no. 15. Another possible example, whose authenticity has not been verified: Christie's New York, 12 December 2002, sale no. 1163, lot 303.

[34] 1) Cleveland Museum of Art, Cleveland, acc. no. 1964.359 (Fig. 9.8) (see n. 19); 2) Yale University Art Gallery, New Haven, acc. no. 1931.138 (Fig. 9.12) (see n. 41); 3) Nelson-Atkins Museum of Art, Kansas City, acc. no. 65-2 (Fig. 9.14) (see n. 46); 4) fragment, illicitly excavated and recovered by Syrian Archaeological Service, reported 29 March 2014: <http://www.dgam.gov.sy/index.php?d=239&id=1199> [accessed 10 October 2021].

[35] Metropolitan Museum of Art, New York, acc. no. 65.126. Harper 1966.

[36] National Museum, Damascus, inv. no. 2840. Schlumberger 1951, 55 no. 15, 145 no. 4, pl. 21.2.

[37] Schlumberger 1951, 13–22.

[38] Teixidor 1979, 80–82.

[39] Seyrig and Stucky 1949, 23–35, pl. 12 (from Djoubb el-Djerrah, near Ḥoms); Sartre-Fauriat 2012, 188, 189, fig. 3 (Dura-Europos); 190, 191, fig. 6 (from Khirbet Hammam).

[40] Ploug 1995, 74 under no. 14.

Figure 9.12. 'Small banquet relief', from Palmyra. Limestone, c. AD 230. New Haven, Yale University Art Gallery, acc. no. 1931.138 (Yale University Art Gallery, Open Access Policy).

Figure 9.13. Relief of the priest Narkissos, entrance to the Lower Great Temple, Niha (Bekaa, Lebanon). Limestone, c. AD 200. In situ (Institut français du Proche-Orient: <https://medihal.archives-ouvertes.fr/medihal-00489378v1> [accessed 10 October 2021], under 'Open License').

for an individual taking part in an important activity. The origin is local, ultimately coming from Persia, and not a Graeco-Roman source, which likewise implies a long-standing, pre-classical tradition behind its use. One may speculate that the hairstyle we are examining is an arrangement specifically worn by attendants at religious offerings and banquets.

The Image of the Attendant: The Conical Cap

One further attribute reinforces those claims already established for dress and hairstyle — a local and ultimately Eastern source, a religious reference, and the reflection of a tradition originating prior to Palmyra's existence as an urban community. On a small banquet relief now in the Yale University Art Gallery, we see the reclining banqueter wearing a short, conical hat (Fig. 9.12).[41] Such a hat is not the standard headdress for a Palmyrene priest, which is the larger, more cylindrical felt hat,[42] seen in this same relief resting on a pedestal. A conical headdress is more typical of priests at other Syrian sites during the Roman period, as evidenced by representations of priests from Hierapolis, Dura-Europos, Doliche, Hamman, Yazili, and Mashara.[43] Although this Syrian version is generally much taller than its Palmyrene counterpart, a form closer in size to that appearing on the Yale banquet relief is found on a votive relief from the Temple of Aphlad at Dura-Europos, where the inscription tells us that a certain Adiabos, son of Zabdibolos, is making an offering.[44] The evidence establishes that there is a Syrian tradition for this conical hat as an attribute of a priest. The fact that only one example from Palmyra depicts an adult male wearing such a hat suggests, however, that its use at Palmyra is different than that found in other Syrian cities. Often on representations of Palmyrene priests, the cylindrical-shaped hat is distinctly rendered with a double border or lining at its base. One may speculate whether this denotes the lower border of a short conical cap worn underneath the cylindrical hat as a means to stabilize what clearly would be an otherwise unstable headdress.

---

[41] Yale University Art Gallery, New Haven, acc. no. 1931.138. Ingholt 1935, 70–71; Brody and Hoffman (eds) 2011, 376, pl. 75; Albertson 2014, 31 no. 6, pl. 3.1; Raja 2019, 111 no. 24, 110, fig. 19.

[42] See most recently Raja 2018 (with previous bibliography).

[43] Stucky 1976; Blömer 2015.

[44] National Museum, Damascus, inv. no. 4488. Downey 1977, 7–9 no. 1, pl. 1.1.

Figure 9.14. 'Small banquet relief', from Palmyra. Limestone, c. AD 230. Nelson-Atkins Museum of Art, Kansas City, acc. no. 65-2 (image courtesy of The Nelson-Atkins Museum of Art, Media Services/Jamison Miller).

Figure 9.15. Stele with two male children, from Palmyra. Limestone, c. AD 150–200. Archaeological Museum, Istanbul, inv. no. 3729 (© Osama Shukir Muhammed Amin FRCP (Glasg)/Wikimedia Commons. CC BY–SA 4.0).

However, in contrast to other Syrian sites, at Palmyra the conical cap is a feature distinctly associated with male youths, which explains why the attendant on the Yale relief is also wearing such a cap. Although its conical shape is the same as that worn by the banqueter, the attendant's version appears to be made of a softer material, with creases visible on either side of an embroidered vertical band of small circles running down its centre. Embroidered caps such as this seem to have been worn by the priests associated with the Temple of Hadaranes and Atargatis at Niha in the Bekaa Valley, as illustrated by the relief representing the priest Narkissos, dating to the late second or the early third century AD (Fig. 9.13).[45] There are other examples of this distinctive cap at Palmyra. On another small banquet relief exhibited in the Nelson-Atkins Museum of Art in Kansas City, the attendant on the right wears an embroidered cap while serving a reclining banqueter wearing his cylindrical priestly hat (Fig. 9.14).[46] The same cap appears on a head in Copenhagen, detached from what originally must have been a large banquet relief forming the lid of a sarcophagus and thus suggesting that it must have originally represented a family member, specifically the son of the reclining patriarch.[47] It should also be noted that the attendant figures wearing caps on the Yale and Kansas City reliefs also wear the same hairstyle seen in connection with other attendants on the sarcophagi — parted in the middle above the forehead, brushed to the sides in wavy strands, and gathered into corkscrew curls along the sides. One may cite three additional examples of this soft-sided conical cap worn by a male youth. The first is a stele in Istanbul depicting two children; the male youth on the left, who wears the cap, holds a cluster of grapes in each hand, clearly signifying he is a boy (Fig. 9.15).[48]

---

[45] In situ. Stucky 1976, 134, 133, fig. 2; Krumeich 1998, 172–73, pl. 49.1–3; Freyberger 1999, 571–73, fig. 2. On the site, Paturel 2019, 165–93.

[46] Nelson-Atkins Museum of Art, Kansas City, acc. no. 65–2. Vermeule 1981, 385 no. 334 with fig.; Parlasca 1984, 285, 287 fig. 4; Albertson 2014, 31 no. 5; Raja 2019, 125–26 no. 47 fig. 27.

[47] Ny Carlsberg Glyptotek, Copenhagen, inv. no. IN 1097. Seyrig 1937, 25–26, pl. 3.2; Ploug 1995, 243 no. 113 with fig.

[48] Archaeological Museum, Istanbul, inv. no. 3729. Ingholt 1928, 154 PS 527; Bobou and others 2021, 336 PS 527, 504 fig. 523, 521.

On a *loculus* plaque in the British Museum, a boy wearing an embroidered cap stands above the left shoulder of an adult who is most assuredly his father.[49] On a third example, a fragmentary stele in the Palmyra Museum, the cap itself is damaged, and although its outline is visible, it is impossible to determine if the cap was decorated or plain.[50] However, the figure wearing the cap is clearly a youth, as he holds the attribute of a bird. Furthermore, the inscription, 'Odainat, his son, alas!', identifies the boy as the son of the missing father. These reliefs, taken as a group, would confirm that at Palmyra the cap is worn not only by male youths but also by the sons of prominent Palmyrenes, not slaves. It also seems apparent that this embroidered cap may be more than a mere fashion item and instead denotes the status of belonging to a particular group and performing a particular function, most likely religious in nature.

Identification

Summarizing all the evidence presented up to this point, several issues become clear regarding these attendants. Being male and being an adolescent seem to be specific requirements for membership, as all representatives of this group are depicted without beards or any signs of adulthood. In addition, there are clear criteria as to dress and hairstyle. In both instances, the source of these defining features is Syrian, and ultimately Persian royal and divine iconography. This would suggest the intention behind the selection of dress and hairstyle is to visually categorize a distinctive group and one of high social and political status. What we have been analysing may also reflect a tradition associated with Palmyra's pre-urban roots, specifically equestrian gods of the desert. It thus reflects a tradition that looks to the East as opposed to the West.

It is proposed here that what at Palmyra have been labelled 'servants' should instead be identified as religious attendants comparable to the *camilli* found in Roman religion — young adolescent males serving as assistants to the various priesthoods of Rome and also, at times, participating in other religious activities such as banqueting.[51] In a Hellenized Syrian context, such individuals would be called 'acolytes', and at Hatra, the Aramaic ʾAQLT, a direct transliteration of the Greek ἀχόλουθος, occurs.[52] Although no textual equivalent occurs at Palmyra, we can conjecture that a similar group would have existed in the city.[53] Therefore, such attendants represent young males performing duties as part of a civic group, not due to a status of servitude. Interestingly, Ernest Will connected these Palmyrene attendants with Roman *camilli* on the basis of dress, noting the similarities of the short, knee-length tunic with a fringed undergarment.[54]

The rejection of an identification of the assistants as slaves or servants also suggests that they are most likely individuals drawn from elite families. In the scenes of both offerings and banquets, in many cases the assistant is probably the adolescent son of the sacrificer or the banqueter. This conclusion would then compare to the evidence already known at Palmyra from the so-called large banquet reliefs, such as the example from the main exedra of the Hypogeum of the Family of Artaban.[55] As is typical of these reliefs and confirmed in this specific case by inscriptions, the activity represented is a family affair, where the young man extending a wreath and the girl holding a plate of fruits are the grandson and granddaughter of the reclining banqueter, the patriarch Artaban, wearing a priest's headdress. The grandchildren hold the place of honour as the servers, evidently because the relief itself was commissioned by their father, ʿOggâ, the son of Artaban. Such a link between family and banqueting would also tie Palmyra into the larger Syrian and northern Mesopotamian tradition. The so-called 'Funerary Couch Mosaic', found in a tomb at Edessa, illustrates a banquet where the family patriarch, Zealot, is being served by two of his young sons, a fact confirmed by the inscriptions.[56] From Hatra, represented

---

[49] British Museum, London, no. 125046 (reg. no. 1889.1012.2). Ingholt 1928, 111 PS 191; Bobou and others 2021, 251 PS 191, 421 fig. 194.

[50] Palmyra Museum, Palmyra, inv. no. 2281/8273. Al-Asʿad, Gawilkowski, and Yon 2012, 172 no. 28. Another example of a *loculus* plaque with a boy wearing an undecorated conical cap standing over the right shoulder of a bearded man comes from Tomb C: Higuchi and Izumi 1994, pl. 45; Yon 2013, 345 no. 50.

[51] As in the case of the banquet of the Arval Brothers. On the *camillus* in Roman religion, see Mantle 2002, 91–99.

[52] Tubach 1986, 258–59 n. 24; Hoftijzer and Jongeling 1995, I, 99–100; Contini and Pagano 2015, 131.

[53] Vuolanto 2019, 207, 209. The assumption that the word [ʾ]AQLTʾ appears at Palmyra in *CIS* no. 3927 has been corrected; see Hillers and Cussini 1996, 65 PAT 0273.

[54] Will 1951, 98.

[55] In situ. Main exedra, Hypogeum of the Family of Artaban, Palmyra. Tanabe 1986, 31, pls 229–32; Sadurska and Bounni 1994, 37–39 no. 41, figs 222–24; Raja 2019, 143–44 no. 84. For the inscriptions, Hillers and Cussini 1996, 308–09 PAT 2666–70. See the discussion in Vuolanto 2019, 207–10.

[56] Now lost, reproduced as drawings: Drijvers 1980, 25–26, pl. 17. For the inscriptions: Segal 1959, 37–39 no. 9.

in relief on a lintel from sanctuary 5 is the Hatrean king Nasru attended by his son, Vologash.[57] We can now be relatively assured that in the case of a ritual banquet at Palmyra, the elder diners most likely would be served by younger family members as well.

Further confirming evidence for linking these youthful servers or attendants with family members comes not directly from Palmyra but from Dura-Europos. Surprisingly it was mentioned by Ingholt in his discussion of these 'servants' or 'pages' but then ignored.[58] The evidence comes in the form of a wall-painting discovered during the excavations undertaken in 1922–1923 under the directorship of Franz Cumont of a side chapel or dining-hall, known as room K, in the so-called 'Temple of the Palmyrene Gods' (Fig. 9.16).[59] It was part of a remodelling of the room done c. AD 220. The temple's name, as coined by Cumont, comes from the fact that although this structure was not patronized exclusively by Palmyrenes and was not a site exclusively devoted to the worship of Palmyrene gods, people of Palmyrene origin figure prominently in the inscriptions, graffiti, and paintings of this structure, especially from the late second century onwards.

Figure 9.16. 'Otes-fresco', from room K of the Temple of the Palmyrene Gods, Dura-Europos. Fresco, c. AD 220. Now lost, preserved through excavation photograph (reproduced from Cumont 1926, pl. 55).

Our knowledge of the fresco, since it no longer survives, relies on the photograph originally published in Cumont's excavation report of 1926. It depicts, on the left, two individuals making an offering over a *thymiaterion* (incense burner) in the presence of five deities standing on globes to the right. The painting is called the 'Otes fresco', from the inscription in Greek accompanying the figure to the right of the altar, which reads 'Otes, the eunuch, the founder of the room'.[60] We are most likely dealing here with a freedman, a one-time slave within a prominent Palmyrene family at Dura and himself being of considerable wealth.[61] This would then explain his role as benefactor to the Palmyrene gods. The figure standing behind is identified simply by name as 'Gorsak'.

The figures that concern us most are those standing to the left of the altar. The Greek inscription identifies the larger individual as Iabsumsos, son of Abdaathes, the *bouleutáis*, literally a member of the *boulé* or town council.[62] The Aramaic name Abdaathes is known from Palmyra and, when combined with the context, would suggest that Iabsumsos's family ultimately came from Palmyra. The smaller attendant standing behind Iabsumsos is identified by the inscription immediately below, 'Abdaathes, son of Iabsumsos'.[63] So, clearly the attendant to Iabsumsos is his very own son, Abdaathes, named in customary fashion after his grandfather. And the costume of our Abdaathes is the same long-sleeved short tunic worn by the attendants on the sarcophagi from Palmyra.

Not unexpectedly, the family associations occurring in the ceremony involving Iabsumsos and his son, Abdaathes, place Palmyrene religious practices within the larger Syrian tradition. Another well-known example also comes from the Temple of the Palmyrene Gods at Dura-Europos, where we observe the fresco depicting

---

57   Dirven 2005, 62–63, 80, fig. 1.

58   Ingholt 1935, 72.

59   Cumont 1926, 122–34, pls 55–58; Dirven 1999, 295–302, pl. 12.

60   For the inscriptions, see Cumont 1926, 364–66 no. 9; Dirven 1999, 296–300 no. 48a–d.

61   Dirven 1999, 296–97.

62   Dirven 1999, 298–99 no. 48c.

63   Dirven 1999, 299–300 no. 48d.

Figure 9.17. Short side of sarcophagus, reclining woman with attendant, from Tomb 176, Palmyra. Limestone, *c.* AD 230. Palmyra Museum, Palmyra, inv. no. B 2677/8983 (© Dossemann/Wikimedia Commons. CC BY–SA 4.0).

Konôn performing his priestly duties with the assistance of his daughter, three sons, a grandson, and at least one additional son or grandson.[64] Konôn's tall conical hat, instead of the cylindrical Palmyrene priestly cap, places him in the larger Syrian sphere of religious activities.

One final point may also be addressed concerning these attendants at Palmyra. Returning to the sarcophagus in the garden of the Palmyra Museum depicting a sacrifice on the front (Figs 9.1–9.2), we now need to examine the short sides. On the short side to the left, a female figure is represented reclining on a *kline* joined by a female attendant bringing a large jewelled necklace, presumably taken from the large polygonal jewellery box in the centre of the composition (Fig. 9.17).[65] The only other examples of this scene come from, not coincidentally, 'small banquet reliefs', where it appears in only three out of the over forty surviving examples.[66] As recently pointed out by Rubina Raja and Signe Krag, although the women on these banquet reliefs are reclining, they are not actually banqueting.[67] Instead, it is actu-

ally a woman's toiletry scene, depicting the presumed matron of the family in an act of personal adornment, with domestic items prominently displayed in the background, such as a large jewellery box or a wool basket. The source may be Graeco-Roman funerary art, where in such a domestic scene, often with a jewellery box to one side, the matron is attended by servants.[68] However, the hairstyles and dress have led Raja and Krag to identify the female attendants on the Palmyrene reliefs as the adolescent daughters of the more mature reclining woman,[69] clearly corresponding to the sons serving fathers on comparable reliefs. Although the scene may not be banqueting, it must certainly be connected to banqueting, as evidenced on a relief from the Hypogeum of Taʾaî, where both male and female — in this case brother and sister — recline on a *kline*, with a large elaborate jewellery box in the background, just as on the 'small banquet reliefs' with a single female reclining figure.[70]

The opposite right end depicts a standing female figure dressed in a long chiton partially covered by a himation looping over the upper chest and falling over the left shoulder (Fig. 9.18). Unfortunately, the head is damaged. She holds a spear in her extended right arm and with her left arm holds the reins of a camel who trails behind. Andreas Schmidt-Colinet, who has published this sarcophagus extensively, identifies this figure as the goddess Astarte, in her guise as protectress of the caravans.[71] The identification is problematic, as images of this Astarte from Palmyra and the Palmyrene

---

[64] Cumont 1926, 41–56, 359–60 no. 5, pls 31–41; Kaizer 2019, 84.

[65] Schmidt-Colinet and al-Asʿad 2007, 273, pl. 86.1–2; Schmidt-Colinet 2009, 223–24, 230, fig. 5.

[66] Albertson 2014, 32 nos 22–24, pl. 3.3; Krag and Raja 2017, 202 n. 37.

[67] Krag and Raja 2017, 202.

[68] Zanker 1994, 222–24, figs 10, 20–23 (grave stelai from Hellenistic Smyrna).

[69] Krag and Raja 2019, 252–53.

[70] National Museum, Damascus, inv. no. 18802. Charles-Gaffiot, Lavagne, and Hofman (eds) 2001, 367–68 no. 255, 314 fig. 255 (J.-B. Yon).

[71] Schmidt-Colinet and al-Asʿad 2007, 273, pl. 86.3–5; Schmidt-Colinet 2009, 224, 230, fig. 6.

Figure 9.18. Short side of sarcophagus, woman with camel, from Tomb 176, Palmyra. Limestone, c. AD 230. Palmyra Museum, Palmyra, inv. no. B 2677/8983 (© Livius.org. CC BY–SA 4.0).

generally depict her without any object or a sceptre.[72] Nevertheless, regardless of who the figure actually is, the iconography shown here brings to mind the previously mentioned 'preparation for a hunt' illustrated on the sarcophagus found in excavations of the Camp of Diocletian (Fig. 9.5). The figure holding the camel and carrying a lance can be seen as the male counterpart to our female spear-bearer and camel tender. It is clear from all this that the same set of three thematic scenes associated with our male attendants — sacrifice, banquet, and a problematic 'preparation for a hunt or caravan' — exist also for women. Thus, there is a strong possibility that a group of female attendants, performing similar religious duties as their male counterparts, also existed at Palmyra.

Conclusion

In summary, the evidence drawn primarily from funerary art would suggest that those adolescent males previously labelled as slaves acting as 'servants' or 'pages' should now be identified as the children of prominent Palmyrenes serving as attendants at religious ceremonies and banquets, thus performing functions similar to Roman *camilli*. This would then explain the apparent criteria of age and gender within the group, the similarities of dress with the banqueters they are supposedly serving, and why they could wear swords. It would explain also the selection of certain forms of local dress and hairstyles. In particular, there is one hairstyle — where the hair is parted in the middle above the forehead, then brushed to the sides in wavy strands, and ultimately gathered into snail-shell curls at the sides — which is almost non-existent on *loculus* plaques but occurs proportionately often among these attendants on sarcophagi and small banquet reliefs. As this hairstyle is otherwise associated with equestrian protector gods of the desert and Parthian-Sasanian royalty, its appearance among Palmyrene attendants only serves to support the conclusions that these attendants are from wealthy and politically prominent families. The added presence of an embroidered cap, associated with a local Syrian priestly tradition, reinforces their position of status. And finally, addressing the theme of this conference, the tradition we have examined has its origins in Palmyra's links to the East, where hairstyle, dress, and attributes have parallels from other sites of Syria and northern Mesopotamia and can ultimately be traced to Persia.

---

[72] Dirven and Kaizer 2013, 397–98.

Works Cited

al-Asʿad, W. 2013. 'Some Tombs Recently Excavated in Palmyra', *Studia Palmyreńskie*, 12: 15–24.
al-Asʿad, K., M. Gawlikowski, and J.-B. Yon. 2012. 'Aramaic Inscriptions in the Palmyra Museum: New Acquisitions', *Syria*, 89: 163–83.
Albertson, F. 2014. 'A Distribution Scene on a Palmyran Funerary Relief', *Antike Kunst*, 57: 25–37.
Audley-Miller, L. 2016. 'The Banquet in Palmyrene Funerary Contexts', in C. Draycott and M. Stamatopoulou (eds), *Dining and Death: Interdisciplinary Perspectives on the 'Funerary Banquet' in Ancient Art, Burial and Belief*, Colloquia antiqua, 16 (Leuven: Peeters), pp. 553–89.
Blömer, M. 2015. 'Images of Priests in North Syria and Beyond', in M. Blömer, A. Lichtenberger, and R. Raja (eds), *Religious Identities in the Levant from Alexander to Muhammed: Continuity and Change*, Contextualizing the Sacred, 4 (Turnhout: Brepols), pp. 185–97.
Bobou, O. and others (eds). 2021. *Studies on Palmyrene Sculpture: A Translation of Harald Ingholt's Studier over Palmyrensk Skulptur*, Studies in Palmyrene Archaeology and History, 1 (Turnhout: Brepols).
Brody, L. and G. Hoffman (eds). 2011. *Dura-Europos: Crossroads of Antiquity* (Boston: McMullen Museum of Art).
Charles-Gaffiot, J., H. Lavagne, and J.-M. Hofman (eds). 2001. *Moi, Zénobie reine de Palmyre: Paris, Place de Panthéon. 18 septembre – 16 décembre 2001* (Milan: Skira).
Colledge, M. 1976. *The Art of Palmyra* (Boulder: Westview).
Contini, R. and P. Pagano. 2015. 'Notes on Foreign Words in Hatran Aramaic', in A. Butts (ed.), *Semitic Languages in Context* (Leiden: Brill), pp. 126–57.
Cumont, F. 1926. *Fouilles de Doura-Europos (1922–1923)* (Paris: Geuthner).
Cussini, E. 2016. 'Family Banqueting at Palmyra: Reassessing the Evidence', in P. Corò and others (eds), *Libiamo ne' lieti calici: Ancient Near Eastern Studies Presented to Lucio Milano on the Occasion of his 65th Birthday by Pupils, Colleagues and Friends*, Alter Orient und Altes Testament, 436 (Münster: Ugarit), pp. 139–59.
Dentzer-Feydy, J. and J. Teixidor. 1993. *Les antiquités de Palmyre au Musée du Louvre* (Paris: Réunion des musées nationaux).
Dirven, L. 1999. *The Palmyrenes of Dura-Europos: A Study of Religious Interaction in Roman Syria*, Religions in the Graeco-Roman World, 138 (Leiden: Brill).
—— 2005. 'Banquet Scenes from Hatra', *ARAM*, 17: 61–82.
Dirven, L. and T. Kaizer. 2013. 'A Palmyrene Altar in the Cincinnati Art Museum', *Syria*, 90: 391–408.
Downey, S. 1977. *The Stone and Plaster Sculpture*, The Excavations at Dura-Europos: Final Report, 3.1.2, Monumenta archaeologica, 5 (Berkeley: University of California Press).
Drijvers, H. 1980. *Cults and Beliefs at Edessa* (Leiden: Brill).
Freyberger, K. 1999. 'Les temples de Niha: Témoins de cultes locaux d'influence romaine au Liban', *Topoi: Orient-Occident*, 9: 569–77.
Gawlikowski, M. 1984. *Palmyre*, VIII: *Les principia de Dioclétien, 'Temple des Enseignes'* (Warsaw: PWN-Éditions scientifiques de Pologne).
Harper, P. 1966. 'Portrait of a King', *Metropolitan Museum of Art Bulletin*, 25: 136–46.
Higuchi, T. and T. Izumi. 1994. *Tombs A and C, Southeast Necropolis, Palmyra, Syria*, Publications of the Research Center for Silk Roadology, 1 (Nara: Research Center for Silk Roadology).
Hillers, D. and E. Cussini. 1996. *Palmyrene Aramaic Texts* (Baltimore: Johns Hopkins University Press).
Hoftijzer, J. and K. Jongeling. 1995. *Dictionary of North-West Semitic Inscriptions*, 2 vols (Leiden: Brill).
Ingholt, H. 1928. *Studier over Palmyrensk Skulptur* (Copenhagen: Reitzel).
—— 1935. 'Five Dated Tombs from Palmyra', *Berytus*, 2: 13–120.
—— 1938. 'Inscriptions and Sculptures from Palmyra, II', *Berytus*, 5: 93–140.
Kaizer, T. 2019. 'Family Connections and Religious Life at Palmyra', in S. Krag and R. Raja (eds), *Women, Children and the Family in Palmyra*, Palmyrene Studies, 3 (Copenhagen: The Royal Danish Academy of Sciences and Letters), pp. 82–94.
Kohlmeyer, K. 2018. 'Palmyra: City in the "Desert"', in R. Abdellatif, J. Gonnella, and K. Kohlmeyer (eds), *Syria Matters* (Milan: Silvana), pp. 60–71.
Krag, S. 2018. *Funerary Representations of Palmyrene Women from the First Century BC to the Third Century AD*, Studies in Classical Archaeology, 3 (Turnhout: Brepols).
Krag, S. and R. Raja. 2017. 'Representations of Women and Children in Palmyrene Banqueting Reliefs and Sarcophagus Scenes', *Zeitschrift für Orient-Archäologie*, 10: 196–227.
—— 2019. 'Unveiling Female Hairstyles: Markers of Age, Social Roles, and Status in Funerary Sculpture from Palmyra', *Zeitschrift für Orient-Archäologie*, 11: 243–77.
Krumeich, R. 1998. 'Darstellungen syrischer Priester an den kaiserzeitlichen Tempeln von Niha und Chehim im Libanon', *Damaszener Mitteilungen*, 10: 171–200.

Long, T. 2017. 'The Use of Parthian Costume in Funerary Portraiture in Palmyra', in T. Long and A. H. Sørensen (eds), *Positions and Professions in Palmyra*, Palmyrene Studies, 2 (Copenhagen: The Royal Danish Academy of Sciences and Letters), pp. 68–83.

Mantle, I. 2002. 'The Roles of Children in Roman Religion', *Greece & Rome*, 49: 85–106.

Michałowski, K. 1962. *Palmyre: fouilles polonaises 1960* (Warsaw: PWN-Éditions scientifiques de Pologne).

Parlasca, K. 1984. 'Probleme der palmyrenischen Sarkophage', in B. Andreae (ed.), *Symposium über die antiken Sarkophage: Pisa, 5.–12. September 1982*, Marburger Winckelmann-Programm, 1984 (Marburg: Verlag des Kunstgeschichtlichen Seminars), pp. 283–96.

Paturel, S. 2019. *Baalbek-Heliopolis, the Bekaa, and Berytus from 100 BCE to 400 CE*, Mnemosyne, Supplements, 426 (Leiden: Brill).

Ploug, G. 1995. *Catalogue of the Palmyrene Sculptures: Ny Carlsberg Glyptotek* (Copenhagen: Ny Carlsberg Glyptotek).

Raja, R. 2017. 'To Be or Not to Be Depicted as a Priest in Palmyra: A Matter of Representational Spheres and Societal Values', in T. Long and A. H. Sørensen (eds), *Positions and Professions in Palmyra*, Palmyrene Studies, 2 (Copenhagen: The Royal Danish Academy of Sciences and Letters), pp. 115–30.

—— 2018. 'The Matter of the Palmyrene "Modius": Remarks on the History of Research into the Terminology of the Palmyrene Priestly Hat', *Religion in the Roman Empire*, 4: 237–59.

—— 2019. 'It Stays in the Family: Palmyrene Priestly Representations and their Constellations', in S. Krag and R. Raja (eds), *Women, Children and the Family in Palmyra*, Palmyrene Studies, 3 (Copenhagen: The Royal Danish Academy of Sciences and Letters), pp. 95–156.

Sadurska, A. and A. Bounni. 1994. *Les sculptures funéraires de Palmyre*, Rivista di archeologia, suppl. 13 (Rome: G. Bretschneider).

Sartre-Fauriat, A. 2012. 'Une stèle au dieu cavalier au Musée des Beaux-Arts de Lyon', *Syria*, 89: 185–94.

Schlumberger, D. 1951. *La Palmyrène du Nord-Ouest*, Institut français d'archéologie de Beyrouth, Bibliothèque archéologique et historique, 49 (Paris: Geuthner).

Schmidt-Colinet, A. 1992. *Das Tempelgrab Nr. 36 in Palmyra: Studien zur palmyrenischen Grabarchitektur und ihrer Ausstattung*, Damaszener Forschungen, 4 (Mainz: Von Zabern).

—— 2009. 'Nochmal zur Ikonographie zweier palmyrenischer Sarkophage', in M. Blömer, M. Facella, and E. Winter (eds), *Lokale Identität im Römischen Nahen Osten: Kontexte und Perspektiven, Erträge der Tagung 'Lokale Identitäten im Römischen Nahen Osten' Münster 2007*, Oriens et Occidens, 18 (Stuttgart: Steiner), pp. 223–34.

Schmidt-Colinet, A. and K. al-As'ad. 2007. 'Zwei Neufunde Palmyrenischer Sarkophage', in G. Koch (ed.), *Akten des Symposiums des Sarkophag-Corpus 2001: Marburg, 2.–7. Juli 2001*, Sarkophag-Studien, 3 (Mainz: Von Zabern), pp. 271–78.

Segal, J. 1959. 'New Syriac Inscriptions from Edessa', *Bulletin of the School of Oriental and African Studies*, 22: 23–40.

Seland, E. 2017. 'The Iconography of Caravan Trade in Palmyra and the Roman Near East', in T. Long and A. H. Sørensen (eds), *Positions and Professions in Palmyra*, Palmyrene Studies, 2 (Copenhagen: The Royal Danish Academy of Sciences and Letters), pp. 106–14.

Seyrig, H. 1933. 'Antiquités syriennes, 12: Textes relatifs à la garnison romaine de Palmyre', *Syria*, 14: 152–68.

—— 1937. 'Antiquités syriennes, 20: Armes et costumes iraniens de Palmyre', *Syria*, 18: 4–31.

Seyrig, H. and R. Stucky. 1949. 'Genneas', *Syria*, 26: 248–57.

Stucky, R. 1976. 'Prêtres syriens II: Hiérapolis', *Syria*, 53: 127–40.

Tanabe, K. 1986. *Sculptures of Palmyra*, I, Memoirs of the Ancient Orient Museum, 1 (Tokyo: The Ancient Orient Museum).

Teixidor, J. 1979. *The Pantheon of Palmyra* (Leiden: Brill).

Tubach, J. 1986. *Im Schatten des Sonnengottes: Der Sonnenkult in Edessa, Ḥarrān und Ḥaṭrā am Vorabend der christlichen Mission* (Wiesbaden: Harrassowitz).

Vermeule, C. 1981. *Greek and Roman Sculpture in America* (Berkeley: University of California Press).

Vuolanto, V. 2019. 'Children and Religious Participation in Roman Palmyra', in S. Krag and R. Raja (eds), *Women, Children and the Family in Palmyra*, Palmyrene Studies, 3 (Copenhagen: The Royal Danish Academy of Sciences and Letters), pp. 201–13.

Wielgosz, D. 2004. 'Osservazioni sul sarcofago palmireno', in M. Fano Santi (ed.), *Studi di archeologia in onore di Gustavo Traversari*, Archaeologica, 141 (Rome: G. Bretschneider), pp. 929–55.

Will, E. 1951. 'Le relief de la tour de Kithôt et le banquet funéraire à Palmyre', *Syria*, 28: 70–100.

Yon, J.-B. 2013. 'Palmyrene Epigraphy after PAT, 1996–2011', *Studia Palmyreńskie*, 12: 333–79.

Zanker, P. 1994. 'The Hellenistic Grave Stelai from Smyrna: Identity and Self-Image in the Polis', in A. Bulloch and others (eds), *Images and Ideologies: Self-Definition in the Hellenistic World* (Berkeley: University of California Press), pp. 212–31.

10. Notes on Some Palmyrene Religious Imagery

Ted Kaizer

Durham University, Department of Classics and Ancient History (ted.kaizer@durham.ac.uk)

Introductory Remarks

This contribution merely aims to offer brief reflections on some of the religious images from Palmyra which are not commonly taken into account in discussions of the cults of the oasis.[1] As such, this is not a proper paper with an overall argument and conclusions. But the various pieces which are considered here, all perhaps a bit more obscure than the oft-studied monuments, are worth being brought together for the very simple reason that they all throw further light on the intricate religious life of the city by making the overall picture of Palmyrene civilization even more complicated than it already is (counterbalancing processes of harmonization[2]), and hence more complete. It is hoped that the modest observations made here will provoke further debate and ensure that the respective imagery will henceforth be borne in mind in future discussions.

A Palmyrene Statue of IOMH from as-Sukhnah

The first object to be discussed here does not even come from Palmyra itself: it was found at as-Sukhnah, a locality within Palmyra's territory, a good seventy kilometres north-east of the oasis, about one third of the way to the Euphrates River. The beautiful sculpture, clearly carved in the typical Palmyrene style, is nowadays kept in the Museum of Archaeology in Istanbul (Figs 10.1–10.2).[3] The limestone statue is accompanied by a Latin inscription which records a dedication to Jupiter Optimus Maximus Heliopolitanus[4] by Sextus Rasius Proculus, prefect of the Second Syrian Cohort of the Thracians.[5] As is well known, the cult of this Jupiter had its home sanctuary at Heliopolis, the city of the sun, nowadays known as Baalbek in the Lebanese Bekaa Valley, and situated in the hinterland of the first Roman colony in the Near Eastern lands, Berytus.[6] From there, this toponymic deity, borrowing his honorary titles 'Best' and 'Greatest' from the Jupiter who was worshipped on the Capitol in Rome, spread throughout the empire where he enjoyed particular popularity amongst the military. He was depicted according to a nearly 'canonical' type,[7] as a beardless person with curly hair, crowned with a calathos, standing on a plinth, flanked by bulls, holding a whip in his right hand and an ear in his left, and most often enclosed in a kind of sheath which was neatly divided in a number of sections displaying busts. That IOMH — his common epigraphic abbreviation, as on the sculpture here under discussion — was worshipped by a prefect of an auxiliary unit of the imperial army passing through the Palmyrena is in itself not surprising. Indeed, the type seems to be recognizable (though not identified by an accompanying inscription) on two

---

[1] Many thanks to Rubina Raja and Ken Lapatin for their kind invitation to participate in the symposium held in the splendid settings of the Getty Villa. This contribution combines part of the paper I gave at Malibu in April 2019 with part of a public lecture presented in Copenhagen in January 2020 at a symposium on 'Palmyra – Pearl of the Syrian Desert' (the invitation to which I owed once more to Rubina) in the Ny Carlsberg Glyptotek, to accompany the exhibition on 'The Road to Palmyra'. I am grateful to Julien Aliquot, Michał Gawlikowski, Maurice Sartre, Andreas Schmidt-Colinet, and Jean-Baptiste Yon for helpfully responding to my queries, but my main debt is to my Durham colleague Edmund Thomas, whose initial questions about some of the imagery discussed here sparked off my efforts and who has continued to give generous feedback.

[2] See Kaizer 2019a.

[3] Hajjar 1977, I, 211–14, no. 186; II, pl. LXX, no. 186.

[4] In fact, as Millar 1993, 127 and 284, emphasized, this concerns one of only two 'IOMH figures' which are unequivocally identified as such by an inscription.

[5] *AE* 1911, 124: 'I(ovi) O(ptimo) M(aximo) H(eliopolitano) Sex(tus) Rasius Proculus praef(ectus) coh(ortis) II Thr(acum) Syr(iacae)', following the reading in As'ad and Delplace 2002, 396, no. 28. The final three letters had originally been read as 'v(ovit) s(ua) p(ecvnia)'.

[6] See, most recently, Paturel 2019.

[7] See Kaizer 2006, 41, on the 'orthodoxy of iconography' which was 'often recognisable, although usually liable to a variable use of motifs and deviating details'.

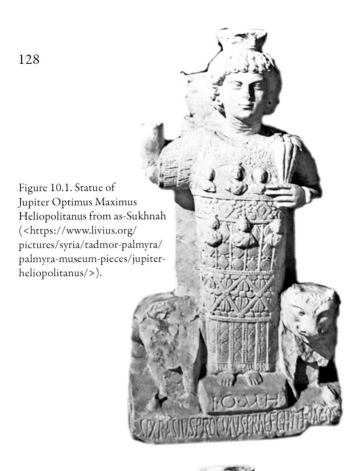

Figure 10.1. Statue of Jupiter Optimus Maximus Heliopolitanus from as-Sukhnah (<https://www.livius.org/pictures/syria/tadmor-palmyra/palmyra-museum-pieces/jupiter-heliopolitanus/>).

Figure 10.2. Statue of Jupiter Optimus Maximus Heliopolitanus from as-Sukhnah (<https://www.worldhistory.org/image/8721/statue-dedicated-to-jupiter-heliopolitanus/>).

Palmyrene tesserae, the small tokens which provided access to religious dining occasions.[8]

On closer inspection, however, the statue from as-Sukhnah deviates quite a bit from the expected iconographic pattern. Sextus Rasius Proculus seems to have ordered the sculpture from a workshop specializing in the typical Palmyrene art style, as is particularly visible in the execution of the god's face and hairstyle.[9] The deity is accompanied by bulls and wears a calathos, but this IOMH is not clothed in a sheath-like dress divided in multiple sections, but wears a patterned garment with two rows above each other of three little busts, resembling depictions from Palmyra, notably on the city's coinage, of a constellation of three gods with a central figure wearing a calathos flanked by a radiated sun god and a moon deity with a crescent on his shoulders.[10] It can perhaps be viewed as a sign of the strength and depth of Palmyra's idiosyncratic culture that an otherwise relatively fixed way of representing the local Jupiter from Baalbek was adjusted when an officer happened to make his dedication within the sphere of influence of the oasis city.

A Relief of the She-Wolf from the Temple of Bel

The second monument under consideration clearly relates to what can only be described as Roman imperial culture. It concerns a monument which seems to have been published just once, unfortunately not accompanied by a clear photograph (Fig. 10.3), by Cécile Dulière in her book on the *Lupa Romana*.[11] But it is still possible to recognize, towards the bottom of the relief, the she-wolf suckling Romulus and Remus, the mythical twin-founders of Rome. According to Dulière's acknowledgements, the image had been sent to her directly by the then director of the Palmyra Museum, Khaled al-As'ad. It seems to have been kept in the storage rooms of the museum and is recorded to have been found some-

---

[8] Ingholt, Seyrig, and Starcky 1955, no. 397, with pl. XXI; no. 1088, with pl. XLVII; cf. du Mesnil du Buisson 1962, 531. For a series of recent articles on the tesserae, see Raja 2015a; 2015b; 2016; 2019b; and for some observations about the way in which the divine world could be portrayed on them, see Kaizer 2022. Note that Hajjar 1977, I, 209–11; II, pls LXVII–LXIX, also listed a four-sided altar with damaged imagery related to Jupiter Optimus Maximus Heliopolitanus as possibly coming from Palmyra, but this attribution had already been judged 'douteuse' by Dussaud 1903, 360.

[9] See also Millar 1993, 128 and 298.

[10] Du Mesnil du Buisson 1962, 719–23; Krzyżanowska 2002, 173, no. I; Kaizer 2019b, 17 with fig. 2.

[11] Dulière 1979, 46–47 (and cf. 228), no. 120, with fig. 297.

Figure 10.3. Relief of she-wolf from the Temple of Bel at Palmyra (Dulière 1979, fig. 297).

Figure 10.4. Relief of she-wolf from the Temple of Bel at Palmyra (© Institut français du Proche-Orient).

where within the temenos of the great Temple of Bel. A different photo is preserved in the archives of the Institut français du Proche-Orient (Fig. 10.4). The visible remains of the vegetative decoration on the sides are said to make the monument contemporaneous with the construction of the temple in the early Julio-Claudian period.[12] It will be clear that the two available photographs do not allow for more precise judgement, but it has been suggested that the now empty space above the relief had originally framed a bronze plaque recording the regulations that were put in place once Palmyra, in the early years of the reign of the emperor Tiberius, had come to be integrated within the provincial structure of Rome's empire.[13] It is in any case tempting to propose a connection with a Latin inscription from this period,

also found in the temenos of the Temple of Bel, which once accompanied a statue group, set up by the *legatus* of *Legio X Fretensis*, of Tiberius flanked by his son Drusus the Younger and his nephew and adopted son Germanicus.[14] The damaged relief from Palmyra depicting the *lupa* suckling the twins nearly stands on its own in the lands of the Near East, but not quite: in the garden of the National Museum of Damascus, a large lintel from Fiq in the Hauran region, executed in the local black basalt stone and accompanied by a Greek dedication to Zeus, contains another specimen.[15]

To this meagre harvest of depictions of she-wolf plus twins from the Roman Near East may also be added another item from Palmyra itself: among the thousands of Palmyrene tesserae there is one single item which on

---

[12] Seyrig 1940, 336 n. 1; Gawlikowski 1973, 68 n. 13: 'ce monument serait contemporain du temple'.

[13] Picard 1934, 187–88: 'un relief représentant les Jumeaux et la Louve, près du figuier ruminal, au-dessous d'un encastrement de stèle de bronze (vide: traité entre Rome et Palmyre?)'; Seyrig 1940, 336 n. 1: 'Cette stèle portait […] une plaque de bronze dont il ne reste que l'encadrement. Il est très possible que ce document ne fût autre que l'acte qui réglait les rapports de Rome et de Palmyre.'

[14] See Gawlikowski 1973, 68 n. 13. For the inscription, see Yon 2012, no. 3.

[15] Dulière 1979, no. 121, with fig. 296; Weber 2006, 69–70, no. 52, with pl. 38. The inscription is acknowledged, though not read, by Meyernsen 2003, 132 with n. 75. The catalogue of the Greek and Latin inscriptions in the Damascus Museum, which does not have an *IGLS* number, had originally (before the civil war of recent years) been planned as a special issue in the series.

Figure 10.5. Arch with bust opposite eastern nymphaeum, opening up street leading from colonnade to agora. View towards the north (© E. V. Thomas).

one of its sides seems to depict the *lupa* suckling Romulus and Remus.[16] It has to be admitted, though, that the image is not entirely unequivocal, although the specimen is not dissimilar in conception to other tesserae. Its reverse side depicts the head of a bearded figure, but as there is no accompanying inscription any further interpretation must remain open. In any case, the relief of the she-wolf, possibly in combination with the tessera, leaves no doubt that in a city whose distinctive religious life seems in many ways untouched by Roman influence,[17] cultural elements closely connected to the empire's Latin culture could still be present. To what degree the Roman *lupa* was thought by Palmyrene viewers to resemble another suckling animal which has been recognized on coins from the oasis city remains an open question.[18]

Figure 10.6. Detail of bust on Fig. 10.5 (© E. V. Thomas).

Figure 10.7. Detail of bust on Fig. 10.5 (© Institut français du Proche-Orient).

---

[16] Ingholt, Seyrig, and Starcky 1955, no. 1072, with pl. XLVII. See also du Mesnil du Buisson 1962, 695.

[17] Gawlikowski 1990; Kaizer 2002.

[18] Krzyżanowska 2002, 173, nos IX–X; du Mesnil du Buisson 1962, 736–38. It may be tempting to connect these images with a relief from Tyre showing a suckling animal — listed by Dulière 1979, no. 122, with fig. 298 — although the latter does not seem to represent a she-wolf. Cf. Seyrig 1963, 23–25, esp. n. 34.

10. NOTES ON SOME PALMYRENE RELIGIOUS IMAGERY

Figure 10.8. Arch with bust opposite eastern nymphaeum, opening up street leading from colonnade to agora. View towards the south (© E. V. Thomas).

Divine (?) Busts on Arches in the Colonnade

The third and final case study concerns a small group of images, displayed in public spaces of Palmyra, which have thus far been overlooked. It ought to be stressed at the outset, however, that it must remain unclear whether these *are* actually images of deities. A couple of small arches within the colonnade, and also some other monuments, were decorated with busts. In a city where divine representations were hardly visible 'in the streets', and instead confined to either sanctuaries, tombs, or domestic settings, these busts stand out.[19] Firstly, an arch opposite the eastern nymphaeum and opening up the street leading from the colonnade to the north-eastern entrance to the agora, has a bust on either side (Figs 10.5–10.10).[20] Comparing the two busts, their frag-

Figure 10.9. Detail of bust on Fig. 10.8 (© E. V. Thomas).

Figure 10.10. Detail of bust on Fig. 10.8 (© Institut français du Proche-Orient).

---

[19] If the two reliefs reused in the later bastion which encloses the propylaea of the Temple of Bel, of Heracles and Hermes figures, did indeed come from the local gymnasium (of which these two gods were traditionally considered protectors), as postulated by Seyrig 1944/45, 75–76 and pl. IV, and if they had indeed been originally located on the outside of that now lost building, they would form another exception.

[20] For the location, see Schnädelbach 2010, 54, opposite C301.3.

Figure 10.11. Arch with bust in western half of colonnade. View towards the north (© E. V. Thomas).

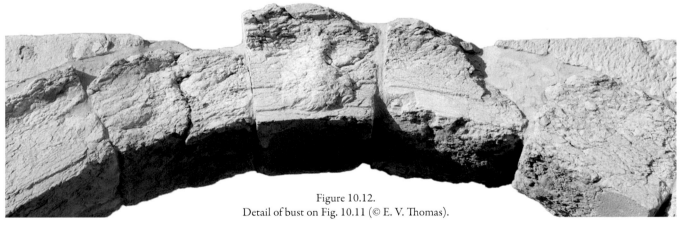

Figure 10.12. Detail of bust on Fig. 10.11 (© E. V. Thomas).

mentary state notwithstanding, they seem to be dressed in different styles: the bust on the south side which looks out towards the agora (i.e. the view taken towards the north, Figs 10.5–10.7) appears to wear more indigenous clothing, with the pattern still visible,[21] than the bust on the north side which looks out towards the nymphaeum (i.e. the view taken towards the south, Figs 10.8–10.10). Naturally, it is hard to say anything definite about these busts, and various options must be kept open. It remains a possibility that they were meant to represent the donors of the arches, although in that case the typical honorary inscriptions (ubiquitous on the consoles on the columns of the colonnade which used to support standing statues of notables) would be lacking. Priestly imagery does not seem likely either, as there are no remains of the characteristic cylindrical sacerdotal hat. This would leave the option that they are divine busts. There is a similar arch in the western half of the colonnade with busts on either

---

[21] As regards the indigenous dress, one may be reminded of the relief of a divine figure wearing Parthian costume and accompanied by a little dog, who has been interpreted by Gawlikowski 1966 as a variant on the Heracles figure, since he is also carrying club and lion skin; Drijvers 1976, pl. XV, 2; Tanabe (ed.) 1986, pl. 134.

Figure 10.13. Arch with bust in western half of colonnade. View towards the south (© T. Kaizer).

Figure 10.14. Ruins of the eastern nymphaeum with bust (© T. Kaizer).

side which are even worse preserved (Figs 10.11–10.13), and another bust is visible on the remains of the eastern nymphaeum (Fig. 10.14).

Perhaps to be compared with those busts are the images which can be recognized on two cornices in the area around the theatre, not too far from the first of the above-mentioned arches in the colonnade. The first concerns the decorative moulding crowning the central door of the scaenae frons, entering from the colonnade road (Fig. 10.15); the second was part of the entrance to the building commonly referred to as the Caesareum, in front of which it was last seen lying on the ground (Fig. 10.16). Both of these lintels show bull protomes at the left and on the right end, and a number of busts in

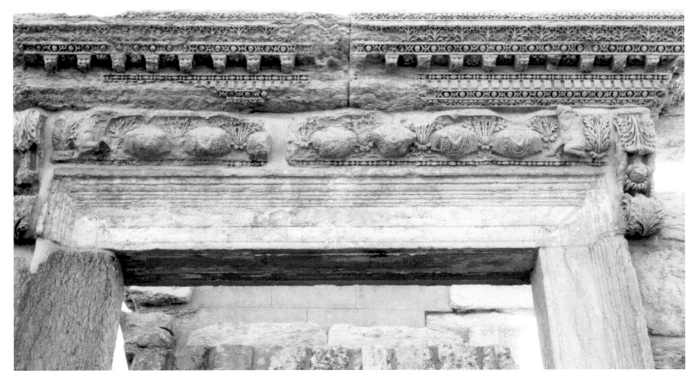

Figure 10.15. Cornice above central door of scaenae frons, entering from colonnade (© A. Schmidt-Colinet).

between, separated by scrolls. It is particularly the framing by the bulls (sacrificial victims, as on some Palmyrene reliefs?[22]) which suggests strongly that at least in these two cases the busts ought to be understood in some sort of religious context.[23] Andreas Schmidt-Colinet has shown how, in the late eighteenth century, these cornices inspired Louis-François Cassas, famous for his drawings of Palmyrene monuments, when he created his reproductions of some of the tomb facades (Fig. 10.17).[24] Cassas interpreted some of them as bearded males, and others as females with their breasts exposed (in other words, rather unlike the way in which Palmyrene women were depicted on the funerary busts, and hence most likely as goddesses), although from the remains of the original sculptures it cannot be said with certainty what sort of figures had been represented by the busts.[25]

But it may be noted that, on one of the busts from the so-called Caesareum, the remains of indigenous clothing a bit similar to that worn by the above-mentioned bust on the arch can still be seen.[26]

The busts on the arches in the colonnade must remain open to interpretation. But if it is indeed correct to view them as religious imagery, they raise questions with regard to their potential presence at cultic occasions,[27] notably at processions. Again, our evidence is perhaps not as good as some have made it out to be, but it is likely that divine images were carried through the streets of Tadmor-Palmyra on given days in the religious calendar,[28] be it in a sedan-chair, in a wagon, or in

---

[22] See e.g. Dentzer-Feydy and Teixidor 1993, 137, no. 147; Charles-Gaffiot, Lavagne, and Hofman 2001, 194, no. 34; cf. Ingholt 1928, 43 n. 2 (*PS* 532–33), with the new edited translation by Bobou and others 2021, 115.

[23] Schmidt-Colinet 1996, 369, for comments on the 'nach innen gewandte Stierprotomen, die wohl als Opfertiere zu interpretieren sind.'

[24] Schmidt-Colinet 1996, 368. For Cassas's drawings of the tombs in general, see now also Henning 2016.

[25] See Schmidt-Colinet 1996, 368: 'wahrscheinlich handelt es sich aber ausschließlich um männliche Büsten'.

[26] Schmidt-Colinet 1996, 483, Abb. 213.

[27] Note the solar bust hanging above the sacrificial scene on a Palmyrene relief, found at the city gate of Dura-Europos, which depicts the goddess Nemesis: Downey 1977, 29–31, no. 9; 191–92, with pl. IV. Similarly, a tessera showing a reclining priest includes the bust of a radiated divinity in the background (though religious dining would have taken place in secluded settings): Ingholt, Seyrig, and Starcky 1955, no. 381; Raja 2019a, no. 150.

[28] For a confident discussion of the meagre evidence, see Le Bihan 2015, 66–71; Kaizer 2002, 200–03 was more sceptical (and argued in particular against those who saw 'nomadic' influence behind the Palmyrene rite). Scholars had traditionally assumed that the central colonnade fulfilled the function of a 'processional way', connecting the Temple of Allat in the western part of the town with

10. NOTES ON SOME PALMYRENE RELIGIOUS IMAGERY

Figure 10.16. Cornice originally above entrance to so-called Caesareum (© A. Schmidt-Colinet).

Figure 10.17. Drawing by Cassas of a frieze with three busts (from Ketelsen 2016, Abb. 22, Kat. 36).

the form of so-called divine 'standards'.[29] In the context of processions, however, the most often discussed piece of evidence is of course the famous relief on the beam from the Temple of Bel which shows a group of veiled women observing a slowly moving camel carrying on its back a covered block.[30] The camel is preceded by a donkey, and Michał Gawlikowski has recently put forward the hypothesis that the left part of the relief, which is preserved only dimly, represents the fixing of a *tropaion*, 'a trophy consisting of armour and helmet' with an 'apo-

---

the Temple of Bel in the east. However, as a much later addition to the urban plan of the city, the colonnade cannot have formed the route of more 'original' processional rites. Jakubiak 2013 has argued for a *via sacra* south of the wall of Diocletian, following the course of the wadi, which, as is now known from soundings near the agora and near the Temple of Nebu, was paved all the way (and which may have gone past four shrines).

[29] Sedan-chair: as mentioned in a Greek inscription which honours a benefactor for, among other things, plating with silver the whole surface of the φορεῖον of the god Bōrroaōnos, see Yon 2012, no. 308. Wagon: as depicted on a fragmentary sculpture from the Temple of Allat, see Tanabe (ed.) 1986, 155; Dirven 1999, pl. XIX; and on coinage from elsewhere in the Near East, such as at Sidon

(*RPC* I, nos 4606, 4608; III, nos 3871–72, 3875, 3877) and at Philadelphia (*RPC* IV.3, nos 6295, 6651, 11635). Standards: as suggested by a small Palmyrene relief found in a building along the main road in Dura-Europos, see Dirven 1999, 273–78, with pl. X, and by depictions on tesserae, see Ingholt, Seyrig, and Starcky 1955, nos 177–78, 180.

[30] Tanabe (ed.) 1986, pls 42–44. See Dirven 1998; 1999, 81–86, for the now conventional interpretation of the scene as the investiture of Allat which was ceremonially repeated on an annual basis.

tropaic' meaning, 'laden with a deterrent divine force'.[31] The alleged sacred image carried on the back of the camel is covered and hidden from view — indeed in contrast to the busts on display in the public space. Taking into account that not all representations of deities fulfilled an actively cultic function, it might therefore be best to interpret the onlooking busts on the arches and the cornices (similarly to the *tropaion* on the relief) as apotropaic imagery, having the power to avert evil influences or bad luck, notably at liminal places. If this hardly seems to be a startling conclusion, it must at least be emphasized that, at Palmyra, such apotropaic divine images are not widely attested in public, and that the available source material from the oasis polis does not permit for a situation to be sketched similar to the Roman Empire at large, where the depiction of gods and goddesses near boundaries and thresholds was widespread. Whether this is simply a function of the evidence, or whether it is the result of a different religious mentality, is a question that is left open for further debate.

---

[31] Gawlikowski 2016, 345.

Works Cited

As'ad, K. and C. Delplace. 2002. 'Inscriptions latines de Palmyre', *Revue des études anciennes*, 104: 363–400.

Bobou, O. and others. 2021. *Studies on Palmyrene Sculpture: A Translation of Harald Ingholt's 'Studier over Palmyrensk Skulptur', Edited and with Commentary*, Studies in Palmyrene Archaeology and History, 1 (Turnhout: Brepols).

Charles-Gaffiot, J., H. Lavagne, and J.-M. Hofman. 2001. *Moi, Zénobie reine de Palmyre* (Paris: Centre culturel du Panthéon).

Dentzer-Feydy, J. and J. Teixidor. 1993. *Les antiquités de Palmyre au Musée du Louvre* (Paris: Éditions de la Réunion des musées nationaux).

Dirven, L. 1998. 'The Arrival of the Goddess Allat in Palmyra', *Mesopotamia*, 33: 297–307.

—— 1999. *The Palmyrenes of Dura-Europos: A Study of Religious Interaction in Roman Syria*, Religions in the Graeco-Roman World, 138 (Leiden: Brill).

Downey, S. B. 1977. *The Stone and Plaster Sculpture*, The Excavations at Dura-Europos Conducted by Yale University and the French Academy of Inscriptions and Letter: Final Report, 3.1.2, Monumenta archaeologica, 5 (Los Angeles: The Institute of Archaeology, University of California).

Drijvers, H. J. W. 1976. *The Religion of Palmyra*, Iconography of Religions, Section 15, Mesopotamia and the Near East, 15 (Leiden: Brill).

Dulière, C. 1979. *Lupa Romana* (Rome: Institut historique belge de Rome).

Dussaud, R. 1903. 'Notes de mythologie syrienne', *Revue archéologique*, 4th ser., 1: 347–82.

Gawlikowski, M. 1966. 'Un nouveau type d'Héraclès à Palmyre', *Études et travaux*, 3: 141–49.

—— 1973. *Palmyre*, VI: *Le temple Palmyrénien: études d'épigraphie et de topographie historique* (Warsaw: Państwowe Wydawnictwo Naukowe).

—— 1990. 'Les dieux de Palmyre', in H. Temporini and W. Haase (eds), *Aufstieg und Niedergang der römischen Welt*, II.18.4 (Berlin: De Gruyter), pp. 2605–58.

—— 2016. 'Gods in Armour in Roman Syria', *La Parola del Passato*, 71: 333–51.

Hajjar, Y. 1977. *La triade d'Héliopolis-Baalbek: son culte et sa diffusion à travers les textes littéraires et les documents iconographiques et épigraphiques*, 2 vols (Leiden: Brill).

Henning, A. 2016. 'Zwischen Realität und Phantasie: Louis-François Cassas und die Turmgräber von Palmyra', in T. Ketelsen (ed.), *Palmyra: Was bleibt? Louis-François Cassas und seine Reise in den Orient*, Der ungewisse Blick, 20 (Cologne: Wallraf-Richartz-Museum), pp. 22–34.

Ingholt, H. 1928. *Studier over Palmyrensk Skulptur* (Copenhagen: Reitzel).

Ingholt, H., H. Seyrig, and J. Starcky. 1955. *Recueil des Tessères de Palmyre*, Bibliothèque archéologique et historique, 58 (Paris: Geuthner).

Jakubiak, K. 2013. '*Via sacra* or Sacral Space in Palmyra', *Zeitschrift für Orient-Archäologie*, 6: 144–55.

Kaizer, T. 2002. *The Religious Life of Palmyra*, Oriens et Occidens, 4 (Stuttgart: Steiner).

—— 2006. 'In Search of Oriental Cults: Methodological Problems concerning "the Particular" and "the General" in Near Eastern Religion in the Hellenistic and Roman Periods', *Historia*, 55: 26–47.

—— 2019a. 'Gods, Temples, and Cults: Religious Life in Palmyra', in A. M. Nielsen and R. Raja (eds), *The Road to Palmyra* (Copenhagen: Ny Carlsberg Glyptotek), pp. 205–20.

—— 2019b. 'Patterns of Worship at Palmyra: Reflections on Methods and Approaches', in R. Raja (ed.), *Revisiting the Religious Life of Palmyra*, Contextualizing the Sacred, 9 (Turnhout: Brepols), pp. 7–24.

—— 2022. 'Some Thoughts on Divine Representations on Palmyrene Coins and Tesserae', in R. Raja (ed.), *The Small Stuff of the Palmyrenes: Coins and Tesserae from Palmyra*, Studies in Palmyrene Archaeology and History, 5 (Turnhout: Brepols), pp. 89–98.

Ketelsen, T. (ed.). 2016. *Palmyra: Was bleibt? Louis-François Cassas und seine Reise in den Orient*, Der ungewisse Blick, 20 (Cologne: Wallraf-Richartz-Museum).

Krzyżanowska, A. 2002. 'Les monnaies de Palmyre: leur chronologie et leur rôle dans la circulation monétaire de la région', in C. Augé and F. Duyrat (eds), *Les monnayages syriens: quel apport pour l'histoire du Proche-Orient hellénistique et romain?*, Bibliothèque archéologique et historique, 162 (Beirut: Institut français d'archéologie du Proche-Orient), pp. 167–73.

Le Bihan, A. 2015. 'Rites et identité religieuse en Syrie romaine', in C. Abadie-Reynal and J.-B. Yon (eds), *Zeugma*, VI: *La Syrie romaine: permanences et transferts culturels*, Travaux de la Maison de l'Orient et de la Méditerranée, 68 (Lyon: Maison de l'Orient et de la Méditerranée Jean Pouilloux), pp. 55–74.

Mesnil du Buisson, R. du. 1962. *Les tessères et les monnaies de Palmyre: un art, une culture et une philosophie grecs dans les moules d'une cité et d'une religion sémitiques* (Paris: Bibliothèque nationale/Boccard).

Meyernsen, S. F. 2003. 'Zwischen "Fremdeinfluß" und "Eigenständigkeit": Hellenistisch-kaiserzeitliche Tierplastik in Südsyrien', in K. S. Freyberger, A. Henning, and H. von Hesberg (eds), *Kulturkonflikte im Vorderen Orient an der Wende vom Hellenismus zur römischen Kaiserzeit*, Orient-Archäologie, 11 (Rahden: Leidorf), pp. 125–42.

Millar, F. 1993. *The Roman Near East, 31 BC – AD 337* (Cambridge, MA: Harvard University Press).

Paturel, S. E. 2019. *Baalbek-Heliopolis, the Bekaa, and Berytus from 100 BCE to 400 CE: A Landscape Transformed*, Mnemosyne Supplements, History and Archaeology of Classical Antiquity, 426 (Leiden: Brill).

Picard, C. 1934. 'Chronique de la sculpture étrusco-latine', *Revue des études latines*, 12: 173–206.

Raja, R. 2015a. 'Staging "Private" Religion in Roman "Public" Palmyra: The Role of the Religious Dining Tickets (Banqueting Tesserae)', in C. Ando and J. Rüpke (eds), *Public and Private in Ancient Mediterranean Law and Religion*, Religionsgeschichtliche Versuche und Vorarbeiten, 65 (Berlin: De Gruyter), pp. 165–86.

—— 2015b. 'Cultic Dining and Religious Patterns in Palmyra: The Case of the Palmyrene Banqueting Tesserae', in S. Faust, M. Seifert, and L. Ziemer (eds), *Antike. Architektur. Geschichte: Festschrift für Inge Nielsen zum 65. Geburtstag*, Gateways, Hamburger Beiträge zur Archäologie und Kulturgeschichte des antiken Mittelmeerraumes, 3 (Aachen: Shaker), pp. 181–99.

—— 2016. 'In and Out of Contexts: Explaining Religious Complexity through the Banqueting Tesserae from Palmyra', *Religion in the Roman Empire*, 2: 340–71.

—— 2019a. *The Palmyra Collection: Ny Carlsberg Glyptotek*, Catalogue (Copenhagen: Ny Carlsberg Glyptotek).

—— 2019b. 'Dining with the Gods and the Others: The Banqueting Tickets from Palmyra as Expressions of Religious Individualisation', in M. Fuchs and others (eds), *Religious Individualisation: Historical Dimensions and Comparative Perspectives* (Berlin: De Gruyter), pp. 243–55.

Schmidt-Colinet, A. 1996. 'Antike Denkmäler in Syrien: Die Stichvorlagen von Louis François Cassas (1756–1827) im Wallraf-Richartz-Museum in Köln', *Kölner Jahrbuch*, 29: 343–548.

Schnädelbach, K. 2010. *Topographia Palmyrena*, I: *Topography*, Documents d'archéologie syrienne, 18 (Damascus: Direction Générale des Antiquités et des Musées de la République Arabe Syrienne).

Seyrig, H. 1940. 'Remarques sur la civilisation de Palmyre (à propos des fragments récemment découverts)', *Syria*, 21: 328–37.

—— 1944/45. 'Héraclès-Nergal', *Syria*, 24: 62–80.

—— 1963. 'Les grands dieux de Tyr à l'époque grecque et romaine', *Syria*, 40: 19–28.

Tanabe, K. (ed.). 1986. *Sculptures of Palmyra*, I, Memoirs of the Ancient Orient Museum, 1 (Tokyo: The Ancient Orient Museum).

Weber, T. M., in cooperation with Q. al-Mohammed. 2006. *Sculptures from Roman Syria in the Syrian National Museum at Damascus*, I: *From Cities and Villages in Central and Southern Syria* (Worms: Werner).

Yon, J.-B. 2012. *Inscriptions grecques et latines de la Syrie*, XVII.1: *Palmyre*, Bibliothèque archéologique et historique, 195 (Beirut: Institut français du Proche-Orient).

11. A Palmyrene Child at Dura-Europos

Lisa R. Brody
Yale University Art Gallery
(lisa.brody@yale.edu)

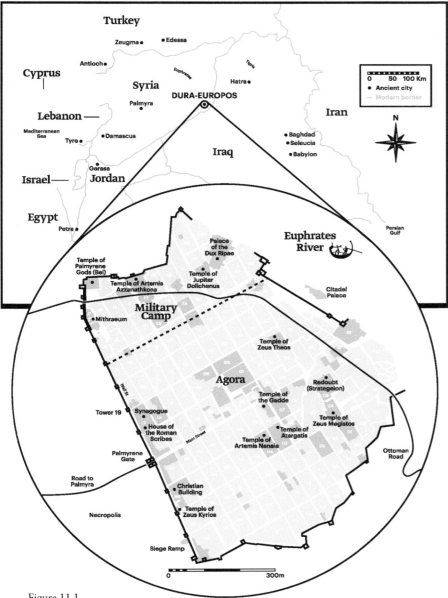

Figure 11.1.
Regional map and city plan of Dura-Europos (image courtesy of the Graphic Design Department, Yale University Art Gallery).

The site of Dura-Europos (Fig. 11.1) is situated on the west bank of the middle Euphrates River in present-day Syria, approximately 250 kilometres from the region's major caravan city, Palmyra. Connections between the two cities in Antiquity are well attested. People from Palmyra comprised a significant element of the Durene community; they continue to use Palmyrene Aramaic script for inscriptions and to identify themselves as Palmyrenes.[1] Several temples and altars in Dura-Europos were dedicated to Palmyrene gods and were likely frequented primarily by people who came from Palmyra.[2] Although the archaeological evidence on this subject is scarce, particularly prior to the Roman era, it is likely that Palmyrenes were already living in Dura in the late first century BC. An inscription records that two men from Palmyra were responsible for the foundation of the Temple of Bel in the necropolis, just outside the city wall, in 33 BC.[3]

Once the Roman garrison was established at Dura-Europos, it certainly included Palmyrene soldiers. In fact the earliest attested military unit stationed in the city is the group of Palmyrene archers who founded the Mithraeum in AD 168–171.[4] By AD 192, the garrison included the *cohors XX Palmyrenorum*, a large regiment recruited from Palmyra that is well documented in the papyrus documents found at the site.[5] Aside from the soldiers, the majority of Palmyrenes living in Dura-Europos were most likely merchants. Both regional and long-distance commerce were important elements in the city's economy, as it was positioned along major trade routes that ran north–south along the Euphrates to Babylon, and east–west through Palmyra to the Mediterranean coast.

Over the course of ten annual campaigns in the 1920s and 1930s, the site of Dura-Europos was excavated by archaeologists from Yale University in New Haven,

---

[1] Dirven 2011, 203.

[2] See Dirven 2011 for a full discussion about Palmyrenes in Dura-Europos with a focus on religious contexts.

[3] Dirven 2011, 199–202; *PAT*, no. 1067.

[4] Dirven 1999, 13.

[5] Welles, Fink, and Gilliam 1959, 26–36; Dirven 1999, 14; James 2019, 245–47.

Figure 11.2. Upper fragment of figure of a Palmyrene child (Dura-Europos Collection, Yale University Art Gallery, dura-e92~01).

Figure 11.3. Lower fragment of figure of a Palmyrene child (Dura-Europos Collection, Yale University Art Gallery, dura-e93~01).

Figure 11.4. Figure of a Palmyrene child (Dura-Europos Collection, Yale University Art Gallery, dura-e91~01).

Connecticut, USA, in collaboration with the Académie des Inscriptions et Belles-Lettres in Paris, France.[6] The project initially was overseen by French field director Maurice Pillet (1928–1931); then by Clark Hopkins of Yale (1932–1935); and finally by Frank E. Brown, also of Yale (1936–1937). During the fifth excavation season (October 1931 to March 1932), field director Clark Hopkins decided to investigate a large section of the city centre, and several private houses were revealed in the area around the Agora.[7] One of these was a structure in Block G1 that was designated as House C.[8] House G1-C was relatively small, approximately 111 m², with five rooms on the ground floor. As the exterior walls abut Houses G1-A, G1-B, and G1-D, it appears that House C was built in the space available between these existing structures.[9] Among the finds in this house were two fragments of a free-standing statue of a child (the shoulders

---

[6] Brody 2011, 17–32.

[7] Rostovtzeff 1934, 31–72. For the most comprehensive recent research on the houses at Dura-Europos, see Baird 2006 and 2014.

[8] Rostovtzeff 1934, 55–58.

[9] Baird 2014, 323 (Appendix).

11. A PALMYRENE CHILD AT DURA-EUROPOS 141

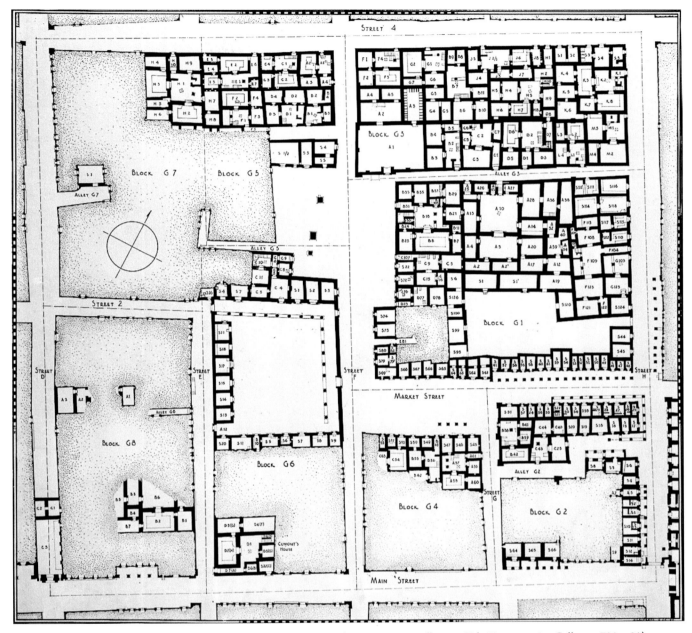

Figure 11.5. Plan of Blocks G1–G8 in Dura-Europos Excavation (Dura-Europos Collection, Yale University Art Gallery, y-721a~01).

and legs). The fragments were discovered in different rooms (rooms 5 and 22) in November 1931 (Figs 11.2 and 11.3).[10]

A few months later, in February 1932, the third fragment of this statue was discovered down the street, in Block G6 of the Agora (Fig. 11.5).[11] In the published preliminary report of the excavation season, Hopkins notes that

it is worthy of remark how widely scattered the parts of [...] this statue were. One might not be surprised to find parts of the same object in different rooms of a house but the fragments could scarcely be carried half a block or so without some special agency.[12]

The fragmentary statue was shipped to the Yale University Art Gallery as part of the *partage* agreement established for the campaign, which dictated a 50/50 division of all finds between the two participants.[13] The three

---

10 These were given field numbers E177 and E368.
11 Field number E1260.

12 Rostovtzeff 1934, 55.
13 This document is preserved in the Dura-Europos excavation

Figure 11.6. Figure of a Palmyrene child from Dura-Europos, Yale University Art Gallery. AD 100–150. Excavated by the Yale-French Excavations at Dura-Europos, present-day Syria, 1928–1937 (photo courtesy of the Yale University Art Gallery).

pieces were joined in 1933 by Robert G. Eberhard, a professor of sculpture in the Yale School of Fine Arts and curator at the Yale Art Gallery, and the statue was acces-

archives at the Yale University Art Gallery, held at Yale's West Campus Collection Studies Center and available for research; this major collection of photographs, drawings, field notebooks, and object registers provides invaluable information about the expedition and its personnel as well as the context and conservation of finds. The Gallery's Dura-Europos Collection includes thousands of artefacts discovered during the excavations, including architectural fragments, sculpture, wall paintings, arms and armour, leather objects, textiles, jewellery, and coins. The majority of these artefacts are available to students and scholars alike at the Margaret and Angus Wurtele Study Center at West Campus. The Académie's share of the finds remained in Syria, at the National Museum in Damascus, as Syria was under French mandate at the time.

sioned into the museum's collection (Fig. 11.6).[14] The head is still missing. In publishing the statue, Hopkins gave a full description of its appearance, noted its Palmyrene characteristics, identified the figure as a girl, and dated it to the first half of the second century AD. He concluded that the close relationship of the statue with Palmyrene works indicated 'parallel schools of work' rather than demonstrating that it was imported.[15]

The statue was subsequently published several times. In her 1973 book, *The Art of Dura-Europos*, Ann Perkins made the observation that the area where the fragments were discovered is located in the vicinity of the Temple of the Gadde, a sanctuary closely connected to Palmyrene cult and the Palmyrene community at Dura, and she theorized that the statue originally was a votive offering in this shrine. Indeed, although there is no surviving dedicatory inscription associated with the statue, it is indeed likely to have been votive in nature. Perkins also commented that 'the material is not Palmyrene limestone, so the statuette was probably made at Dura, but certainly by a sculptor familiar with the art of Palmyra'.[16] Susan Downey's publication of the statue in her 1977 final report on the sculpture from Dura-Europos also addressed the issue of the stone and its carving. She reached some strikingly different conclusions:

> Various factors suggest that the statue was imported from Palmyra. The stone is apparently Palmyrene. The short mantle is common at Palmyra, but is otherwise unknown at Dura. While I have been unable to find an exact parallel for the ornament on the right sleeve of the tunic, elaborately ornamented clothing is common at Palmyra. The style also is Palmyrene. In particular, the treatment of the mantle over the left arm and shoulder in wide, flat folds is a Palmyrene, not a Durene convention. Probably the statue was made around the middle of the second century AD.[17]

It is telling that these two scholars — both experts in Durene sculpture — studied this statue and arrived at essentially opposite deductions about it, including the stone itself and where it was carved. It is possible that these issues will never be settled decisively, but the development of analytical technologies and continuing research on both Palmyrene and Durene sculpture and

---

[14] Yale University Art Gallery, New Haven, inv. no. 1932.1214.
[15] Rostovtzeff 1934, 58.
[16] Downey 1977, 111.
[17] Downey 1977, 112.

11. A PALMYRENE CHILD AT DURA-EUROPOS 143

Figure 11.7. Mary and James Ottaway Gallery of Ancient Dura-Europos (photo courtesy of Jessica Smolinski, Yale University Art Gallery).

the relationship between the two cities certainly calls for reconsideration of this object and its archaeological context.

The statue, currently on display in the Mary and James Ottaway Gallery of Dura-Europos at the Yale University Art Gallery, represents an important piece in the ongoing study of the interactions between Palmyra and Dura-Europos (Fig. 11.7). Despite its extensive publication history, many questions about the statue remain unresolved. Recent research on Palmyrene sculpture provides some new parallels and insights into its iconography, while technological advances in artefact analysis may be a means of gathering new information about its source and context.

The surviving statue, with the three fragments joined, stands 0.68 m high from shoulders to feet (it would originally have been approximately three-quarters of a metre tall including the head), is 0.32 m wide across the chest, and 0.17 m in depth. The figure appears in a stiff, frontal pose with the weight evenly distributed on both legs. It is clearly meant to be viewed from the front, as it is flat and unfinished in back (Fig. 11.8).

The arms are held close to the body and are bent at the elbows so that both hands are in front of the torso. The figure wears a long-sleeved, ankle-length tunic or chiton. The garment hangs in suspended, semi-regular, elliptical folds over the chest. Between the legs, the material hangs straight down in vertical pleats; each leg is modelled by suspended U-shaped folds. The neckline and sleeves are ornamented with what appear to

Figure 11.8. Figure of a Palmyrene child from Dura-Europos (left and right side views) (photo courtesy of the Yale University Art Gallery).

Figure 11.10. Silver bracelet with carnelian intaglio from Dura-Europos, Yale University Art Gallery. Second or early third century AD. Excavated by the Yale-French Excavations at Dura-Europos, present-day Syria, 1928–1937 (photo courtesy of the Yale University Art Gallery).

Figure 11.9. Figure of a Palmyrene child from Dura-Europos (detail) (photo courtesy of the Yale University Art Gallery).

be rows of beads or embroidery; additional decorative rows are evident on the right upper arm. All of these elements would originally have been highlighted by elaborate polychromy; additional decoration on the fabric may also have been painted. The feet (wearing plain closed-toe shoes) protrude from underneath the hem of the floor-length garment.

Over the chiton is a mantle or himation that covers the figure's left shoulder and arm, curves across the abdomen, and is decorated with tassels. Close examination indicates that the sculptor may have had some confusion about rendering this garment; its exact arrangement is difficult to ascertain. It clearly hangs over the left shoulder and drapes around the back of the torso, coming around the front of the body at the right hip. In at least two locations the edge of the himation is adorned with a tassel (signifying the individual's high social status). It wraps around the left forearm at least once but apparently twice, hanging down from where it is pinned between the left wrist and the body, but the drapery does not precisely correspond to the way such a garment would really fall. The object certainly would have been painted in Antiquity, and it is possible that some of this ambiguity would have been clarified by the artist's choice of pigments and patterns.

The figure holds a bird in the right hand and bunch of grapes in the left (Fig. 11.9). The index and middle fingers of the right hand are extended. Jewellery includes a necklace with a trapezoidal pendant, a heavy twisted bracelet on each wrist, and a ring on the index finger of the left hand. Several bracelets very similar in design to the ones rendered in the sculpture, in both bronze and silver, were discovered in the Dura-Europos excavations (Fig. 11.10).[18]

An important source of evidence and comparanda for the Durene statue is the Palmyra Portrait Project, directed by Dr Rubina Raja of Aarhus University.[19] This ongoing compilation of all surviving examples of Palmyrene funerary sculpture held in museums and private collections around the world currently contains over 3700 works of art. An invaluable corpus of ancient portraiture, the project has already facilitated many significant new research projects and publications. In studying works of art such as the statue from Dura-Europos, for which the closest comparanda are children depicted in Palmyrene sculpture, the Palmyra Portrait Project is clearly an invaluable resource. Using the database, Sara Ringsborg of Aarhus University determined in 2017 that approximately 7 per cent of surviving Palmyrene funerary portraits depict children. The children often are shown along with one or both parents, most frequently the mother.[20] Despite the increased research and scholarship on Palmyrene portraits made possible by the Palmyra Portrait Project, it remains true that 'overall fairly little is known about children and childhood in Palmyra, as these themes have received little attention in scholarly research publications on the city'.[21]

---

[18] For example: Yale University Art Gallery, New Haven, inv. nos 1929.405a–b; 1933.632b; 1938.5207; 1938.5999.1793.

[19] <https://projects.au.dk/palmyraportrait/> [accessed 10 October 2021]. Raja is Professor of Classical Archaeology and Art, School of Culture and Society at Aarhus University as well as Centre director of the Danish National Research Foundation's Centre of Excellence, Centre for Urban Network Evolutions.

[20] Ringsborg 2017, 67.

[21] Krag and Raja 2019, 7.

Figure 11.11. Palmyrene funerary relief with a man and his two nephews, Seattle Art Museum. Second century AD. Eugene Fuller Memorial Collection (photograph by Nathaniel Willson; photo courtesy of the Seattle Art Museum).

Among the recent studies on Palmyrene sculpture that examine and interpret images of children are most notably those published by Sara Ringsborg, Signe Krag, and Rubina Raja. One recurring theme in this research addresses the problem of identifying the child's sex in these representations. When the subjects of Palmyrene art are named by accompanying inscriptions, the identification of them as male or female is obviously straightforward. When no inscription is present, however, even making this basic determination is frequently problematic. Krag and Raja state that:

> In representations with women and the children the actual gender of boys and girls is often challenging to judge. It can be rather hard or impossible to tell the difference between boys and girls when inscriptions are not accompanying the representations or when they are not preserved.[22]

Ringsborg reaches the same conclusion after examining numerous examples and observing that children of both genders wear the same garments, have the same short hairstyles, and wear the same jewellery.[23]

Both boys and girls in Palmyrene sculpture are depicted holding bunches of fruit (generally either grapes or dates) and birds. These attributes very rarely appear in images of grown men and women, so they appear to have special relevance to children. They can be useful, therefore, in confirming the youth of a subject even when, as is sometimes the case, the figure is rendered with adult-like proportions. Francis Pierson, in fact, declared the presence of a bunch of grapes and/or a bird to be one of the best means of recognizing a figure in Palmyrene sculpture as a child, in addition to those instances where small figures are shown together with a larger one (generally a parent) in a funerary relief composition.[24] The precise significance of these attributes, however, remains unclear. The fact that the figure from Dura holds a bunch of grapes and a bird serves both to identify it as a child and to connect it iconographically with Palmyrene portrait sculpture.

Similarly, the gesture made by the Durene figure, with the index and middle fingers of one hand extended, is one that has been shown by Maura Heyn to be quite common in Palmyrene portraiture.[25] It appears in portraits of various individuals, including adults and children, males and females, including one of two boys depicted with their uncle on a relief now in the Seattle Art Museum (Fig. 11.11).[26]

Heyn's research is inspired by several published discussions on gesture in Roman art.[27] As she notes, however, Palmyrene art has its own systems of iconography and interpretation that are distinct from those in other realms of Roman art, and it thus requires its own analysis. Her compiled statistics are useful in connecting certain hand gestures to certain groups of individuals — arranged by gender, age, status, and role. While there are certain gestures or arm positions that appear to be used exclusively by a distinctive social group, for many gestures it remains difficult to ascertain the precise meaning

---

22 Krag and Raja 2016, 143.

23 Ringsborg 2017, 68.

24 Pierson 1984, 90.

25 Heyn 2010, 631–61.

26 <https://art.seattleartmuseum.org/objects/23742/tomb-seal-portrait-of-a-man-and-two-children> [accessed 10 October 2021]; Albertson 2000, 162; Fuller 1946, 22; Heyn 2010, 639; Seattle Art Museum 1951, 111; Parlasca 1990, 133–44.

27 Brilliant 1963; Kleiner 1977.

behind an artist's choice (or even if the choice necessarily had a particular meaning).[28]

In the absence of an identifying inscription for a portrait, scholars of ancient sculpture generally look to hairstyles and garments for identification of gender; this holds true for Palmyrene portraits as well as Greek and Roman ones. Obviously and unfortunately, the head of the figure from Dura is missing. Accordingly, since there are no traces of hair evident on the preserved shoulders, nothing is known about its hairstyle other than that it did not hang down in front of the shoulders. There do exist images of young girls in Palmyrene art that have short hair, so the apparent lack of long hair on the Durene figure is not evidence for its being male. Further, the fact that it is unfinished in the back and, to a large degree, on the sides, means that even if the figure did have hair that cascaded down its back, this would only be evident on the completed statue if some of the locks hung in front of the shoulders.

The next and perhaps most potentially useful element of the statue to examine is its costume: a long chiton with decoration along the sleeves and neckline, a himation adorned with tassels, and jewellery including a necklace with a trapezoidal pendant, bracelets, and a ring.

Some past researchers have made the claim that long tunics were worn only by girls. Francis Pierson, for one, stated this as though it were an accepted fact but in the same article pointed out examples of boys wearing long tunics (attributing this to the fact that they are particularly young children).[29] Recent scholars, however, have come to recognize that the surviving evidence does not support such broad assumptions. In publishing a Palmyrene relief in the Colket collection at the University of Washington, for example, Fred Albertson asserts that 'often [...] boys and girls are indistinguishable, with both wearing a simple, sleeveless tunic, and so the missing head of the Colket stele makes a gender designation all the more difficult'.[30] Ringsborg also comes to the same frustrating conclusion that 'it can be difficult to distinguish gender if the inscription does not mention the child, as portraits of both sexes have virtually identical clothing, hairstyles, and jewelry'.[31]

---

[28] As Heyn notes (2010, 640): '[I]t does not follow [...] that every gesture was significant'.

[29] Pierson 1984, 101.

[30] Albertson 2000, 162.

[31] Ringsborg 2017.

Figure 11.12. Palmyrene funerary relief with a brother and a sister, The State Hermitage Museum, St Petersburg, c. AD 114. Donated by the Patriarch of Antioch in 1909 (© The State Hermitage Museum; photo by Leonard Kheifets).

Figure 11.13. Palmyrene funerary relief with a mother and child, British Museum, London, c. AD 184. Museum Purchase in 1891 (© Trustees of the British Museum).

11. A PALMYRENE CHILD AT DURA-EUROPOS

A Palmyrene funerary relief in the Hermitage Museum shows a brother and sister holding hands (Fig. 11.12).[32] Both children are identified by the inscription between their heads. Each holds a bird and, in their clasped hands, a bunch of grapes. Their garments are nearly identical. The boy's chiton is long-sleeved and belted, his himation adorned with tassels. The girl's tunic is short-sleeved. Both wear twisted bracelets on each wrist; the girl also wears wide, elaborate cuff bracelets. Both have a row of what appear to be beads along the neckline of the chiton — either sewn to the garment itself or suspended from a necklace. The girl has an additional adornment around her neck. With the exception of the belt, the arrangement of clothing and jewellery worn by the boy on this relief are closer to those of our figure than those worn by the girl. The tunics on both of the Hermitage figures are shorter than that worn by the figure from Dura.

As an aside, boys in Palmyrene portraiture do seem to wear belts more frequently than girls, but even this is not a consistent and reliable rule. A relief now in Leiden, for example, depicts a woman and a child.[33] The child wears a long-sleeved tunic and a necklace and holds a tablet and a bunch of grapes. The inscription identifies the child as the woman's daughter, and her tunic is belted. The fact, then, that the statue from Dura does not appear to include a belt is not necessarily an indication that it represents a boy.

A Palmyrene relief in the British Museum depicts a woman holding a spindle and distaff, a veil draped over her head (Fig. 11.13).[34] To her right stands a child on a plinth. Visually, one might initially identify the child as a girl: the figure wears earrings and a necklace, and the himation is draped over the shoulders with a diagonal overfold and is grasped at the neck in a way that echoes the gesture of the woman. Indeed, in 2016, Krag and Raja called the child a girl. The inscriptions are somewhat confusing, as the longer one states: 'Alas, Shalmat

Figure 11.14. Palmyrene funerary relief of a family, Metropolitan Museum of Art, New York. Second or third century AD. Museum Purchase in 1902 (public domain).

her mother, alas, Shalmat daughter of Shamshigeram, in the month of Elul, year 495 [September, AD 184]'. This seems to indicate that the figures are mother and daughter, both named Shalmat. Another inscription, however, appears next to the child: 'Hairan her son'. Perhaps the figures do indeed represent the two Shalmats and Hairan was buried in the tomb at a later date? Or did the son commission the relief for his mother and sister? In any case, Krag's 2018 publication chooses the gender-neutral term 'child', as does the current object entry in the online collection catalogue of the British Museum.

A Palmyrene banquet relief in the Metropolitan Museum of Art features the reclining figure of a man named in the inscription by his left elbow: Zabdibol (Fig. 11.14).[35] He is accompanied by three standing figures, all of whom are also identified by inscriptions: Aliyat, his daughter; Moqimu, his son; and Tadmor, his daughter. The son, in the centre of the three, appears to be the youngest. Indeed, Krag describes the standing figures as two women and a child. The son, Moqimu, wears a long-sleeved tunic and holds a bird in his left hand, a bunch of grapes suspended from his right. Around his neck is a necklace with a central oval pendant, from which are suspended three smaller ornaments. A belt, apparently made of rope, is knotted low around his hips. The tunic hangs

---

[32] State Hermitage Museum, St Petersburg, ΔB-4177, AD 114. Donated by the Patriarch of Antioch in 1909. H: 79 cm.

[33] Rijksmuseum van Oudheden, Leiden, 1977/4.1, AD 200–273. Krag 2018, 356, cat. no. 723.

[34] British Museum, London, no. 125150, AD 184. Purchased by the museum in 1891. Colledge 1976, 260; Heyn 2010, app. 4, cat. no. 9; Krag and Raja 2016, 162, cat. no. 19; Krag 2018, 297, cat. no. 490.

[35] Metropolitan Museum of Art, New York, acc. no. 02.29.1, AD 140–180. Purchased by the museum in 1902. Krag 2018, 312–13, cat. no. 551.

Figure 11.15. Palmyrene funerary relief of a mother and two children, Harvard Art Museums. Mid-second century AD. Harvard Art Museums/Arthur M. Sackler Museum, Gift of Alden Sampson, Richard Norton, and Edward W. Forbes in 1908 (© Harvard Art Museums).

in suspended folds across his torso and each leg, hanging straight down vertically between the legs.

A relief in the Harvard Art Museum shows a woman flanked by two children (Fig. 11.15).[36] The woman herself is extravagantly adorned with an elaborate headdress, several necklaces, earrings, an elaborate fibula, and a twisted bracelet very similar to that on the Durene sculpture. She holds a spindle and distaff. Both of the children wear bracelets (apparently simpler than the one on the woman's wrist, but perhaps just less detailed due to their smaller scale). They both carry fruit (grapes and dates, respectively). Both wear a chiton and himation; the figure on the proper right seems to also wear a belt. It is difficult to be certain of the length of their garments, as they are partially concealed behind the woman's shoulders. The publication of the relief in 1990 by Cornelius Vermeule and Amy Brauer, however, plainly demonstrates the difficulty of gender identification of children in Palmyrene sculpture. The authors accurately transcribe the inscriptions and state that they clearly identify the children as the woman's sons:

> There are three inscriptions on the relief. The one belonging to the woman is located to the right of the veil and extends to the left side of the head of the child on the right. It reads 'daughter of Hayran, Alas!' The inscription to the right of the child on the right, belongs to that child and reads 'Hayran, her son'. The inscription on the left, belonging to the child on the left, reads 'Simon, her son'.

Their visual description and identification of the children, however — on the very same page of the publication — directly contradicts this statement: 'The children [...] seem to be a young girl with a necklace or apron of fruits, on her right, and a slightly older boy, a ceremonial tassel in his left hand, on her left'.[37]

The bottom line, in examining a variety of examples, seems to be (as other scholars previously have noted) that young boys and girls in Palmyrene portrait sculpture are virtually indistinguishable without an identifying inscription. Neither jewellery nor clothing nor held attributes are distinctive for one gender or the other. The younger the child depicted, the more true this appears to be.

Yale Limestone Project

One of the outstanding questions about the figure of a child from Dura-Europos (and many other examples of sculpture found in the excavations) has been whether or not the stone is from a Palmyrene quarry. While the iconography and style clearly connect the figure with Palmyra, identifying the source of the stone would bring scholars one step closer to understanding the connection between this piece and its original context and would further be evidence for understanding the broader relationship between the two cities in Antiquity.

In the summer of 2018, with the goal of determining the type of limestone used for this sculpture and others, a project was initiated at the Yale University Art Gallery to analyse works of limestone in the museum's collection.[38] The project's aim is to begin creating a database of limestone isotopic signatures that may ultimately aid in determining quarry sources for ancient sculptures in

---

[36] Harvard Art Museums, Cambridge, MA, no. 1908.3. c. AD 150. Harvard Art Museums/Arthur M. Sackler Museum, Gift of Alden Sampson, Richard Norton, and Edward W. Forbes.

[37] Vermeule and Brauer 1990, 163.
[38] Brody and Snow 2019, 76–83.

collections worldwide. The enterprise is inspired by the well-established process for investigating marbles based on their stable isotopic signature and the proven usefulness of this information for linking sculpted objects with a particular marble quarry.

In order to understand the application of stable isotope analysis to the study of ancient limestone, a brief scientific explanation is useful. Every chemical element has one or more isotopes — variants of chemical elements whose atoms contain the same number of protons but different numbers of neutrons in the nucleus. Unstable isotopes are generally radioactive and decay over time (^{14}C, for example, which is used for radiocarbon dating), but there are around three hundred known stable isotopes that do not undergo radioactive decay or change. The ratios of the stable isotopes of carbon and oxygen ($^{13}C/^{12}C$ and $^{18}O/^{16}O$) have been successfully used to study ancient marble and to link objects with possible quarry sources.

Since the 1950s, marble samples have been analysed using mass spectrometers into clusters of data that correspond to quarry sources. The technique ionizes the carbon and oxygen isotopes, gives the atoms a positive or negative charge, and separates them according to their mass-to-charge ratios. Utilizing and interpreting the results has allowed ancient marble sculptures and architectural pieces from around the Mediterranean to be linked with particular marble quarries based on their stable isotopic signatures. This process has had a significant impact on scholarly understanding of marble craftsmanship, workshops, and trade practices in Antiquity. The first analyses of marble isotopes were published by Harmon and Valerie Craig in 1972. Subsequent significant work by Norman Herz, Lorenzo Lazzarini, and others in the 1980s resulted in the creation of a substantial database containing isotopic signatures of quarries around the Mediterranean that can be used to suggest sources for marble sculptures.[39]

Limestone, like marble, is a calcium carbonate ($CaCO_3$) stone and can be analysed using exactly the same technique to obtain an isotopic signature, or fingerprint. The analysis is destructive, but the required sample size is minute: 100 μg, about the size of the head of a pin. There is the same potential for identifying quarry sources and creating a database of known isotopic signatures as there is for marble. Despite the importance of limestone as a material for sculpture as well as for inscriptions and architecture in the Roman world, particularly in the Roman Near East, such isotope studies of limestone have not yet been undertaken.

Yale's important archaeological collection excavated from Dura-Europos includes over two hundred sculptural and architectural stone fragments, most of which were carved locally in the first few centuries AD. The stones represent a wide range of qualities in their crystal size, hardness, and colour. While simple hardness tests make it possible to distinguish between soft gypsum and hard limestone, further identification is difficult without more comprehensive analysis. Publication of these objects to date has relied solely on visual observation to identify the stones, which have been called variously 'Palmyrene limestone', 'white limestone', 'powdery limestone', 'gypsum', 'alabaster', or 'marble'.

Scholars have long been interested in the interaction between Dura-Europos and Palmyra in the Roman era. While it is clear that trade took place between the two prosperous cities, connected by caravan routes, the precise nature of their exchange of raw materials and works of art, including limestone sculptures, remains a topic for investigation. Were blocks of raw limestone imported to Dura from Palmyra and carved there, or were finished sculptures sent from Palmyra to Dura? What other types of stones were carved at Dura? Were the sculptors themselves from Palmyra, or Dura, or elsewhere? If not originally from Palmyra, were the sculptors at least being trained in Palmyrene workshops, as some of their artworks closely reproduce techniques and styles from known Palmyrene artistic traditions?

Focusing initially on works of art from Palmyra and Dura-Europos, samples were taken to the Yale Analytical and Stable Isotope Center for analysis. The first group of samples were analysed in September 2018, with a focus on pieces in storage in Yale's Collection Study Center. Ten limestone objects were sampled: three Palmyrene funerary reliefs, a fragmentary relief from the Temple of the Gadde at Dura, and six other fragments of sculptures and architectural elements from Dura that appeared, upon visual observation, to be carved of a variety of stones.[40] The samples, taken by Carol Snow, then Deputy Chief Conservator and the Alan J. Dworsky Senior Conservator of Objects at the Yale University

---

[39] See for example Gorgoni and others 2002.

[40] Palmyrene reliefs: inv. nos 1954.30.1, 1954.30.2, 1957.7.6; Malakbel: inv. no. 1938.5373; draped figure: inv. no. 1935.52; Arsu leading a camel: inv. no. 1938.531a–b; statue fragments of draped figure: inv. no. 1938.5374; statue fragments of hand and drapery: inv. no. 1938.5999.3086; stele fragment of nimbate figure: inv. no. 1938.5354; architectural fragment: inv. no. 1938.5999.4556.

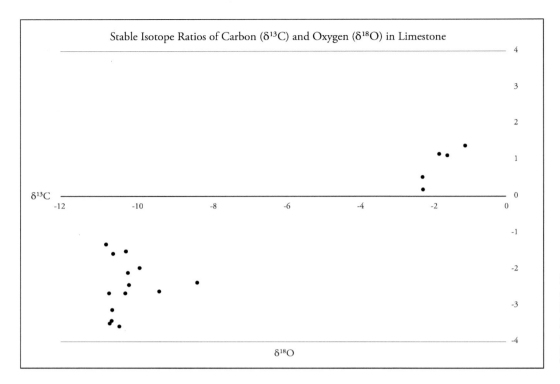

Figure 11.16. Graph showing clusters of stable isotope ratios for limestone objects from Durene and Palmyrene quarry sources (photo courtesy of the Graphic Design Department, Yale University Art Gallery).

Art Gallery, were analysed at Yale's Analytical and Stable Isotope Center by Facility Manager and Research Associate Brad Erkkila. The initial results were exciting. Clusters of isotopic signatures appeared to indicate distinct groups of Palmyrene and Durene limestone (Fig. 11.16).

Four of the analysed objects — including three funerary reliefs from Palmyra and one fragmentary relief from the Temple of the Gadde at Dura — had carbon isotopes between -2.08 and -2.64 and oxygen isotopes between -8.32 and -10.68. This created a distinct cluster (visible in the lower left of the graph). The isotope signature grouping presumably represents objects carved from a single quarry source. Another cluster, with carbon isotopes between 0.53 and 1.12 and oxygen isotopes between -1.58 and -2.25, included two of the higher-quality reliefs from Dura. This seemed to indicate clearly that these objects represent a second distinct source of limestone, perhaps one near Dura itself. One fragment, which visually looked quite different from all of the others, was an outlier with carbon 2.73 and oxygen -7.10. Three other samples did not react with acid, possibly an indication that the stone is gypsum (calcium sulphate) rather than limestone (calcium carbonate).

Due to the extremely promising results from the initial set of analyses, additional samples were taken in December 2018 from several works of sculpture that are currently on view in the Mary and James Ottaway Gallery of Ancient Dura-Europos. This group included the statue of a child from Dura as well as seven cult reliefs from Dura and five Palmyrene funerary reliefs.[41] Prior to analysis, certain of the Durene sculptures were hypothesized to be carved of Palmyrene limestone, while others were thought to have come from different quarry sources solely on the basis of visual observation of the stone (colour, crystal size, hardness, inclusions, etc.).

The results from the second set of samples were consistent with those received in the initial round, with the isotope signatures essentially falling into the two distinct clusters that had appeared in the first round, supporting the interpretation of these clusters as representative of Palmyrene and Durene quarry sources. The five Palmyrene reliefs, the two cult reliefs from the Temple of the Gadde, the relief of Nemesis, and the statue of the Palmyrene child all fell within the first cluster from the preliminary set of samples, with carbon isotopes between

---

[41] Palmyrene reliefs: Yale University Art Gallery, New Haven, inv. nos 1930.6; 1931.135; 1931.138; 1954.30.3; 1954.30.4; Gad of Palmyra: Yale University Art Gallery, inv. no. 1938.5313; Gad of Dura: Yale University Art Gallery, inv. no. 1938.5314; Nemesis: Yale University Art Gallery, inv. no. 1938.5373; Atargatis: Yale University Art Gallery, inv. no. 1935.42; Zeus-Kyrios Baalshamin: Yale University Art Gallery, inv. no. 1935.45; Arsu standing: Yale University Art Gallery, inv. no. 1938.5311; Arsu riding a camel: Yale University Art Gallery, inv. no. 1935.44; Palmyrene child: Yale University Art Gallery, inv. no. 1932.1214.

-1.3 and -3.57 and oxygen isotopes between -8.32 and -10.68. It appears quite likely that these results represent a single quarry source, probably one near Palmyra. Other analysed sculptures from Dura had isotopic signatures that fell into the second cluster: the reliefs of Atargatis had a carbon isotope of 1.17 and an oxygen isotope of -1.8, while the relief of Zeus Kyrios-Baalshamin had a carbon isotope of 0.20 and an oxygen isotope of -2.23.

Although still very preliminary, this analysis seems to have great potential for linking ancient limestone sculptures with quarry sources. The isotopic signatures of the Palmyrene reliefs formed a distinct cluster with those sculptures that had been hypothesized to be Palmyrene stone through visual observation or stylistic features or archaeological context. The values of this cluster presumably represent a Palmyrene quarry source. A second distinct cluster is formed by the isotopic signatures of several other Durene sculptures, carved of stones that appear, upon observation, to have different characteristics and are of relatively fine quality, and this cluster may represent a quarry source near Dura-Europos.

With the Palmyrene reliefs in the first cluster are the cult reliefs from the Temple of the Gadde (a religious meeting place for Palmyrenes in Dura) and the cult relief of the goddess Nemesis (the inscription on which says that it was dedicated to Nemesis by a man from Palmyra). In her study of Palmyrenes at Dura-Europos, Lucinda Dirven states unequivocally that the Gad of Dura relief 'was produced in Palmyra',[42] and that all of the Gadde reliefs 'testify to the intimate economic relations between Palmyra and Dura-Europos'.[43] Susan Downey, in her publication of the sculpture from Dura, outlines the many connections that she sees between these reliefs and Palmyrene works, including the stone itself as well as stylistic elements of the composition.[44] Downey and Michael Rostovzeff both theorized that these reliefs were imported from Palmyra, based on the appearance of the stone, the style of the carving, and the ethnicity of the dedicants. While such assumptions have been repeated by numerous scholars, it was not until the isotopic signatures of the three reliefs were identified that it is now possible to use scientific evidence to identify the quarry source for the Gad reliefs as being the same as that for the Palmyrene funerary reliefs in the Gallery's collection — thus presumably one near Palmyra itself.

Identifying the source of the stone unfortunately does not reveal when or where a sculpture was carved. It is possible that these works were imported from Palmyra to Dura-Europos in a finished state. It is also quite possible, however, that the raw material may have been imported and the objects carved in Dura by a sculptor from Palmyra (or at least trained there). In any event, the confirmation of the limestone as Palmyrene provides scholars with important information about the contact and trade that flourished in the Roman period between Dura-Europos and Palmyra.

The cluster of isotopic signatures that likely represent a Palmyrene quarry source also includes one other object of interest: the so-called Palmyrene child from Dura. While still in its preliminary research phases, this analysis seems to suggest that it is now possible to assert with confidence that the statue is carved of Palmyrene limestone. As with the other objects of Palmyrene stone that were excavated in Dura, of course, this does not reveal exactly where the piece was carved or by whom, just that the material itself is connected to Palmyrene sculptural workshops. This scientific data, together with the iconographic interpretation of the statue, creates a strong link between the material culture of Dura-Europos and that of Palmyra.

Ancient Pigment

One other potential query about the statue of a child is whether any traces of ancient pigment can be ascertained using advanced imaging techniques. As is clearly seen in the Ny Carlsberg Glyptotek's 'Beauty of Palmyra',[45] Palmyrene reliefs, like all ancient sculptures, were once decorated with elaborate polychromy to enhance and emphasize details of hair colour, facial features, and drapery adornment. It is safe to assume that the Durene sculpture was also originally painted, despite the fact that no visible traces of pigment remain.

Collaborative studies at Yale and elsewhere have been utilizing various imaging techniques to detect traces of pigment on ancient sculptures.[46] It is unclear, however, what sort of conservation was performed on this sculpture in the field; microscopic traces of pigment may have been cleaned off if they were not immediately visible to

[42] Dirven 1999, 111.
[43] Dirven 1999, 127.
[44] Downey 1977, 17.

[45] Ny Carlsberg Glyptotek, Copenhagen, IN 2795. Bought in Syria in 1929 from a private collection. See analysis done at <http://www.trackingcolour.com/objects/36> [accessed 10 October 2021].
[46] Lauridsen 2014; Vlassopoulou 2008; McCouat 2008; Dyer and Sotiropoulou 2017.

Figure 11.17. Figure of a Palmyrene child from Dura-Europos photographed with Visible-Induced (infrared) Luminescence (VIL) (photo courtesy of Richard House, Yale University Art Gallery).

the archaeologists at the time. Thus far only a preliminary test has been conducted on this statue.

The figure of a Palmyrene child from Dura-Europos was photographed in April 2019 using advanced imaging in an attempt to test whether any traces of ancient pigment remain on the surface, despite none being visible to the naked eye (Fig. 11.17). The photograph was taken with an IR converted camera filtered to only record above 780 nm, to the limit of the sensor at approximately 1200 nm (aka the 'near infrared' wavelengths). The light source has been filtered so that only visible light is illuminating the sculpture. A BG38 filter on the source cuts out any ultraviolet or infrared illumination, so that any response in the resulting image is considered to be 'visible induced infrared luminescence' or VIL. This is a technique known to reveal Egyptian blue pigment; you can see a vial of Egyptian blue to the lower right of the statue and the level to which it fluoresces. This initial test did not immediately reveal any obvious traces of Egyptian blue pigment remaining on the surface. It is hoped that future additional tests with VIL will be possible, as well as tests utilizing other multispectral imaging techniques at different wavelengths. Examination of the surface using X-ray Fluorescence Spectroscopy (XRF) might also be potentially useful for determining whether any ancient pigment remains. Considering the extraordinary preservation of archaeological materials at Dura-Europos, and the relatively high amount of pigment surviving on other objects found there, it is reasonable to expect that some traces of ancient pigment that are not visible to the naked eye may be found.

The array of fascinating papers presented in this publication shows clearly that there remains tremendous potential for exciting research on Palmyra and the East. Even with objects and sites that were systematically excavated decades ago, new perspectives and new technologies allow for reanalysis and reinterpretation. The Dura-Europos collection at the Yale University Art Gallery has provided many opportunities for new research, including collaborations with specialist colleagues in art history and archaeology, conservation, digital imaging, and conservation science. Relating the knowledge achieved from further study of the excavated remains from Dura-Europos to those from Palmyra will continue to enhance scholars' understanding of the sophisticated networks of cultural connections and trade in the Roman East as well as contact and workshop practices throughout the provinces of the Roman Empire.

Works Cited

Albertson, F. C. 2000. 'Three Palmyrene Reliefs in the Colket Collection, University of Wyoming', *Syria*, 77: 159–68.

Baird, J. A. 2006. 'Housing and Households at Dura-Europos: A Study in Identity on Rome's Eastern Frontier' (unpublished doctoral thesis, University of Leicester).

—— 2014. *The Inner Lives of Ancient Houses: An Archaeology of Dura-Europos* (Oxford: Oxford University Press).

Brilliant, R. 1963. *Gesture and Rank in Roman Art: The Use of Gestures to Denote Status in Roman Sculpture and Coinage* (New Haven: Connecticut Academy of Arts and Sciences).

Brody, L. R. 2011. 'Yale University and Dura-Europos: From Excavation to Exhibition', in L. R. Brody and G. Hoffman (eds), *Dura-Europos: Crossroads of Antiquity* (Chestnut Hill: McMullen Museum of Art, Boston College), pp. 17–32.

Brody, L. R. and C. E. Snow. 2019. 'Quarries at the Crossroads: Sourcing Limestone Sculpture from Dura-Europos and Palmyra at Yale', *Yale University Art Gallery Bulletin*, 2019: 78–85.

Colledge, M. A. R. 1976. *The Art of Palmyra* (Boulder: Westview).

Dirven, L. 1999. *Palmyrenes in Dura-Europos: A Study of Religious Interaction in Roman Syria* (Leiden: Brill).

—— 2011. 'Strangers and Sojourners: The Religious Behavior of Palmyrenes and Other Foreigners in Dura-Europos', in L. R. Brody and G. Hoffman (eds), *Dura-Europos: Crossroads of Antiquity* (Chestnut Hill: McMullen Museum of Art, Boston College), pp. 201–20.

Downey, S. 1977. *The Stone and Plaster Sculpture*, The Excavations at Dura-Europos: Final Report, 3.1.2 (Los Angeles: Institute of Archaeology, University of California).

Dyer, J. and S. Sotiropoulou. 2017. 'A Technical Step Forward in the Integration of Visible-Induced Luminescence Imaging Methods for the Study of Ancient Polychromy', *Heritage Science*, 5: 24.

Fuller, R. E. 1946. *Seattle Art Museum* (Seattle: Seattle Art Museum).

Gorgoni, C. and others. 2002. 'An Updated and Detailed Mineropetrographic and C-O Stable Isotopic Reference Database for the Main Mediterranean Marbles Used in Antiquity', in J. Herrmann, N. Herz, and R. Newman (eds), *ASMOSIA 5: Interdisciplinary Studies on Ancient Stone; Proceedings of the Fifth International Conference of the Association for the Study of Marble and Other Stones in Antiquity, Museum of Fine Arts, Boston, June 1998* (London: Archetype), pp. 115–31.

Heyn, M. K. 2010. 'Gesture and Identity in the Funerary Art of Palmyra', *American Journal of Archaeology*, 114: 631–61.

James, S. 2019. *The Roman Military Base at Dura-Europos, Syria: An Archaeological Visualization* (Oxford: Oxford University Press).

Kleiner, D. E. E. 1977. *Roman Group Portraiture: The Funerary Reliefs of the Late Republic and Early Empire* (New York: Garland).

Krag, S. 2018. *Funerary Representations of Palmyrene Women from the First Century BC to the Third Century AD*, Studies in Classical Archaeology, 3 (Turnhout: Brepols).

Krag, S. and R. Raja. 2016. 'Representations of Women and Children in Palmyrene Funerary *loculus* Reliefs, *loculus stelae*, and Wall Paintings', *Zeitschrift für Orient-Archäologie*, 9: 134–78.

—— 2019. 'Families in Palmyra: The Evidence from the First Three Centuries CE', in S. Krag and R. Raja (eds), *Women, Children, and the Family in Palmyra*, Palmyrene Studies, 3 (Copenhagen: The Royal Danish Academy of Sciences and Letters), pp. 7–18.

Lauridsen, H. 2014. '"Digging" for Color: The Search for Egyptian Blue in Ancient Reliefs' <https://news.yale.edu/2014/05/05/digging-color-search-egyptian-blue-ancient-reliefs> [accessed 16 April 2021].

McCouat, P. 2018. 'Egyptian Blue: The Colour of Technology', *Journal of Art in Society*: <http://www.artinsociety.com/egyptian-blue-the-colour-of-technology.html> [accessed 16 April 2021].

Parlasca, K. 1990. 'Palmyrenische Skulpturen in Museen an der amerikanischen Westküste', in G. Koch (ed.), *Roman Funerary Monuments in the J. Paul Getty Museum*, I (Malibu: J. Paul Getty Museum), pp. 133–44.

Pierson, F. 1984. 'Recherches sur le costume des enfants dans l'iconographie palmyrénienne', *Revue des archéologues et historiens d'art de Louvain*, 17: 85–111.

Ringsborg, S. 2017. 'Children's Portraits from Palmyra', in R. Raja (ed.), *Palmyra: Pearl of the Desert* (Aarhus: SUN-Tryk), pp. 67–76.

Rostovtzeff, M. I. (ed.). 1934. *The Excavations at Dura-Europos Conducted by Yale University and the French Academy of Inscriptions and Letters: Preliminary Report of Fifth Season of Work, 1931–1932* (New Haven: Yale University Press).

Seattle Art Museum. 1951. *Handbook, Seattle Art Museum: Selected Works from the Permanent Collections* (Seattle: Seattle Art Museum).

Vermeule, C. and A. Brauer. 1990. *Stone Sculptures: The Greek, Roman and Etruscan Collections of the Harvard University Art Museums* (Cambridge, MA: Harvard University Art Museum).

Vlassopoulou, C. 2008. 'Neue Untersuchungen zur Farbigkeit des Parthenon', in B. Götter (ed.), *Die Farbigkeit antiker Skulptur: Eine Ausstellung der Liebieghaus Skulpturensammlung, Frankfurt am Main in Kooperation mit der Stiftung Archäologie, München, 8.10.2008–15.2.2009* (Frankfurt: Liebieghaus), pp. 145–47.

Welles, C. B., R. O. Fink, and J. F. Gilliam. 1959. *The Parchments and Papyri*, The Excavations at Dura-Europos: Final Report, 5.1 (New Haven: Yale University Press).

12. Edessa and the Sculpture of Greater North Mesopotamia in the Romano-Parthian Period

Michael Blömer
*University of Münster, Forschungsstelle Asia Minor im Seminar
für Alte Geschichte (michael.bloemer@uni-muenster.de)*

Introduction

In the discussion of Palmyrene sculpture, the eastern connection plays a crucial role. Distinctive elements of Palmyrene style and iconography have always been explained by eastern influences and, most importantly, by an exposure to what is commonly referred to as 'Parthian art'. On the other side, in most studies of 'Parthian sculpture' and 'Parthian art', monuments from Palmyra take centre stage.[1] The same applies to the rich sculptural finds from Dura-Europos and Hatra. The excavations at Dura-Europos in the 1920s and 1930s can even be regarded as the starting point for the study of 'Parthian art'. At a time when knowledge about the material culture of Syria, Mesopotamia, and Iran in the Hellenistic and Romano-Parthian period was still limited, the excavations at Dura-Europos yielded a trove of objects that did not easily fit in the traditional categories of Hellenistic and Graeco-Roman art. In an ingenious essay, the great historian Mikhail Rostovtzeff interpreted these finds as expressions of Parthian culture and took them as a point of departure for a first comprehensive study of 'Parthian art' and its principles.[2] He saw frontality, spirituality, and a veristic, ornamental, and linear style as key characteristics that defined this art. Rostovtzeff's study proved to be extremely influential and his ideas still reverberate in modern scholarship. However, soon after the publication, an increasing number of new discoveries from different parts of the Parthian realm and neighbouring regions allowed for a more nuanced discussion, to which eminent scholars, most importantly Henri Seyrig,[3] Daniel Schlumberger,[4] Ernest Will,[5] and Roman Girshman[6] contributed. They diverged from many of Rostovtzeff's ideas, but still tried to preserve the notion of a 'Parthian art' that evolved from an oriental Hellenism and pervaded the diverse artistic articulations that can be grasped in the empire's vast territories.[7]

Subsequently, however, alternative perspectives on Parthian art developed. The idea of unity was abandoned, and emphasis was put on the great regional variety of styles and motifs within the Parthian realm.[8] This was explained as a result of the decentralized organization of the state. From this perspective, 'Parthian art' as a category was a by-product of a political reality rather than the result of a shared cultural heritage. What was produced within the borders of the Parthian Empire was filed under the header 'Parthian art'.[9]

Another branch of research took this approach even further and distinguished between the artistic production in the territories of the Parthian commonwealth and the art of the royal court. The latter was labelled 'Arsacid art' to get rid of any overarching ethnic implica-

---

* This research has partly been funded by the Danish National Research Foundation (DNRF grant 119).

[1] This is encapsulated in a statement by Malcolm Colledge: 'By an amusing trick of fate, the earliest known examples of truly "Parthian" art were found on a site not strictly Parthian at all. They were discovered at Palmyra' (Colledge 1967, 148). See also Colledge 1987.

[2] Rostovtzeff 1935. For a discussion of this book and its contemporary context, see Dirven 2016. Before Rostovtzeff, the period of Parthian rule was seen as a period of artistic decline bereft of any originality. The contemporary disdain transpires in Hans Henning von der Osten's assessment (Osten 1926, 170): 'The decline of Hellenism in Parthian art resulted in a kind of barbarization rather than in the rise of a new style. [...] Parthian art was moribund.' For a more nuanced view, however, see Herzfeld 1920; Debevoise 1931.

[3] Seyrig 1937.

[4] Schlumberger 1960.

[5] Will 1962.

[6] Ghirshman 1962.

[7] The course of the debate has been traced and discussed variously, Baratin 2011; Hauser 2014; Dirven 2016.

[8] Colledge 1986.

[9] Baratin 2011; Mathiesen 1992. At the same time, the latter largely denied creativity and, most importantly, originality to the art production of the Parthian Empire: 'Catalyst and generator of its stylistic development seems always to have been inspiration from the Graeco-Roman areas. Consequently, Parthian art is most static in periods when it is most uninfluenced by western art' (Mathiesen 1992, 13).

tions.[10] Along these lines, Michał Gawlikowski concluded already in 1979 that the sculpture, which was produced in an area between the Tigris region and the Syrian steppe in the second and third centuries AD, followed regional trajectories that were rooted in local traditions. He did not challenge Rostovzeff's characterization of the art of Dura and Palmyra, but he disagreed with his conclusion that it bears a strong Parthian imprint.[11] In the same vein, if more cautiously, Han Jan Willem Drijvers emphasized the autochthonous origin of art in Syro-Mesopotamia — not denying, however, the strong impact of increased connectivity, exchange, and changing political realities on the formation of this art.[12]

More recently, Bruno Jacobs analysed the development of sculpture in the territories of the Parthian Empire and convincingly showed how local rulers and elites fostered the introduction of sculptural representation.[13] He emphasized that in contrast to the Achaemenid period no Arsacid *Hofkunst* existed that they could have emulated. Yet, they drew from a repertoire of icons of prestige and power that was also recognized at the Arsacid court — a fact that added authority and legitimacy.

The emphasis on local trajectories in the development of art in the Syro-Mesopotamian realm (and in other parts of the Parthian Empire, as the Elymais) provoked strong criticism, too, and the idea of a unifying Parthian culture and identity that transpired in the material culture and the practices in the 'Parthian Commonwealth' has been reinvigorated.[14] This is, to some extent, a legitimate response to Romanocentric and orientalizing approaches that still linger on in the study of the material culture of Mesopotamia in the Romano-Parthian period, a field that remains dominated by scholars trained in Greek and Roman archaeology. In some circles, however, any criticism of the validity of the term 'Parthian art' rings alarm bells and is perceived a priori as an attempt to doubt the vigour of Iranian culture. Moreover, the matter has become mixed up with another dispute: the extent of Parthian rule over the principalities of Mesopotamia. Whether Hatra, Edessa, Adiabene, but also Mesene in the south were integral parts of the Parthian Empire or just loose allies that acted independently is a bone of contention.[15] In this context, any claim that the art of Syro-Mesopotamia (as well as other areas linked to the Parthian Empire) followed trajectories that had only weak links to the Arsacid centres of power is quickly considered as favouring the idea of a weak Parthian state and limited Parthian political control.

In general, the situation is very complex and, because sometimes ideological concerns overshadow the debate, even murky. Yet, it is remarkable that research in Palmyrene (and, to a lesser degree, Durene) sculpture has preserved a rather naive stance on the problem. Without much further discussion, certain elements of this sculpture continue to be labelled 'Parthian'.[16] The criteria, however, have changed over time. Instead of style and expression, iconography has become the most important marker of Parthian connections. Central in this respect is the trouser suit worn by men, which is commonly referred to as 'Parthian' dress.[17] This is an umbrella term applied to male garments that have no parallels in Graeco-Roman traditions: trousers, sometimes worn with leggings, and various types of shirts, usually long-sleeved and with rich embroidery. In Palmyra, a mantle is worn with this trouser suit; in Dura, Hatra, and beyond, long-sleeved cloaks are more common. In 1950, Henri Seyrig put the underlying notion in a nutshell by stating that 'strangely enough no Palmyrene ever seems to have thought of letting himself be portrayed in native dress'.[18] In his opinion, the funerary, religious, and honorary monuments showed the Palmyrene people either in Iranian or in Greek garments. This view still pervades research in Palmyrene sculpture and iconography today.

---

[10] Invernizzi 2011; Hauser 2014; Fowlkes-Childs and Seymour 2019, 3–23.

[11] Gawlikowski 1979, 325: 'Le nom del'art parthe, consacré par l'usage, est tout de convention.'

[12] Drijvers 1980, 4: 'Leaving aside the vigorous discussions on the origin of this special art which in all likelihood has nothing to do with Parthia and Parthian artistic traditions it should be stated that this art only appears in the cities edging the Syrian-Mesopotamian desert and seems to be restricted to that area.' See also Drijvers 1977.

[13] Jacobs 2014.

[14] For very strong opposition to the idea of an independent development of art in Mesopotamia, see Jong 2013. He considers the (in his view 'frivolous') focus on indigenous traditions and local culture as an ahistoric insistence of unchanging predetermination and, at the same time, as Romanocentric. For a more moderate stance, see Dirven 2016.

[15] On the question of the extent and efficiency of Parthian rule, see Keall 1994; Sommer 2018; Gregoratti 2017; Fabian 2020.

[16] It is notable, though, that the term Parthian is now frequently put in inverted commas or modified by putting 'so-called' in front of it. Yet, the reasons for doing so are rarely discussed.

[17] The classic article on the 'Parthian' costume in Palmyra and beyond is Seyrig 1937. For recent studies in this dress, see Curtis 1998; 2017.

[18] Seyrig 1950, 2.

Emphasis is put on Palmyrene agency and deliberate processes of code-switching, but the presupposition still is that Palmyrenes, men in particular, chose between Greek, Parthian, and in rare instances Roman fashions.[19] A 'native' dress is only postulated for Palmyrene women.[20] To some extent, images of priests constitute an exception, as they are distinguished by headgear that has no direct parallels outside of Palmyra and is therefore considered 'native'.[21]

What does it mean, however, that men in Palmyra, Dura, and Hatra wear 'Parthian' dress? Why do they wear it and since when? And why is there no female equivalent to the 'Parthian' dress? These questions have rarely been discussed in recent studies. Instead, rather simplistic dichotomies between East and West are perpetuated. This is to some degree the result of habitualized research traditions. Here, the strong division between Romanocentric and, to a lesser degree, but not less dangerous, Iranocentric approaches to the topic plays a crucial role. Even though serious attempts have been made during the last decades to overcome this partition and to stress the connectivity of the region, the Euphrates continues to be perceived as a barrier.[22] Not an impenetrable one, but still a demarcation line between different *Kulturlandschaften*.

Another issue that fosters the lack of in-depth studies on the relation between Palmyrene and Mesopotamian sculpture is the generally poor knowledge of Mesopotamian material culture in the Romano-Parthian period. Consequently, most discussions centre on a limited canon of monuments that has been codified long ago. The majority come from Dura, Hatra, and to a lesser extent Seleucia on the Tigris. In recent times, no effort was made to provide a comprehensive conspectus of sculpture from the region in the Romano-Parthian period. The last attempt was Hans Erik Mathiesen's book *Sculpture in the Parthian Empire*.[23] However, his decisions to include or to omit material from his catalogue seem arbitrary at times. As the title of the book indicates, the study only considers sculpture from within the Parthian Empire. Therefore, he excludes finds from territories west of the Euphrates, like Palmyrene and Commagene. This distinction proves difficult to maintain, however, and many of the pieces that he discusses were made after Parthian rule over the respective territories had ended.[24] Moreover, because he is mainly concerned with questions of chronology, Mathiesen treats the bulk of sculpture from Greater Mesopotamia in a very superficial way only. Concentrating on hand-picked specimens that serve his line of argumentation, he does not aim to provide a full catalogue of sculpture from the Parthian period.

Even at smaller scale, overviews that allow for a full appreciation of the sculptural production of a city or a region of Greater Romano-Parthian Mesopotamia do not exist. The exception is Dura-Europos, for which Susan Downey has published catalogues of sculptures in stone and terracotta figurines.[25] For Hatra, however, neither a corpus nor an in-depth discussion of the large number of sculptures that were discovered at this site exists.[26] Other areas of north Mesopotamia have hardly been included in the discussion of Palmyrene and north Mesopotamian sculpture at all. This is most evident in the case of the city of Edessa, modern Sanliurfa in Turkey, and the surrounding region of Osrhoene. Monuments from Edessa do rarely feature in studies of 'Parthian art' and Palmyrene material culture.[27] However, they clearly form part of a Syro-Mesopotamian *koine* of sculpture and iconography and may contribute significantly to the understanding of this *Kunstlandschaft* and its networks.

Edessa and Osrhoene

Osrhoene is an ancient name of the western part of northern Mesopotamia, but it is difficult to define the borders of its territory with precision (Fig. 12.1). In the liter-

---

[19] See for example Heyn and Raja 2019.

[20] For an overview of female representations at Palmyra, see Krag 2018 The particularities of the female dress in Palmyra and beyond are discussed in Blömer 2014 and Rumscheid 2019.

[21] On priests and priestly dress in Palmyra, see Stucky 1973; Raja 2016; 2017a.

[22] More recently, the history and culture of the north Mesopotamian plains and the valleys of the Khabur and Balikh started to receive more attention, see Jong and Palermo 2018; Palermo 2019.

[23] Mathiesen 1992.

[24] Mathiesen 1992. To justify this procedure, Mathiesen invented the category of 'sub-Parthian' art for the final decades of Hatra. However, sculptures from Roman Dura and late Edessa are simply filed under 'late Parthian'.

[25] Downey 1977; 2003.

[26] The fullest account of Hatrene sculpture is still the well-illustrated overview by Safar and Mustafa 1974 in Arabic. The situation is even more disparate for minor sites like Assur and Nineveh.

[27] Mathiesen 1992 has included a small and random choice of sculptures as examples of his late Parthian-period sculpture, but he does not discuss them at any length, see Mathiesen 1992, 9, 39–41, 216.

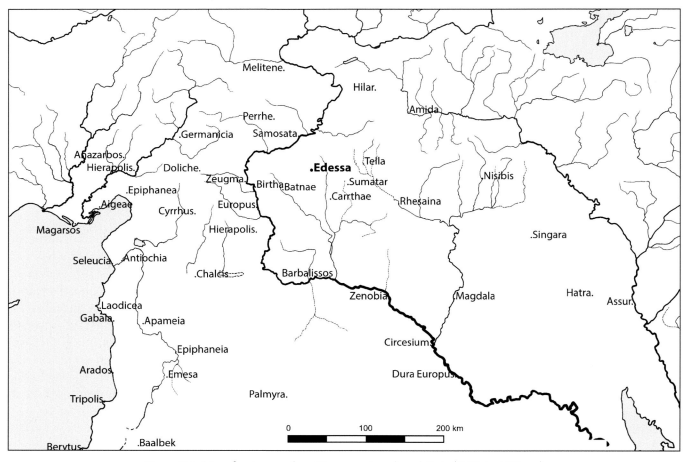

Figure 12.1. Map of ancient northern Mesopotamia and north Syria (© Michael Blömer).

ary sources, all the land between the Taurus Mountains in the north, the Euphrates in the west, and the River Khabur in the east may be referred to as Osrhoene. The heartland of Osrhoene, however, may have been largely identical with the modern Turkish province of Şanlıurfa and stretched from the east bank of the Euphrates to the plain of Harran and the rugged Tek Tek Mountains.

The main city of Osrhoene was Edessa, modern Şanlıurfa. Edessa became the centre of an autonomous principality after the Seleucids retreated from this area in the 130s BC.[28] It was ruled by a local family, called the Abgarids after the name Abgar that was common among Edessa's rulers. With few interruptions, the dynasty stayed in power for about 350 years. The lords of Edessa were allies of the Parthian king, but after Rome had annexed Syria in 63 BC, allegiance shifted between the two empires. Osrhoene became a main zone of contact between the Parthian and Roman realms, and the region benefitted immensely from the trade between East and West. Yet, Osrhoene was frequently dragged into conflicts between the two superpowers and had to side with either Rome and Parthia. Nevertheless, the rulers of Edessa successfully retained independence for a long period and took on the title of kings. Even after Septimius Severus had formally annexed large parts of northern Mesopotamia to the Roman Empire, the kingdom of Edessa continued to exist, even though it was reduced to the city of Edessa and her immediate surroundings.[29]

In AD 213, however, Caracalla annexed Edessa and gave her the status of a Roman colony. In a surprising turn of events, Emperor Gordian restored royal rule over Edessa in AD 239, and Abgar VIII became king of Osrhoene. At that time, the Sasanian king Ardashir attacked the Roman Empire, and the re-establishment of the local dynasty obviously was an attempt to mobilize local elites in the fight against the Persians. This was a short-lived episode and already in AD 241 the Romans dethroned him again and abolished the king-

---

[28] For the history and culture of Edessa and Osrhoene, see Segal 1970; Ross 2001; Blömer 2019a; Sommer 2018; Edwell 2017.

[29] Speidel 2007.

Figure 12.2. Column monuments of the third century AD on the citadel of Şanlıurfa (Edessa) (© Michael Blömer).

dom for good. In the ensuing period, domination over Osrhoene was fiercely contested between Rome and the Sasanian Empire. In AD 260, the Roman emperor Valerian was captured by the Persians in a battle south of Edessa. Eventually, the Romans prevailed in the fight and secured rule over northern Mesopotamia. Over the following centuries, the city developed into the most important political, cultural, and religious centre of late Roman Mesopotamia.[30] Subsequently medieval and modern buildings have obscured almost all traces of Antiquity. The most conspicuous monuments from that period are two tall columns that rise on the citadel of Şanlıurfa (Fig. 12.2). One of the columns bears a dedicatory inscription to a member of the royal family.[31] Apart from the columns, various rock-cut tombs can be attributed to the second and third centuries AD.

Evidence for other settlements in Osrhoene is even scarcer. Late antique literature conveys the image of a vivid urban landscape, but there is little information about the layout and organization of towns in the pre-Christian period.[32] We may assume that Batnai/Marcopolis(?) (modern Suruç), Antioch/Constantia/Tella (modern Viransehir), and Birtha (modern Birecik) were major settlements, but none of these sites have yielded archaeological remains from the time of the Abgarid kingdom. Carrhae (modern Harran), located in the plain south of Edessa was an eminent urban centre and internationally renowned for her sanctuary of the moon god Sin. Unfortunately, like in Edessa, buildings of later periods obscure earlier strata.[33]

The only site of Osrhoene that preserves substantial remains from the time of the Abgarid kingdom is Sumatar in the Tek Tek Mountains east of Edessa (Fig. 12.3).[34] Various Syriac inscriptions from the site reveal that in the second century AD Sumatar was the seat of the governor of ʿArab. The name probably refers

---

[30] Segal 1970. The recent discovery of a sixth-century AD Byzantine building with outstanding mosaic decoration is a vivid reminder of the otherwise lost splendour of late ancient Edessa, see Karabulut, Önal, and Dervişoğlu 2011.

[31] Drijvers and Healey 1999, 45–48.

[32] For a general overview of the urban settlements in northern Mesopotamia, see Cohen 2006.

[33] It is also not clear whether the rulers of Edessa exerted direct rule over the city. Carrhae minted its own autonomous coinage in the second century AD and propagated allegiance to Rome already before the reign of Septimius Severus, see Blömer (forthcoming).

[34] For descriptions of the site, see Segal 1953; Drijvers 1973; 1980, 122–44; Odrobiński 1995; Ross 2001, 39–43. For the inscriptions, see Drijvers and Healey 1999, 87–139 with further references.

Figure 12.3. View of Sumatar from the west with the höyük at the centre (© Michael Blömer).

to the nomad population of this rugged district.[35] The modern village of Sumatar occupies the former lower city at the northern foot of a tell. Ancient remains, among them two sanctuaries, are scattered over the village and its surroundings. Apart from the sanctuaries, many rock-cut graves and sumptuous tomb monuments attest to the importance of Sumatar in Antiquity.[36]

In general, new excavation and survey projects have gathered new data on settlements and material culture of the region, but so far, no attempts have been undertaken to synthesize this information. A comprehensive account of the topography and archaeology of Edessa and Osrhoene that collects and re-examines legacy data and combines it with the results recently made remains to be written.

Sculpture from Edessa

A growing corpus of statues and reliefs is known from Edessa and the surrounding region, but these have attracted only limited attention so far.[37] One reason for this neglect certainly was the political division of north Mesopotamia in the aftermath of the First World War that entailed the emergence of separate research trajectories in Turkey, on the one hand, and Syria/Iraq, on the other. If monuments of the Hellenistic and Romano-Parthian period in Turkish north Mesopotamia were studied, they were frequently considered in the context of 'Anatolian' archaeology.[38] Scholars working in modern Iraq and Syria, on the other hand, have rarely engaged with sites and finds from Turkey. Only recently, has the artificial division created by modern political borders started to break down.

Another reason is the general disregard of Hellenistic and Romano-Parthian sites in south-east Turkey. For decades, not even the main urban sites of northern Mesopotamia — Edessa, Harran, Amida, and Nisibis — received attention. To some extent, this appears to have been the result of political considerations, too. Moreover, partisan unrest and lack of accessibility hampered research. Over the last two decades, however, the situation has improved significantly.

A consequence of the protracted research history is that a large number of finds of statues and reliefs from Edessa were reported already in the Late Ottoman period, when travellers and researchers frequently passed through the city of Urfa.[39] However, they were studied only in a haphazard way. It is also important to realize that research in ancient Edessa was for a long

---

[35] For the use of the name Arab in Antiquity and its meaning, see Retsö 2003.

[36] For recent excavations in the necropolis, see Albayrak and others 2019; Albayrak 2019.

[37] For a first attempt to appreciate the Edessean sculpture in a comprehensive way, see Çobanoğlu 2021.

[38] Parlasca 1982b.

[39] Sachau 1882; Renan 1883; Chabot 1906; Pognon 1907; Euting 1909.

Figure 12.4. Statue of a nobleman from Osrhoene, limestone, second–third centuries AD, Archaeological Museum of Şanlıurfa (© D-DAI-IST-R29912, D-DAI-IST-R29910, D-DAI-IST-R29913 [D. Johannes]).

raphy and the position of Edessa in the sculptural network of the Near East.

As in most other areas of the ancient Near East, the majority of the extant sculptures come from funerary contexts. Various cemeteries with rock-cut tombs — the prevailing type of elite burial in north Mesopotamia as in north Syria — have been identified in the barren limestone hills that surrounded the ancient city.[43] Many of these tombs are still accessible in the modern city of Şanlıurfa. In some of them, the rear walls of the burial niches are decorated with funerary banquet scenes carved in the rock.[44] In addition, free-standing statues and a few funerary reliefs with busts of the deceased have been retrieved from the necropoleis.

time dominated mainly by linguists and epigraphers, who were interested in the inscriptions that accompany the sculptures. They are written in the Aramaic dialect spoken in Edessa, which is commonly referred to as Old Syriac.[40] This dialect eventually evolved into the Classic Syriac that became the lingua franca of large parts of Syria and Mesopotamia in the Byzantine period. As a result, the most comprehensive catalogue of sculpture and ancient monuments from Edessa is the corpus of the Syriac inscriptions compiled by John Healey and Han Drijvers, which appeared in 1999.[41] In recent times, the situation improved greatly and research and fieldwork activities in the region, spearheaded mainly by Turkish scholars, intensified substantially. They uncovered various new monuments and yielded new data that allow for a better appreciation of ancient Edessene culture and sculpture.[42] The total number of monuments is still relatively small, especially when compared to the thousands of sculptures from Palmyra, but it is significant enough to convey a clear idea of the prevailing style and iconog-

The stone material used for most statues and stelai was the chalky and very soft limestone that is characteristic of north Syria and north Mesopotamia. It can be easily carved but is ill-suited for the rendering of delicate details and free-ranging body parts. To stabilize statues in the round, massive supports were necessary, which make the statues look clumsy. Moreover, the backsides are usually left unworked. To a much lesser extent, basalt has been used for sculpture production.

Most sculptures depict men. Best attested is an aristocratic 'warrior' type, equipped with a long sword that hangs on the left hip (Fig. 12.4).[45] Low-slung leather belts serve to suspend the sword. Either the left hand or both hands are seizing the hilt. Statues of this type wear loose trousers and a long-sleeved girdled shirt. Both mantles fastened with brooches and long-sleeved cloaks are attested. Some wear leggings over their trousers.[46]

---

[40] For Old Syriac, see Gzella 2018.

[41] Drijvers and Healey 1999.

[42] See, for example, Karabulut, Önal, and Dervişoğlu 2011; Önal 2017; Önal, Mutlu, and Mutlu (eds) 2019.

[43] Segal 1970, 27–28.

[44] Drijvers and Healey 1999, For a recently discovered relief, see Demir 2019, 253, fig. 3.

[45] See Winkelmann 2009. See also Winkelmann 2004 for a catalogue of statues of this type from Hatra.

[46] A well-studied example of male statue with trouser suit and leggings is a statue from northern Osrhoene, see Jacobs and Schütte-

Figure 12.5. Statue of an archer, from Edessa, limestone, second–third centuries AD, Archaeological Museum of Şanlıurfa (© D-DAI-IST-R33768 [D. Johannes]).

Figure 12.6. Statue of a nobleman, Bir el-Kantari, limestone, second–third centuries AD, Archaeological Museum of Aleppo (after Seyrig 1971, fig. 4).

Singular is the occurrence of the statue of an archer with bow and quiver (Fig. 12.5).[47]

The most fascinating representations of this type are two almost identical monumental statues that were discovered during the clearing of the Kızılkoyun necropolis in 2015.[48] They were standing in niches flanking the entrance to a tomb.[49] One of them was still in situ. His head had been chopped off, but it was lying next to the statue with the facial features erased. The head of the second statue is missing.

Both wear wide trousers, a long shirt, and a long-sleeved cloak. The shirts are decorated with vertical and horizontal bands that are decorated with beads. The latter most likely represent embroidery. Identical bands of beads adorn the men's trousers and the shoes. Moreover, the latter are tied by straps fixed with a very distinctive pair of massive buckles.[50]

Another characteristic feature is the headgear worn by Edessean men, a tiara without flaps or neck-piece made of a very soft fabric. The tip bends forward like a 'Phrygian cap' (Figs 10, 14–15).[51] This hat can be found in reliefs, statues, and mosaics. It is worn by adult men and in some instances by young boys. In other regions of Syro-Mesopotamia the tiara has few parallels, but it occurs in some sculptures of Hatra.[52] Furthermore, it is slightly reminiscent of decorated caps worn by some young Palmyrene men in funerary reliefs.[53] In Edessa, other types of male headgear are not attested, but there are various examples of bare-headed images. The coin images of the kings, however, show that they wore a richly embroidered high tiara, the *tiara orthe*, that closely resembles the tiara of the lords of Hatra.[54]

The new finds from Edessa allow the identification of statues as Edessean that were found in other parts of

---

Maischatz 1999.

   47 Jacobs and Schütte-Maischatz 2006.

   48 Demir 2019.

   49 Demir 2019, 253–54, fig. 4.

---

50 For similar straps with buckles at Hatra, see Safar and Mustafa 1974.

51 For a discussion of this headgear, which is frequently identified as a 'turban', see Leroy 1957, 337–39.

52 See, for example, Safar and Mustafa 1974, 267.

53 See Raja 2019, 313.

54 In a funerary mosaic from Edessa, a man who is identified as Abgar, the lord, wears a soft tiara, see Drijvers 1982. He is frequently interpreted as king of Edessa. If this interpretation is correct, the king would have worn the same headgear as the other members of the elite. In the mosaic, he is distinguished by his richly decorated mantle.

Figure 12.7. Fragmented statue from Ain Arous, limestone, whereabouts unknown (© Slg. Oppenheim 10/6 S.41b, Max Freiherr von Oppenheim Stiftung).

Figure 12.8. Funerary banquet scene, tomb of Seluk, Kırk Mağara necropolis, Edessa, second–third centuries AD (© Slg. Oppenheim 29/15.20 S.90b, Max Freiherr von Oppenheim Stiftung).

Figure 12.9. Funerary banquet scene, Kırk Mağara necropolis (?), Edessa, second–third centuries AD (Slg. Oppenheim 29/15.20 S.91a, Max Freiherr von Oppenheim Stiftung).

the region but have not yet been recognized as such. The best example is a statue of a man from Bir el-Kantari north of Deir ez-Zor in Syria, which Henri Seyrig published in 1971 (Fig. 12.6).[55] Many details of this statue match the recently found statues from the Edessa necropolis almost exactly. Especially the decoration of the trousers and the shirt, the weapons, and the shoes are so similar that an origin of the statue from the same Edessean workshop can be taken for granted. This is further supported by the almost relief-like rendering of the statue, which is characteristic for statues carved from the chalky limestone of Edessa. Not attested so far in Edessa is the raising of the right hand, a gesture of adoration, which is well known from Hatra. It indicates that the statue was standing in a sanctuary, not in a tomb.

Seyrig interpreted the statue as the representation of a local ruler. At the time he wrote his article, the closest comparison he could find was the lower part of the statue of a seated man, which Max von Oppenheim had discovered already in 1899 at Ain Arous, south of Harran (Fig. 12.7).[56] Yet, Seyrig did not link both sculptures to Edessa, but to Hatra and Palmyra.[57] Indeed,

---

[55] Seyrig 1971.

[56] Seyrig 1971, 120. For illustrations, see Herzfeld 1920, pl. 25 (identified as a Parthian king). Herzfeld, based on a mistake made by Oppenheim, identified the find place as Ras el-Ain (ancient Rhesaina), which Seyrig corrected to Ain Arous.

[57] The statue has been discussed as an example of Parthian fashion and in the context of Palmyrene sculpture more recently, too, see Curtis 2001, 301–02, pl. 10e; 2017, 63, fig. 16, where the statue is considered unprovenanced.

Figure 12.10. Funerary relief with a male half figure, Edessa, limestone, second–third centuries AD, Archaeological Museum Istanbul (after Segal 1970, pl. 14b).

Figure 12.11. Funerary relief (?) with a male and female half figure, Edessa, limestone, second–third centuries AD, whereabouts unknown (© Slg. Oppenheim 29/15.4 S.74a, Max Freiherr von Oppenheim Stiftung).

iconography and style show a generic resemblance to Hatrean sculpture, indeed, but the Edessean provenance is beyond doubt.

In addition to the statues in the round, an unspecified number of funerary reliefs exist that were cut in the back walls of burial niches in rock-cut tombs (Figs 12.8–12.9). Nineteenth-century travelogues mention them frequently, and it seems that many of them are destroyed or obliterated today.[58] Apparently, all of them show funerary banquet scenes.[59] At the centre are reclining men in trousers and long-sleeved shirts with drinking cups. They are accompanied by their wives and sometimes children, who are seated in a chair next to them. The arrangement follows the standard pattern of funerary banquet scenes as observed in Palmyra and elsewhere in the Roman Near East.[60]

Two funerary reliefs surfaced in Şanlıurfa in the late nineteenth century and were taken to Istanbul. The odd shape of the slabs suggests that they were cut out of the living rock. The reliefs show half figures in curved niches, each accompanied by a Syriac inscription. The first relief depicts a single man (Fig. 12.10).[61] He is clad in a himation and wears a soft tiara. The second relief shows a man in the same guise next to a woman, Qaymi, probably his wife, who wears a chiton, a massive necklace with a medallion, and a veil that covers her head and falls over her shoulders.[62] Another relief that Max von Oppenheim photographed in 1899 seems to be lost (Fig. 12.11). It is an ashlar block with the projecting half figures of a couple. In this relief, the woman's head is not covered at all. This is unusual for Edessean images of women, which are not numerous. No statues in the round have been discovered; there are only a small number of reliefs and stelai. The most prominent is a large limestone stele with the image of a

---

58 Most mentions are rather unspecific, and it remains unclear how many and which reliefs exactly the visitors saw.

59 Segal 1970, pls 25–26; Drijvers and Healey 1999, 68–75.

60 For the funerary banquet in Palmyra, see Audley-Miller 2016.

61 Parlasca 1982, 14; Drijvers and Healey 1999, 49–50.

62 Parlasca 1982; 14–15, pl. 17, 2; Drijvers and Healey 1999, 57–58.

Figure 12.12. Funerary stele of Šalmat and Rabbayta, limestone, second–third centuries AD, Archaeological Museum of Şanlıurfa (© D-DAI-IST-R33935 [H. Hauptmann]).

Figure 12.13. Votive stele (?) of Zabedibol, Şanlıurfa/Karaköprü, basalt, 176/77 AD, H. 1.23 m, Archaeological Museum of Şanlıurfa (© Michael Blömer).

seated woman and her daughter in high relief.[63] A Syriac inscription identifies them as ʿAni and Matašada.[64] ʿAni is seated on a throne. She wears high conical headgear, covered by the himation, which is pulled over the head. The tall hat is the most distinctive feature of female images in Edessa. Similar hats have been worn in Hatra, too, but they are not attested in other parts of Syro-Mesopotamia.[65]

Another relief shows Šalmat and her daughter Rabbayta (Fig. 12.12).[66] The latter is depicted as a standing figure but at a significantly smaller scale. She is fully dressed and wears a high conical hat. Her mother's headgear has a different shape. It is not conical, but cylindrical. Both women wear the standard apparel of Edessean women, a long-sleeved undergarment and a 'himation', a long rectangular piece of cloth that is wrapped around the body, pulled over the head, and fastened by a fibula on the left shoulder. Very similar dress is worn in Hatra and Palmyra, but also in Hierapolis in north Syria.[67] The women in the banquet reliefs mentioned above look very similar and wear the same dress (Figs 12.8–12.9). As in Palmyra, they are seated next to their reclining husbands.

The vast majority of Edessean statues and reliefs are connected to the funerary realm. In comparison, sculpture from the religious sphere is extremely rare.[68] A possible exception is a basalt stele depicting two bare-headed men in trouser suits, who are sacrificing on incense

---

[63] Parlasca 1982, pl. 17. The stele is on display in the Archaeological Museum of Diyarbakır today.

[64] Drijvers and Healey 1999, 206–07.

[65] See, for example, Safar and Mustafa 1974.

[66] Parlasca 1982, 15, pl. 17; Drijvers and Healey 1999, 208; Laflı 2016, 444–45. The latter compares the female headgear to a Palmyrene modius, which, however, was a type of male headgear.

[67] For this costume, see Rumscheid 2019, 76–77. Despite the long tradition of research in Palmyrene sculpture, a precise analysis of the female apparel is still lacking.

[68] On the religious life of Edessa, see Drijvers 1980; Tubach 1986; Healey 2019.

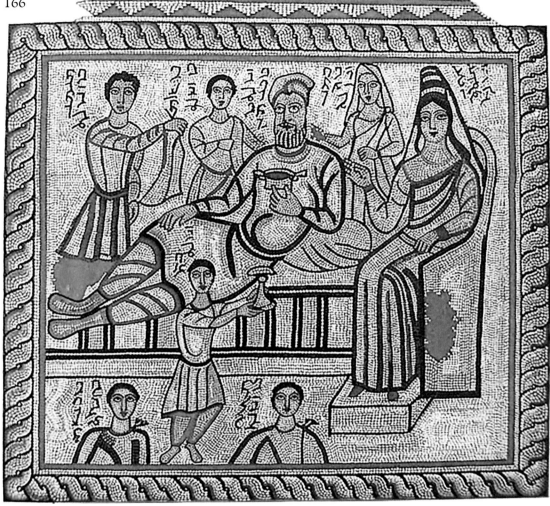

Figure 12.14. Funerary mosaic with funerary banquet scene, Edessa, second–third centuries AD, now lost (after Segal 1970, fig. 2).

burners (Fig. 12.13).[69] Even rarer are images of deities.[70] A relief from Edessa with two seated figures flanking a cult object had been interpreted by Drijvers as an image of Atargatis, Hadad, and the semeion.[71] However, its iconography differs considerably from other images of this triad. More importantly, the dating of the relief to the Romano-Parthian period is not convincing, and it should therefore be excluded from the discussion.

Considering the large number of divine images from Hatra, Palmyra, but also from minor sites of north Mesopotamia, their absence at Edessa is surprising. To some extent, this might be an accident of transmission, but it seems also possible that aniconic objects of worship played an important role at Edessa.[72] However, images of the moon god in a local style exist at the Sumatar in the territory of Edessa (see below).

Funerary Mosaics of Edessa

At Edessa, a very peculiar mode of funerary representation that has no counterpart in other parts of Syro-Mesopotamia can be found. In some of the rock-cut tombs, funerary mosaics with figural scenes and funerary inscriptions cover the floors of the central chamber(s). Travellers to Edessa reported of casual discoveries of funerary mosaics in Urfa since the late nineteenth century.[73] In recent times, the number has increased considerably. By now more than thirty mosaics are known, but a

---

69 Laflı and Christof 2014. The interpretation as a funerary stele seems unconvincing.

70 For the locally produced statue of Dionysos, see Filges 2001. The find-spot is said to be Birtha at the Euphrates. Filges interprets the statue as an *interpretatio graeca* of the local god Bar Maren. In some of the mosaics of Edessa and Osrhoene, gods and mythological figures of Greek origin are depicted.

71 Drijvers 1980, 80–82, pl. 22.

72 Rare coins from the royal period show an aniconic rectangular object inside a temple. Moreover, an aniconic cult object seems to have been at the centre of the cult of Sin at Carrhae.

73 Sachau 1882; Renan 1883; Chabot 1906; Euting 1909.

12. EDESSA AND THE SCULPTURE OF GREATER NORTH MESOPOTAMIA IN THE ROMANO-PARTHIAN PERIOD 167

Figure 12.15. Funerary mosaic of Aphtuha and his family, Edessa, second–third centuries AD, Istanbul, Archaeological Museum, inv. 1605 (after Salman 2008, fig. 5).

comprehensive study is still lacking.[74] Many bear inscriptions in Syriac, some of which give a precise date and even the names of the mosaicists. Based on these dates and on palaeographical considerations, it has been concluded that the mosaics date to the period between the later second and the fourth centuries AD.[75] The bulk of mosaic floors appear to date to the early third century AD.

Different categories of representations can be discerned. Some of them show mythological scenes connected to the funerary sphere, most prominently Orpheus, but most common are images of the deceased and their families.[76] In the latter, the repertoire of motifs and the iconography are very similar to the funerary sculpture, and the colourful details provide information that cannot otherwise be obtained. For this reason, it is important to include the mosaics in the discussion of north Mesopotamian sculpture.

Male figures wear trousers, shirts, and frequently, but not always, long-sleeved coats or mantles. However, the 'warrior' type with sword, dagger, and leggings is not attested in the mosaics. The focus apparently is on family and on piety. Best attested are funerary banquet and sacrificial scenes (Fig. 12.14). In addition, some mosaics show half figures, either inscribed in square fields or

---

[74] The best overviews of the mosaics in Edessa are provided in Colledge 1994; Salman 2008; Rumscheid 2009; 2013; Önal 2017. For discussions of iconography, see also Leroy 1957.

[75] Healey 2006. In recent times, mosaics of Christian tombs of the third/fourth century have been discovered, see Önal 2017, 136–37.

[76] On the mythological mosaics, see Balty and Briquel-Chatonnet 2000; Possekel 2008.

Figure 12.16. Cave sanctuary at Sumatar, rear wall with niche flanked by cultic standards and adorants, third century AD (© Michael Blömer).

Figure 12.17. Open-air sanctuary with rock-cut reliefs and inscriptions at Sumatar (© Michael Blömer).

dispersed over the floor (Fig. 12.15).[77] They seem to be directly inspired by funerary reliefs with half figures.

Images of women are numerous in the family scenes. They provide important information on the details of the female dress. They wear tall hats of either a conical or a cylindrical shape.

An interesting detail is the curious coiffure of young girls. They have their hair collected in three buns that stick out from the head.[78]

In addition to sculptures and mosaics, paintings must have adorned many of the tombs, but traces of painted decoration have survived only in some recently discovered late antique tombs.[79] However, reports from the nineteenth century indicate that the walls of the pagan tombs could be covered with plaster and embellished with paintings and painted inscriptions.[80]

Beyond Edessa and Hatra: The Sculptural Habit in Greater North Mesopotamia

Beyond Edessa, few sites of Osrhoene have yielded sculptures so far. The statue of a nobleman from the banks of the Euphrates has been mentioned already. Two funerary reliefs with banquet scenes have been observed next to a tower tomb in the hills south of Edessa.[81] Sumatar is the only site of Osrhoene where a substantial number of sculptures were discovered. As mentioned above, this was the seat of a governor who ruled over the mountainous region east of Edessa. The site is best known for an underground sanctuary that is carved in the rock. The rectangular main room has a large niche at the front end that must have contained the cult object (Fig. 12.16). Reliefs of cult standards — poles with tassels surmounted by crescents — frame the niche. Various more-than-life-size male figures in local dress are carved in the side walls.[82] Some of them have small altars in front of them and perform sacrifices. They wear trousers, long-sleeved coats, and tall, slightly convex hats, which might identify them as priests.[83] Syriac inscriptions indicate the names and offices of these men.[84]

An open-air sanctuary with rock reliefs and various inscriptions is located on a hilltop south of the tell. Inscriptions identify the place as a sanctuary for the moon god Sin, the lord of the gods, who had his main sanctuary in the nearby city of Harran. Two heavily weathered and defaced reliefs in an open-air sanctuary can be identified as the portraits of the moon god (Fig. 12.17).[85]

In addition to the religious sculpture, various fragmented stelai and a torso of a statue have been found at Sumatar. All of them were discovered in the area of the necropolis and therefore should be considered as funerary sculpture. The finds display a close affinity to the sculptures from Edessa. The statue torso and a stele with a male half figure represent the aristocratic 'warrior' type.[86] Another badly weathered relief, lost today, depicts the half figure of a headless man wearing a shirt and a long-sleeved coat.[87] Likewise lost is a fragmented stele with a male head surmounted by an eagle.[88] There is only one stele, most likely a funerary stele, that depicts women.[89] Three defaced busts can be discerned, all of them wearing high hats. All other details are beyond recognition.

For good reasons, the statues and reliefs found at Sumatar are usually treated as examples of Edessean sculpture. At the same time, they witness the proliferation of sculpture in Osrhoene beyond Edessa, and it is to be expected that the vast and unexplored region of the Tek Tek Mountains, where Sumatar is located, will yield further statues and reliefs in the future. In general, the sculptural habit in north Mesopotamia was not confined to the large centres Edessa and Hatra. While the main workshops supposedly were urban, indeed, a small but growing number of sculptures that

---

[77] Önal 2017.

[78] For examples, see Rumscheid 2009, 263; Önal 2017, 25. A similar hairstyle is attested in figurines of young girls in Seleucia on the Tigris.

[79] Önal 2017, 122–25.

[80] Walpole 1851, 290–91; Sachau 1882, 162.

[81] One relief with a banquet scene (?) has been variously mentioned since the nineteenth century and still seems to be at the site, see Deichmann and Peschlow 1977, pl. 20.2. This is a curious relief, because the man seems to be lying outstretched on his back. Euting drew an unpublished sketch of a second funerary banquet relief in his diary during his visit in 1883.

[82] For this cave, see Pognon 1907, 23–38; Segal 1953.

[83] Tall conical hats are typical for priests of autochthonous cults in (north) Syria, see Blömer 2015.

[84] Drijvers and Healey 1999, 125–39.

[85] Drijvers and Healey 1999, 87–94, pls 17, 20. Two reliefs of eagles are probably related to the cult of the sun god, see Drijvers 1980, pl. 30; Çelik and Albayrak 2019.

[86] For the statue, see Segal 1953, 100, pl. 11, 1 (whereabouts unknown). The relief is published in Drijvers and Healey 1999, 153–54; Laflı 2016, 446 (incorrectly identified as a man grasping a *schedula*).

[87] Drijvers 1973, 2–6.

[88] Drijvers 1973, 11.

[89] Drijvers 1973, 6–7, pl. 4; Drijvers and Healey 1999, 124, pl. 31.

Figure 12.18. Funerary statue (?) of man, from Carrhae/Harran, limestone, second–third centuries AD, Archaeological Museum of Şanlıurfa (© Michael Blömer).

closely resemble the styles and iconographies of Edessa and/or Hatra have been discovered in rural areas. The finds of statues at Ain al-Arous and Bir al-Kantari — mentioned above — and a fragmented female statue from a cemetery at Mishrife attest to the proliferation of sculptures in the south of Osrhoene.[90] A high-quality statue of a nobleman in riding costume was discovered further north, close to the Atatürk dam on the banks of the Euphrates (Fig. 12.4).[91] The distance to Edessa is 55 km as the crow flies. At Carrhae, modern Harran, evidence for sculpture production is very limited, but we must presume that workshops were active at this eminent city and its sanctuary (Fig. 12.18).[92]

The high quality of workmanship of these statues and reliefs suggests that urban workshops were commissioned with their production. However, locally produced sculpture that follows similar patterns existed, too. The little-known necropolis of Hilar may serve as an example. The site is located far north at the foothills of the Taurus chain that separates north Mesopotamia and Anatolia near the Turkish city Ergani.[93] In Antiquity, this region must have been part of Sophene.[94] Traces of a settlement have not been registered so far, but adjacent to the modern village of Hilar, a large number of chamber tombs that can be dated to the second and third centuries AD are carved into a limestone ridge.[95] Next to the entrance of some of the tombs, funerary banquet scenes, single figures, and altars have been carved in the rock surfaces (Fig. 12.19). The reliefs show a generic connection to the funerary sculpture of Edessa. This link is also supported by Old Syriac funerary inscriptions.[96] The style and the execution, however, is much coarser, and the position of the reliefs outside of the graves does not find parallels in Edessa.

Further east, in the Tigris gorge, rock reliefs at Finik and further north between Dağyeli and Koçtepe show a close resemblance to the sculpture of Hatra.[97] The figures of the latter are very worn, but an inscription in North Mesopotamian Aramaic

---

[90] For the statue of a seated woman from Mishrife in the area of the Tabqa dam, see Egami, Masuda, and Iwasaki 1979.

[91] Jacobs and Schütte-Maischatz 1999.

[92] At Harran, a male statue in trouser suit has been found, see Segal 1970, pl. 13a. For the recent find of the statue of a seated woman, see Önal and Desremaux 2019.

[93] In Antiquity, this region was part of the Armenian kingdom of Sophene, see Marciak 2017. This is important as it underlines the close entanglement between Armenia and Syro-Mesopotamia.

[94] For Sophene, see Marciak 2017.

[95] Equini-Schneider 1992; Spanu, Bejor, and Equini-Schneider 1992–1993.

[96] Drijvers and Healey did not include them in the corpus of Old Syriac inscriptions, because they considered them closer to Hatrean and other scripts of north Mesopotamia, see Drijvers and Healey 1999, viii.

[97] See Nogaret 1984 for the Finik relief and Lightfoot and Naveh 1991.

Figure 12.19. Rock reliefs in the necropolis of Hilar, second–third centuries AD (© Michael Blömer).

identifies a standing male next to the figure of an eagle as the god Nergal. Even more intriguing is the recent find of a fragment of a male statue at the village of Beşikkaya/Fafı in the Tur Abdin mountains.[98] Only parts of the left leg with trousers and tunic are preserved, but the high-quality embroidery — wine scrolls adorn the trousers, lozenges made of beads filled with rosettes on the shirt — closely resembles the finest Hatrean statues of the second century.[99] So far, little research has been conducted in the Tur Abdin mountains, a region that has been unruly and inaccessible for a long time. It would not be a surprise if more sculptures emerge from this region in the future.

The upper Tigris region and the Tur Abdin were affiliated with of the kingdom of Adiabene in the first two centuries AD.[100] The nearest large city was Nisibis, an eminent urban centre.[101] Close to nothing is known about the archaeology and topography of Nisibis, but the finds of sculptures in the city's hinterland suggest that it was a centre of sculpture production like Hatra and Edessa.[102] Moreover, we must assume that more than just one workshop was active in Adiabene, which extended over a large territory. The core areas were located east of

---

[98] Comfort 2017, 204–05, fig. 26a. Comfort cautiously identified the piece as headgear.

[99] See Safar and Mustafa 1974, 70, 208. In this context it is also noteworthy that at Fafı, Gertrude Bell photographed a tower tomb with human busts protruding from the outer walls, which resembles the sculptural decoration at Hatra, see Comfort 2017, 204. The tomb is completely destroyed today. Max von Oppenheim recorded a similar tower tomb with protruding portrait busts at Çatalat in the Tek Tek Mountains, but it remains unpublished. Better known are the tower tombs of Serrin, in modern Syria, see Gogräfe 1995.

[100] For the kingdom and its topography, see Marciak 2017.

[101] Palermo 2014.

[102] For a different perspective, see Jong and Palermo 2018. They conclude 'it is highly unlikely that inscriptions, stelae, honorific sculpture, or imported marble, in any quantities, or evidence for investments in water management from the steppe, remain unreported. It is far more likely that they never were there'. However, for the reasons mentioned here, it is no surprise that there is little information about such objects and installations.

the Tigris with Arbela as capital, and included the former Assyrian centres of Nineveh and Ashur.[103] For several centuries, the kingdom was an important regional power, and it is very likely that the royal court and the cities of Adiabene exerted a strong impact on the principalities of Mesopotamia as Hatra and also Edessa.[104] The material culture of Adiabene remains elusive, but the kings of Adiabene commissioned sculptures, and they did so already before the advent of Parthian rule in Mesopotamia.[105] The oldest example is the rock relief at Batas-Herir in northern Iraq that most probably displays the image of king Abdissares, who took power over Adiabene in the 160s BC.[106] He is wearing a long-sleeved shirt, trousers, a mantle, and a soft tiara. The style is different from the later sculpture and shows a stronger Hellenistic imprint that resembles Commagenean sculpture, but it shows that the local production of sculpture was not completely abandoned in the region. In general, Persian and Persianizing traditions that thrived in the royal courts of Adiabene, Sophene, Greater Armenia, and Commagene in the Hellenistic period must not be disregarded as sources of inspiration for the elite cultures of the neighbouring Syro-Mesopotamian realm.[107] The statues and relief of late Hellenistic Commagene and the Batas-Harir relief mark the western and the eastern borders of this region. Moreover, the latter relief demonstrates that the Iranian or 'Parthian' dress had been adopted by local rulers of Greater Mesopotamia prior to the arrival of the Arsacids.

After this brief survey, we may conclude that the sculptural habit was more pervasive in north Mesopotamia during the Romano-Parthian period than has so far been postulated. New and old finds attest to a prominent role of Edessa, but there is compelling evidence for the existence of other centres of production, which have gone largely unrecorded so far. Workshops must have existed in Nisibis and Carrhae, but also in the cities of Adiabene that are located east of the Tigris.

Scattered examples of statues and, most of all rock reliefs, go back to Hellenistic times, but it remains to be explored whether the early occurrences of locally produced sculpture were insular phenomena or manifestations of an artistic network that paved the way for the flourishing sculpture production in the subsequent period. In any case, the main revival of the sculptural habit happened only in the second and early third centuries AD. At that time, we can grasp the development of a characteristic style and iconographic repertoire in greater north Mesopotamia. The sculptural habit did not develop in a void, though, but was deeply rooted in local Mesopotamian and Hellenistic traditions. At the same time, the rise of the Arsacid kings as a major power in Mesopotamia had an impact and fostered the choice of certain images and patterns. This becomes manifest mostly in the sphere of elite representation, while it is much weaker in religious imagery. Yet, more efforts are necessary to discriminate between Arsacid influence, undercurrents of more ancient Iranian impact, and universal fashions that developed in the Hellenistic East. The 'Parthian' trouser suit is a case in point. It was Parthian apparel, but it was also common among many people from Anatolia to Central Asia and India. We might also surmise that it was common among the Arabs of Mesopotamia already before the Parthians arrived in Mesopotamia in the second century BC.[108] It is therefore difficult to consider this apparel as a marker of Parthian identity or even as a sign of allegiance to Parthia in a political sense, especially since there is no indication that the proliferation of certain dress codes was initiated or fostered by Parthian elites. It rather seems that by the second century AD, the trouser suit had lost its Iranian character in greater north Mesopotamia. It had become a 'native' garment, void of political and cultural connotations.

This change of perspective has repercussions for the assessment of Palmyrene dress codes, too. It means that contrary to the statement of Henri Seyrig mentioned above, the people of Palmyra let themselves be portrayed in native dress.[109] Wearing trousers, leggings, and long-sleeved tunics with rich embroidery was not referring

---

[103] At Nineveh, a fragmented pedestal with a foot of a statue has been found that closely resembled Hatrean sculpture, see Reade 1998, 76, fig. 14. Possibly also from Nineveh is a male head, see Reade 1998, 81, fig. 22. At Ashur, three large stelai with worshippers from the first century AD have been found, see Mathiesen 1992, 190–91.

[104] In the same vein, it has recently been proposed that the Hatrean language and script followed models from Adiabene, see Pennacchietti 2019.

[105] For rock reliefs of the Romano-Parthian period in Adiabene, see Mathiesen 1992, 182–86; Reade and Anderson 2013; Marciak and Wójcikowski 2016; Miglus, Brown, and Aguilar Gutiérrez 2018; Brown and others 2018.

[106] Grabowski 2011; Marciak and Wójcikowski 2016. For coin images of king Abdissares, see Kovacs 2016, 2–3.

[107] For the concept of Persianism, see Strootman and Versluys (eds) 2017.

[108] The large number of 'Persian rider' figurines from the Achaemenid period onwards attest to the popularity of the riding costume in Mesopotamia and also in Syria, see Elayi 1991; Moorey 2000.

[109] Seyrig 1950, 2.

to a distant Iranian culture, but was a local fashion and expressed participation in the cultural sphere of greater north Mesopotamia. Similar is the case of the alleged Greek dress, chiton and himation. In the course of the centuries, this apparel had been transformed into a local fashion, too, and it is doubtful whether the people of Palmyra still regarded it as something Greek.[110]

Analogous problems can be seen in other categories of material culture that are commonly referred to as 'Parthian', as, for example, green-glazed pottery that was very popular in large parts of Mesopotamia in the Parthian period. It has traditionally been deemed a key marker of Parthian culture, but this tableware was also popular in Palmyra, and it has surfaced at various sites of central and north Syria. Moreover, it is becoming increasingly evident that its production commenced before the Parthian advent in Mesopotamia.[111] It might therefore rather be viewed as a class of autochthonous Mesopotamian pottery that developed in the Parthian period. Despite the predilection for green-glazed wares in territories under Arsacid rule, the Parthian links might have been rather weak.

In general, the material culture and the images that were produced in the cities and principalities of greater north Mesopotamia reflect modes of representation that developed locally.[112] The direct impact of the imperial powers — Rome and Iran — should not be exaggerated. That does not imply that they were strictly localized, though. Quite the contrary, the formulation and manifestation of the material culture of greater north Mesopotamia were the results of an increasingly globalized world. The region is frequently pictured as divided between two empires, but in fact it constituted a *koine* with strong interregional ties.[113] If the notion of imperial periphery — both from a western and eastern perspective — is abandoned, the central position of greater north Mesopotamia comes to the fore.[114]

An assemblage of twenty-one papyri that surfaced on the art market in the 1980s demonstrates how close the links between the Middle Euphrates and Mesopotamia were.[115] The exact find-spot of the assemblage is not clear, but the documents clearly suggest that they were deposited in the archive of the town of Appadana/Neapolis. Where the latter is located has not been ascertained, but it was not too far north of Dura-Europos, probably on the left bank of the Euphrates.[116] The nature of the documents is administrative, and many of them deal with the affairs of inhabitants of villages in the surrounding area. Significant is that a majority of the places that are mentioned in the documents are located in north Mesopotamia, and the transactions referred to highlight how the network of village dwellers in the vicinity of Dura-Europos extended as far as Batnae, Edessa, Carrhae, and Nisibis. The Khabur River appears as a vital link that tied the urban centres of north Mesopotamia to the Euphrates. Western connections play a minor role only.

The close entanglement of the region is also palpable in other areas. All over the region, people spoke dialects of Aramaic and shared religious traditions. While the panthea of the main cities of the regions certainly were distinct, they all have features in common that are rooted in ancient Near Eastern traditions, but were transformed under the impact of Hellenism.[117] An example of the longevity and vitality of Mesopotamian religion is the goddess Nanaja.[118] As has recently been shown, her popularity grew immensely in the Partho-Roman period, and her veneration can be traced well beyond the ancestral centres of her cult. This is not merely an example of the continuity of pre-Hellenistic traditions, but attests to the vitality and creativity of contemporary Mesopotamian culture.[119]

---

110 The situation is different with the toga, which was much more exclusive and closely tied to Roman citizenship, see Schmidt-Colinet 2009.

111 Clarke and others 2019, 273–75; Römer-Strehl 2013. It appears that the use of the label 'Parthian' for green-glazed pottery has turned into a self-fulfilling prophecy. Finds of this pottery have been used to date assemblages to the Parthian period a priori, without entertaining the possibility that glazed sherds could be attributed of an earlier period.

112 For an alternative view, see Jong 2013.

113 For further examples of this bricolage of Mesopotamian, Greek, and Iranian traditions in the wider region, see, for example, Messina 2014; Fowlkes-Childs and Seymour 2019.

114 How important and fruitful changes of perspective are, see Versluys 2017.

115 For these fascinating documents, see Feissel and Gascou 1989; 1995; 2000; Teixidor, Feissel, and Gascou 1997. See also Sommer 2018.

116 Gnoli 1999.

117 Drijvers 1980; Tubach 1986. For Palmyra, see Kaizer 2002.

118 Ambos 2003.

119 For more examples from Hatra, see Dirven 2009.

Conclusion

It is not yet possible to fully grasp the scale and scope of sculptural production in north Mesopotamia in the Romano-Parthian period, but in recent years evidence has started to mount that suggests that statues and reliefs were much more prolific than has previously been assumed. By the later second century AD, various centres of production had emerged in Osrhoene, Hatrene, and Adiabene. They were tied together by distinctive forms of style and iconography, but they also shared many characteristics with the sculpture from Dura and Palmyra. This supports the idea that north Mesopotamia and the Syrian Middle Euphrates region must be considered a coherent cultural landscape. In this region, elites shared concepts of male and female virtues, religious beliefs, language, and lifestyle. In terms of sculpture and iconography, the prominence of an apparel consisting of trousers, a long-sleeved shirt with embroidery, and a mantle or cloak as a popular mode of elite male representation is distinctive. For women, a dress that included headgear, a turban or high hat, a long-sleeved undergarment, and an upper garment that is fastened by a fibula on the left shoulder is characteristic. Various types of jewellery were typical for both men and women. With regard to style, a predilection for frontality can be observed.

There are differences, too. The formalistic precision in the rendering of details and the hypertrophic routine that characterizes Palmyrene craftmanship find no direct counterpart in Mesopotamia. The elongation of body parts and the expressive appearance are particular to Hatra and smaller centres in the vicinity of Hatra. There is little stylistic homogeneity discernible in the sculpture of Edessa and Osrhoene, but this might be a result of the relatively small sample size. It seems, however, that the predilection for abstraction is less pronounced than in Palmyra and Hatra. In terms of style, the sculpture of Zeugma and Hierapolis in Syria, two important cities that share borders with Osrhoene, may have exerted influence on the sculpture of Edessa.[120] However, some of the stylistic differences may also result from the varying properties of the locally available stone material.

The variety of iconographic details is significant, too. If men wear trouser suits, the length of the shirts and the design of the cloaks vary. It is also important to keep in mind that at Palmyra the by far best-attested male apparel is chiton and himation. The types of headgear differ, too. The soft tiara worn by men appears almost exclusively in Edessa, and the priestly hat at Palmyra has no counterpart in Mesopotamia. Moreover, the female tall hats of Edessa and Hatra contrast considerably with the embroidered turbans worn in Palmyra; yet the fact that women wore headgear and pulled a himation over it firmly link Palmyra to north Mesopotamia.

Purpose and context of sculptures varied in the different regions of greater north Mesopotamia, too. At Palmyra, loculus reliefs and sarcophagi were used to commemorate the dead. Thousands of portraits were carved.[121] At Edessa, however, statues in the round, rock-cut reliefs, and mosaics prevailed as means of funerary representation. In Hatra and Dura-Europos, on the other hand, funerary sculpture is hardly attested at all. At both cities, most sculptures come from religious contexts, while religious sculpture seems to be absent at Edessa. This variety is no surprise. Modes of funerary commemoration and religious representation were highly localized and differed strongly even in regions that were politically, religiously, and economically closely entangled.[122]

All these variances complicate trans-local comparisons of the sculptural habit in greater north Mesopotamia, but they cannot obscure the fundamental similarities. In a region as closely entangled as Syro-Mesopotamia, peer polity interaction at various levels and economic ties fostered the transmission of ideas and the emergence of comparable and compatible symbolic systems, while the different cities and principalities at the same time sported local differences.[123] Labelling key features of artistic production in north Mesopotamia 'Parthian' is just as inadequate as calling them 'Graeco-Roman'. The sculptural tradition that emerged in the Late Hellenistic period and gained traction in Roman-Parthian times was not uniform, self-sufficient, or idiosyncratic. The sculptures reflect a persistent interaction with the neighbouring regions. At varying speed and intensity, the centres of production responded to features and fashions of the main political powers. Nonetheless, during the second century AD, a distinctive form of artistic expression and style pervaded north Mesopotamia which transcended political boundaries. Edessa and Osrhoene were part of this cultural *koine*, and so was Palmyra.

---

[120] For the sculpture of north Syria, see Parlasca 1982; Blömer 2014; Rumscheid 2019. The predilection for mosaics at Edessa certainly has also been fostered by the contemporary flourishing of tessellated floors in north Syria.

[121] So far, more than 3500 funerary portraits from Palmyra are known, see Kropp and Raja 2014; Raja 2017b.

[122] For a similar situation in neighbouring north Syria, see Blömer 2019b.

[123] For the concept of peer polity interaction, see Renfrew and Cherry (eds) 2009.

Works Cited

Albayrak, Y. 2019. 'Soğmatar', in M. Önal, S. I. Mutlu, and S. Mutlu (eds), *Harran ve Çevresi Arkeoloji* (Şanlıurfa: Şurkav Yayınları), pp. 271–84.

Albayrak, Y. and others. 2019. 'Soğmatar'da sunaklı kaya oyuğu mezarlar', *Karadeniz*, 41: 263–74.

Ambos, C. 2003. 'Nanaja: Eine ikonographische Studie zur Darstellung einer altorientalischen Göttin in hellenistisch-parthischer Zeit', *Zeitschrift für Assyriologie und vorderasiatische Archäologie*, 93: 231–72.

Audley-Miller, L. 2016. 'The Banquet in the Palmyrene Funerary Context', in C. M. Draycott and M. Stamatopoulou (eds), *Dining and Death: Interdisciplinary Perspectives on the 'Funerary Banquet' in Ancient Art, Burial and Belief* (Leuven: Peeters), pp. 553–90.

Balty, J. and F. Briquel-Chatonnet. 2000. 'Nouvelles mosaïques inscrites d'Osrhoène', *Monuments et mémoires: Fondation Eugène Piot*, 79: 31–72.

Baratin, C. 2011. 'Le rayonnement oriental de la culture parthe : enjeux historiographiques et perspectives', *Topoi*, 17: 179–88.

Blömer, M. 2014. *Steindenkmäler römischer Zeit aus Nordsyrien: Identität und kulturelle Tradition in Kyrrhestike und Kommagene* (Bonn: Habelt).

—— 2015. 'Images of Priests in North Syria and Beyond', in M. Blömer, A. Lichtenberger, and R. Raja (eds), *Religious Identities in the Levant from Alexander to Muhammed: Continuity and Change*, Contextualizing the Sacred, 4 (Turnhout: Brepols), pp. 185–97.

—— 2019a. 'Edessa and Osrhoene', in O. Tekin (ed.), *Hellenistic Kingdoms in Anatolia: Kings, Emperors, City States* (Istanbul: Yapı ve Kredi Yayınları), pp. 196–221.

—— 2019b. 'The Diversity of Funerary Commemoration in Roman Commagene and Cyrrhestice', in M. Blömer and R. Raja (eds), *Funerary Portraiture in Greater Roman Syria*, Studies in Classical Archaeology, 6 (Turnhout: Brepols), pp. 45–64.

—— (forthcoming). 'Notes on the Coinage of Mesopotamia in the Romano-Parthian Period', in R. Raja (ed.), *The Small Stuff of Palmyra*, Studies in Palmyrene Archaeology and History, 5 (Turnhout: Brepols).

Brown, M. and others. 2018. 'Portraits of a Parthian King: Rock-Reliefs and the Mountain Fortress of Rabana-Merquly in Iraqi Kurdistan', *IRAQ*, 80: 63–77.

Çelik, B. and Y. Albayrak. 2019. 'Soğmatar'dan ele geçen bir kartal figürü', *Karadeniz Uluslararası Bilimsel Dergi*, 42: 60–67.

Chabot, J.-B. 1906. 'Notes sur sur quelques monuments épigraphiques araméens', *Journal asiatique*, 7.1: 281–304.

Clarke, G. and others. 2019. 'The Trading Links of a Seleukid Settlement: Jebel Khalid on the Euphrates', in R. Oetjen (ed.), *New Perspectives in Seleucid History, Archaeology and Numismatics* (Berlin: De Gruyter), pp. 264–83.

Çobanoğlu, D. 2021. 'Osrhoene Bölgesi: Edessa Roma Dönemi Heykeltraşlık Eserleri' (unpublished doctoral thesis, Antalya Akdeniz University).

Colledge, M. A. R. 1967. *The Parthians* (London: Thames & Hudson).

—— 1986. *The Parthian Period* (Leiden: Brill).

—— 1987. 'Parthian Cultural Elements at Roman Palmyra', *Mesopotamia: rivista di archeologia*, 22: 19–28.

—— 1994. 'Some Remarks on the Edessa Funerary Mosaics', in J.-P. Darmon and A. Rebourg (eds), *La mosaïque gréco-romaine*, IV: *Trèves, 8–4 aout 1984: IV. Colloque international pour l'étude de la mosaïque antique* (Paris: Association internationale pour l'étude de la mosaïque antique), pp. 189–97.

Cohen, G. M. 2006. *The Hellenistic Settlements in Syria, the Red Sea Basin and North Africa* (Berkeley: University of California Press).

Comfort, A. 2017. 'Fortresses of the Tur Abdin and the Confrontation between Rome and Persia', *Anatolian Studies*, 67: 181–229.

Curtis, V. S. 1998. 'The Parthian Costume and Headdress', in J. Wiesehöfer (ed.), *Das Partherreich und seine Zeugnisse. The Arsacid Empire: Sources and Documentation: Beiträge des internationalen Colloquiums, Eutin (27.–30. Juni 1996)* (Stuttgart: Steiner), pp. 61–74.

—— 2001. 'Parthian Belts and Belt Plaques', *Iranica antiqua*, 36: 299–327.

—— 2017. 'The Parthian Haute-Couture at Palmyra', in T. Long and A. H. Sørensen (eds), *Positions and Professions in Palmyra* (Copenhagen: The Royal Danish Academy of Sciences and Letters), pp. 52–66.

Debevoise, N. C. 1931. 'Parthian Problems', *The American Journal of Semitic Languages and Literatures*, 47.2: 73–82.

Deichmann, F. W. and U. Peschlow. 1977. *Zwei spätantike Ruinenstätten in Nordmesopotamien: Vorgelegt von Hans-Georg Beck am 5. 11. 1976* (Munich: Verlag der Bayerischen Akademie der Wissenschaften).

Demir, M. 2019. 'Şanlıurfa Kızılkoyun ve Kale eteği nekropolü kurtama kazı ve temizlik çalışması', in M. Önal, S. I. Mutlu, and S. Mutlu (eds), *Harran ve Çevresi Arkeoloji* (Şanlıurfa: Şurkav Yayınları), pp. 251–70.

Dirven, L. 2009. 'My Lord with his Dogs: Continuity and Change in the Cult of Nergal in Parthian Mesopotamia', *Mesopotamia*, 50: 243–60.

—— 2016. 'The Problem with Parthian Art at Dura', in T. Kaizer (ed.), *Religion, Society and Culture at Dura-Europos* (Cambridge: Cambridge University Press), pp. 68–88.

Downey, S. B. 1977. *The Stone and Plaster Sculpture* (New Haven: Yale University Press).

—— 2003. *Terracotta Figurines and Plaques from Dura-Europos* (Ann Arbor: University of Michigan Press).

Drijvers, H. J. W. 1973. 'Some New Syriac Inscriptions and Archaeological Finds from Edessa and Sumatar Harabesi', *Bulletin of the School of Oriental and African Studies*, 36: 1–14.

—— 1977. 'Hatra, Palmyra und Edessa: Die Städte der syrisch-mesopotamischen Wüste in politischer, kulturgeschichtlicher und religionsgeschichtlicher Bedeutung', in H. Temporini (ed.), *Aufstieg und Niedergang der römischen Welt*, 2.8 (Berlin: De Gruyter): 799–906.

—— 1980. *Cults and Beliefs at Edessa*. Leiden: Brill.

—— 1982. 'A Tomb for the Life of a King: A Recently Discovered Edessene Mosaic with a Portrait of King Abgar the Great', *Le muséon: revue d'études orientales*, 95: 167–89.

Drijvers, H. J. W. and J. F. Healey. 1999. *The Old Syriac Inscriptions of Edessa and Osrhoene* (Leiden: Brill).

Edwell, P. 2017. 'Oshroene and Mesopotamia between Rome and Arsacid Parthia', in J. M. Schlunde and B. B. Rubin (eds), *Arsacids, Romans, and Local Elites: Cross-Cultural Interactions of the Parthian Empire* (Oxford: Oxbow), pp. 111–35.

Egami, N., S. Masuda, and T. Iwasaki. 1979. *Rumeilah and Mishrifat: Excavations of Hellenistic Sites in the Euphrates Basin, 1974–1978* (Tokyo: Ancient Orient Museum).

Elayi, J. 1991. 'Deux "ateliers" de coroplastes nord-phéniciens et nord-syriens sous l'Empire perse', *Iranica antiqua*, 26: 181–206.

Equini-Schneider, E. 1992. 'Rilievi funerari dalla necropoli di Hilar', *Rivista di archeologia*, 16: 28–35.

Euting, J. 1909. *Notulae epigraphicae* [n.p.].

Fabian, L. 2020. 'The Arsakid Empire', in S. von Reden (ed.), *Handbook of Ancient Afro-Eurasian Economies* (Berlin: De Gruyter), pp. 205–40.

Feissel, D. and J. Gascou. 1989. 'Documents d'archives romains inédits du Moyen Euphrate (IIIe s. ap. J.-C.)', *Comptes-rendus des séances de l année: Académie des inscriptions et belles-lettres*, 133: 535–61.

—— 1995. 'Documents d'archives romains inédits du Moyen Euphrate (IIIe s. après J-C) [I. Les pétitions (T. Euphr. 1 à 5)]', *Journal des savants*, 1995: 65–119.

—— 2000. 'Documents d'archives romains inédits du Moyen Euphrate (IIIe s. après J.-C.) [III. Actes divers et Lettres (P. Euphr. 11 à 17)]', *Journal des savants*, 2000: 157–208.

Filges, A. 2001. 'Der Dionysos-Bar Marên von Şanlıurfa', in R. M. Boehmer and J. Maran (eds), *Lux orientis: Archäologie zwischen Asien und Europa; Festschrift für Harald Hauptmann zum 65. Geburtstag* (Rahden: Leidorf), pp. 133–37.

Fowlkes-Childs, B. and M. Seymour. 2019. *The World between Empires: Art and Identity in the Ancient Middle East* (New York: Metropolitan Museum of Art).

Gawlikowski, M. 1979. 'L'art "parthe" et l'art arsacide', in W. Kleiss (ed.), *Akten des VII. internationalen Kongresses für iranische Kunst und Archäologie* (Berlin: Reimer), pp. 323–26.

Ghirshman, R. 1962. *Iran: Parthes et Sassanides* (Paris: Gallimard).

Gnoli, T. 1999. 'I papiri dell'Eufrate. Studio di geografia storica', *Mediterraneo antico: economie, società, culture*, 2: 321–58.

Gogräfe, R. 1995. 'Die Grabtürme von Sirrin (Osroëne)', *Damaszener Mitteilungen*, 8: 165–201.

Grabowski, M. 2011. 'Abdissares of Adiabene and the Batas-Herir Relief', *Swiatowit*, 9: 117–38.

Gregoratti, L. 2017. 'Sinews of the Other Empire: Parthian Great King's Rule over Vassal Kingdoms', in H. F. Teigen and E. H. Seland (eds), *Sinews of Empire: Networks in the Roman Near East and Beyond* (Oxford: Oxbow), pp. 95–104.

Gzella, H. 2018. 'The Syriac Language in the Context of the Semitic Languages', in D. King (ed.), *The Syriac World* (London: Routledge), pp. 205–21.

Hauser, S. R. 2014. '"Parthian Art" or "Arts in the Arsacid Empire": Hatra and Palmyra as Nodal Points for Cultural Interaction', in B. Jacobs (ed.), *'Parthische Kunst': Kunst im Partherreich; Akten des internationalen Kolloquiums in Basel, 9. Oktober 2010* (Düsseldorf: Wellem), pp. 127–78.

Healey, J. F. 2006. 'A New Syriac Mosaic Inscription', *Journal of Semitic Studies*, 51: 313–27.

—— 2019. 'The Pre-Christian Religions of the Syriac-Speaking Regions', in D. King (ed.), *The Syriac World* (London: Routledge), pp. 47–67.

Herzfeld, E. 1920. *Am Tor von Asien: Felsdenkmale aus Irans Heldenzeit* (Berlin: Reimer).

Heyn, M. and R. Raja. 2019. 'Male Dress Habits in Roman Period Palmyra', in M. Cifarelli (ed.), *Fashioned Selves: Dress and Identity in Antiquity* (Oxford: Oxbow), pp. 41–54.

Invernizzi, A. 2011. 'Parthian Art – Arsacid Art', *Topoi*, 17: 189–207.

Jacobs, B. 2014. 'Repräsentative Bildkunst im Partherreich', in B. Jacobs (ed.), *'Parthische Kunst': Kunst im Partherreich; Akten des internationalen Kolloquiums in Basel, 9. Oktober 2010* (Düsseldorf: Wellem), pp. 77–126.

Jacobs, B. and A. Schütte-Maischatz. 1999. 'Statuette eines Adligen aus der nördlichen Osroëne', *Istanbuler Mitteilungen*, 49: 431–42.

—— 2006. 'Statue eines Bogenschützen aus dem Stadtgebiet von Urfa', *Istanbuler Mitteilungen*, 56: 359–69.

Jong, A. de. 2013. 'Hatra and the Parthian Commonwealth', in L. Dirven (ed.), *Hatra: Politics, Culture and Religion between Parthia and Rome* (Stuttgart: Steiner), pp. 143–60.

Jong, L. de and R. Palermo. 2018. 'Living on the Edge: The Roman Empire in the North Mesopotamian Steppe', in B. S. Düring and T. D. Stek (eds), *The Archaeology of Imperial Landscapes: A Comparative Study of Empires in the Ancient Near East and Mediterranean World* (Cambridge: Cambridge University Press), pp. 240–71.

Kaizer, T. 2002. *The Religious Life of Palmyra: A Study of the Social Patterns of Worship in the Roman Period* (Stuttgart: Steiner).

Karabulut, H., M. Önal, and N. Dervişoğlu. 2011. *Haleplibahçe Mozaikleri: Şanlıurfa Edessa* (İstanbul: Arkeoloji ve Sanat Yayınları).

Keall, E. J. 1994. 'How Many Kings Did the Parthian King of Kings Rule?', *Iranica antiqua*, 29: 253–72.
Kovacs, F. L. 2016. *Armenian Coinage in the Classical Period* (Lancaster: Classical Numismatic Group).
Krag, S. 2018. *Funerary Representations of Palmyrene Women*, Studies in Classical Archaeology, 3 (Turnhout: Brepols).
Kropp, A. J. M. and R. Raja. 2014. 'The Palmyra Portrait Project', *Syria: archéologie, art et histoire*, 91: 393–408.
Laflı, E. 2016. 'Five Old Syriac Inscriptions from the Museum of Şanlıurfa', *ARAM*, 28: 443–51.
Laflı, E. and E. Christof. 2014. 'Die Basaltgrabstele des Zabedibolos für Gennaios und Zebeis in Edessa/Şanlıurfa', in E. Olshausen and V. Sauer (eds), *Mobilität in den Kulturen der antiken Mittelmeerwelt* (Stuttgart: Steiner), pp. 355–66.
Leroy, J. 1957. 'Mosaïques funéraires d'Édesse', *Syria: revue d'art oriental et d'archéologie*, 34: 306–42.
Lightfoot, C. and J. Naveh. 1991. 'A North Mesopotamian Aramaic Inscription on a Relief in the Tigris Gorge', *ARAM*, 3: 319–36.
Marciak, M. 2017. *Sophene, Gordyene, and Adiabene: Three Regna Minora of Northern Mesopotamia between East and West* (Leiden: Brill).
Marciak, M. and R. S. Wójcikowski. 2016. 'Images of Kings of Adiabene. Numismatic and Sculptural Evidence', *IRAQ*, 78: 79–101.
Mathiesen, H. E. 1992. *Sculpture in the Parthian Empire: A Study in Chronology* (Aarhus: Aarhus University Press).
Messina, V. 2014. 'Parthian Mesopotamia', in P. Leriche (ed.), *Art et civilisations de l'Orient hellénisé: rencontres et échanges culturels d'Alexandre aux Sassanides; hommage à Daniel Schlumberger* (Paris: Picard), pp. 191–99.
Miglus, P. A., M. Brown, and J. Aguilar Gutiérrez. 2018. *Parthian Rock-Reliefs from Amādiya in Iraqi-Kurdistan* (Berlin: Mann).
Moorey, P. R. S. 2000. 'Iran and the West. The Case of the Terracotta "Persian" Riders in the Achaemenid Empire', in R. Dittmann and others (eds), *Variatio delectat: Iran und der Westen: Gedenkschrift für Peter Calmeyer* (Münster: Ugarit), pp. 469–86.
Nogaret, M. 1984. 'Le relief parthe de Finik', *Syria: revue d'art oriental et d'archéologie*, 61: 257–66.
Odrobiński, P. 1995. 'A Note on the Remains of the Old Syriac Monuments at Sumatar Harabesi', *Études et travaux* 17: 265–77.
Önal, M. 2017. *Urfa: Edessa Mozaikleri* (Şanlıurfa: Şanlıurfa Büyükşehir Belediyesi).
Önal, M. and A. Desremaux. 2019. 'The Fragment of Woman Statue with Syriac Inscription Was Found in Harran Excavation', in M. Önal, S. I. Mutlu, and S. Mutlu (eds), *Harran ve Çevresi Arkeoloji* (Şanlıurfa: Şurkav Yayınları), pp. 241–49.
Önal, M., S. I. Mutlu, and S. Mutlu (eds). 2019. *Harran ve Çevresi Arkeoloji* (Şanlıurfa: Şurkav Yayınları).
Osten, H. H. von der. 1926. 'Seven Parthian Statuettes', *The Art Bulletin*, 8: 168–74.
Palermo, R. 2014. 'Nisibis, Capital of the Province of Mesopotamia: Some Historical and Archaeological Perspectives', *Journal of Roman Archaeology*, 27: 457–72.
—— 2019. *On the Edge of Empires: North Mesopotamia during the Roman Period (2nd–4th c. CE)* (London: Routledge).
Parlasca, K. 1982. *Syrische Grabreliefs hellenistischer und römischer Zeit: Fundgruppen und Probleme*, Trierer Winckelmannsprogramme, 3 (Mainz: Von Zabern).
Pennacchietti, F. A. 2019. 'The Adiabene as Culture Background to the Language and Script of Hatra', in M. Morriggi and I. Bucci (eds), *Aramaic Graffiti from Hatra: A Study Based on the Archive of the Missione archeologica italiana* (Leiden: Brill), pp. 141–48.
Pognon, H. 1907. *Inscriptions sémitiques de la Syrie de la Mésopotamie et de la région de Mossoul* (Paris: Imprimerie nationale).
Possekel, U. 2008. 'Orpheus among the Animals: A New Dated Mosaic from Osrhoene', *Oriens Christianus*, 92: 1–35.
Raja, R. 2016. 'Representations of Priests in Palmyra: Methodological Considerations on the Meaning of the Representation of Priesthood in the Funerary Sculpture from Roman Period Palmyra', *Religion in the Roman Empire*, 2: 125–46.
—— 2017a. '"You Can Leave your Hat on." Priestly Representations from Palmyra: Between Visual Genre, Religious Importance and Social Status', in R. L. Gordon, G. Petridou, and J. Rüpke (eds), *Beyond Priesthood: Religious Entrepreneurs and Innovators in the Roman Empire* (Berlin: De Gruyter), pp. 417–42.
—— 2017b. 'Powerful Images of the Deceased: Palmyrene Funerary Portrait Culture between Local, Greek and Roman Representations', in D. Boschung and F. Queyrel (eds), *Bilder der Macht: Das griechische Porträt und seine Verwendung in der antiken Welt* (Paderborn: Fink), pp. 319–48.
—— 2019. *Catalogue: The Palmyra Collection; Ny Carlsberg Glyptotek* (Copenhagen: Ny Carlsberg Glyptotek).
Reade, J. E. 1998. 'Greco-Parthian Niniveh', *IRAQ*, 60: 65–83.
Reade, J. E. and J. R. Anderson. 2013. 'Gunduk, Khanes, Gaugamela, Gali Zardak: Notes on Navkur and Nearby Rock-Cut Sculptures in Kurdistan', *Zeitschrift für Assyriologie und vorderasiatische Archäologie*, 103: 69–123.
Renan, E. 1883. 'Deux monuments épigraphiques d'Édesse', *Journal asiatique*, 8.1: 246–51.
Renfrew, C. and J. F. Cherry (eds). 2009. *Peer Polity Interaction and Socio-Political Change* (Cambridge: Cambridge University Press).
Retsö, J. 2003. *The Arabs in Antiquity: Their History from the Assyrians to the Umayyads* (London: Routledge Curzon).
Römer-Strehl, C. 2013. 'Keramik', in A. Schmidt-Colinet and W. al-As'ad (eds), *Palmyras Reichtum durch weltweiten Handel: Archäologische Untersuchungen im Bereich der hellenistischen Stadt* (Vienna: Holzhausen), pp. 7–80.
Ross, S. K. 2001. *Roman Edessa: Politics and Culture on the Eastern Fringes of the Roman Empire, 114–242 CE* (London: Routledge).
Rostovtzeff, M. 1935. *Dura and the Problem of Parthian Art*, Yale Classical Studies, 5 (New Haven: Yale University Press), pp. 158–304.
Rumscheid, J. 2009. 'Familienbilder im Haus der Ewigkeit: Zu Grabmosaiken aus Edessa', in L. Greisiger and others (eds), *Edessa in hellenistisch-römischer Zeit: Religion Kultur und Politik zwischen Ost und West: Beiträge des internationalen Edessa-Symposiums in Halle an der Saale 14. – 17. Juli 2005* (Würzburg: Ergon), pp. 255–65.
—— 2013. 'Mosaiken aus Grabanlagen in Edessa', *Kölner und Bonner Archaeologica*, 3: 109–32.

——2019. 'Different from the Others: Female Dress in Northern Syria Based on Examples from Zeugma and Hierapolis', in M. Blömer and R. Raja (eds), *Funerary Portraiture in Greater Roman Syria*, Studies in Classical Archaeology, 6 (Turnhout: Brepols), pp. 66–82.

Sachau, E. 1882. 'Edessenische Inschriften', *Zeitschrift der Deutschen Morgenländischen Gesellschaft*, 36: 142–67.

Safar, F. and M. A. Mustafa. 1974. *Hatra: The City of the Sun God* (Baghdad: Directorate General of Antiquities = Wizarat al-Alam, Mudiriya al-Athar al-Amma).

Salman, B. 2008. 'Family, Death and Afterlife According to Mosaics of the Abgar Royal Period in the Region of Osroene', *Journal of Mosaic Research*, 1–2: 103–15.

Schlumberger, D. 1960. 'Descendants non-méditerranéens de l'art grec', *Syria: revue d'art oriental et d'archéologie*, 37: 253–319.

Schmidt-Colinet, A. 2009. 'Nochmal zur Ikonographie zweier palmyrenischer Sarkophage', in M. Blömer, M. Facella, and E. Winter (eds), *Lokale Identitäten im Römischen Nahen Osten: Konzepte und Deutungsmuster*, Oriens et Occidens, 18 (Stuttgart: Steiner).

Segal, J. B. 1953. 'Pagan Syriac Monuments in the Vilayet of Urfa', *Anatolian Studies*, 3: 97–119.

——1970. *Edessa: 'The Blessed City'* (Oxford: Clarendon).

Seyrig, H. 1937. 'Antiquités syriennes', *Syria: revue d'art oriental et d'archéologie*, 18: 1–53.

——1950. 'Palmyra and the East', *Journal of Roman Studies*, 40: 1–7.

——1971. 'Quatre images sculptées du Musée d'Alep', *Syria: revue d'art oriental et d'archéologie*, 48: 115–20.

Sommer, M. 2018. *Roms orientalische Steppengrenze: Palmyra – Edessa – Dura-Europos – Hatra; Eine Kulturgeschichte von Pompeius bis Diocletian* (Stuttgart: Steiner).

Spanu, M., G. Bejor, and E. Equini-Schneider. 1992–1993. 'Nuove ricerche nella Mesopotamia settentrionale', *Scienze dell'Antichità*, 6–7: 343–85.

Speidel, M. A. 2007. 'Ein Bollwerk für Syrien: Septimius Severus und die Provinzordnung Nordmesopotamiens im dritten Jahrhundert', *Chiron*, 37: 405–33.

Strootman, R. and M. J. Versluys (eds). 2017. *Persianism in Antiquity* (Stuttgart: Steiner).

Stucky, R. A. 1973. 'Prêtres syriens, 1: Palmyre', *Syria: revue d'art oriental et d'archéologie*, 50: 163–80.

Teixidor, J., D. Feissel, and J. Gascou. 1997. 'Documents d'archives romains inédits du Moyen Euphrate (IIIe siècle après J-C) [II. Les actes de vente- achat (P. Euphr. 6 À 10)]', *Journal des savants*, 1997: 3–57.

Tubach, J. 1986. *Im Schatten des Sonnengottes: Der Sonnenkult in Edessa Ḥarrān und Ḥaṭrā am Vorabend der christlichen Mission* (Wiesbaden: Harrassowitz).

Versluys, M. J. 2017. *Visual Style and Constructing Identity in the Hellenistic World: Nemrud Dağ and Commagene under Antiochos I* (Cambridge: Cambridge University Press).

Walpole, F. 1851. *The Ansayrii and (or Assassins,): With Travels in the Further East, in 1850–51; Including a Visit to Nineveh* (Whitefish: Kessinger).

Will, E. 1962. 'L'art sassanide et ses prédécesseurs', *Syria: revue d'art oriental et d'archéologie*, 39: 45–63.

Winkelmann, S. 2004. *Katalog der parthischen Waffen und Waffenträger aus Hatra* (Halle: Orientwissenschaftliches Zentrum).

——2009. 'Partherzeitliche Waffenträger in Edessa und Umgebung', in L. Greisiger and others (eds), *Edessa in hellenistisch-römischer Zeit: Religion, Kultur und Politik zwischen Ost und West: Beiträge des internationalen Edessa-Symposiums in Halle an der Saale 14. – 17. Juli 2005* (Würzburg: Ergon), pp. 313–65.

Index

Abgal: 117
Abgarids: 158–59
Acts of Thomas: 51–54
Adda: 49
Adiabene: 156, 171–72, 174
al-Walid, Khalid b.: 62–63
Anastasius, Saint: 62
Appian: 29, 30, 33
Arabian Peninsula, Arabians: 26–27, 36, 42, 46–47
Aramaic: 3–19, 29, 33, 47, 50, 120, 161, 173
   inscriptions: 3–19, 31–33, 76, 85–86, 93, 139, 170–71
   names: 33, 48, 121
   script: 139
Ardaxšīr: 39–40, 42
aristocracy *see* elites
Arsacid Empire: 39–43, 53, 156, 172–73
   see also Parthian Empire
Ashurbanipal: 97–98, 105–06
Assur: 31, 50–51
Astarte: 122–23
attendants: 101–02, 105, 109–123
attributes:
   bird: 92, 109, 110, 120, 144–45, 147
   bracelet: 84–85, 92, 94–96, 144, 146–48
   drinking cup; vessel: 74–78, 99–106, 113, 164
   earrings: 25, 93, 95–96, 147–48
   fruit: 76–77, 84, 92, 95, 109, 110, 113, 120, 145, 148
   grapes: 87, 91, 119, 144–45, 147–48
   jewellery, jewellery boxes: 25, 74–77, 95, 122, 144–48, 174
   necklace: 25, 84–85, 87–89, 92–93, 95–96, 122, 144, 146–48, 164
   patera: 91–92, 109–10, 113
   ship: 26, 111
   spindle and distaff: 147–48
   sword: 91, 115, 123, 161, 167
   vessel *see* attributes, drinking cup
Aurelian: 43, 45–47, 54

Baalbek: 127–28
Baalshami, Ba'alshamin
   inscription to: 10
   sanctuary of: 30, 59, 64, 65, 103
   with Zeus, Zeus-Kyrios: 7, 32, 151
Babylonia, Babylon: 29, 31–35
Bahrain: 26–27, 41, 42
banquet scenes: 17, 73–78, 84–89, 93–96, 97–107, 109, 111–20, 122–23, 147, 161, 163–67, 169–70
Barateh: 101
Bel, Bol: 31–32
   temple/sanctuary of: 11, 29–31, 35, 62, 103, 105, 129, 135, 139

camels: 23, 35
   camel-drivers: 33, 117
   depictions of: 90, 111, 122–23, 135–36
caravans, caravan trade: 9, 11, 23, 34–36, 43, 53, 60–63, 65, 109, 111, 114, 122–23, 149
   leaders of: 34, 114
   depictions of: 109, 111, 123
cataphracts: 48, 53
code-switching: 157
coins, coinage: 39, 41, 46, 50, 60, 65, 128, 130, 162
Coptic: 13–14

Diocletian: 61
   Camp of: 59–60, 63–64, 111, 123
   Edict of: 24
dress
   belt: 91–92, 94, 100–01, 115, 147–48, 161
   brooch: 84, 86, 88, 91, 95–96, 115, 161
   cap, hat: 88, 90, 100–01, 105, 111, 115, 118–20, 122–23, 132, 162, 165, 169, 174
   chiton: 90, 122, 143, 144, 146–48, 164, 173–74
   chlamys: 84, 88, 91, 104
   cloak: 99–101, 104, 162, 174
   hat *see* dress, cap; dress, turban
   himation: 84–96, 115, 122, 144, 146–48, 164–65, 173–74
   leggings: 156, 161, 167, 172
   mantle: 110, 115, 116, 142, 144, 156, 161–62, 167, 172, 174
   pendant: 84–85, 88–89, 91–94, 96, 144, 146–47
   priestly: 115, 118
   tiara: 162, 164, 172, 174
   toga: 85, 92, 109–10
   trousers: 50, 90–91, 99, 101, 104, 111, 115, 156, 161–65, 167, 169–70, 172, 174
   tunic: 84–96, 99–101, 104, 111, 115–16, 120–21, 142–43, 146–47, 171–72
   turban: 89, 93, 95–96, 101, 162, 174
   veil: 78, 84–85, 87–89, 92–93, 95–96, 100–01, 135, 147–48, 164
   see also Parthian dress
Dura-Europos: 3–4, 6–7, 14–19, 32–33, 39–43, 48, 51, 53–54, 104, 117, 121, 139–152, 155–157, 173–74

Edessa: 31–33, 51, 53, 78, 120, 155–66, 169–74
Egypt: 23, 27
Elites, elite culture: 25, 41, 49, 50–52, 54, 61–62, 65, 73, 75–78, 97, 99, 104, 113, 120, 156, 158, 161, 169, 172, 174
Euphrates River: 14, 23, 26–27, 29, 32–33, 36, 39, 42, 49, 51, 53, 62–65, 127, 139, 157–58, 173

frontality: 30–31, 98, 154, 174

Gallienus: 45, 46
Germanicus: 33–34, 129
gestures: 99, 106, 145–47, 163
goods, exotic or luxury: 3, 23, 25, 60, 74
graffiti: 5, 6, 8, 9, 17–18, 26, 54, 121
Great Colonnade: 64–65

hairstyles: 85, 91–96, 105, 113, 115–20, 122–23, 127–28, 145–46, 169
Hatra: 7, 32, 39–43, 50–51, 53, 117, 120–21, 155–57, 162–63, 165, 169–71, 174
Hilarus, Manlius Publicius: 25
Historia Augusta: 45–46
hunting scenes: 31, 101, 109–11, 123
Hypogeum of Bôlbarak: 101

Jupiter: 127–28

Kerdir: 50, 52, 54

loculus plaque *see* reliefs, *loculus*

Malikû, son of Nešâ: 28, 34
Mani; Manichaeans: 49, 50, 54
mints: 39–40
mosaics: 25, 49, 78, 104, 120, 162, 166–67, 169, 174

Nabatean Kingdom: 3, 23, 41
Nabu: 32
Nanai: 32
Nanaja: 173
Nemesis: 16, 150–51
Nisibis: 48, 51–52, 61, 171–72

Odainath; Odeanathus: 42–43, 45–51, 53–54
Oman: 41–42
onomastics: 32, 36, 40, 48
Osrhoene: 33, 157–60, 169–70, 174

Palmyra Portrait Project: 71–73, 144
Parthian Empire, Parthians: 3, 14, 23, 31, 33, 36, 39, 41, 46–50, 52–53, 155–58, 172–73
  Parthian art: 9, 31, 98, 113, 155–57, 173–74
  Parthian dress: 46–47, 90–91, 94, 101, 104–05, 115, 132 n. 21, 156–57, 172
  see also Arsacid Empire

pearls: 23–27, 42
Periplus Maris Erythraei: 36, 41
Persian Empire; Persians: 40, 45–54, 105, 158–59
Persian Gulf: 23, 25–27, 29, 35, 39, 41–43, 111
Peter the Patrician: 42–43, 45
Petra: 23, 98
polychromy: 144, 151–52
priests
  depictions of: 32, 88, 103, 109, 110, 116, 118–19
  Zoroastrian: 50
Proculus, Sextus Rasius: 127–28
propaganda: 46–47

reliefs
  loculus: 102, 117, 120, 123, 174
  sarcophagus: 72–76, 78, 84–92, 101, 109–17, 119, 121–23, 174
Roman Empire, Romans: 3, 5, 8, 14, 23–24, 30, 33, 39–43, 46–48, 50–52, 54, 62, 136, 152, 158–59
royalty: 50–53, 97, 117, 123, 172
  inscriptions of: 51, 54, 158
  iconography of: 97, 113, 120

Saracens, *Saracenoi*: 47, 62, 65
sarcophagus lids *see* reliefs, sarcophagus
Sasanian Empire: 39–40, 42–43, 48–54, 63, 158–59
sculpture, funerary: 25, 71–78, 97–107, 109–15, 122–23, 134, 144–45, 147–51, 161–67, 169–70, 174
Seleucid Empire: 33
Seleukeia: 35
Septimius Severus: 158
Septimius Worod: 48–49, 61
Shapur I; Šāpūr I: 39–43, 45, 49, 51–52, 54
Ships, sea-going vessels: 23, 26–27, 41, 111
silk: 23–27, 43
Silk Road: 39, 43
Socotra: 26–27, 36

Sol Invictus: 46–47
Spasinou Charax; Spasinu Charax: 23, 25, 41–43
Strabo: 33, 35
Sumatar: 159–60, 166, 168–69

Tax Law, Tax Tariff: 5, 9, 12–13, 34, 48
Temple of the Gadde: 142, 149–51
tesserae: 9, 32, 49, 73, 77, 99, 102–04, 106, 114, 128–30
tombs: 9, 11, 25, 26, 30, 33, 53, 75–76, 97–104, 106, 109–14, 116, 131, 134, 147, 159–64, 166, 169, 170
  Cantineau: 75–76, 84–86
  chamber: 170
  of ʿAtênaten: 110–11
  of Aviation: 75, 112–13, 116
  of Julius Aurelius Marona: 26, 111, 113
  of Kithôt: 99–100
  rock-cut: 160–61, 164, 166
  temple: 75
  tower: 99–100, 169
trade
  in the Indian Ocean: 23, 25, 26, 27, 41
  maritime: 23–27
  via Egypt: 24, 25, 36
  via the Red Sea: 23, 25–27, 36
  via the Silk Road: 39, 43
  with China: 23–24
  with India: 23–27, 29, 41
  with the Nabateans: 36
tropaion: 135–36

Umayyad Dynasty, Umayyad caliphate: 61, 63–64

Wahaballat; Wahballath: 5, 49

Yale Limestone Project: 148–49
Yarḥai: 115

Zenobia: 43, 45–54, 59–62
Zoroastrianism: 42, 50–54

Studies in Palmyrene Archaeology and History

All volumes in this series are evaluated by an Editorial Board, strictly on academic grounds, based on reports prepared by referees who have been commissioned by virtue of their specialism in the appropriate field. The Board ensures that the screening is done independently and without conflicts of interest. The definitive texts supplied by authors are also subject to review by the Board before being approved for publication. Further, the volumes are copyedited to conform to the publisher's stylebook and to the best international academic standards in the field.

Titles in Series

Studies on Palmyrene Sculpture: A Translation of Harald Ingholt's Studier over Palmyrensk Skulptur, *Edited and with Commentary*, ed. by Olympia Bobou, Jesper Vestergaard Jensen, Nathalia Breintoft Kristensen, Rubina Raja, and Rikke Randeris Thomsen (2021)

Production Economy in Greater Roman Syria: Trade Networks and Production Processes, ed. by Rubina Raja and Julia Steding (2021)

Individualizing the Dead: Attributes in Palmyrene Funerary Sculpture, ed. by Maura Heyn and Rubina Raja (2021)

Rubina Raja, Julia Steding, and Jean-Baptiste Yon, *Excavating Palmyra. Harald Ingholt's Excavation Diaries: A Transcript, Translation, and Commentary* (2 vols) (2021)

The Small Stuff of the Palmyrenes: Coins and Tesserae from Palmyra, ed. by Rubina Raja (2022)

In Preparation

Julia Steding, *Carvers and Customers in Roman Palmyra: The Production Economy of Limestone Loculus Reliefs*

Exchange and Reuse: Economy and Circularity at Palmyra, ed. by Nathanael J. Andrade and Rubina Raja

Odds and Ends, ed. by Maura K. Heyn and Rubina Raja